Advances in Japanese Business and Economics

Volume 36

Advances in Japanese Business and Economics (AJBE) showcases the work of Japanese and non-Japanese scholars researching the Japanese economy and Japanese businesses. Published in English, the series highlights for a global readership the unique perspectives of Japan's most distinguished and emerging scholars of business and economics. It covers research of either theoretical or empirical nature, in both authored and edited volumes, regardless of the sub-discipline or geographical coverage, including, but not limited to, such topics as macroeconomics, microeconomics, industrial relations, innovation, regional development, entrepreneurship, international trade, globalization, financial markets, technology management, and business strategy. At the same time, as a series of volumes written by Japanese and non-Japanese scholars studying Japan, it includes research on the issues of the Japanese economy, industry, management practice, and policy, such as the economic policies and business innovations before and after the Japanese "bubble" burst in the 1990s.

AJBE endeavors to overcome a historical deficit in the dissemination of Japanese economic theory, research methodology, and analysis. The volumes in the series contribute not only to a deeper understanding of Japanese business and economics but to revealing underlying universal principles.

Overseen by a panel of renowned scholars led by Editor-in-Chief Professor Ryuzo Sato, AJBE employs a single-blind review process in which the Editor-in-Chief, together with the Managing Editors and specialized scholars designated by the Editor-in-Chief or Managing Editors, rigorously reviews each proposal and manuscript to ensure that every submission is a valuable contribution to the global scholarly readership.

All books and chapters in AJBE are indexed in Scopus.

Iichiro Uesugi

The Economics of SME Finance

Springer

Iichiro Uesugi
Institute of Economic Research
Hitotsubashi University
Kunitachi, Tokyo, Japan

ISSN 2197-8859 ISSN 2197-8867 (electronic)
Advances in Japanese Business and Economics
ISBN 978-981-96-3192-6 ISBN 978-981-96-3193-3 (eBook)
https://doi.org/10.1007/978-981-96-3193-3

The original submitted manuscript has been translated into English. The translation was done using artificial intelligence. A subsequent revision was performed by the author(s) to further refine the work and to ensure that the translation is appropriate concerning content and scientific correctness. It may, however, read stylistically different from a conventional translation.

Translation from the Japanese language edition: "Chusho kigyo kinyu no keizaigaku: Kinyu kikan no yakuwari, seifu no yakuwari" by Iichiro Uesugi, © Iichiro Uesugi 2022. Published by Nihon Keizai Shimbun Shuppan. All Rights Reserved.

This Springer imprint is published by the registered company Springer Nature Singapore Pte Ltd.
The registered company address is: 152 Beach Road, #21-01/04 Gateway East, Singapore 189721, Singapore

Preface

The starting point for the author's research on small business finance was the establishment of a study group at the Research Institute of Economy, Trade and Industry (RIETI) in 2004. The purpose of the group was to provide a forum for members to present their research and to host workshops attended by domestic and foreign researchers. At that time, Japan was finally emerging from the financial crisis caused by the non-performing loan problem. While the government was implementing large-scale financial support measures, it was also the case that there were many listed zombie firms that could not survive without the support of financial institutions. In addition, the credit market was undergoing major changes due to a series of bank mergers that occurred during this period. All of these events were the subject of the study group's analysis, and the desire to conduct such research was a strong motivation for the author. Since then, the study group has been active as the "Study Group on Corporate Finance and Firm Dynamics". The unique feature of this study group is that it has not limited itself to research using government statistics, but has also conducted a series of surveys on the actual state of SME financing. By collecting and examining information during periods such as the global financial crisis and the COVID-19 pandemic, it is possible to evaluate the impact of these shocks from a long-term perspective. RIETI's understanding and support has been extremely helpful in continuing these activities. It has provided a wide range of support and advice.

The author has also been involved in other research projects. In order to study the role played by financial institutions in SME financing, such as the impact of mergers, it is necessary to obtain comprehensive information on bank-firm relationships and on the firms themselves. To this end, it has been helpful to conduct a joint project with Teikoku Databank under the "Social Science Empirical Research Project for Near-Future Problem Solving" (FY2008-2012) funded by the Ministry of Education, Culture, Sports, Science and Technology of Japan. The author has also been involved in an ongoing research project between Teikoku Databank and Hitotsubashi University.

The author has studied the role of government financial institutions since 2012, using anonymized loan-level data provided by the SME Unit of Japan Finance Corporation. The SME Unit staff are motivated to examine the effectiveness of government banks. The author also worked as a special researcher for the Financial Services Agency, using bank branch-level information on loans and deposits to examine concentration in the local loan and deposit market and to construct indicators for the interregional flow of funds. The results in this book do not represent the views of the data providers.

The Institute of Economic Research at Hitotsubashi University, of which the author is a member, is a cadre of highly active researchers. In recent years, the Institute has welcomed a group of young researchers, whose contributions have invigorated the author's own research. The administrative staff of the Institute has also provided invaluable assistance and encouragement.

In the preparation of this book and the papers on which it is based, the author has received a great many useful comments and suggestions from researchers and policy and business practitioners. As it is impractical to acknowledge all of the individuals who have provided assistance, he extends his sincerest gratitude to a select few:

Naohito Abe, Yoshiyuki Arata, Kazuyoshi Ishiga, Tokuo Iwaisako, Ichiro Iwasaki, Hiromichi Iwaki, Kozo Ueda, Kenichi Ueda, Hirofumi Uchida, Taisuke Uchino (deceased), Naoki Ohgo, Hiroshi Ohashi, Kazuo Ogawa, Yoshiaki Ogura, Arito Ono, Daiji Kawaguchi, Ryo Kambayashi, Hiroshi Gunji, Makoto Saito, Koji Sakai, Masaya Sakuragawa, Susumu Sato, Ikuko Samikawa, Etsuro Shioji, Chihiro Shimizu, Peng Xu, Shigenori Shiratsuka, Ryo Jinnai, Toshitaka Sekine, Yuta Takahashi, Naoki Takayama, Daisuke Tsuruta, Kensuke Teshima, Takeshi Nakata, Masashi Nakanishi, Tomoya Nakamura, Makoto Nirei, Tadanobu Nemoto, Makoto Hazama, Masazumi Hattori, Kozo Harimaya, Kazuki Hiraga, Tomohiro Hirano, Kyoji Fukao, Hikaru Fukanuma, Shin-ichi Fukuda, Hiroshi Fujiki, Takeo Hoshi, Kaoru Hosono, Tomohito Honda, Masashi Manabe, Takeshi Mizuta, Daisuke Miyakawa, Chiaki Moriguchi, Masayuki Morikawa, Hodaka Morita, Yukihiro Yasuda, Nobuyoshi Yamori, Jiro Yoshida, Naoyuki Yoshino, Naoki Wakamori, Wako Watanabe, Tsutomu Watanabe, Hans Degryse, Andrea Presbitero, Gregory F. Udell, Teng Wang, Alberto Zazzaro.

This book is based on Chusho Kigyo Kinyu no Keizaigaku: Kinyu Kikan no Yakuwari, Seifu no Yakuwari, a Japanese-language publication of the Nikkei Newspaper Press which was released in June 2022. The book was awarded the 65th Nikkei Prize for Excellent Books in Economic Science, the 29th Zengin Foundation Award, and the FY2022 Awards for Studies on Small Business. The author would like to express gratitude to Nikkei Newspaper Press for allowing the publication of this English edition. The author would like to express his gratitude to Guy M. Yamashiro for his invaluable contributions, including detailed comments and meticulous proofreading, which were instrumental in the development of this book. Furthermore, the author is indebted to Juno Kawakami of Springer Japan for her invaluable assistance in facilitating the publication of this book. On a personal note, the author would like to express gratitude to his family for respecting his freedom to pursue the research and for their endurance throughout this project.

The author is grateful to acknowledge the financial support provided by the Grant-in-Aid for Scientific Research (B) (Nos. 24K00271 and 21H00729) from the Ministry of Education, Culture, Sports, Science, and Technology of Japan.

The field of finance has the potential to influence the resource allocation within an economy. It is this author's hope that financial institutions and the government will fulfill their respective roles, with the result that SME finance will contribute to the overall growth of the economy. The author further hopes that this book will contribute to the ongoing discussion on how to achieve this goal from an economic point of view.

Tokyo, Japan
November 2024

Iichiro Uesugi

Contents

About the Author

Iichiro Uesugi is a professor at the Institute of Economic Research of Hitotsubashi University and a faculty fellow at the Research Institute of the Economy, Trade and Industry. Before joining Hitotsubashi, he had worked for the Ministry of Economy, Trade and Industry of the Japanese government for 18 years. His main areas of research interest are banking, corporate finance, and firm dynamics. He has published papers in scholarly journals including International Economic Review, Journal of Money, Credit, and Banking, Journal of Banking & Finance, Journal of Financial Stability, and Journal of the Japanese and International Economies. Professor Uesugi received a B.A. in economics from the University of Tokyo and a Ph.D. in economics from the University of California, San Diego.

Chapter 1
Role of SME Finance—Liquidity Provision in Crises and Efficient Allocation of Funds

Abstract This introductory chapter explains the motivation of the book, its analytical approach, and the contents of each chapter.

Keywords Liquidity provision · Efficient fund allocation · Small and medium enterprises (SMEs)

1.1 Introduction

1.1.1 Small and Medium Enterprises: Important but Problematic for the Japanese Economy

Small and medium enterprises (SMEs) account for more than 99% of all Japanese firms, approximately 70% of employment, and 50% of value added. Their performance is thus directly related to the performance of the Japanese economy. They are the source of growth in the corporate sector, as evidenced by the fact that they account for the majority of entries and exits and as most of the large firms that are now well-known were SMEs in their initial stages. On the other hand, the low productivity of SMEs relative to large firms has also been frequently pointed out.

1.1.2 Importance of Finance for SMEs

For SMEs, which have such multifaceted characteristics, financing is critical to their survival. SMEs have lower profit margins and less cash flow than their larger corporate counterparts, and need to raise funds from external sources to finance their business activities. SMEs often rely on borrowing from banks, Shinkin banks, and credit cooperatives in the loan market to raise funds, as it is difficult for them to issue stocks or bonds.

I. Uesugi, *The Economics of SME Finance*, Advances in Japanese Business and Economics 36, https://doi.org/10.1007/978-981-96-3193-3_1

Borrowing, however, often proves difficult for SMEs, particularly during recessions, due to information asymmetries. To alleviate these financial constraints the government sector is deeply involved in the loan market.

The recent COVID-19 pandemic, which caused a drastic reduction in economic activity due to stay at home orders or requests, has once again revealed the importance of finance for the survival of SMEs. The most common strategy to cope with the crisis used by SMEs was to obtain new funds for working capital from financial institutions. Government support contributed greatly to these financing efforts. Credit-guaranteed loans, in which the government guarantees the loans extended by private financial institutions to SMEs, and direct loans from government-affiliated financial institutions to SMEs amounted to over 50 trillion yen (as of the end of June 2021). This is more than the amount of SME loans of similar types extended during past crises, and is equivalent to about 20% of Japan's total outstanding loans to SMEs. The number of corporate bankruptcies is at its lowest level in 30 years thanks to the ample and prompt business support measures provided by financial institutions and the government. The provision of liquidity by financial institutions and the government has proven to be a very effective policy in increasing the viability of firms, particularly SMEs.

1.1.3 What Role Should SME Finance Play?

However, the role of SME finance is not just to reduce the number of bankruptcies and maximize the viability of existing firms through the provision of liquidity. If financial support is provided only for the survival of existing SMEs it would not be possible to adequately fund startup firms and firms with growth potential, and thus will not be able to promote the growth of the corporate sector as a whole. What is expected of SME finance, in addition to short-term liquidity provision, is to alleviate financial constraints caused by asymmetric information between borrowers and lenders through screening and monitoring, and to efficiently allocate funds that contribute to the growth of the economy as a whole, taking into account the risks associated with the provision of funds. An efficient allocation of funds that contributes to economic growth means supplying more funds to high-productivity firms than to low-productivity firms, and channeling funds to firms that are expected to generate high value-added. Only when such an allocation is achieved can SME financing stimulate growth across the entire economy.

1.1.4 Purpose of This Book and its Analytical Approach

The purpose of this book is to empirically examine whether small business financing provides the necessary liquidity and allocates funds efficiently. Focusing on financial institutions as well as the government that play an important role in this area, we closely examine the following aspects of SME financing: the size and efficiency of the allocation of funds to firms and regions; the role of government; and the behavior of financial institutions in the loan market. This is because in each of these three areas there are many important but unexplored questions that need to be addressed. In the analysis we will also clarify the role played by SME finance in Japan.

To conduct a comprehensive analysis it is not enough to simply focus on individual representative episodes. Despite a number of episodes of SMEs making hard management efforts and bankers extending loans to credit-constrained but promising firms, these episodes alone, no matter how persuasive, cannot be used to infer the entire state of SME finance. On the other hand, even if data is used, meaningful inferences cannot be obtained simply by presenting the aggregated amount of loans being extended to SMEs. That alone does not tell us where financial institutions channeled funds to SMEs and how much, the proportion of the funds allocated to productive firms, and how firm behavior changed as a result.

This book therefore accesses data from various sources including government statistics, databases accumulated by private credit research firms, administrative data, and surveys of firms. We also obtain data at various levels of aggregation including firms, loan contracts, and financial institution branches. All of this is probably the most comprehensive dataset we are able to access for the examination of SME finance in Japan. We then adopt two analytical approaches to answer the research questions in this book.

The first is an analytical approach based on quantitative methods using a variety of data at the firm level and firm-bank level. This will help determine whether liquidity is being provided to firms that need it, whether funds are being allocated efficiently, and whether the government is contributing to this.

The second approach reorganizes micro-level data in a manner different from how they are usually aggregated and constructs new indicators and statistics. The information includes the shares of zombie firms and zero leverage firms, the allocation of loans among firms, the interregional flow of funds, and the extent of loan market concentration. Each one of these statistics allows us to understand the current status of the liquidity provision and fund allocation efficiency among SMEs. Some of the information (interregional flow of funds indicators and market concentration) is publicly available and can be used by researchers and practitioners.

1.2 Background for Each Part and the Summary of Each Chapter

In what follows we will present an overview of the research questions that have not been addressed so far in each aspect of SME finance: allocation of funds to SMEs and its efficiency (Part 1 of Chapters 2 to 4); the role of the government (Part 2 of Chapters 5 to 9); and the behavior of financial institutions in the loan market (Part 3 of Chapters 10 to 11). We then briefly explain the contents of each chapter. This book will focus on debt financing, the most important part of SME finance in Japan, and will not primarily analyze equity or trade credit.

1.2.1 Part 1 (Chapters 2 to 4): Allocation of Funds to SMEs and Their Efficiency

The first question we will focus on in Part 1 is whether Japanese SMEs are provided with an adequate amount of funds and whether the allocation of funds among firms and regions is efficient.

Japanese firms as a whole were in savings deficit in the 1980s but after the asset bubble burst in the mid-1990s they changed to being in savings surplus, and the dependence on interest-bearing debt has continued to decline even among SMEs.

Note, however, that this is only the trend among average firms and does not necessarily capture the whole picture regarding corporate financing in Japan. At one end of the distribution regarding the dependence on debt there are firms labeled as zombie firms which are dependent on such a large amount of debt that they are not able to continue their businesses without the help of financial institutions. After the bubble burst in the 1990s large zombie firms listed in the stock exchange were said to be a serious problem for the economy as they had a negative spillover effect on non-zombie firms. Peek and Rosengren (2005), Caballero, Hoshi and Kashyap (2008), and Fukuda and Nakamura (2011), among other studies of Japanese listed companies, have pointed to the existence of zombie firms as an example of the inefficient allocation of funds by financial institutions.

However, these analyses were conducted only for listed companies around the 2000s. There are no studies that clearly answer the question of to what extent zombie SMEs existed from the 1990s up to the present.

In addition to the allocation of funds across firms, the interregional allocation of funds and its efficiency has not been well studied until now. It has long been pointed out that economic activities are concentrated in Tokyo. Furthermore, it has been widely recognized that cross-border lending by regional financial institutions, in which deposits collected in regional areas are provided as loans in Tokyo, is on the rise. However, there has been a lack of quantitative knowledge among practitioners, policy makers, and researchers as to whether such cross-border lending is efficient and, moreover, how funds are allocated among regions via loans and deposits.

Chapter 2 presents the characteristics and changes in the average financing structure of SMEs and overviews their trends, focusing on groups at both ends of the distribution: firms that do not borrow and firms that are over-indebted. Among SMEs the average reliance on financial institution loans declined as the firm sector has become more in a state of saving surplus and the number of zero leverage firms with no borrowings on their balance sheets has increased.

On the other hand the share of negative net worth SMEs remains high and there are a certain percentage of zombie firms that are unable to survive without support from financial institutions. Under the COVID-19 pandemic zombie firms tended to take advantage of government-provided financial support measures more than non-zombie firms and the zombie ratio began to rise. Not all zombie firms are forced to exit, as some later emerge from zombie status. However, a certain portion of them will be required to take steps to restructure their businesses, debt, and management.

In Chapter 3 we focus on the reallocation of credit among firms by adding up the increase and decrease in interest-bearing debt of individual firms, respectively, and analyze the relationship between the size of such reallocation and productivity. One of the characteristics of credit reallocation in Japan is that the degree of reallocation becomes smaller during economic downturns. In addition, looking at the relationship between the credit reallocation and productivity among SMEs there is no clear tendency for funds to flow from firms with low productivity to those with high productivity. This is in contrast to the efficient credit reallocation among large firms, with the exception of the "lost decade" following the burst of the bubble economy in the early 1990s. Productivity growth in the SME sector through the reallocation of funds does not appear to have occurred.

In Chapter 4 we examine the allocation of funds among regions and analyze the relationship with productivity. Using information on branch-level loan and deposit balances, which has not been used in research to date, we create a new indicator for the interregional allocation of funds via loans and deposits by financial institutions. We then examine the actual distribution of funds across regions by financial institutions, the degree of concentration of funds in Tokyo, and the efficiency of the interregional allocation of funds. We find that, while deposits collected in each region are most frequently used for lending within each prefecture, a certain percentage of collected deposits are also used for cross-border lending to other prefectures. In recent years the inflow of deposits from the regions, which are the source of lending in Tokyo, has begun to decline and the flow of funds within the same prefecture has relatively increased. The allocation of funds through loans and deposits has not necessarily moved in the direction of more concentration of funds in Tokyo. There is a negative relationship between regional productivity and the flow of funds between regions and deposits tend to be provided as loans from regions where productivity is rising to those where it is declining.

1.2.2 Part 2 (Chapters 5 to 9): The Role of the Government

The second part of the book assesses the support measures the government has undertaken to facilitate the financing for SMEs and to improve efficiency of this financing.

Financial support for SMEs in Japan, although scaled back during the period of reform of the government-affiliated financial institutions in the mid-2000s, expanded in both coverage and intensity in each of the major economic crises that occurred in the past 30 years, including Japan's financial crisis (late 1990s to early 2000s), the Global Financial Crisis (fall 2008–2009), the Great East Japan Earthquake (March

2011), and the COVID-19 pandemic (since early 2020). The government has provided generous support measures in response to these major crises. At the same time, however, there are several issues that are remained to be discussed: whether these support measures are effective; whether there are side effects of these measures; and whether the government financial support measures substitute for the activities of private financial institutions.

Among the various types of government financial support measures for SMEs in Japan there two major policy tools: credit guarantees, with which private financial institutions provide loans to SMEs; and direct lending by government-affiliated financial institutions to SMEs. Until recently there had been a paucity of empirical analyses of these measures due to the limited availability of firm-level and loan-level data on the use of these programs. Further, there had been no empirical analysis comparing these two measures in a unified framework even though they are supposed to be similarly effective as financial support measures for SMEs. There was also no empirical analysis that examined the validity of the criticism that government-affiliated financial institutions are suppressing lending that could be done more efficiently by private financial institutions.

Chapter 5 overviews the various measures taken by the government in the area of SME finance. We focus on the two major pillars of government involvement, direct lending by government financial institutions and credit guarantees and present predictions based on a simple theoretical model regarding which of the two measures firms prefer and how their borrowing and capital investment are affected by the use of these measures. The actual data shows that firms with higher credit risk prefer credit guarantees to government loans, which is consistent with the prediction, but that there was no empirical evidence that is consistent with the theoretical prediction that the credit guarantees stimulate borrowing and investment more than the direct government bank loans.

Following up with the inconsistency between the theoretical prediction and the empirical finding in Chapter 5, Chapters 6 and 7 examine the effects of credit guarantees and direct lending by government financial institutions, respectively. What the theoretical model in Chapter 5 does not take into account is the possibility that private financial institutions substitute "proper" loans, loans that are not guaranteed by the credit guarantee scheme, for credit guaranteed loans.

An examination of the effects of the two massive credit guarantee programs offered during the previous two crises in Chapter 6 shows that such substitution did indeed occur, with a smaller improvement in the credit availability for firms that used credit-guaranteed loans. In contrast, the analysis in Chapter 7 using data on the loans extended by one of the government-affiliated financial institutions shows that such substitution of the private sector by the government sector is less likely to occur and that firms that use loans from the government financial institution increase their capital investment.

Chapter 8 examines more rigorously whether there is a substitutive or complementary relationship between government-affiliated financial institutions and private financial institutions in lending, an issue which is also discussed in Chapter 7. The chapter focuses on an exogenous institutional change in the way the government financial institution sets its loan interest rates.

In times of crisis, such as the COVID-19 pandemic, government-affiliated financial institutions are not seen as a problem because the risk-taking capacity of the private sector declines. But if government-affiliated institutions substitute for private sector lending in normal times despite the lending capacity of the private sector then criticism that they are "squeezing private industry" will emerge. We focus on a change in the interest rate structure at Japan Finance Corporation's (JFC's) SME Unit, which extends loans to relatively large SMEs, a sector that is most criticized by the private sector among the government-affiliated financial institutions. Even with exogenously lower interest rates by the JFC to firms with less credit risk we do not find evidence for the substitution of private sector loans by those extended by the JFC.

In Chapter 9 we focus on the policies that work on the qualitative aspects of lending and examine their effects. The focus is on the policy objective of promoting lending that is not overly dependent on collateral and personal guarantees. The government has set this objective partly in reflection of the fact that during the bubble period financial institutions extended loans without evaluating the business prospects of borrower firms, relying heavily on real estate collateral. Also, it has promoted lending without excessive use of personal guarantees partly in order to facilitate business succession in SMEs. An analysis of the loan programs introduced by a government-affiliated financial institution to achieve these objectives reveals that covenants (agreements that outline the behavior of borrowers and included in a loan contract) may be a useful alternative to personal guarantees in helping to discipline borrowers.

1.2.3 Part 3 (Chapters 10 to 11): Behavior of Financial Institutions in the Loan Market

The question we address in Part 3 is how the behavior of financial institutions in the loan market has affected the availability of financing for firms, including SMEs. In recent years, interest margins, the difference between loan and deposit rates, have continued to decline in the corporate loan market, raising concerns about the sustainability of financial institutions, especially regional financial institutions. Against this backdrop there are indications that the ongoing mergers and consolidation of financial institutions will increase their market power and worsen the financing environment for SMEs. However, there has been no comprehensive study on the impact of these mergers on the availability of financing for firms that used to transact with the merged banks or those that were located within geographic areas of the merged banks. Furthermore, there was no accurate and comprehensive information on the concentration of financial institutions which could serve as an indicator of the degree of competition in regional loan markets, due to the limited access to data on outstanding loans at the regional level.

Chapter 10 calculates for the first time accurately and comprehensively the extent of concentration in the regional loan and deposit markets in Japan. Then we discuss the relationship between concentration and the market power of financial institutions. For each prefecture and urban employment area we calculate the Herfindahl–Hirschman index (HHI, the sum of the squares of the financial institutions' market shares, which indicates market power under certain assumptions) in the loan market to examine its nature. The results show that while the overall loan HHI has been increasing, there has been a polarization, with the level of loan HHI declining more strongly in the metropolitan areas. In addition, an examination of the relationship between regional HHI and borrowing interest rates of firms located in these areas reveals that interest rates tend to increase slightly and gradually as the HHI increases.

In Chapter 11 we focus on bank mergers, which have a significant impact on the competitive environment in the loan market, and examine the impact they have on the financing environment faced by the firms with which they transact. The first merger to be analyzed is the 2006 merger between two megabanks, Bank of Tokyo-Mitsubishi and UFJ Bank. This merger resulted in both a larger increase in interest rates and a decline in the borrowing ratios of non-listed firms which used to transact with the merged banks. Next we consider all the mergers among financial institutions from 2004 to 2018, including mergers among megabanks. We find that the financing environment for firms that used to transact with the merged bank improved on average, with the megabank merger resulting in higher interest rates being one of a few exceptions.

In the final chapter, based on the results of the empirical analyses throughout the book, we provide a perspective on the future of SME finance to the greatest extent possible.

1.3 Structure of Each Chapter and Additional Remarks

This book uses data at various levels, including firms, loan contracts, and financial institution branches, to the best of the authors' ability, thanks to the cooperation and generosity of all parties involved. However, the views expressed in this book are those of the authors and not those of the organizations that provided the data.

The research presented here is a reorganization of academic papers published by the author and his coauthors, while new analyses by the author are added in a number of places. The book also presents some research results by the members of the Research Institute of Economy, Trade and Industry's Study Group on Corporate Finance and Firm Dynamics, for which the author has been the organizer since 2004. Contents of the book also show the current status of the knowledge on SME finance in Japan.

Each of Chapters 2 through 11 is divided into sections that are arranged as an introduction, overview of the results, and subsequent details. This structure enables readers to get a rough idea of the findings in each chapter within its opening pages. In addition, this introductory Chapter 1 and the concluding Chapter 12 should provide some idea of the motivation and background of the study and the policy implications of the results obtained. We believe that this book can be read and understood not only by researchers but also by practitioners, policy makers, and students who are interested in the fields of SMEs and finance.

Chapter 2
SME Financing Structure and Changes

Abstract Since small and medium enterprises (SMEs) are less likely than large firms to raise funds from the stock and bond markets and have relatively lower profit margins they rely more heavily on borrowing from financial institutions. Japanese SME borrowing increased through the 1980s and 1990s but since then SMEs' dependence on borrowing has been declining, reflecting a trend towards savings surplus among Japanese firms.

Considering the diversity of SMEs, we focus on firms at both ends of the distribution in terms of their dependence on debt, namely, zero leverage firms and insolvent or zombie firms. The proportion of zero leverage firms has significantly increased over time, particularly in the 2000s. Zero leverage SMEs are characterized by high profit margins but low capital investment and growth orientation. Therefore, even though these firms do not borrow it is unlikely that they face strong financial constraints. An important issue is how to best stimulate these firms' demand for funds. There also exist a number of insolvent and zombie firms. While the ratio of insolvent firms in the Japanese economy has remained high since the late 1990s the ratio of zombie firms declined from the 2000s until the COVID-19 pandemic.

Keywords Dependence on loans · Savings surplus · Zero leverage firms · Zombie firms · Business revitalization · SME Financing Facilitation Act

2.1 Introduction

2.1.1 Importance of SMEs in the Overall Economy and Their Characteristics

Many people have the perception that while SMEs are numerous their aggregate share in the economy is small. Despite their small individual size, however, the share of SMEs in the overall economy is actually substantial. Roughly speaking, SMEs account for over 99% of the total number of firms in Japan's corporate sector, 70% of employment, and about half of sales and value added.

I. Uesugi, *The Economics of SME Finance*, Advances in Japanese Business and Economics 36, https://doi.org/10.1007/978-981-96-3193-3_2

Table 2.1 Definition of SMEs

Definition of SMEs based on the SME Basic Act			
	SMEs (satisfies either one or both of the conditions)		Micro businesses
	Number of employees	Amount of paid-in capital (for incorporations)	Number of employees
Manufacturing and other industries	300 or smaller	300 million yen or smaller	20 or smaller
Wholesale industry	100 or smaller	100 million yen or smaller	5 or smaller
Retail industry	50 or smaller	50 million yen or smaller	5 or smaller
Services industry	100 or smaller	50 million yen or smaller	5 or smaller

Definition of firm size (employed by the author for the explanation of results)				
	Large firms	Medium-sized firms	SMEs	Micro businesses
Amount of paid-in capital	1 billion yen or larger	100 million yen to 1 billion yen	10 million yen to 100 million yen	Less than 10 million yen

Based on the Economic Census there were 3.59 million firms in Japan as of 2016, of which 1.61 million were incorporations and 1.98 million were sole proprietorships. The majority of these firms were SMEs. The most common definition of an SME is based on the Small and Medium Enterprise Basic Act (see Table 2.1).[1] SMEs with fewer than a certain number of employees are classified as micro businesses. In addition, since the threshold for the reduced corporate tax rate is 100 million yen in capital some statistics distinguish between large enterprises and SMEs based on whether their capital is around 100 million yen.[2] Table 2.2 shows the number of SMEs as a proportion of the number of enterprises, number of employees, sales, and value added.

There are economic implications to classifying firms by size and treating SMEs separately from large firms. The reason for this is that firms of different sizes have different attributes and thus respond differently to shocks. Moreover, the impact of firm performance on the overall economy differs depending on firm size.[3] There are three unique features of SMEs: (1) they are sensitive to external shocks and thus

[1] The Small and Medium Enterprise Basic Act was enacted in 1963. The current definition of SMEs is based on the 1999 amendment.

[2] In this chapter, when presenting results using the Annual/Quarterly Financial Statements Statistics of Corporations by Industry reported by the Ministry of Finance we will use designations classified at the bottom of Table 2.1.

[3] As a result of the size-dependent policy which provides preferential treatment to smaller firms and a subsequent change in firm behavior after the treatment, the attributes of SMEs may differ from those of large firms. Public credit guarantees and loans by government-affiliated financial

Table 2.2 SMEs' share in the economy

	SMEs	Micro businesses	Large firms	Sum
Number of firms	3,578,176	3,048,390	11,157	3,589,333
Share (%)	99.7	84.9	0.3	100
Number of workers	32,201,032	10,437,271	14,588,963	46,789,995
Share (%)	68.8	22.3	31.2	100
Amount of sales (100 million yen)	6,290,133	1,359,085	7,986,085	14,276,218
Share (%)	44.1	9.5	55.9	100
Amount of value added (100 million yen)	1,351,106	357,443	1,205,336	2,556,442
Share (%)	52.9	14.0	47.1	100

Note Agriculture, forestry, and fishery industries are excluded. Figures in June 2016 are for the number of firms and number of workers and those in 2015 are for sales and value added
Source Economic Census—Activities survey

while a large number of SMEs achieve high growth many others are forced out of business. Most of the large, listed companies in Japan started as SMEs. At the same time almost all bankruptcies (99.9%) in the country are attributed to SMEs[4]; (2) many SMEs have relatively low productivity due to the lack of economies of scale. In the 2020 White Paper on SMEs the labor productivity of SMEs with less than 100 million yen in capital, which is measured by the amount of value added per employee, was only 40% that of large firms with more than 1 billion yen in capital, and the gap has been widening over time[5]; (3) even after controlling for firm characteristics the degree to which management attributes affect firm performance is significant.[6]

2.1.2 *The Financial Environment for SMEs is Very Different from that of Large Firms*

Due to these features the financing environment faced by SMEs differs from that faced by large corporations. Since SMEs tend to have relatively lower, and more

institutions are provided to SMEs as defined by the SME Basic Act. Reduced corporate tax rates are also applied to firms with capital of 100 million yen or less.

[4] According to the bankruptcy report issued by the Teikoku Databank, 7310 of the 7314 bankruptcies in FY2020 were of SMEs.

[5] For more information see Small and Medium Enterprise Agency (2020). The white paper comprehensively compares the labor productivity of SMEs to that of large firms and shows that even within industries there are substantial productivity differences across firm size and that the differences in labor productivity are attributed to capital equipment ratios.

[6] Bennedsen et al. (2020) focus on the exogenous event of SME CEOs' hospitalization and show how important the CEOs are to firm performance. They find that profitability and investment decreases in firms where the CEO is hospitalized.

variable, performance than large enterprises investors are often hesitant to provide funds to these firms. In addition, many SMEs do not disclose financial information, such as that included in balance sheets, which makes it difficult for prospective lenders to assess credit risk. If there is asymmetric information about their credit risk SMEs cannot raise funds in either the stock or bond market or attract funds from individual investors.

Instead, SMEs rely on financial institutions such as commercial banks, Shinkin banks, and credit cooperatives for funds. These financial institutions accumulate information on SMEs' quality and solvency through transactions of loans, deposits, foreign exchange, and other services in order to make lending decisions.[7]

This does not mean, however, that these institutions will always accept the credit risk and extend loans to SMEs. During recessions, when the credit risk of SMEs increases and the risk-bearing capacity of financial institutions decreases, it becomes difficult for SMEs to borrow and an increasing number of them face financing difficulties.[8]

How can we characterize the current financial environment faced by SMEs and how has it changed over time? The Japanese economy has experienced various macroeconomic episodes since the 1980s including the growth and collapse of the asset price bubble and a prolonged period of stagnation that began with the massive non-performing loan problem. Each of these events has had a significant impact on the financing environment of SMEs.

2.2 Overview of the Financing Structure of SMEs

In this chapter, based on government statistics, firm surveys, and previous studies, we detail the financing structure of SMEs by using data compiled for different firm sizes. On average the ratio of borrowings from financial institutions to total assets increased for SMEs from the 1980s through the late 1990s. Thereafter the ratio declined as the corporate sector shifted towards savings surpluses in response to the Japanese financial crisis and the economic stagnation that followed. While the ratio of loans

[7] Theoretical models emphasize that financial institutions are superior in that they establish relationships with borrower firms and learn about their quality (i.e., produce information), thereby reducing moral hazard and adverse selection. Diamond (1984) argues the importance of financial institutions as a delegated monitor, which collects funds from a large number of depositors and channels those funds to a limited number of borrowers. Such a delegated monitor is able to cover the fixed costs of both monitoring and information production. Some theoretical models focus on the advantage of financial institutions over the bond market. Diamond (1991) and Holmstrom and Tirole (1997) respectively present models in which borrower firms, depending on their reputation and net worth, choose between borrowing from financial institutions and raising funds from bond markets. Both papers find that it is appropriate for firms that have not yet fully established their reputations or that have little net worth to first borrow from financial institutions.

[8] Such situations provide a justification for some form of government intervention in SME financing. Chapters 5 to 9 in Part 2 of the book will discuss the specifics and effects of these interventions.

did increase during the COVID-19 pandemic there has been no reversal of the overall downward trend.

Averages alone, however, do not accurately capture the diverse characteristics of SMEs. Therefore, we focus not only on "average" SMEs but also on SMEs with extreme financing situations such as those that have not borrowed at all, those that are insolvent on a book value basis, and zombie firms that have difficulty continuing operations without the support of financial institutions. Since some firms perform poorly and thus accumulate a large amount of debt, focusing on firms at both ends of the spectrum allows us to examine the efficiency of the allocation of funds.

In Japan the ratio of zero leverage firms, regardless of size, has increased over time, especially in the 2000s. Zero leverage SMEs are characterized by high profit margins but low growth orientation due to little capital investment. While some zero leverage firms did borrow during periods of high liquidity demand, such as the Global Financial Crisis and drew down their cash and deposits, it cannot be said that these firms faced strong financial constraints.

Next there are a certain number of SMEs that fall into either the insolvent or zombie categories. While the ratio of insolvent firms has remained high since the late 1990s the ratio of zombie firms declined from the beginning of the 2000s until just prior to the COVID-19 pandemic. It is a strong possibility, however, that the ratio of zombie firms will increase due to the large-scale business support measures taken during the pandemic. Since a number of these firms need serious business restructuring, more drastic policy measures should be introduced to facilitate such restructuring.

The remainder of the chapter is organized as follows. Section 2.3 describes the financing structure of SMEs, comparing it to that of large firms. Section 2.4 reveals the extent to which the corporate sector is surplus or deficit in savings based on corporate balance sheet information and shows how changes in the financing trends of Japanese firms have been related to their savings-investment balance. From Section 2.5 onwards we focus on the variation in borrowing across firms. In Section 2.6 we discuss the trend of zero leverage firms and in Section 2.7 we present the characteristics of firms that are insolvent, in book value, or zombies. Section 2.8 summarizes the chapter.

2.3 Comparison of Firm Financing Structures Across Firm Sizes

In this section we compare the financing structure of SMEs to large firms through the pre-COVID period using balance sheet data from the Ministry of Finance's Annual Financial Statements Statistics of Corporations by Industry. We also compare financing structures within SMEs themselves using the Small and Medium Enterprise Agency's Basic Survey on SMEs. Since SMEs are divided into corporations and sole proprietorships, and only corporations have balance sheets, the following discussion only applies to corporations.

2.3.1 Firm Debt Structure

Figure 2.1 displays the composition of firm liabilities by their level of capital based on FY2018 figures from the Annual Financial Statements Statistics of Corporations by Industry. The statistics are population estimates which aggregate the assets and liabilities of firms within each size category for Japan as a whole. In terms of total assets, large firms (with capital larger than or equal to 1 billion yen) hold the most at 922 trillion yen, followed by SMEs (capital between 10 million to 100 million yen) at 522 trillion yen, medium-sized firms (capital between 100 million yen and 1 billion yen) at 233 trillion yen, and micro businesses (capital less than 10 million yen) at 122 trillion yen.

Larger firms have a higher share of equity capital. This is due to their ability to raise funds in the stock market, as well as their higher profit margins, resulting in more retained earnings. Both medium-sized firms and SMEs have equity ratios of over 40% while micro businesses have less than 20%. While corporate bonds account for about 8% of funding for large firms this accounts for less than 1% of SME financing.

SMEs and micro businesses are highly dependent on financial institutions for funds. Loans from financial institutions account for about 25% of total assets for SMEs and 40% for micro businesses. In addition, the share of loans from non-financial firms and individuals is 8% for SMEs and 20% for micro businesses, which is also higher than large and medium-sized firms.

Trade payables, consisting of accounts payables and notes payables, represent the gap between delivery and settlement of goods and services in commercial transactions between firms, and indicates the extent to which firms obtain trade credit. The ratio

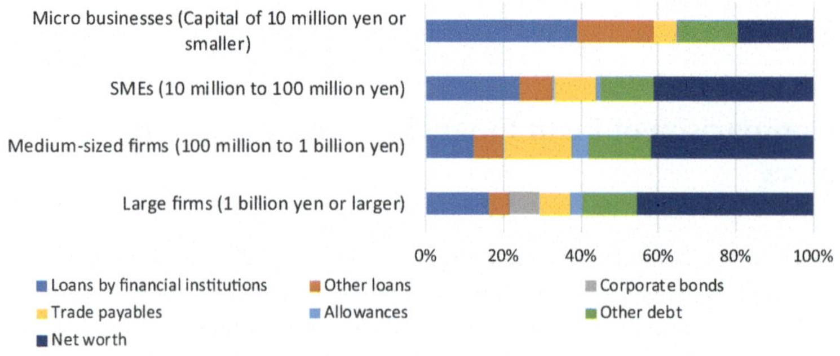

Fig. 2.1 Debt structure of corporations (FY2018, by capital size) (*Source* Tabluated by the author based on Ministry of Finance's Financial Statements Statistics of Corporations by Industry)

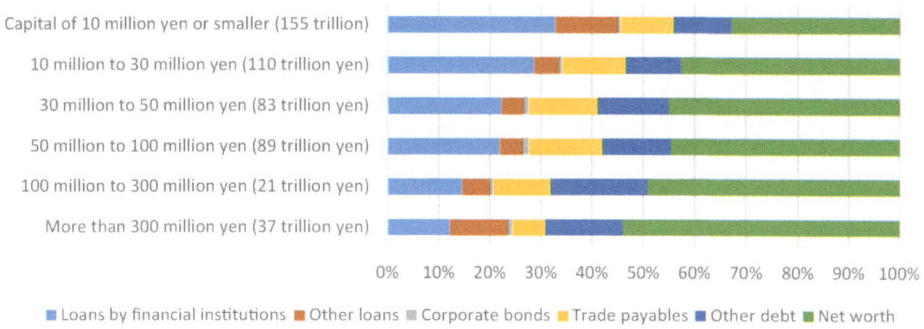

Fig. 2.2 Debt structure of SMEs (Year 2019, by capital size) (*Note* Figures in parentheses are population-estimated total asset size. *Source* Tabulated by the author based on Ministry of Finance's Financial Statements Statistics of Corporations by Industry)

of trade payables to total assets is the highest for medium-sized firms while it is the smallest for micro businesses followed by large firms and SMEs. On one hand, the larger a firm becomes the stronger its bargaining position with suppliers. For instance, large firms are likely to be allowed longer intervals between delivery and settlement. As a result large firms tend to have a larger share of trade payables. On the other hand, large firms may have the ability to handle a wide variety of inter-firm transactions more efficiently and thus may need less trade payables than small firms. These are thought to be the two key factors in determining the pattern of dependence on trade payables across firms of different sizes.[9]

To this point we have only compared large and medium-sized firms with SMEs and micro businesses. When we make more detailed comparisons between SMEs and micro businesses what differences do we observe?

Figure 2.2 shows the debt composition as of the 2019 Survey (FY2018) for firms by level of capitalization, based on the Basic Survey of Small and Medium Enterprises covering SMEs under the Small and Medium Enterprise Basic Act. Among SMEs, the smaller they are the lower their equity ratio and the higher the share of financial institution loans.[10]

---

[9] In addition to transaction costs and bargaining power, several other determinants of interfirm trade credit have been theoretically identified. This includes information production capacity, substitution for loans from financial institutions, and price discrimination. See Uchida (2011) for a theoretical overview and Uchida, Uesugi and Hotei (2010) and Tsuruta and Uchida (2019) for empirical analyses.

[10] The debt composition of firms with capitalization of less than 10 million yen in the Annual Financial Statements Statistics of Corporations by Industry and the Basic Survey on Small and Medium Enterprises are different in that the capital ratio is much lower in the former (19% in FY2018) than in the latter (33% in FY2018). This is despite the fact that they both cover almost the same group of firms. This may be due to substantial differences in the populations of these two surveys, especially for micro businesses.

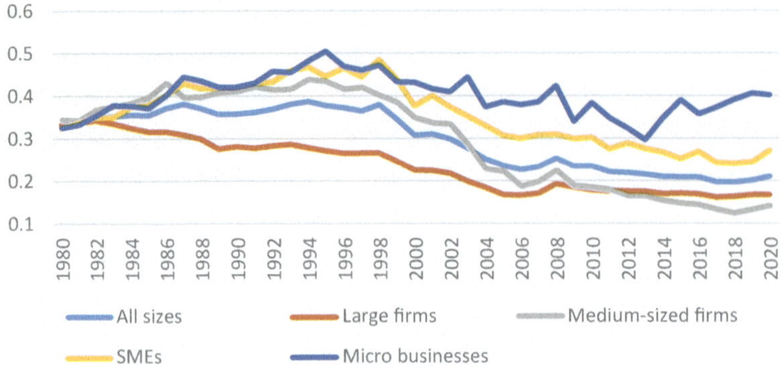

Fig. 2.3 Ratio of loans by financial institutions to total assets (by capital size) (*Note* Ratio = loans extended by financial institutions/total assets. *Source* Tabluated by the author based on Ministry of Finance's Financial Statements Statistics of Corporations by Industry)

2.3.2 Change in the Dependence on Loans

These figures, for the period just before the COVID-19 pandemic, show that SMEs are more dependent on loans from financial institutions and loans from other sources and have lower equity ratios than larger firms. The current financing structure of SMEs is actually a result of changes that occurred in the past. As shown in Figure 2.3, if we focus on changes in the level of dependence on loans from financial institutions from FY1980 to the present we see that the direction and degree of change differ depending on the time period and the size of the firm.

Large firms decreased their dependence on loans from financial institutions throughout the 1980s and 1990s. In the first half of this period financial liberalization that included deregulation of corporate financing led large firms to pivot to the securities markets, resulting in a significant decline in their reliance on loans from financial institutions.[11] In contrast, the dependence on financial institution loans among SMEs and micro businesses increased during the 1980s and 1990s. This is due to the fact that large financial institutions, such as city banks and long-term credit banks, increased their lending to smaller firms in response to the reduced demand for borrowing by large firms.[12]

In the late 1980s real estate-based loans increased alongside loans to SMEs and micro businesses, leading to the creation of an asset price bubble. Its eventual collapse

[11] On the other hand, the total sum of the dependence on corporate bonds and loans has been almost unchanged during this period, with corporate bonds making up for the decline in loans from financial institutions. Okazaki and Hoshi (2002) explain deregulation as a driving force behind these changes. In particular, they cite the liberalization of the corporate bond market since the late 1970s, the 1980 amendment of the Foreign Exchange Law to liberalize financial transactions with foreign countries, and the 1984 abolition of the so-called real demand principle for international financial transactions.

[12] Hoshi and Kashyap (1999) describe this situation.

led to a massive non-performing loan problem and a severe financial crisis in Japan in the late 1990s and early 2000s. During this period (i.e., from FY1998 to FY2000), firms' dependence on financial institution loans declined regardless of size. This coincided with a reluctance to lend by the financial institutions that were damaged by non-performing loans.[13]

The decline in financial institution loans, regardless of firm size, continued into the 2000s. The decline during this period was particularly pronounced for medium-sized firms and SMEs. Then, in FY2008, in the midst of the Global Financial Crisis, dependence on financial institution loans increased temporarily for firms of all sizes, indicating that financial institutions actively supplied funds in response to firms' financing needs. Subsequently, however, firm dependence on loans from financial institutions has declined, with the exception of micro businesses after FY2013. For SMEs, dependence peaked at nearly 50% (FY1998), but by FY2019 it had fallen roughly by half to 25%.[14]

There was a slight change in the trend in FY2020 (as of March 2021) due to the crisis caused by the COVID-19 pandemic. In particular, the dependence on loans by financial institutions increased by 3% for SMEs. However, the increase was not large enough to reverse the overall downward trend.

2.4 Prolonged Savings Surplus in the Firm Sector

The decline in the dependence on loans from financial institutions, especially among medium-sized firms and SMEs since the beginning of the 2000s, can be attributed to the fact that real investment in the corporate sector has been low and exceeded by savings. We obtain this result by using the methodology of Nakamura (2017) who uses aggregate data from the Annual Financial Statements statistics of Corporations by Industry of Japan, and compares internal capital, which corresponds to corporate savings, and the amount of real investment by firm size.

Firms' surplus or deficit in savings is determined by whether the internal funds held by firms exceed, or fall short, of the level of real investment implemented. The

[13] Based on a review of the related literature Uchida (2018) describes how the growth and collapse of asset price bubbles led to the non-performing loan problem, resulting in a financial crisis.

[14] The decline in the firm sector's reliance on financial institution lending after the 2000s was somewhat anticipated. Hoshi and Kashyap (1999) projected the size of bank loans in Japan and predicted that loans to firms would shrink by more than 30% in the medium to long term. This forecast was based on the assumption that Japanese firms' reliance on borrowing would converge to a level similar to that of U.S. firms and that the total assets of the corporate sector would remain unchanged. They based their projection on the Quarterly Financial Statements Statistics of Corporations by Industry. When we examine their prediction using current statistics 20 years later the total assets of the firm sector increased by 35% over the past 20 years but the outstanding balance of loans to firms by financial institutions decreased by almost 30%. The fact that the size of total corporate assets expanded while outstanding loans declined almost as expected means that the extent of decline in the reliance of Japanese firms on financial institution loans was greater than expected.

magnitudes of internal funds and real investment can be determined by looking at balance sheet changes. Internal funds are defined as follows.

$$\begin{aligned}\text{Internal funds} = {} & \text{Net income} - \text{Special profits} + \text{Special losses} \\ & + \text{Depreciation and amortization} \\ & - \text{Increase in required working capital}\end{aligned}$$

Depreciation is added because it is an expense item that does not involve an outflow of funds. Similarly, special losses are added and special profits are subtracted because they contain items that do not involve cash inflows or outflows. Required working capital, which is calculated by subtracting accounts payables from accounts receivables and inventories, represents the amount of bridge capital needed by a firm. Thus, required working capital is subtracted from net income. Note that, as in Nakamura (2017), we treat dividends as part of internal capital and their disbursement is one of the uses of surplus savings. It should also be noted that this treatment results in large firms, which usually make higher dividend payments, reporting more internal funds and, thus, a larger savings surplus. Real investment is defined as follows.

$$\begin{aligned}\text{Real investment} = {} & \Delta\begin{pmatrix}\text{Tangible fixed assets(land and other tangible fixed assets)} \\ +\text{Intangible assets}\end{pmatrix} \\ & + \text{Depreciation and amortization}\end{aligned}$$

Figure 2.4 compares internal funds to real investment by firm size to see whether investment exceeds savings or savings exceed investment in the Japanese firm sector in the FY1980 to FY2019 period. Internal funds and real investment are divided by total assets at the end of the previous period. Internal funds is shown as a bar above the horizontal line, while real investment is shown as a bar below the line. The difference between the two is displayed as a line. The bar chart shows that the level of internal funds has been fluctuating, between 2% and 6% of total assets, and gradually increasing, and that the level of real investment increased to over 6% of total assets in FY1992 but has declined sharply since.

The same figure makes clear that the corporate sector has had a savings deficit since FY1980, which only intensified during the asset price bubble of the late 1980s, finally reaching −3.8% in FY1990. Following the bursting of the bubble, however, the deficit shrank significantly, reflecting the sharp decline in real investment. Due to the increase in internal funds the savings deficit turned into a savings surplus by FY1996. After expanding to about 2% in the 2000s the surplus has subsequently remained flat.

Figure 2.5 shows the savings surplus by firm size. We see that the shift from a savings deficit in the 1980s to a savings surplus is common across all firm size categories. The timing and magnitude of the saving surplus, however, differ considerably across size groups.

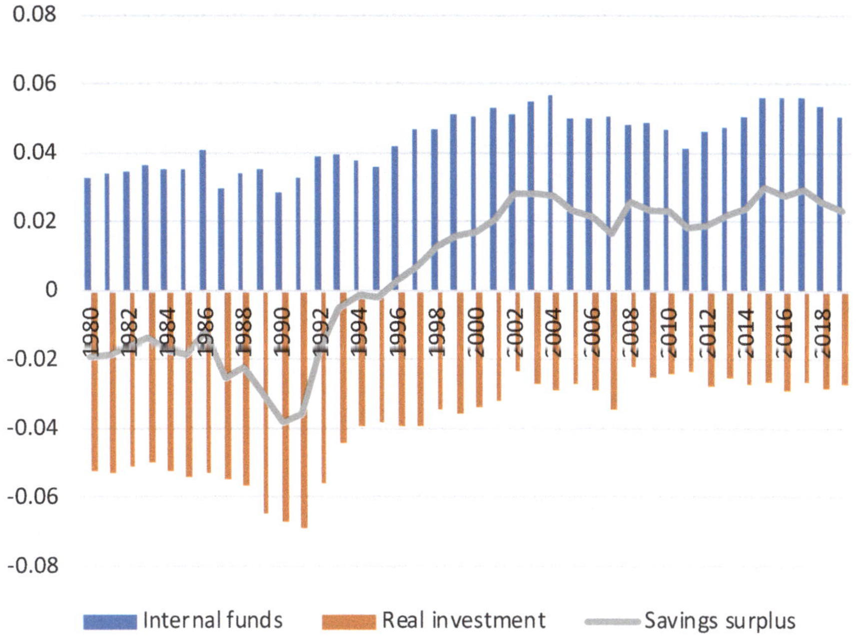

Fig. 2.4 Savings surplus of corporations (all firm sizes) (*Source* Tabluated by the author based on Ministry of Finance's Financial Statements Statistics of Corporations by Industry)

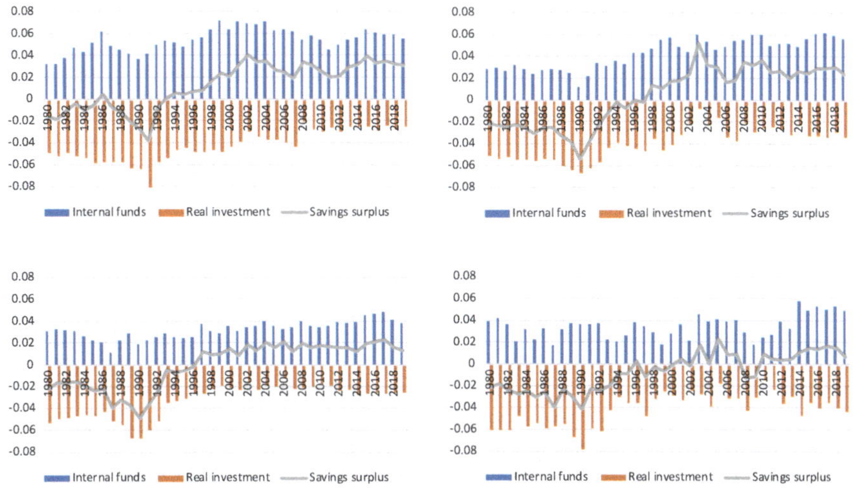

Fig. 2.5 Savings surplus of corporations by capital size (*Source* Tabluated by the author based on Ministry of Finance's Financial Statements Statistics of Corporations by Industry)

Large firms switched from a deficit to a surplus in FY1993 and SMEs followed suit several years later, FY1996 to FY1998. Micro businesses, on the other hand, alternated between a savings surplus and a savings deficit even after the late 1990s into the 2010s.

Next, when we consider the magnitude of the savings surplus since the late 1990s medium-sized firms had the largest, reaching 5.3% of total assets in FY2003, exceeding the level held by large firms, SMEs, and micro businesses.

Since the total amount of assets must always equal the total amount of liabilities in the financial statements, changes in the balance sheet that result in a surplus of savings should always be offset by changes in other items on the balance sheet. One such adjustment is the decrease in loans from financial institutions. The long-term decline in firms' dependence on loans, including SMEs, coincides with the long-term increase in the savings surplus.[15]

2.5 Importance of Focusing on the Variation in Borrowing Among Firms

The previous sections have examined trends in financing, particularly interest-bearing debt, including loans from financial institutions, among Japanese firms. In addition to the overall trend in firms' dependence on loans, what is important is its variation across firms. Even when the ratio of loans to total assets declines for all firms some firms may still be highly dependent on loans while others may have no loans at all on their balance sheet. These "extreme debt ratio" firms are difficult to reconcile with the standard view of optimal capital structure based on the trade-off theory.[16] The existence of these kinds of firms may lead to a larger, or smaller, propagation of shocks through the economy than if there were only firms with average debt ratios. For example, firms with extremely high debt ratios are likely to file for bankruptcy or go out of business when there is a negative shock, resulting in a larger economic downturn. In contrast, firms with low debt ratios, for reasons that cannot be explained by

[15] In addition to the decrease in loans from financial institutions other balance sheet changes that adjust for the savings surplus include a decrease in other interest-bearing debt, an increase in cash and deposits, an increase in stock and bond investments, and dividends. The most notable changes on balance sheets since the mid-1990s have been increased dividends (for large and medium-sized firms), an increase in stock and bond investments (for large firms), and increased cash and deposits in the 2010s (for micro businesses, SMEs, and medium-sized firms).

[16] The trade-off theory of capital structure focuses on the two effects of a firm's debt holdings and argues that debt holdings are determined by the balance between their benefits and costs. The benefit of holding debt is a reduction in corporate taxes. The more debt a firm raises the greater the interest payments, which reduces taxable profits and the amount of taxes, thereby increasing tax savings and firm value. On the other hand, the cost of holding debt is the increased likelihood of financial distress. The higher the debt ratio the higher the firm's repayment burden and the greater the likelihood that it will default on its repayments. Financial distress is costly to the firm as it often leads to bankruptcy or the sale of the business. The optimal debt ratio is determined by the point at which the benefits and costs of holding debt are equal.

economic motives as assumed by theory, may be unresponsive to economic stimulus implemented by the government, or negative macroeconomic shocks. The presence of these firms may lead to smaller fluctuations in the economy. In the following section we focus on firms with no debt and firms with high levels of debt to better understand their behavior.

2.6 Zero Leverage Firms

The first type of firms we discuss are those that do not borrow. In Japan zero leverage firms are often mentioned in the press perhaps because there is support among firms for a zero leverage management policy. For example, the Nihon Keizai Shimbun, a newspaper, focuses on listed companies whose combined amount of cash and deposits and short-term securities holdings exceed their interest-bearing debt. It defines these firms as effectively zero leverage. It then indicates that the share of these effectively zero leverage firms reached 59% by the end of FY2017 (Nihon Keizai Shimbun Morning Edition, June 26, 2018).

Yamori (2007) found that a significant number of firms are sympathetic towards zero leverage management. The study uses the results of a survey conducted by the Research Institute of Economy, Trade and Industry (RIETI) in 2005 on listed and unlisted companies headquartered in the Kansai region to tabulate and estimate the extent to which firms are oriented towards zero leverage management and the reasons for this. When asked in the survey how much they are sympathetic with the statement "zero leverage management is ideal," 29% of responding firms answered "strongly sympathetic" and 60% said "somewhat sympathetic." With "hardly sympathetic" and "not sympathetic at all" at 12%, clearly many firms consider it ideal to be zero leverage. Yamori (2007) employs a firm's response to the statement "zero leverage management is ideal" as the dependent variable and firm attributes and management conditions as explanatory variables to estimate the determinants of sympathy to zero leverage management. Results show that the smaller the firm and the higher the equity ratio the higher the degree of sympathy for zero leverage management.

Zero leverage firms are not unique to Japan, however. They have been attracting more attention and have been increasing in number overseas as well. In what follows we overview the current research in both Japan and abroad to better understand the state of zero leverage firms.

It should be noted that there are several definitions of "zero leverage" firms. In some cases it refers to the complete absence of outstanding debt, such as loans and bonds on the balance sheet, while in other cases, as in the Nikkei survey, it refers to a virtually zero leverage status where cash and cash equivalents and other cash reserves exceed interest-bearing debt. We use both criteria in what follows.

2.6.1 *Zero Leverage Ratio Among Listed Companies in the World*

Strebulaev and Yang (2013), who first brought attention to the existence of zero leverage firms among U.S. publicly traded companies, use several criteria to first identify zero leverage firms and then measure the share of these firms in the firm sector annually from 1962 to 2009.[17] Their primary definition of zero leverage is that the sum of short-term and long-term debt on a firm's balance sheet is zero. They call these firms zero leverage (ZL) firms. Other definitions of zero leverage include zero long-term debt (ZLTD) where long term debt amount outstanding is zero, almost zero leverage (AZL) where the sum of short-term and long-term debt is 5% or less of total assets, and non-positive net debt (NPND) where the total of short-term and long-term debt is equal to or less than the cash and deposit balance. The NPND category is roughly equivalent to Nihon Keizai Shimbun's "effectively zero leverage" definition.[18] The criteria for being categorized as zero leverage is more stringent than that for non-positive net debt since zero leverage requires the debt balance itself to be zero, while non-positive net debt allows firms to carry a positive debt balance.

Strebulaev and Yang (2013) show that in 1980 the percentage of U.S. listed firms categorized as ZL, ZLTD, AZL, and NPND was 4%, 7%, 11%, and 19%, respectively. By 2009 these ratios were 20%, 27%, 34%, and 48%, substantially larger than at any point over the past 30 years.[19]

The increase in the number of ZL firms is not just limited to the U.S. but appears to be a relatively common phenomenon across countries. Bessler et al. (2013) calculate the percentage of listed firms that are zero leverage for 20 advanced economies, including Japan as well as the U.S., and find that the ratio of ZL firms increased from 6% in 1988 to 26% in 2011. El Ghoul et al. (2018) measure the ratio of listed ZL firms in 73 countries, both developed and developing, and find that while the overall level of these firms is low the zero leverage ratio has been increasing from the mid-1990s to 2010.

---

[17] They exclude financial services, electricity, gas, and water, foreign firms, privately held firms, and subsidiary firms from the analysis. They also exclude firm-years with total assets of less than $10 million on a year 2000 basis.

[18] Strebulaev and Yang (2013) define a firm with a positive difference between cash and deposits and liabilities as being a non-positive net debt firm, which differs from the criterion set by the Nikkei Newspaper, which includes not only cash and deposits but also short-term securities holdings.

[19] To account for the possible overestimation by including firms that are only temporarily zero leverage, Devos et al. (2012) calculate the percentage of U.S. listed firms that remained zero leverage for three consecutive years. Even so, the number of zero leverage firms increased from 4% in 1990 to 11% in 2008.

2.6.2 Zero Leverage Ratio Among Listed Companies in Japan

What about Japan? Bessler et al. (2013) found that the average ratio of ZL firms across developed countries is 18% (1988-2011 average) while it is 19% for Japan, which is nearly the same. Khoo and Durand (2017), in their study of the evolution of the ratio of ZL firms in Japan, found that the ratio of ZL firms on the Tokyo Stock Exchange rose from 3% in 1990 to 8% in 2005 and then fell to 4% in 2014. The ratio of AZL firms, in contrast, rose from 7% in 1990 to 22% in 2007 and remained at that level through 2014.[20] Takami (2013) examined the ratios of ZL, ZLTD, and NPND firms for listed manufacturing firms from 1999 to 2009. Perhaps because the analysis is limited to the period immediately following the Global Financial Crisis that began in fall 2008, all the ratios increased. The ratio of ZL firms went from 3% in 1999 to 8% in 2009, similar to the findings in Khoo and Durand (2017). They also found that the already high ratio of NPND firms rose even further, from 31% in 1999 to 40% in 2009.

If we compare Japan to the U.S. the ratio of ZL firms in the U.S. tended to be higher than in Japan until around 2010. However, at least for the ratio of NPND firms, Japan appears to have surpassed the U.S. since then. Takata (2018) tracks the ratio of listed firms in Japan and the U.S. that satisfy the criterion close to the definition of non-positive net debt through FY2017. He shows that the ratio in Japan has continually increased, approaching 60% as of FY2017, while in the U.S. it has fallen to just over 30%.

2.6.3 Zero Leverage Ratio Including Unlisted SMEs in Japan is Rising

Up to this point the statistics presented for zero leverage firms were solely based on listed firms, both in Japan and abroad. There are studies, however, including Miwa (2011), Tsuruta (2016), and the Small and Medium Enterprise Agency (2016), which focus on unlisted SMEs in Japan. All of these analyses use firm-level data from the Annual Financial Statements Statistics of Corporations by Industry which includes information not only listed firms but also unlisted SMEs. The studies all focus on loans from financial institutions, among interest-bearing debt holdings, to measure the ratio of zero bank debt firms. If a firm does not borrow from financial institutions it is considered a zero bank debt firm even if it borrows from other sources, and thus more firms satisfy this condition than the no outstanding interest-bearing debt condition.

The SME Agency (2016) splits firms by size, those with capital of 100 million yen or less and those with capital exceeding 100 million yen and defines a firm as being in a zero bank debt status when it has zero outstanding loans from financial

[20] Khoo and Durand (2017) refer to zero leverage firms and almost zero leverage firms as all equity firms and nearly all equity firms, respectively.

institutions in both the previous and current fiscal years. It then tracks changes in this status over time. Among SMEs and micro businesses with capital of 100 million yen or less, the percentage of firms with zero bank debt went from 17% in FY1983 to reaching 37% in FY2008 before leveling off at 35% in FY2014. In contrast, among medium-sized and large firms with capital of more than 100 million yen, the share of zero bank debt firms rose continually from 12% in FY1983 to 35% in FY2008, and then 42% in FY2014.

This analysis reveals an important fact. The number of firms that do not have loans from financial institutions continues to increase regardless of firm size, reaching more than one-third of all firms by the mid-2010s. On the other hand, there are several remaining issues that need further examination in light of previous studies on listed firms. First, the SME Agency (2016) and Tsuruta (2016) focus only on loans from financial institutions, making it difficult to compare to Takami (2013) and Khoo and Durand (2017), which both examine listed firms with zero outstanding interest-bearing debt, including loans from nonfinancial institutions. Second, there may be substantial heterogeneity among firms whose capital is 100 million yen or less. Previous studies have ignored this possibility. Thus, it is not possible to precisely identify in which size category ZL firms are increasing.

Against this background and based on Sakai and Uesugi (2021) who use firm-level data from the Quarterly Financial Statements Statistics of Corporations by Industry, we show how the shares of ZL, ZBD, and NPND firms evolved from FY1980 to FY2014. The data is similar to what has been used in previous studies, except that Sakai and Uesugi (2021) use quarterly rather than annual financial statements statistics in which firms with the capital amount of 10 million yen or less are excluded. The firms in their study are divided into three categories: SMEs with capital between 10 million yen and 100 million yen; medium-sized firms with capital between 100 million yen and 1 billion yen; and large firms with capital of 1 billion yen or more. Further, in addition to ZBD firms they also identify ZL firms and NPND firms. The respective ratios are presented in Figure 2.6.

There are several interesting things to note. First, the ratios of zero leverage firms have increased for all size categories under all three definitions of zero leverage. For zero leverage firms and zero bank debt firms they have risen from around 6% to 8% in FY1980 to 21% to 34% in FY2014, respectively. Also, the ratios of these firms have risen monotonically over time, with the increase being particularly strong in the 2000s. In contrast, the ratios of non-positive net debt firms, while increasing from 21% to 34% during the period, have moved with the business cycle as opposed to continually increasing. For large firms the ratio rose during the boom period of the late 1980s followed by a fall during the subsequent period of recession, while it also declined slightly during the Global Financial Crisis. The ratio moves with the business cycle because firms whose cash and deposit balance exceeds their debt attempt to overcome financial distress by increasing debt and reducing cash.

Second, among large firms with at least 1 billion yen in capital, which includes many listed firms, the percentage of zero leverage firms was about 25% as of 2014, which is considerably higher than the 8% Takami (2013) reported for listed manufacturing firms in 2009. The difference between the numbers may be due to the fact

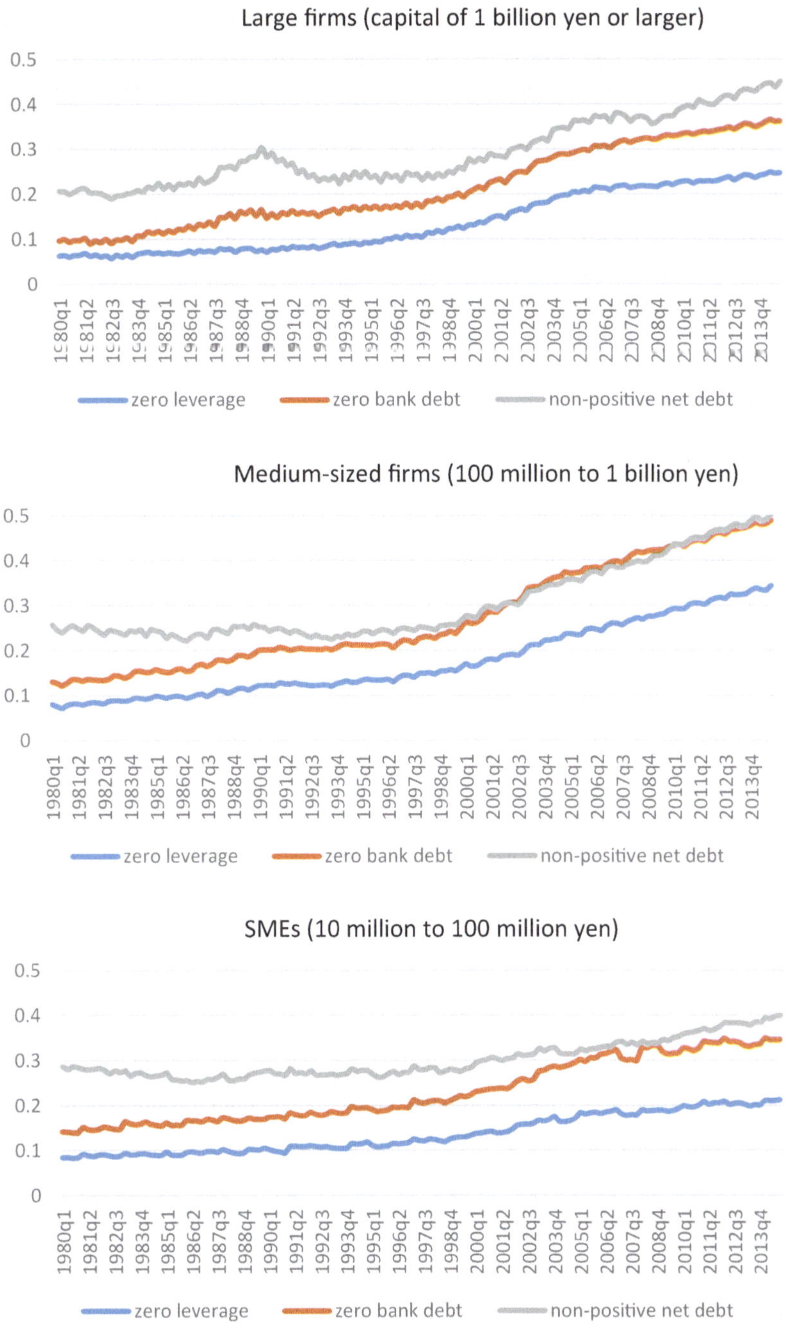

Fig. 2.6 Ratio of zero leverage firms (by capital size) (*Source* Appendix Figure H-1 in Sakai and Uesugi (2021))

that the Financial Statements Statistics of Corporations by Industry used by Sakai and Uesugi (2021) tabulates non-consolidated financial statements, while Takami (2013) uses consolidated statements. In fact, when we check non-consolidated and consolidated financial statement information for the same listed firms a considerable number of firms that have no interest-bearing debt balance on their non-consolidated statement have a positive balance on their consolidated statement.[21] Therefore, for large firms that are likely to have subsidiaries or affiliated companies the importance of the increasing percentage of zero leverage firms in the stand-alone financial statements should be somewhat discounted.

Third, the share of zero leverage medium-sized firms has increased substantially regardless of the criteria. As of 2014 half of the sample firms were in a non-positive net debt position and one-third of them were in a zero leverage position. In Section 2.3 we examined the average firm's financing environment based on the aggregate statistics and found a declining dependence on loans from financial institutions beginning at the end of the 1990s. This indicates that many of these firms did not just reduce their debt but reduced it to zero. This was particularly the case for medium-sized firms.

To summarize, the number of zero leverage firms has been on the rise worldwide, at least since the 2000s and at least among listed firms. In Japan, in addition to the presence of non-positive net debt firms whose existence was widely known, the number of zero leverage firms has increased. Medium-sized firms have seen the largest increase in zero leverage firms followed by SMEs. For listed firms the ratio of zero leverage firms may be overestimated in non-consolidated financial statements because a substantial number of subsidiaries or affiliated firms actually borrow funds even when the large listed firms are themselves zero leverage.

2.6.4 Characteristics of Zero Leverage Firms

What are the common characteristics of zero leverage firms? Here we present the results of previous studies for Japan, U.S., and other countries, which examine the types of firms that are zero leverage. While most look only at listed firms, some analyses in Japan focus on non-listed firms as well. In most of these studies the dependent variable is a dummy variable that takes the value of 1 if the firm is zero leverage and 0 otherwise. We can categorize the explanatory variables employed by these studies into two groups: those that are common across almost all the studies and those that are not. The former includes profit margins, tangible fixed asset ratios,

[21] Many of the large firms included in the Annual Financial Statements Statistics of Corporations by Industry are publicly listed and disclose their financial information on a consolidated basis, which includes subsidiaries and affiliates, rather than on a non-consolidated basis. The ratio of zero leverage firms on a consolidated basis is about half that on a non-consolidated basis.

firm size, price-to-book ratios (for listed firms only), and cash and deposit ratios.[22] These are also the variables used to identify the determinants of leverage in general.[23]

The estimation results are summarized in Table 2.3. The coefficient on profit margin is generally positive. We interpret this to mean that if profit margins are high and internal capital is abundant then there is no need to borrow and the firm is more likely to be zero leverage. Another possibility is that firms with higher profit margins but weak corporate governance are more averse to intervention by creditors and are more likely to be zero leverage through the use of other sources of financing than debt. However, as far as U.S. listed firms are concerned, Devos et al. (2012) do not find evidence of weak governance in zero leverage firms, making it difficult to reconcile the findings with this interpretation.

The coefficients on the tangible fixed asset ratio and firm size are negative in all the previous studies. This implies that firms with assets that could be offered as collateral and firms that are large, and thus considered less likely to go bankrupt in the event of adverse shocks, are more likely to finance themselves with debt. The coefficient on the price-to-book value ratio is generally positive, indicating that listed firms with high growth potential prefer to raise capital through equity rather than debt. The sign of the coefficient, however, may become negative when variables measuring a firm's growth opportunities, such as the growth rate of total assets, R&D investment, and capital expenditures, are included. This implies that the higher a firm's growth potential the higher the demand for financing through debt. Tsuruta (2016), who examined SMEs that have difficulty financing through equity, finds a negative coefficient on capital investment. Cash and deposit ratios have positive coefficients in all the studies, implying that firms with more liquid assets on hand tend to have less need for debt financing.

In summary, smaller firms, firms with high profit margins, and firms with few assets that can serve as collateral tend to be zero leverage. Publicly traded firms are also more likely to be zero leverage when they have positive growth prospects and advantageous conditions for equity issuance. In contrast, for smaller firms with limited access to the stock market, high growth potential does not necessarily mean that they can issue equity. Rather, smaller firms that make fewer capital investments and have less of a growth orientation are more likely to be zero leverage.

2.6.5 Do Zero Leverage Firms Face Financial Constraints?

Table 2.3 shows that highly profitable firms with little need for outside financing tend to choose to be zero leverage regardless of their size, while firms with low

[22] In addition, variables related to governance structure, management attributes and relationships with the firm, financing from the stock market, and legal and cultural factors are sometimes included. Variables related to governance structure include the presence of outside directors and whether institutional investors are shareholders.

[23] For example, Rajan and Zingales (1995), in an international comparison of the determinants of debt ratios in developed countries, explain the impact of these variables on debt ratios.

Table 2.3 Estimation results for the determinants of zero leverage firms in the previous studies

	Strebulaev and Yang (2013)	Devos et al. (2012)	Bessler et al. (2013)	ElGhoul et al. (2018)	Takami (2013)	Tsuruta (2016)
Countries	US	US	20 developed countries	46 countries	Japan	Japan
Types of firms	Listed firms	Listed firms	Listed firms	Listed firms	Manufacturing listed firms	SMEs and medium-sized firms mostly unlisted
Dependent variables	Almost zero leverage	Zero leverage	Zero leverage	Zero leverage	Zero leverage	Zero bank debt (positive debt in the previous period)
Number of tables in the study	Table4,11	Table3	Table4	Table5	Table11	Table4
Profitability	+		+	+		+
Tangibility	–	–	–	–		–
Size	–	– (Table2)	–	–		–
Market to book ratio	+		+	(+)	+	
Asset growth			–			
Fixed tangible asset growth						–
R&D investment					–	
Investment	+	–	–	+	–	
Age	(–)	–			–	
Cash ratio	+ (Table2)	+	+	+	(–)	+

Note Signs of coefficients in the estimation. Signs with parentheses indicate non-significance. For Strebulaev and Yang (2013) we present results for the cash and deposit ratio. The variable is not included as an explanatory variable in their estimations, but the descriptive statistics in their Table 2.2 show that the cash and deposit ratio significantly differs between almost zero leverage firms and other firms. Devos et al. (2012) do not use total assets in their estimations, but instead present descriptive statistics in their Table 2.2 and test for the difference in total assets between zero leverage and other firms. Takami (2013) does not employ multivariate regressions, but instead conducts variable-by-variable two-group comparisons for Japanese listed manufacturing firms. Finally, Tsuruta (2016) focuses only on firms with 500 or fewer employees

Source Made by the author based on these previous studies

creditworthiness due to their small size and firms without tangible fixed assets that can be used as collateral are also more likely to be zero leverage. While highly profitable firms may voluntarily choose to be zero leverage, small and asset-poor firms are financially constrained and, as a result, may be forced to be zero leverage. For instance, Bessler et al. (2013) and Devos et al. (2012) examine listed firms in the U.S. and other developed countries and find that there may be a significant number of firms that are zero leverage due to financial constraints. They develop indicators to identify financial constraints and find that zero leverage firms are more likely to face constraints than other firms.

Note, however, that these indicators focus only on the relative position of firms within a sample to judge whether firms that have difficulty obtaining a corporate bond rating, or have a low firm age and small size, are facing financial constraints. In fact, it is difficult to identify firms' financial constraints in a direct manner because we cannot observe the success/failure of debt issuance attempts for all firms.

2.6.6 Japan's Zero Leverage SMEs Have Little Demand for Funds

The SME Agency (2016) and Tsuruta (2016) provide quantitative evidence on whether zero bank debt SMEs in Japan either had loan applications rejected or did not have a demand for loans. The SME Agency (2016) tabulates the results of a survey conducted for the White Paper on SMEs in which SMEs that refrained from borrowing from financial institutions were asked why they did so.[24] The most common response was "no need to borrow funds," which accounted for 69.7% of the total, which was followed by "parent firm/affiliated firm has requested to do so" (23.4%), "can borrow on more favorable terms than borrowing from financial institutions" (5.2%), "the procedure for borrowing from financial institutions is complicated" (1.7%), and "daily interactions with financial institutions are cumbersome" (1.4%). While 70% of the firms indicated no need for funds only a limited number of firms did not borrow due to supply-side factors.

Tsuruta (2016), using firm-level data from the 2004 Basic Survey on SMEs, finds that firms with zero bank debt do not apply for loans in the first place. More specifically, in response to a question about applications for loans from their main bank in the previous year, 0.4% said that their applications were rejected, or had the loan amount reduced, 0.1% said that they were able to borrow the amount they applied for without changes in loan terms and conditions, while 99.5% answered that they did not apply for a loan. Although the survey was limited to loans from financial institutions it is clear that the majority of zero bank debt firms have no loans because they do not apply, not because their loan applications were rejected.

[24] The survey was conducted by Mizuho Research Institute in December 2015 as part of the "Survey on Financing of SMEs" commissioned by the SME Agency. Among all responding firms, the sample is limited to 1,152 firms that have no loans from financial institutions.

2.6.7 *Is Zero Leverage Status in Preparation for Future Borrowing Needs?*

In the preceding analysis we looked at whether firms are zero leverage as a result of facing financial constraints or whether they are zero leverage of their own volition. This contrasts with the analysis for foreign listed firms, including those in the U.S, which showed that zero leverage firms were relatively more likely to face financial constraints.

The remaining question is, "Why do firms that are not currently facing borrowing constraints choose to be zero leverage despite the ability to borrow?" In response to this, Bessler et al. (2013) test the hypothesis that zero leverage firms have zero outstanding debt in order to increase their financial flexibility and ensure that, when future needs arise, they are able to raise the necessary funds.[25]

Specifically, they focus on when zero leverage firms begin to borrow and examine how much their liabilities, tangible fixed assets, capital expenditures, and cash holdings change as a result. They find that the longer a firm has been zero leverage before taking out a new loan the smaller the increase in debt and assets upon borrowing. It is also the case that zero leverage firms not facing financial constraints experience shorter periods of being zero leverage. Given this fact, Bessler et al. (2013) argue that firms without financial constraints choose to remain zero leverage temporarily in order to increase their financial flexibility and when they borrow again they use that flexibility to borrow more and make larger capital investments.

Is it also true that zero leverage SMEs in Japan currently choose zero leverage management to increase their future financial flexibility? Using a different methodology from that of Bessler et al. (2013), Tsuruta (2016) compares the borrowing behavior of zero bank debt firms to other firms when there is a need for funds. He focuses on the change in loans from financial institutions and cash and deposits. If the increase in borrowing by zero bank debt firms exceeds that of other firms then being a zero bank debt firm has increased financial flexibility, allowing the firm to borrow more when needed. On the other hand, if the increase in borrowing by zero bank debt firms is smaller then having zero bank debt has a negative impact on the firms' subsequent financing environment.

The results are consistent with the latter. Tsuruta (2016) uses the change in working capital requirements as an explanatory variable measuring an increase in the demand for funds. He then examines the firm's financing environment by looking at the extent to which bank loans increase in response to an increase in demand for working capital. He finds that the coefficient on working capital is positive but smaller for zero bank debt firms than for other firms.

Further, in an additional estimation with the change in cash and deposits as the dependent variable the coefficient on the change in working capital is negative and greater in absolute value for zero bank debt firms than for other firms. In other

---

[25] This empirical study is based on the theoretical model of DeAngelo, DeAngelo, and Whited (2011) which predicts that not borrowing in the present will reduce future borrowing costs.

words, zero bank debt firms needed to withdraw more cash and deposits to meet their increased working capital needs.

Zero bank debt firms, relative to other firms, respond to actual increases in the demand for funds by drawing down their accumulated cash and deposits rather than obtaining loans. This finding for Japanese SMEs implies that the advantages of being zero leverage, as suggested theoretically by DeAngelo et al. (2011) and demonstrated empirically by Bessler et al. (2013) using data from listed firms in advanced economies, namely, "reducing future borrowing costs by not borrowing at the present time," does not hold for Japan.

2.6.8 What is the Problem with the Increase in the Number of Zero Leverage Firms?

Zero leverage firms are highly profitable and have abundant cash and deposits on hand. Since they do not make many capital investments they do not have much need for new capital and do not apply for loans. SMEs and medium-sized firms that are not listed on a stock exchange increasingly have zero outstanding loans for these reasons.

As long as there is no demand for funds the choice to be zero leverage appears to be rational. However, if the majority of firms are unwilling to invest and expand their businesses by borrowing due to past experiences, such as credit crunches during previous recessions, then the growth potential of the economy suffers.

In addition, by reducing their outstanding loans to zero, long-established relationships between firms and financial institutions may be damaged and the information they have accumulated on one another would be lost. The results of Tsuruta (2016) seem to confirm this negative outcome.

The sluggish demand for funds, reflected by the increase in the number of zero leverage firms, also means that financial institutions have not been able to stimulate firms' loan demand. As a result of financial institutions' rush to offer loans to creditworthy firms that do want to borrow the degree of competition in the lending market has intensified, leading to a long-term decline in lending margins.[26]

2.7 Insolvent and Zombie Firms

In this section we turn our attention to firms that, as opposed to being zero leverage, are debt-laden. Until the early 1990s Japanese firms had significantly increased their interest-bearing debt, including loans from financial institutions and corporate

[26] Chapters 10 to 11 in Part 3 analyze the concentration in the loan market and the impact of mergers among financial institutions.

bonds. However, the collapse of the asset price bubble in the early 1990s significantly damaged the value of assets, particularly real estate, held by firms. The result was that a number of firms emerged from the crisis with the value of their assets, as marked to the market, being less than the value of their liabilities. Further, it would have taken a number of years for these firms to pay off their liabilities in full using their profits alone.

Since then, while financial institutions have gradually reduced their holdings of non-performing loans, both large and small firms have generally been reducing their dependence on interest-bearing debt and the number of firms struggling to service their debt has declined, at least until the COVID-19 pandemic.

It is not easy to determine whether a firm holds an excessive amount of debt. This is because of the difficulty in distinguishing between positive net worth firms that aggressively increase their loans and investments and negative net worth firms that simply seek to survive through forbearance loans. Therefore, we do not make a judgment as to whether a firm has excess debt or not. Instead, we just identify firms who have more debt than others: in other words, firms whose book value of liabilities exceeds the book value of assets. We do this based on the Quarterly Financial Statements Statistics of Corporations by Industry, splitting the sample by firm size: large firms with capital of 1 billion yen or more; medium-sized firms with capital between 100 million and 1 billion yen; and SMEs with capital between 10 million and 100 million yen. Figure 2.7 shows the results.

2.7.1 Ratio of Insolvent Firms Still High Among SMEs

Across all firm sizes the ratio of insolvent firms was quite low in the late 1980s and early 1990s, before beginning to increase subsequently. However, following the mid-1990s the trends do differ depending on size. For large and medium-sized firms the ratio of insolvent firms peaked around FY1998 (around 4 and 8%, respectively) before returning to its late 1980s level by FY2005. In contrast, the ratio for SMEs rose throughout the 1990s and remained high (7 to 9%) through the early 2010s. During the Global Financial Crisis the ratio initially rose for large and medium-sized firms before returning to its pre-crisis level shortly thereafter, while there was little change among SMEs.

The decline in the ratio of insolvent firms can be attributed to their own debt repayment efforts, private debt workouts that include debt forgiveness by financial institutions, and legal bankruptcy procedures. The private workouts are facilitated by government-sponsored agencies such as the Industrial Revitalization Corporation, the Small and Medium Enterprise Revitalization Support Council, and the Regional Economy Vitalization Corporation of Japan. Legal bankruptcy procedures are stipulated by the Civil Rehabilitation Act, the Corporate Reorganization Act, and the Bankruptcy Act.

The decrease in the ratio of insolvent firms reflects the trend in corporate bankruptcies. Figure 2.8 displays the number of bankruptcies and the total liabilities of

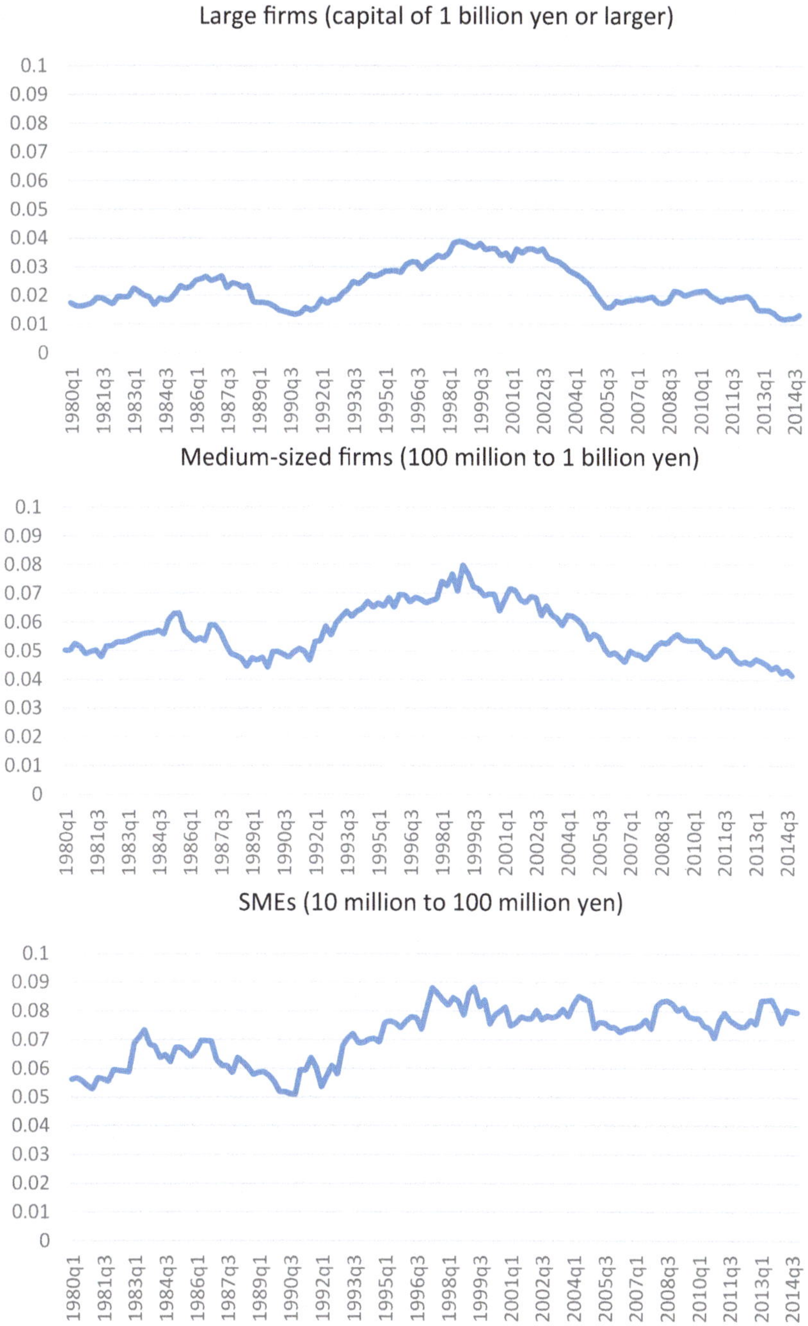

Fig. 2.7 Ratio of negative net worth firms in book value (by capital size) (*Source* Appendix Figure H-2 in Sakai and Uesugi (2021))

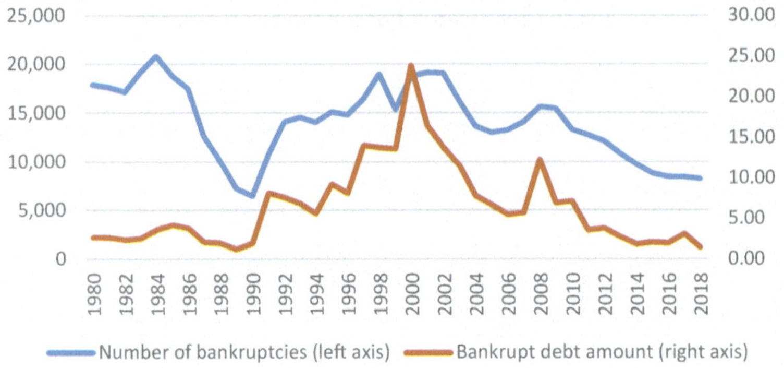

Fig. 2.8 Number of bankruptcy cases and bankrupt debt amount in trillion yen (*Source* Made by the author based on the informaion on the Tokyo Shoko Research webpage, https://www.tsr-net.co.jp/news/status/transition/index.html)

bankrupt firms in Japan from 1980 to 2018. Total liabilities of bankrupt firms exceeded 10 trillion yen for seven years from around 2000 to 2008.[27] In particular, from the end of the 1990s to the early 2000s there were many large bankruptcies including publicly listed firms, which indicates that a number of debt-laden large firms exited the market during this period. On the other hand, the overall number of bankruptcies has been declining since the beginning of the 2000s. In addition, the total amount of liabilities has also been on a downward trend, with the exception of a brief surge during the Global Financial Crisis.

One of the reasons for the ratio of insolvent SMEs remaining high in Japan is that these firms have not negotiated private debt workouts nor have they been exiting the market through bankruptcies.

Fukuda and Koibuchi (2006) identify the characteristics of debt forgiveness and their impact on the Japanese economy by examining cases of private debt restructuring among large listed firms. Debt forgiveness includes debt discharge and debt-equity swaps, with most cases concentrated in the early 2000s. They also find that firms whose main banks are actively involved in debt forgiveness display better ex-post performance.[28]

In contrast SMEs may not have experienced a significant reduction in insolvencies through debt restructuring. It is true that there were a massive number of debt contract renegotiations for SMEs under the SME Financing Facilitation Act, which was in

[27] The TSR's bankruptcy statistics include two categories of firms other than those under judicial bankruptcy procedures: those that are stopped bank transactions and those that are undergoing private out-of-court dissolution. Private out-of-court dissolution includes cases where business is suspended but not legally liquidated and settlements with creditors and other parties are still underway. This is different from out-of-court debt workouts which aim at continuing operations. Note also that the statistics include failures of financial institutions which are out of the scope of our interest.

[28] They measure the level of commitment by the main bank to the firm by the extent to which the share of the main bank for loans that are forgiven exceeds its overall loan share prior to forgiveness.

effect from 2009 to 2013. During the time that the law was in effect 4.14 million debt contracts amounting to 114 trillion yen were renegotiated and modified (see the column at the end of this chapter for more information on the Act). As Uesugi et al. (2015) show, however, only a small number of firms that have undergone modifications in loan terms and conditions are likely to have reduced their debt.

Uesugi et al. (2015) asked firms whether they had received any changes in terms and conditions during the period the Act was in effect and received responses from approximately 6000 firms. The majority of the changes in terms and conditions were for changes in the repayment period and the deferral of principal payments, with very few debt reductions or debt-to-equity swaps. Table 2.4 illustrates this point. The majority of the modifications involved principal payment deferral (38%) and repayment period extensions (55% combined, an extension of one year or less and an extension of over one year) while more drastic measures such as principal debt reductions (8%) and debt-to-equity swaps (0.1%) are rare.

Of course, even if there is no reduction in the amount owed when firms modify the terms and conditions of their debt there is still a possibility that they will be able to repay if their business restructuring turns out to be successful and their business conditions improve as a result of a shift to proactive management, allowing them to escape from insolvency. In fact, according to Uesugi et al. (2015), many firms

Table 2.4 Types of modifications in loan terms and conditions after the introduction of the SME financing facilitation act

Deferral of payment period for one year or less	365
	24.9
Deferral of payment period for more than one year	437
	29.8
Deferral of principal payment	557
	37.9
Reduction in the interest payment	240
	16.3
Reduction in the debt amount	115
	7.8
Debt equity swap	2
	0.1
Debt debt swap	13
	0.9
Other	123
	8.4
Number of responses	1468
	100

Note Number of responses (first row) and the share (second row; %)
Source Table 4–9 in Uesugi et al. (2015)

cite process innovation, product innovation, and business diversification as included in their submitted management improvement plan. If these efforts prove successful firms' business conditions will improve and they will be able to escape insolvency. In addition, nearly half of the firms are engaged in restructuring and we can assume that these firms have reduced their costs, including debt, equipment, and employment.

However, Ono and Yasuda (2017), who used individual data from this same questionnaire to examine changes in firm performance after a change in terms and conditions, find that changes in terms and conditions that go as far as principal and interest rate reductions and forgiveness are necessary to improve business conditions. They divided firms that underwent loan contract modifications into two groups: those that had deferred payments, such as extended repayment periods and deferred principal payments, and those that had forgiven debt payments, such as principal debt reductions, interest rate reductions, and debt-equity swaps. The latter group of firms displayed a greater improvement in their credit ratings. Based on these results it appears that the measures taken by the majority of firms under the SME Financing Facilitation Act, such as extending repayment periods and deferring payments, were not effective enough to help these firms emerge from insolvency.

2.7.2 *Identification of Zombie Firms that Have Difficulty Continuing Operations Without the Support of Financial Institutions*

Thus far, we have identified insolvent firms using the amount of liabilities relative to assets on the balance sheet and discussed the change in the share of these firms over time. As mentioned at the beginning of Section 2.7, however, it is not possible to determine whether a firm has excess debt based on a simple comparison between the book value of assets and liabilities.

Therefore, many studies have tried to find firms that have performed poorly, carry a lot of debt, and have difficulty continuing operations without support from financial institutions in an attempt to identify so-called "zombie firms." Caballero, Hoshi and Kashyap (2008) were the first to present a criterion for identifying zombie firms among Japanese listed firms and since then alternative criteria have been proposed by Fukuda and Nakamura (2011) and Imai (2016). Most analyses focus on large firms but some studies do cover both large and small firms, although the periods of analysis are limited. In recent years interest in zombie firms, mostly among listed firms, has increased overseas and as a result there are a number of studies that focus on a number of countries including Japan.[29] Table 2.5 summarizes the details.

---

[29] See, for example, Banerjee and Hofmann (2020) and El Ghoul, Fu, and Guedhami (2021).

Table 2.5 Criteria for zombie firms and the development of zombie ratio

	Caballero, Hoshi, and Kashyap (2008)	Fukuda and Nakamura (2011)	Imai (2016)	Goto and Wilbur (2018)	Banerjee and Hofmann (2020)
Criterion	Calculate the minimum required interest rate payable (R_it*) based on the long- and short-term prime rates, bond issuance rates in the market, and the amount of long- and short-term debt and bond issuance for each firm. Then, a firm-year in which the actual interest rate R_it being smaller than R_it* is judged as in the zombie status	A firm is considered zombie if it meets one of two criteria Profitability criterion: The firm is considered a zombie under the CHK criterion and has EBIT (= ordinary income + interest expense − interest income) < INT_it* (= minimum required interest payment) Forbearance criterion: EBIT is below INT_it*, debt is more than half of total assets in the previous period, and borrowing has increased from the previous period to the current period	Modify the profitability criterion of FN so that EBIT < INT_it* is established not only for the current year, but also for the past several years. The criteria for forbearance criterion remain unchanged	Use all the three criteria alternately	EBIT < INT_it (=interest payment) and Tobin's q is below the median value of the industry to which the firm belongs for two years
Countries	Japan	Japan	Japan	Japan	14 developed countries indlucing Japan
Firm type	Listed firms	Listed firms	By capital size: large, medium-sized, SMEs, and micro businesses	By capital size: large, medium-sized, SMEs&micro businesses	Listed firms

(continued)

Table 2.5 (continued)

	Caballero, Hoshi, and Kashyap (2008)	Fukuda and Nakamura (2011)	Imai (2016)	Goto and Wilbur (2018)	Banerjee and Hofmann (2020)
Period of analysis	1981–2002	1995–2004	2002–2008	2009–2014	Mid 1980s–2017
Major results	Zombie ratio was around 5% in the 1980s, while it rose sharply in the late 1990s and has remained around 30%	Zombie ratio was on an upward trend since 1995, peaking in 2001 (over 10%) and then declining significantly through 2004	Zombie ratio is highest in micro businesses, followed by large firms, medium-sized firms, and SMEs. The ratio was highest in the real estate industry, where it declined through 2007 and then increased slightly in 2008	Zombie ratio is highest in micro businesses for both criteria, which is followed by medium-sized and large firms for FN and Imai, and followed by large and medium-sized firms for CHK. Decreasing trend during the period for FN and Imai, but increasing for CHK	In Japan, zombie ratio was highest in the early 2000s, followed by 2010. Since then, it has been declining rapidly. Overseas, on the other hand, zombie ratio has been on the rise since 2010 in many countries

Source Summarized by the author based on each paper

Caballero, Hoshi and Kashyap (2008) focus only on the presence of support from financial institutions to identify zombie firms. Specifically, when raising funds through loans or corporate bonds, if the interest payment falls below the most favorable market interest rate the firm is considered to be a zombie in the sense that it is supported by financial institutions, or the corporate bond market, and cannot survive without such support.

Fukuda and Nakamura (2011) instead propose a criterion that includes performance, debt size, and the change in debt in addition to the presence of support from financial institutions. They argue that using only the financial support criterion may lead to errors in classifying non-zombie firms as zombies and zombie firms as non-zombies. In the case of the first error they note the possibility that even the most creditworthy firms borrowing at interest rates below the prime rate may be identified as zombies.

To avoid this Fukuda and Nakamura (2011) restrict zombie firms to those that meet the criteria of Caballero, Hoshi and Kashyap (2008) but also have low profitability. To deal with the latter error they point out a situation in which a firm with high debt and low repayment possibilities and thus a high interest rate would not be identified as a zombie. Therefore, they add a criterion that identifies firms with high, and increasing, outstanding loan balances as zombies.

Imai (2016) uses a slightly modified version of the Fukuda and Nakamura (2011) criterion, while Goto and Wilbur (2019) use all three criteria. Banerjee and Hofmann (2020) argue that in the recent low interest rate environment it may be difficult for zombie firms to obtain negative interest rates even if they receive support from financial institutions, and so they consider firms with an interest coverage ratio (= EBIT/interest expense) less than one and a low Tobin's q to be zombies.

There are two interesting observations in Table 2.5. First, when comparing zombie ratios by size we see that the ratio is highest for micro businesses, followed by large firms. This is similar to what we find in Figure 2.7 for firms with excess debt where the ratio is highest for the smallest size category. This suggests that among SMEs the smaller the firm the more difficult it is for them to survive without support. Large firms, on the other hand, had the lowest ratio of insolvency but a high ratio of zombies. This is likely because many of the large firms received financial support from financial institutions even though they were not insolvent in terms of book value.

Second, if we compare the ratio of zombie firms among listed firms across countries the ratio of zombies in Japan has been declining since 2010 while it has been increasing in most other developed countries. While the presence of zombie firms in Japan was significant through the early 2000s, as Fukuda and Nakamura (2011) point out, many of these firms were able to recover. And, although the ratio rose initially during the Global Financial Crisis, zombie firms may now be less prominent among listed Japanese firms than they are in other countries.

2.7.3 *Ratio of Zombie Firms Among SMEs*

Unlike listed zombie firms there have been, up to this point, no analyses that measured the share of zombie SMEs over a long period. Exceptions are Honda et al. (2023, in English) and Uesugi, Ono, et al. (2022, in Japanese) where they examine the ratio of zombie firms from the 1990s to the present. The results are presented here.[30]

The study focuses on firms that responded to any of the 2008, 2009, 2014, and 2020 surveys conducted by RIETI, which mainly focused on SMEs. These were the same surveys that Uesugi et al. (2009, 2015) and Uesugi, Ono et al. (2021, 2022) used in their papers. The authors obtained financial data of responding firms from the firm-level database of a major credit research firm and calculated the percentage of firms that were identified as zombies.[31] Of the definitions presented in Table 2.5 those based on Caballero, Hoshi and Kashyap (2008) (hereafter referred to as the CHK criterion) and on Fukuda and Nakamura (2011) (hereafter referred to as the FN criterion) are used.

There are a few interesting features in Figure 2.9. The ratio of zombie firms, regardless of criteria, increased from 1995 to 1996 and then declined until the mid-2000s, followed by another rise until 2009 in the wake of the Global Financial Crisis. Subsequently, however, the movements in the ratio depend on the criterion. By the CHK criterion the ratio continued to rise, reaching 37% in 2019, a level comparable to the late 1990s, while by the FN criterion the ratio declined, falling to 11% in 2019, the lowest level in the last 30 years. In 2020, the year of the COVID-19 pandemic, the ratio increased slightly for both criteria.

Uesugi, Ono, et al. (2022) examined whether the CHK criterion or the FN criterion more accurately identifies zombie firms in the current economy. They find that the possibility that firms are mistakenly identified as zombies has increased since the Global Financial Crisis because the actual borrowing rates paid by firms, including prime borrowers, have continued to decline while the prime short-term and long-term loan rate, which is the benchmark for comparison, has remained almost unchanged. In addition, when using more direct information on the support extended by financial institutions, such as changes in the terms and conditions of loan contracts, they find that firms that receive support are more likely to be zombie firms under the FN criterion than the CHK criterion. Therefore, they believe that the FN criterion is more suitable for identifying zombie firms than the CHK criterion in the post-Global Financial Crisis period.

[30] Yamada et al. (2022) calculate the ratio of zombie firms among SMEs since the late 2000s. Compared with Fig. 2.9 the ratio is similar with respect to the FN criterion. On the other hand, their zombie ratio based on the CHK criterion only slightly increased after 2015.

[31] The number of firms in the sample varies from year to year. From about 2200 firms in 1990, the first year, it increased to about 5500 firms in 2000, and has fluctuated between 5800 and 6500 since then.

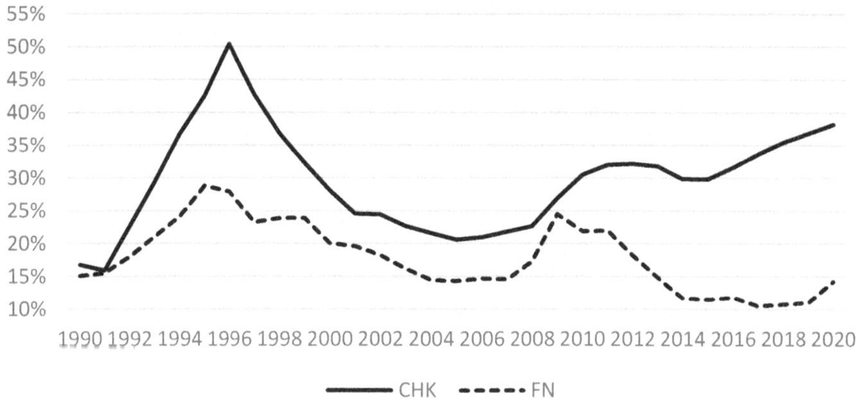

Fig. 2.9 Zombie ratio for SMEs (*Source* Processed by the author based on Uesugi, Ono et al. (2022))

Taking these considerations into account it can be said that the ratio of zombie firms among Japanese SMEs declined after the Global Financial Crisis up to the COVID-19 pandemic. However, by 2021, when the effects of the pandemic became more pronounced, the ratio of zombie firms, as measured by the FN indicator, increased as it did in 2020.

2.7.4 *What's Wrong with Zombie Firms?*

In what sense is the existence of zombie firms problematic for the economy? In previous research, focusing mainly on large firms, the first issue is the negative spillover effects of zombie firms. Caballero, Hoshi and Kashyap (2008) point to crowding-out effects where the survival of zombie firms discourages investment and employment in other firms. Kwon, Narita and Narita (2015) find that the labor hoarding effect of zombie firms is particularly large and that the total productivity growth rate of Japanese firms in the 1990s was lower than it would have been without loans to zombie firms.

The second issue has to do with the behavior of zombie firms themselves. Fukuda and Nakamura (2011) show that many zombie firms were able to emerge from zombie status by cutting costs. Fukuda (2015) notes that while firms were able to escape zombie status by cutting costs they were not proactive enough in improving productivity and competitiveness, and capital investment remained sluggish, suggesting that passive corporate behavior during the emergence process may have contributed to the overall stagnation of the Japanese economy since the 2000s.

SME zombie firms may also have the same negative spillover effects on their neighboring firms as do large zombie firms. There are indications that SMEs with a lot of debt and little chance of survival tend to compete by offering lower prices without adding value to their products or services.[32] However, a quantitative analysis has yet to be conducted on the mechanism or extent of the problem.

2.7.5 Relationship Between Zombie Firms and Government Financial Support Measures

The definition of a zombie firm is that it cannot continue to operate without the support of financial institutions. In response to the COVID-19 pandemic the government provided extensive support measures to assist firms. The purpose of these measures was to help firms facing a temporary liquidity crisis due to the negative COVID-19 shock. Were firms already classified as zombies prior to the crisis more likely to take advantage of these government support measures?

Hoshi, Kawaguchi and Ueda (2022) and Uesugi, Ono et al. (2022) examine the financing support measures implemented during the pandemic and analyze the determinants of their application or use. Both show that firms experiencing larger sales declines after 2020, when the pandemic began, and firms with higher credit risk before 2020 were more likely to apply for and use the support measures.

Additionally, Uesugi and Ono et al. (2022) find that firms classified as zombies by the FN criterion made more use of government support measures. Table 2.6 compares zombie firms and non-zombie firms based on the FN criterion one year before the crisis. We see that the use rates of support measures, such as interest-free unsecured loans from government and private financial institutions, business continuity grants and subsidies, local government support funds for voluntary business closures, employment adjustment subsidies, and rent support grants, are higher for zombie firms than non-zombies.

That zombie firms are more likely than non-zombies to use support measures during a crisis is not just limited to the COVID-19 pandemic. The table shows that zombie firms also made more use of the emergency guaranteed loans provided during the Global Financial Crisis as well.

Is government support for zombie firms inefficient? Given the fact that many firms can emerge from zombie status it does not necessarily follow that the use of support measures by zombie firms is a life-extension measure for firms that are unlikely to ever recover. Moreover, in emergency situations it may be more important to minimize the risk of viable firms not receiving support than to minimize the risk

[32] A practitioner in charge of business restructuring of distressed borrower SMEs in a regional financial institution has indicated that some firms, particularly in the construction industry, are taking such actions ("Roundtable Discussion: Post-COVID-19 Business Restructuring: Issues and Challenges from a Regional Finance Perspective," Business Restructuring and Credit Management, January 5, 2022 issue, in Japanese).

Table 2.6 Use ratios of support measures for financing (zombie firms and non-zombie firms)

Use ratio of support measures provided during the COVID-19 pandemic		
	Non-zombie firms (%)	Zombie firms (%)
Interest-free and unsecured loans by the government-affiliated financial institutions	24.8	35.6
Interest-free and unsecured loans by the private financial institutions	46.5	56.3
Business continuity grant or subsidies	34.4	47.8
Financial support during business closure by the local governments	11.1	17.5
Employment adjustment subsidies	31.9	44.1
Rent payment grant	12.5	16.2
Use ratio of support measures provided during the Global Financial Crisis		
	Non-zombie firms (%)	Zombie firms (%)
Emergency credit guarantee loans	21.6	40.5

Note Calculate zombie ratios based on the FN criterion
Source Produced by the author based on Uesugi and Ono et al. (2022)

of unviable firms receiving support. However, if the performance of zombie firms worsens due to the use of support measures it is important for the government and financial institutions to actively promote efforts toward business restructuring.

2.8 Summary

This chapter provides an overview of the financing environment for Japanese firms, particularly SMEs, by looking at medium- to long-term changes in financing since the 1980s and focusing not just on average firms but on firmst at both ends of the distribution of debt dependence.

There is a growing concern that the number of zombie firms, which are finding it difficult to survive without the support of financial institutions, may be increasing due to the COVID-19 pandemic. Against this background we examined trends in the number of insolvent and zombie firms, including SMEs, as well as trends in the number of zero leverage firms, with a surplus in savings, in the Japanese corporate sector.

Quantifying the scale of insolvent and zombie firms as a percentage of total SMEs has both practical and policy implications. Many firms are able to emerge from zombie status (Fukuda and Nakamura, 2011), and so being identified as a zombie does not necessarily mean that the firm will exit. However, it is the case that a number of these firms must undertake drastic measures to survive such as debt restructuring, business reorganization, and management change.

The Financial Services Agency stated that as of March 2013, the date of the expiration of the SME Financing Facilitation Act, there were 50,000 to 60,000 firms in need of business revitalization out of the 300,000 to 400,000 firms that had amended their loan terms and conditions.[33] On the other hand, since its establishment in 2003 the Small and Medium Enterprise Revitalization Support Councils, which support the formulation of business revitalization plans, have helped approximately 16,000 SMEs to formulate revitalization plans by providing consultations and financial support.

How do these numbers relate to the ratios of insolvent and zombie firms discussed in this chapter? Are the current efforts of financial institutions and the SME Revitalization Support Councils sufficient or insufficient in light of these figures? Can they handle the expected increase in insolvent and zombie firms as a result of the pandemic? These are all important issues for future consideration.

Further, it is noteworthy that the proportion of zero leverage firms, such as those without debt or with non-positive net debt, has increased among SMEs as Japan's firm sector continues to have a saving surplus. From our analysis zero leverage SMEs are characterized by a lack of willingness to invest rather than difficulty in borrowing from financial institutions. The questions as to why the number of zero leverage firms has increased and how to stimulate the borrowing demand of these firms should be important issues for SME finance in the future.

In the next chapter we will examine the efficiency of SME financing. We focus on the relationship between productivity and the allocation of funds among Japanese firms, including SMEs, and use firm-level data to examine the extent to which interest-bearing debt is reallocated and whether funds are reallocated from low-productivity firms to high-productivity firms in accordance with productivity growth.

2.9 Column: SME Financing Facilitation Act

The SME Financing Facilitation Act is officially called the "Act Concerning Temporary Measures to Facilitate Financing for SMEs." The law was enacted in response to strong concerns about the financing environment for SMEs even though the worst part of the recession following the Global Financial Crisis was already over. The law came into effect on December 4, 2009, and was initially a temporary legislation slated to end in March 2011, but was extended twice, partly due to the Great East Japan Earthquake on March 11, 2011.

The main pillar of the law is that financial institutions should endeavor to comply as much as possible with requests from SMEs for changes in loan terms and conditions, such as deferral of repayment deadlines. Furthermore, in order to support the efforts of financial institutions the FSA eased the requirements in its Supervisory Guidelines and Financial Inspection Manual for loans that do not fall under restructured loans,

[33] See Minutes of the Joint Meeting of the 28th General Assembly and the 16th Subcommittee on Finance of the Financial System Council in the Financial Services Agency (held on July 4, 2012, in Japanese).

which are classified as nonperforming loans, even if financial institutions modify the terms of their SME loans.

During the period the law was in effect a large number of applications for changes in terms and conditions were submitted by SMEs to financial institutions, and a high percentage of those applications were approved. According to the "Status of changes in loan terms and conditions under the SME Financing Facilitation Act (final report)" released by the Financial Services Agency in June 2014, a total of 4.37 million applications for debt contract modifications were submitted between the initiation and termination of the Act, amounting to 120 trillion yen in value terms. Of these, 4.15 million requests, or 114 trillion yen in value terms, were approved with a modification of repayment terms, representing an approval rate of more than 97%. It is estimated that between 300,000 and 400,000 firms in Japan have received such modifications. If, as Table 2.4 shows, the majority of the loans are for the deferral of principal payments or an extension of the repayment period then financial institutions do not incur any losses because they are not reducing or exempting the principal or interest rate. These circumstances are likely behind the very high approval rates by financial institutions.

Although the law ended in March 2013 the FSA emphasized that the intent of the law will remain the same and that there will be no change in the behavior of government authorities and financial institutions. This stance has continued to the present time.[34]

There are opposing views on the economic effects of the Facilitation Act, primarily focusing on its economic effects. On one hand there are studies with negative views, including Sakuragawa and Hoshi (2009) and Kondo (2014). Sakuragawa and Hoshi (2009) predict the following problems: financial institutions will no longer provide new loans; healthy firms will not apply for changes in terms and conditions in consideration of their relationship with financial institutions; only high-risk firms will make use of the Facilitation Act resulting in adverse selection; and there will be a potential increase in non-performing loans due to the relaxation of bank asset assessments by the Financial Services Agency. Using bank-level data Kondo (2014) finds that financial institutions that approve more changes in terms and conditions under the Facilitation Act decrease their non-credit guaranteed loans and increase their NPLs. He also finds that the behavior of these financial institutions does not result in an improvement in the SMEs' business conditions, as measured by the diffusion index of sales, or their financing environment.

On the other hand, studies that find mixed results of the Facilitation Act include Yamori (2012) and Uesugi et al. (2015). Yamori (2012) had several findings. First, there was no substantial change in the percentage of firms applying for changes in loan terms and conditions, in the acceptance rate of the applications, or in the ratio of financially distressed firms before and after the Facilitation Act. Second, financial institutions' attitudes toward SMEs were polarized between those who were willing

[34] The FSA's website states that although the Act on the SME Financing Facilitation Act has expired there is no change in the obligation of financial institutions in that they are responsible for the funding of SMEs and for responding to firms' applications for loan contract modifications.

to discuss restructuring and those who were highly unlikely to extend new loans. Third, there was no difference in the frequency of meetings with financial institutions depending on the firm's use of the Facilitation Act.

Uesugi et al. (2015) found that more than half of the firms that received a change in loan terms and conditions reported that they would have gone bankrupt or closed due to financing difficulties if the terms and conditions had not been changed. However, they also found that a substantial number of firms gave negative assessments of the business improvement plans they submitted when they received changes in the terms and conditions as "the plans were necessary only to have the application for a change in loan terms and conditions approved" and "the plans do not fully reflect the firms' business circumstances."

Practitioners and lawyers working on business restructuring for SMEs also seem to have both positive and negative views on the Facilitation Act. On the positive side it has made it easier for debtor firms to request financial institutions to postpone repayments, making it easier for these practitioners to work on business restructuring through private debt workouts. On the negative side, even after entering into the process of private debt workouts, debtors tend to repeatedly change the terms and conditions of their loans without a clear prospect for business recovery rather than undertaking a drastic business restructuring.[35]

[35] "Roundtable Discussion: The current state of formal out-of-court debt workouts and the role of lawyers" (Business Restructuring and Credit Management, April 5, 2020 issue, in Japanese).

Chapter 3
Size and Efficiency of Credit Reallocation Across Firms

Abstract We examine credit reallocation among Japanese firms since the 1980s. We look at both the size (i.e., the extent of credit reallocation as measured by the sum of the increase in firms' outstanding interest-bearing debt and the decrease in their outstanding interest-bearing debt) and the efficiency (i.e., the degree to which interest-bearing debt is redirected from firms with low productivity to those with high productivity) of these reallocations. We find that while the magnitude of reallocation tends to be smaller during short-term recessions and the long-term economic downturn of the 1990s, what is unique to Japan about these reallocations is that we observe both smaller increases and decreases in interest-bearing debt holdings. As for the efficiency of reallocation, large firms experienced inefficient reallocations during the "lost decade" from the early 1990s to the early 2000s mainly due to firms that received financial support from the government. However, in other periods, credit was efficiently reallocated. In contrast, for SMEs there is no clear evidence of credit being reallocated from low-productivity firms to high-productivity firms, either in normal times or in economic downturns. It appears that credit reallocation in the SME sector has made no contribution to SMEs' productivity growth.

Keywords Credit reallocation · Total factor productivity · Interest-bearing debt · Loans · The lost decade

3.1 Introduction: How Does the Allocation of Funds to Firms Affect Productivity?

In Chapter 2 we summarized the changes in the financing environment and holdings of interest-bearing debt of the entire firm sector, including SMEs, using mainly aggregate statistics. We found that for large firms interest-bearing debt increased throughout the 1980s and 1990s before decreasing after the late 1990s, while for SMEs the decrease in interest-bearing debt began later.

I. Uesugi, *The Economics of SME Finance*, Advances in Japanese Business and Economics 36, https://doi.org/10.1007/978-981-96-3193-3_3

The next issue is how the allocation of funds through interest-bearing debt relates to the overall performance of the firm sector. One indicator of performance is productivity. The fact that the average productivity of SMEs is lower than that of large firms is pointed out in the 2020 White Paper on SMEs. Atkinson (2019) attributes Japan's long-term stagnation in productivity to SMEs that have exploited the government's size-dependent support measures. These firms have no incentive to expand their operations and therefore have not been able to take advantage of economies of scale.[1] He further argues that the existence of zombie firms, which have difficulty continuing operations without support from financial institutions, is not a significant cause of the slowdown in productivity growth. However, as he did not provide any convincing evidence for the role of financing in explaining the SMEs' low productivity, an important research question is just how much financial aspects matter in regards to the productivity stagnation of Japanese firms, especially SMEs.

We define efficient capital allocation as an allocation of funds that increases the overall productivity of the firm sector and we measure its "success" based on the following considerations. If there is an increase in funds allocated to high-productivity firms and a decrease in funds allocated to low-productivity firms then the share of high-productivity firms will increase, thus increasing overall productivity. Under these circumstances we can say that an efficient allocation of funds has taken place. Conversely, if less funds are allocated to high-productivity firms and more to low-productivity firms this is an inefficient allocation of funds, and the average productivity of firms will decline.

Aggregate data on overall borrowing trends is insufficient to evaluate the efficiency of credit allocation among firms. What is necessary is firm-level information on the level of productivity and the increase/decrease in interest-bearing debt. In this chapter we assess the efficiency of credit allocation for large firms and SMEs using firm-level data on the increase/decrease of interest-bearing debt and productivity levels from the Ministry of Finance's Financial Statements Statistics of Corporations by Industry. The order of analysis is as follows.

First, we examine the amount of credit reallocation in the firm sector. We sum changes in interest-bearing debt for all firms that recorded an increase in their amount of debt outstanding. Similarly, we sum changes in interest-bearing debt for all the firms that recorded a decrease. We then add these two together to measure the extent of credit reallocation occurring in the firm sector. We use the term "reallocation" because the baseline is the state in which interest-bearing debt has already been allocated to

[1] The main argument of Atkinson (2019) is not about the role that finance plays in improving the productivity of SMEs but that to improve the productivity of the Japanese economy it is necessary to reduce the overall share of SMEs by expanding the size of SMEs through mergers and consolidation. Minato (2021), Kurose (2021), Mitsui (2020), among others, have made a counterargument. They argue that it is important to note that the low productivity of SMEs is due in part to their unfavorable business transaction relationships with large firms, which must be rectified, and that policies aimed at expanding the scale of SMEs were already adopted in the 1960s and did not have any noticeable effect on productivity or on the economy. Guner et al. (2008) posit a theoretical model where the existence of support measures for small firms may distort corporate behavior. Hosono, Takizawa, and Tsuru (2017) and Tsuruta (2020) provide empirical evidence for the distortionary effect of such policies on the size distribution of SMEs.

firms and we examine the increase or decrease from that baseline for our analysis. Since the 1990s a large number of studies have focused on the heterogeneity of characteristics among firms and households and examined how the allocation of resources such as labor, capital, and credit has affected overall economic performance. Several seminal studies examined the reallocation of labor before other studies examined the reallocation of physical capital. Research examining credit reallocation only began in the 2010s.[2]

After defining the reallocation of credit across firms we examine the amount of reallocation, its development over time, and its linkage to the business cycle. Some theoretical models on the relationship between business cycles and the magnitude of reallocation predict that the relationship between firms and financial institutions is more likely to break during recessions, resulting in a greater degree of credit reallocation. Others instead predict less reallocation as financial institutions roll over existing contracts instead of terminating them, leading to a smaller decline in interest-bearing debt outstanding. We will empirically test which of these is true, implementing analyses both for large and medium-sized firms and SMEs.

Second, we identify how the increase or decrease in interest-bearing debt at the firm level relates to productivity. Specifically, we estimate how firm-level total factor productivity is related to changes in interest-bearing debt in the following period. This will verify whether credit is reallocated from low-productivity firms to high-productivity firms or vice versa.[3]

---

[2] In studies on the reallocation of managerial resources, Davis and Haltiwanger (1992) and Davis, Haltiwanger, and Schuh (1996) focus on labor, specifically for the U.S. manufacturing industry, while Genda (2004) summarizes the relevant findings for labor reallocation in Japan. In the area of physical capital Ramey and Shapiro (1998), Eisfeldt and Rampini (2006), and Lanteri (2018) all analyze the U.S. Uesugi et al. (2018) attempt a similar analysis for physical capital reallocation in Japan. Herrera, Kolar, and Minetti (2011) were the first to examine the inter-firm reallocation of credit, using data on U.S. listed firms. Hyun and Minetti (2019) focus on South Korea, showing trends in credit reallocation before and after the 1997 financial crisis and discussing the relationship between credit reallocation and investment efficiency. In Japan, however, there has been no research to date which investigates the scale and nature of credit reallocation.

[3] There are numerous studies in Japan that focus on the firm sector and examine the efficiency of resource allocation, including funds. Fukao and Kwon (2006), Nishimura, Nakajima, and Kiyota (2005), and Sakai, Uesugi, and Watanabe (2010) all analyze the relationship between the entry and exit of firms and their productivity, or profitability. Sekine, Koyabashi, and Saita (2003) and Peek and Rosengren (2005) look at how listed firms' debt is affected by their performance and past levels of debt. The analysis in this chapter is similar to Peek and Rosengren's (2005) approach in that it focuses on surviving firms and the efficiency of the allocation of interest-bearing debt and loans. Most previous studies have focused on the 1990s and early 2000s when there was a severe financial crisis in the country. This chapter is unique in that it analyzes the evolution of the efficiency of credit allocation over the long term, from the 1980s to the 2010s, and compares large firms and SMEs.

3.2 Overview of Results

In terms of the magnitude of reallocation, because SMEs are more likely to face large negative shocks, while at the same time having higher growth potential than large firms, SMEs contribute more to the credit reallocation than large firms.

When we consider changes in the amount of reallocation from the 1980s to the 2010s we see a large drop for both large firms and SMEs, not only during short-term recessions but also during the so-called "lost decade" following the collapse of the bubble economy. The extent of the increase and the degree of the decrease in interest-bearing debt becomes smaller during economic downturns in Japan, which is a distinct feature of credit reallocation in Japan compared to the U.S. and South Korea.

We then turn to the efficiency of credit reallocation. For large firms, during normal times we see an efficient reallocation, where credit flows from firms with low productivity to firms with high productivity. During the "lost decade," however, the opposite occurred, with credit being reallocated from high-productivity firms to low-productivity firms. This is most often observed in firms that received financial assistance and were able to obtain low interest rate loans. In contrast, for SMEs it is difficult to find a statistically significant relationship between productivity and the reallocation of credit. Throughout the period for which we have data we observe no statistically significant productivity gains through credit reallocation. These results suggest that there is still room for financial institutions to provide financial support to SMEs that contribute to an improvement in productivity.

The order of analysis is as follows. We define indicators for credit reallocation in Sect. 3.3. In Sect. 3.4 we present the calculated values for these indicators. We follow this in Sect. 3.5 by tracking changes over time, focusing particularly on economic downturns. In Sects. 3.6 and 3.7 we examine the efficiency of credit reallocation and interpret the results. Section 3.8 summarizes the chapter.

3.3 Credit Reallocation Indicators

3.3.1 Definitions

To understand the extent of credit reallocation in Japan we begin by defining the relevant indicators. The measures of reallocation were first introduced by Davis and Haltiwanger (1992) in their analysis of the labor market. Herrera, Kolar, and Minetti (2011) applied this methodology to the examination of credit reallocation, which we closely follow in this chapter.

As shown in Eq. (3.1), c_{ft} is the average of interest-bearing debt of firm f at the end of period t-1 and the end of period t. Interest-bearing debt consists of loans and corporate bonds. F_{st} denotes the set of firms belonging to sector s (classified by industry, firm size, and region) in period t, and C_{st} is the average of interest-bearing debt at the end of period t-1 and the end of period t for the entire set of firms F_{st}. g_{ft} is the change in interest-bearing debt from t-1 through t for firm f divided by c_{ft}.

Credit creation (POS) is the weighted sum of the debt growth rate g_{ft} for firms in the set of firms F_{st} that increased their interest-bearing debt between t-1 and t. Credit destruction (NEG) is the weighted sum of the absolute value of the debt growth rate g_{ft} for those firms that decreased their interest-bearing debt between t-1 and t. POS is large when the increase in interest-bearing debt by the firm becomes large, while NEG is large, when the decrease in interest-bearing debt by the firm becomes large.

$$POS_{st} = \sum_{\substack{f \in F_{st} \\ g_{ft} > 0}} \left(\frac{c_{ft}}{C_{st}}\right) g_{ft}, \; NEG_{st} = \sum_{\substack{f \in F_{st} \\ g_{ft} < 0}} \left(\frac{c_{ft}}{C_{st}}\right) |g_{ft}| \qquad (3.1)$$

Credit reallocation (SUM) is the sum of credit creation and credit destruction, as shown in Eq. (3.2).

$$SUM_{st} = POS_{st} + NEG_{st} \qquad (3.2)$$

SUM measures the extent to which credit is reallocated across firms as well as the degree of heterogeneity in firms' financing behavior. The larger the increase or decrease in a firm's interest-bearing debt the larger the amount of credit reallocation (SUM). The net change in credit (NET) is the difference between credit creation and credit destruction:

$$NET_{st} = POS_{st} - NEG_{st} \qquad (3.3)$$

The net change in funds (NET) is equal to the weighted sum of the individual firm's debt growth rate g_{ft} for all firms and represents the aggregate growth rate of the amount of interest-bearing debt.

An additional indicator, used similarly to SUM, to measure credit reallocation is excess credit reallocation (EXC). Excess credit reallocation is the absolute value of the net change in funds subtracted from total credit reallocation as shown in Eq. (3.4). EXC measures the extent to which credit reallocation exceeds the minimum required level of credit reallocation (NET) for the entire firm sector.[4]

$$EXC_{st} = SUM_{st} - |NET_{st}| \qquad (3.4)$$

[4] Consider the case where the net credit change (NET) is + 1%. To achieve this with the smallest possible reallocation of funds there should be no firms that decrease debt while all firms increase debt by only 1%. In this case the creation of credit (POS) would be 1%, the decrease in funds (NEG) would be zero, and the reallocation of credit (SUM) would be 1%. In reality there are firms that decrease their debt and, correspondingly, the overall increase in debt will be greater than 1%. In this case the excess credit reallocation (EXC) will be greater than zero and the sum of credit creation (POS) and credit destruction (NEG), which is the amount of credit reallocation (SUM), will exceed the net credit change (NET) of 1%.

3.3.2 Data

Data is from the Ministry of Finance's Quarterly Financial Statements Statistics of Corporations by Industry. The period covered is from the first quarter of FY 1980 (April-June of 1980) to the fourth quarter of FY 2014 (January to March of 2015). Unlike the Annual Financial Statements Statistics of Corporations by Industry, which includes micro businesses in its survey, the Quarterly Financial Statements Statistics cover firms with capital of 10 million yen or more. Variables include interest-bearing debt, which is the sum of long-term loans from financial institutions (over 1 year), short-term loans from financial institutions (within 1 year), other loans (including loans from management), and bonds. In addition to looking at interest-bearing debt overall we also present a credit reallocation index calculated separately for loans from financial institutions, long-term loans from financial institutions, short-term loans from financial institutions, and corporate bonds.

3.3.3 Notes on the Construction and Use of the Credit Reallocation Measures

It is necessary to consider the following two points with regard to the indicators of credit reallocation. First, consideration should be given to the appropriate unit of measurement for an increase and decrease in interest-bearing debt. The question is: when we examine credit reallocation in the firm sector should the reallocation be measured on a per-project or per-contract basis, or on a per-firm basis? Here, as in previous studies on the U.S. and Korea, we use firms as the unit of measurement and identify firms that increase their interest-bearing debt and those that decrease it to calculate the credit creation (POS) and the credit destruction (NEG) variables, respectively. The smaller a firm becomes the more banks are likely to lend based on the profitability and credit risk of the entire firm, rather than on the business potential and risk of each project of the firm. For this reason it is desirable to calculate the credit reallocation measures on a firm-by-firm basis rather than on a project-by-project basis.

Second, it is important to account for the entry and exit of firms when we calculate the reallocation measures. The outstanding amount of interest-bearing debt held by firms changes substantially upon entry and exit. For newly established firms the interest-bearing debt balance, which is zero before entry, jumps to a positive value at the time of entry. On the flip side, for firms exiting the market through bankruptcy or closure a positive debt balance drops to zero upon exit. These discontinuous changes in debt for entering and exiting firms are reflected in g_{ft} and affect the credit creation (POS) and destruction (NEG) measures.[5] However, the impact may be limited because new entrants and exiting firms account for only a small portion of the entire population of firms, and this is especially true in Japan where firm entry and exit ratios are lower than in other developed countries.[6]

Unfortunately, the Quarterly Financial Statements Statistics of Corporations used in this analysis do not contain information on the year of establishment of firms, nor do they contain information on firm exits. Therefore, this dataset alone does not allow us to directly measure the impact of the entry and exit of firms on credit reallocation.

To deal with this issue we merge the Quarterly Financial Statements Statistics with another database that is able to identify the years of entry and exit and calculate the amount of credit reallocation after accounting for firms' entry and exit.

The results indicate that the magnitude of credit reallocation for large firms does not substantially change whether or not we include entry/exit firms in the dataset. In contrast, for SMEs the amount of credit reallocation is substantially larger if we include entry/exit firms in the dataset. Specifically, the credit creation (POS) measure is larger by 0.3 percentage points if we include entering firms and credit destruction (NEG) is larger by 1 percentage point if we include exiting firms.

3.4 Magnitude of Credit Reallocation: Is There Active Reallocation Among Firms?

This section provides an overview of the magnitude of credit reallocation in the Japanese economy. We begin by looking at the reallocation indicators for the firm sector including both large firms and SMEs.

Table 3.1 presents the quarterly average of the credit reallocation indicators for interest-bearing debt from FY1980 to FY2014: credit creation (POS) is 4.2%, credit destruction (NEG) is 3.6%, credit reallocation (SUM), the sum of POS and NEG is 7.7%, net credit change (NET) is 0.6%, and excess credit reallocation (EXC), which indicates the amount of reallocation above the net change is 6.4%. These values indicate how much interest-bearing debt increased or decreased each quarter relative to the total debt held by the firm sector (POS and NEG), how much it changed on a net basis (NET), and how large the combined increase and decrease were (SUM and EXC).

---

[5] In the analysis, g_{ft} is defined as (current period debt outstanding—prior period debt outstanding) / 0.5 (current period debt outstanding + prior period debt outstanding), so the range of possible values for g_{ft} is -2 to $+2$. For new entrants, if they obtain credit at the time of entry, the value of g_{ft} is always $+2$. On the flip side, for exiting firms, the value of g_{ft} is always -2, if the firm had a positive debt balance upon exit.

[6] According to the SME Agency (2018), the annual new business opening rate is 14.6% in the UK (2016), 12.7% in France (2016), 9.1% in the U.S. (2011), and 7.1% in Germany (2015) as compared to 5.6% in Japan (2016). Exit rates are 11.6% in the UK, 9.5% in France, 10.0% in the US, and 7.5% in Germany as compared to 3.5% in Japan over the same period.

Table 3.1 Extent of credit reallocation in Japan (Quarterly rate of change, From FY1980 to FY2014)

Types of liabilities	POS	NEG	NET	SUM	EXC
Interest-bearing debt	0.042	0.036	0.006	0.077	0.064
Loans from financial institutions	0.044	0.039	0.005	0.083	0.069
Short-term loans	0.081	0.078	0.002	0.159	0.133
Long-term loans	0.049	0.042	0.007	0.092	0.071
Corporate bonds	0.04	0.035	0.005	0.075	0.05

Notes POS stands for credit creation, NEG for credit destruction, NET for net credit change, SUM for credit reallocation, and EXC for excess credit reallocation
Source Table 4 in Uesugi and Sakai (2017)

For more than 30 years the net change in interest-bearing debt has been less than 1% per quarter. However, there has been a more dynamic churning of credit at the firm level, as can be seen in the size of the credit creation and destruction indicators, resulting in considerable credit reallocation across firms.

Next we break down the reallocation of interest-bearing debt into its components. How does the amount of credit reallocation vary? As shown in the row for loans extended by financial institutions, and the rows below, in Table 3.1 the magnitude of credit reallocation depends on the duration of debt. For short-term financial institution loans, which are repaid within one year or less, the amount of credit reallocation is large while it is small for long-term loans with duration longer than a year, and for corporate bonds.

In the case of short-term loans, with repayment being made within a year, firms frequently make new loan contracts and repay their debt, and as a result the degree of credit reallocation for short-term financial institution loans is likely to be larger.

How do differences in firm size and industry affect the magnitude of credit reallocation? Table 3.2 shows that the smaller the firm, as measured by the number of employees, the larger the amount of credit reallocation. For the smallest firms, those with less than 50 employees, credit reallocation (SUM) is 8.6%, about 1.5 times that of the largest firms (5.9%) with more than 10,000 employees. The net change in funds (NET) shows little difference across sizes while the size of the increase in funds (POS) and the decrease in funds (NEG) differ substantially depending on firm size. Table 3.3 shows that there are also considerable differences in the magnitude of credit reallocation by industry. In the construction, food manufacturing, electronic machinery manufacturing, and information and communication industries, credit reallocation (SUM) exceeds 10%.

In contrast, credit reallocation (SUM) for the electricity, gas, heat, and water supply industries is less than 4%, and for the transportation, steel, and nonferrous metal manufacturing industries it is around 6%. Excess credit reallocation (EXC), which is adjusted for the considerable differences in the net credit change (NET) across industries, is high in the construction, food manufacturing, and wholesale industries. It is low in the electricity, gas, heat, and water supply industries and

Table 3.2 Extent of credit reallocation (Quarterly rate of change, interest-bearing debt, by employment size)

Number of employees	POS	NEG	NET	SUM	EXC
0–49	0.046	0.04	0.005	0.086	0.07
50–99	0.047	0.037	0.009	0.084	0.065
100–499	0.044	0.037	0.007	0.081	0.063
500–999	0.042	0.037	0.005	0.079	0.06
1000–4999	0.043	0.036	0.007	0.078	0.06
5000–9999	0.036	0.031	0.005	0.067	0.045
10,000–	0.031	0.027	0.004	0.059	0.03

Notes POS stands for credit creation, NEG for credit destruction, NET for net credit change, SUM for credit reallocation, and EXC for excess credit reallocation
Source Table 1 in Uesugi and Sakai (2017)

Table 3.3 Extent of credit reallocation (Quarterly rate of change, interest-bearing debt, by industry)

Industry	POS	NEG	NET	SUM	EXC
Industries with high SUM					
Construction	0.067	0.062	0.005	0.13	0.089
Food processing	0.064	0.059	0.005	0.123	0.087
Electrical and IT machinery	0.059	0.049	0.011	0.108	0.071
Information and telecommunication	0.056	0.049	0.007	0.105	0.057
Wholesale	0.05	0.045	0.005	0.095	0.075
Industries with low SUM					
Iron and steel	0.031	0.029	0.002	0.06	0.031
Non-ferrous metal	0.034	0.028	0.005	0.062	0.042
Pulp and paper	0.036	0.029	0.007	0.064	0.039
Land, water, and other transportation	0.03	0.025	0.005	0.056	0.042
Electricity, gas, heat supply, water	0.021	0.017	0.004	0.038	0.009

Notes POS stands for credit creation, NEG for credit destruction, NET for net credit change, SUM for credit reallocation, and EXC for excess credit reallocation
Source Table 4 in Uesugi and Sakai (2017)

in materials industries such as steel and pulp, paper, and processed paper products manufacturing.

Note that we calculated these credit reallocation indicators only for Japanese firms. While there are clear differences by firm size (number of employees) and industry it is difficult to know whether the scale of reallocation is large or small from these indicators alone. We, therefore, compare these results with previous studies on the U.S. and South Korea. Herrera, Kolar and Minetti (2011) examined listed U.S. firms while Hyun and Minetti (2019) looked at unlisted Korean firms including relatively large SMEs. In contrast, Uesugi and Sakai (2017) examine all Japanese firms included in the Quarterly Financial Statements Statistics of Corporations by Industry and calculate the reallocation indicators for large and medium-sized firms (capital of 100 million yen or more) and SMEs (capital of 10 million yen to less than 100 million yen) based on the amount of capital. Since the studies for the U.S. and South Korea calculated the annual rate of credit reallocation we also calculate the annual rate of reallocation for Japan as well.

Table 3.4 compares the results for Japan, the U.S., and South Korea. For the largest firms across the three countries, aggregated from 1980 onward, the results are similar. The amount of credit reallocation (SUM) for the U.S. and South Korea is comparable at around 20% while it is somewhat lower, at 14%, for large and medium-sized Japanese firms. However, in South Korea net credit change (NET) is large enough to be positive which may be inflating the size of the credit reallocation indicator. Excess reallocation (EXC) has been in the range of 15% to 19% in the U.S. since 1980 while in South Korea and Japan it is lower at around 10%.

Since for Japan and South Korea we have data on unlisted firms and SMEs it is possible to make a comparison between the two countries. We consider firms with capital of less than 100 million yen, the cutoff to be considered an SME in Japan, to be roughly equivalent to firms in the first to fourth quintiles in South Korea. Comparing the two countries, Japanese SMEs (19.2%) consistently underperform their South Korean counterparts (22.4 to 27.9%) in terms of the amount of credit reallocation (SUM). Excess reallocation (EXC) is also lower among Japanese SMEs (13.7%) than for South Korean firms (13.2–15.8%).

Table 3.4 Extent of credit reallocation in Japan, US, and South Korea (Yearly rate of change)

	POS	NEG	NET	SUM	EXC
Japan (1980–2014)	0.092	0.070	0.022	0.162	0.115
Large firms	0.083	0.059	0.024	0.141	0.098
SMEs	0.107	0.084	0.023	0.192	0.137
US (1952–2007)	0.114	0.067	0.047	0.181	0.124
US (1980–1989)	0.131	0.086	0.045	0.217	0.162
US (1990–1999)	0.117	0.086	0.032	0.203	0.155
US (2000–2007)	0.119	0.105	0.014	0.225	0.193
South Korea (1981–2012)	0.142	0.072	0.069	0.214	0.132
Fifth quintile (largest)	0.130	0.062	0.068	0.192	0.107
Fourth quintile	0.164	0.067	0.097	0.231	0.132
Third quintile	0.151	0.073	0.079	0.224	0.139
Second quintile	0.174	0.075	0.099	0.250	0.148
First quintile (smallest)	0.200	0.079	0.121	0.279	0.158

Notes POS stands for credit creation, NEG for credit destruction, NET for net credit change, SUM for credit reallocation, and EXC for excess credit reallocation

Source Processed by the author based on Table 1 in Herrera, Kolar, and Minetti (2011), Tables 1 and 2 in Hyun and Minetti (2019), and Table A1 in Uesugi and Sakai (2017)

Compared to the U.S. and South Korea, Japanese firms, regardless of size, have a relatively small amount of credit reallocation. This does not change substantially even when using the excess credit reallocation (EXC) indicator, which takes into account the net credit change.

3.5 Changes in Credit Reallocation Over Time

In the discussion so far it has been found that in the Japanese corporate sector as a whole, from the 1980s to the present, there has been a mix of firms that have either increased or decreased their interest-bearing debt, resulting in the amount of credit reallocation across firms being larger than the net credit change. How has the scale of such reallocation evolved over time? The Japanese macroeconomy has experienced significant fluctuations since the 1980s. During this period there have been not only short-term economic fluctuations but also medium-term economic changes. In other words, the economic growth rate changed substantially during the bubble economy, the financial crisis triggered by the non-performing loan problem after its collapse, and in subsequent periods. In this section we focus on credit reallocation during the short-term recessionary period and the period of economic stagnation that followed the collapse of the asset price bubble.

We focus our analysis on this period for two particular reasons. First, in recent years Japan has faced not only short-term recessions but also a long-term economic downturn which is often called the "lost decade." It is important to study credit reallocation during downturns of different time horizons. Second, there is a belief among economists that creative destruction, in which old and obsolete production units disappear and new production units are created, is more likely to occur during recessions than during normal times. If we focus on credit as a resource used in production we can make several theoretical predictions regarding the credit reallocation process during recessions. In the following section we review the existing theoretical perspectives.[7]

3.5.1 Magnitude of Credit Reallocation During Recessions: Theoretical Hypotheses

When a negative shock triggers a recession, how does the number of newly generated and disappearing production units change and, as a result, how much does

[7] Several of the theoretical models presented below do not necessarily focus on credit allocation but rather on the allocation of resources needed for production in general. In what follows we will discuss the extent to which credit is reallocated during recessions by considering credit as one of the inputs necessary for production, but it should be noted that such an assumption does not hold in an environment where firms do not face financial constraints.

the reallocation of resources, particularly credit, change? To empirically understand this reallocation it is necessary to examine how the measures of credit reallocation, namely, credit creation (POS), credit destruction (NEG), credit reallocation (SUM), and excess credit reallocation (EXC), change over time.

3.5.1.1 Scrapping Existing Production Equipment Leads to an Increase in Resource Reallocation

Caballero and Hammour (1994) point to the possibility that the reallocation of resources used in production is more active during recessions. In their theoretical model each unit of production equipment is state-of-the-art when it is introduced but becomes obsolete over time and is eventually discarded. When demand declines firms respond by either stopping the installation of new production equipment or by increasing the retirement of incumbent equipment that is not yet obsolete. If it is costly to install new production equipment firms do not change the amount of new equipment installed in response to economic fluctuations but rather absorb demand fluctuations by increasing the amount of scrapping of incumbent production equipment. In other words, during recessions firms dispose of more existing equipment rather than reducing the amount of new production equipment being installed. In this case, the expansionary effect of resource reallocation associated with the disposal of a large number of existing production units exceeds the contractionary effect of resource reallocation associated with the creation of fewer new production units, resulting in a situation in which the amount of resource reallocation increases during a recession.

3.5.1.2 Termination of Bank-Firm Relationships Increases the Size of Credit Reallocation

Den Haan, Ramey, and Watson (2003) present a model that focuses specifically on credit reallocation, which increases during a recession, rather than on the general reallocation of resources due to the creation and destruction of production units. In their model there are households, lenders, and entrepreneurs, and the savings of households are used by lenders to fund entrepreneurs who in turn use the savings to produce. For production resources to be provided by the lender to the entrepreneur a relationship must be established between the two parties through matching.

In such an environment, when a negative productivity shock occurs and the number of relationships declines the flow of funds to entrepreneurs decreases and the rate of return on investment declines, further reducing the number of relationships and the level of investment. Even if there is no change in the number of new relationships being created there is an increase in the number of existing relationships being terminated. As a result the scale of credit reallocation during a recession reflects the increase in credit destruction.

The model suggests that the larger the recession the larger the decrease in credit (NEG) as the existing relationships between firms and financial institutions are terminated, which consequently increases the amount of credit reallocation (SUM). Based on this we can expect that business cycle fluctuations are inversely related to the amount of credit reallocation. This indicates the presence of creative destruction, as Schumpeter calls it, during recessions.

3.5.1.3 Size of Resource Reallocation Becomes Smaller as Distressed Firms Do Not Exit

In contrast, there are theoretical models in which the amount of resource reallocation declines during a recession. Caballero and Hammour (2005) focus on the labor market, specifically on the creation and destruction of jobs. They present an empirical finding that is the opposite of the view that the amount of labor reallocation increases during recessions due to an increase in job destruction. They found that in the U.S. labor market the magnitude of job reallocation declines after a recession rather than increasing. This is based on the fact that job creation declines during a recession and the initial increase in job destruction in the early stages of a recession is followed by a decrease in the later stages. They provided a theoretical model that explains this feature of labor reallocation during a downturn.

Caballero, Hoshi, and Kashyap (2008) construct a theoretical model which focuses on the creation and destruction of production units. Under normal steady state conditions, even if a negative shock leads to a recession, there is no change in the magnitude of resource reallocation used for production units because the decrease in creation and the increase in destruction of production units cancel each other out. However, if there exists a mechanism in which distressed production units are prevented from exiting the amount of resource reallocation of production units during the recession will be affected.[8] Specifically, because the destruction of existing production units cannot be increased to absorb the negative shock, adjustments are made in the direction of reducing the number of production units being created. As a result, the scale of the reallocation of resources used for production shrinks.

3.5.1.4 Reduction in the Size of Credit Reallocation as Existing Loan Contracts are Rolled Over

There is a study that draws a conclusion similar to that of Caballero and Hammour (2005) and Caballero, Hoshi, and Kashyap (2008), which focuses on the reallocation of credit. Chamley and Rochon (2011) develop a theoretical model, similar to den Haan, Ramey and Watson (2003), where matching takes place between banks and entrepreneurs. In direct contrast to den Haan, Ramey and Watson (2003), however,

---

[8] One example of such a mechanism is the financial support provided by banks to zombie firms which are unable to survive without the support of these banks.

their model predicts that the amount of credit reallocation during recessions will shrink.

What distinguishes their model is that they incorporate a feature whereby banks are given the option of rolling over their contracts and continuing to provide long-term loans or terminating their contracts and funding new projects through matching. As a result, two equilibria exist: one in which banks roll over and provide long-term loans to entrepreneurs and another in which they do not and continually seek new entrepreneurs. In the former equilibrium there is very little credit reallocation because there is neither an increase nor a decrease in credit. In contrast, in the latter equilibrium, banks terminate their existing loan contracts, a decrease in credit, and are always looking for new borrowers, an increase in credit, so that credit reallocation is large.

How does credit reallocation differ during recessions relative to normal times? Chamley and Rochon (2011) assume that verification costs are higher in a recession than in normal times. This reduces the rate of return on lending for new projects through matching. As a result, the equilibrium where banks continue to roll over loans becomes more likely and the amount of reallocation is expected to decrease.

In Caballero and Hammour (2005) and Chamley and Rochon (2011) the focus is on production units rather than on credit but both theoretical models do predict that the amount of resource reallocation will be smaller during recessions. Chamley and Rochon (2011), while using the same matching model to focus on the exchange of credit as den Haan, Ramey and Watson (2003), obtain a contrasting theoretical prediction. In other words, during a recession, both credit creation (POS) and destruction (NEG) are smaller, and consequently, total reallocation (SUM) is also smaller.

3.5.2 *Magnitude of Credit Reallocation During Recessions: An Empirical Analysis*

Section 3.5, to this point, has provided an overview of the existing theoretical models on credit reallocation during recessions. Because the models make contrasting predictions, however, it is necessary to empirically verify which of these models is correct.

Since our focus is the Japanese economy since the 1980s we examine the two short-term recessions, as well as the severe economic crisis, which followed the collapse of the bubble economy. This period includes the so called "lost decade" of economic stagnation. To capture short-term economic fluctuations we use the DI (diffusion index) for business sentiment from the Bank of Japan's Short-term Economic Survey of Enterprises (BOJ Tankan).

We identify the "lost decade" by using the peaks and troughs of the business cycle as indicated by the reference dates published by the Economic and Social Research Institute of the Cabinet Office: the period beginning in January-March 1991, the business cycle peak preceding the collapse of the bubble, to January-March 2002,

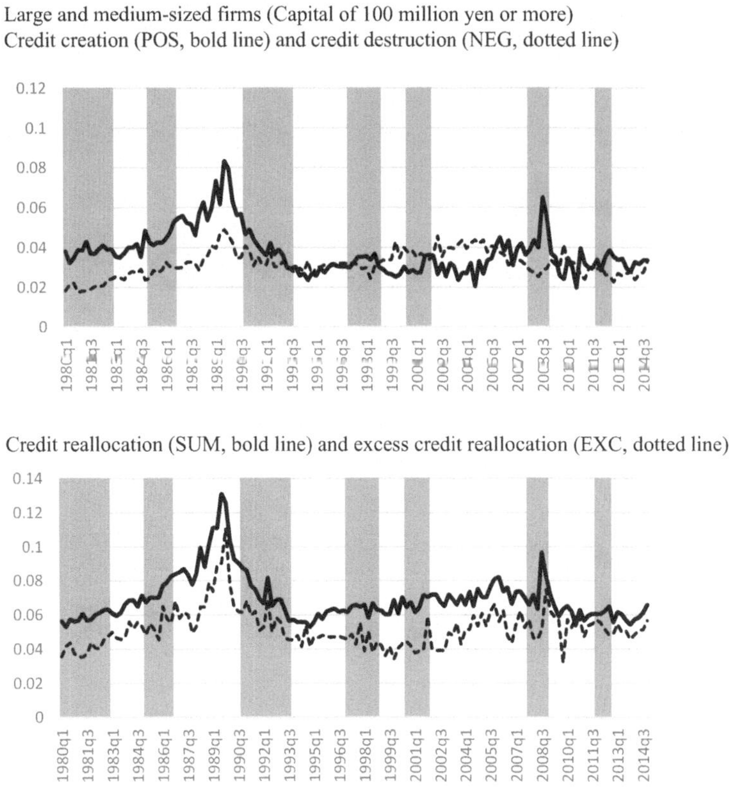

Fig. 3.1 Development of credit reallocation in Japan (Large and medium-sized firms and SMEs) (*Note* A shaded area represents the period of an economic recession. *Source* Fig. 2 in Sakai and Uesugi (2024))

the first business cycle trough of the 2000s. Some argue that the "lost decade" should be extended to the "lost two decades" because the stagnation of the Japanese economy was not just limited to the 1990s but continued well into the 2000s.[9] However, as we will see later, there are significant differences in the magnitude and efficiency of credit reallocation in the 1990s relative to the preceding and following periods. Thus, it makes sense to focus the analysis on the "lost decade," centered on the 1990s.

In the empirical analysis we first overview movements in the credit reallocation index through time by firm size. Figure 3.1 graphs credit creation (POS), credit destruction (NEG), credit reallocation (SUM), and excess credit reallocation (EXC) for large and medium-sized firms with capital of 100 million yen or more and for SMEs with capital between 10 and 100 million yen.

The white areas represent periods of economic expansion while the gray shaded areas represent periods of recession. Regardless of firm size all credit reallocation

[9] Fukao (2012) is a representative study that discusses the Japanese economy during the "lost two decades."

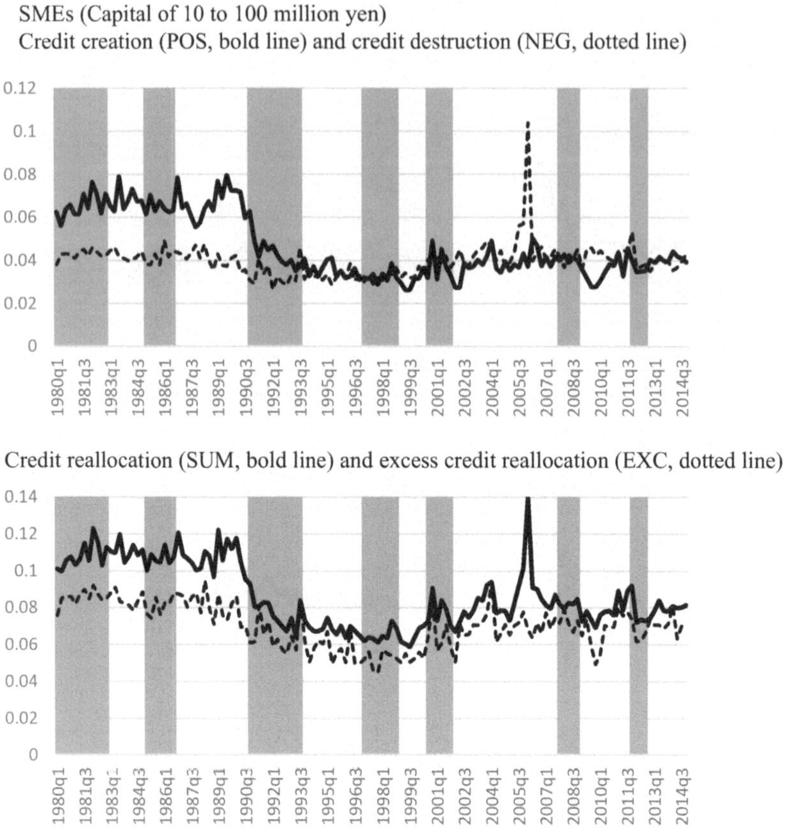

Fig. 3.1 (continued)

indicators significantly decreased shortly after the beginning of the 1990s. For large and medium-sized firms POS, reflecting the rising demand for liquidity, increased during the global financial crisis, after the collapse of Lehman Brothers, in fall 2008.

Next we present correlation coefficients between the DI for business conditions and the credit reallocation index. This allows us to examine trends in credit reallocation over the short-term business cycle. Table 3.5 presents the results by firm size and we find no significant qualitative differences across large firms, medium-sized firms, and SMEs.

Positive and significant correlation coefficients are obtained for credit creation (POS), credit reallocation (SUM), and excess credit reallocation (EXC). This indicates that as business conditions worsen during a recession, either simultaneously or with a lag of up to four quarters (= one year), the amount of credit reallocation also shrinks with most of the reduction in reallocation attributed to the decline in credit creation. In contrast, credit destruction (NEG) is positively correlated with the DI simultaneously but not significantly correlated with a lag. There is a tendency

Table 3.5 Correlation coefficients between business cycle and credit reallocation

Large and medium-sized firms (capital of 100 million yen or more)					
Business condition	DI(t-4)	DI(t-3)	DI(t-2)	DI(t-1)	DI(t)
POS	0.408***	0.362***	0.280***	0.164*	0.083
NEG	0.048	0.083	0.134	0.178**	0.211**
SUM	0.370***	0.343***	0.301***	0.236***	0.193**
EXC	0.257***	0.256***	0.219***	0.179**	0.134
SMEs (capital of 10 million to 100 million yen)					
Business condition	DI(t-4)	DI(t-3)	DI(t-2)	DI(t-1)	DI(t)
POS	0.319***	0.370***	0.371***	0.334***	0.254***
NEG	0.110	0.110	0.129	0.145*	0.131
SUM	0.253***	0.283***	0.297***	0.280***	0.231***
EXC	0.180**	0.207**	0.211**	0.212**	0.154*

***, **, and * represent the rejection of the null hypothesis that coefficients are not different from zero at the 1, 5, and 10%, respectively

Notes POS stands for credit creation, NEG for credit destruction, NET for net credit change, SUM for credit reallocation, and EXC for excess credit reallocation

Source Table 2 in Sakai and Uesugi (2024)

for NEG to decrease during recessions but not to the same extent as credit creation (POS).

Next we analyze the magnitude of credit reallocation during the "lost decade" and the remainder of the period. This allows us to compare the scale of credit reallocation during periods of medium-term economic stagnation with other periods. Table 3.6 presents the magnitude of credit reallocation by firm size for the period from January-March 1991 to January-March 2002 (the "lost decade") and the periods before and after. What is common to both large and medium-sized firms and SMEs is that there was less credit reallocation during the "lost decade" relative to other periods. While this is also true for credit creation (POS) it is not the case for credit destruction (NEG). For large and medium-sized firms NEG does not differ significantly between the "lost decade" and other periods while for SMEs NEG was smaller in the "lost decade" relative to other periods.

These results are consistent with the hypothesis that the amount of credit reallocation in Japan shrinks during recessions. This is primarily attributed to the substantial reduction in credit creation (POS) during recessions. The fact that the level of credit destruction (NEG) also tends to remain the same or decrease rather than increase during recessions also contributes to the decline in credit reallocation. This may be due to the fact that bank-firm relationships are not severed during recessions and rather existing loan contracts tend to continue.

Whether we are examining a short-term recession or a long-term, large-scale downturn, such as the "lost decade," what sets Japan apart from the U.S. and South Korea is the movement in the credit destruction (NEG) indicator. Comparing

Table 3.6 Extent of credit reallocation (During the "lost decade" and periods before and after)

Interest-bearing debt	Large and medium-sized firms (capital of 100 million yen or more)					SMEs (capital of 10 million to 100 million yen)				
	POS	NEG	NET	SUM	EXC	POS	NEG	NET	SUM	EXC
Before or after the "lost decade"	0.040	0.031	0.009	0.071	0.054	0.051	0.043	0.008	0.094	0.075
"Lost decade"	0.032	0.033	0.000	0.065	0.048	0.037	0.034	0.003	0.071	0.059
Null hypothesis: Lost decade = rest of the period	***		***	***	***	***	***	**	***	***

***, **, and * represent the rejection of the null hypothesis that coefficients are not different from zero at the 1, 5, and 10%, respectively

Notes POS stands for credit creation, NEG for credit destruction, NET for net credit change, SUM for credit reallocation, and EXC for excess credit reallocation

Source Table 1 in Sakai and Uesugi (2024)

Table 3.5 with the results of Herrera, Kolar and Minetti (2011), we see that NEG increases during recessions in the U.S., while it does not in Japan.

Comparing Table 3.6 with the 1997 financial crisis episode in South Korea, as shown in Hyun and Minetti (2019), the degree of credit destruction (NEG) in South Korea increased significantly with the onset of the crisis while in Japan during the "lost decade" there was no significant change for large firms, and for SMEs it actually decreased.

The result for Japan, that the extent of credit destruction (NEG) is no greater during recessions than in other periods, may be understood using the argument made by Chamley and Rochon (2011). According to them it is possible that Japanese financial institutions choose to continue with their existing loans during recessions rather than calling in loans and looking for new borrowers. On the other hand, since we did not distinguish supply from demand factors in our analysis the result may be due to the behavior of borrower firms who choose to continue with existing loans rather than ending them.

3.6 Efficiency of Credit Reallocation

After examining the magnitude of credit reallocation, here we examine its efficiency, that is, whether credit flows from low to high productivity firms, or vice versa. Many of the theoretical models introduced in the previous section assume an efficient allocation of resources. There are several studies, however, which have examined whether the tendency toward efficient resource allocation is stronger or weaker during recessions.

3.6.1 *Efficiency of Resource Reallocation During Recessions—Theoretical Hypothesis*

We first overview the discussion on whether the reallocation of resources used in production, such as credit, labor, and capital, is efficient during economic recessions. If the reallocation is efficient then less productive firms will use less resources while more productive firms will use more resources. Most of the studies we have discussed so far assume that the efficient reallocation of resources takes place during normal, non-recessionary periods. However, it is important to consider whether this efficient reallocation is enhanced or weakened during recessions.

One perspective is that recessions result in a more efficient resource reallocation. Becsi, Li, and Wang (2005) consider matching in the credit market under the assumption that there is heterogeneity in the quality (e.g., productivity) of entrepreneurs. In their model, during a recession, the relationships between existing banks and entrepreneurs are more likely to break, especially those with low-quality entrepreneurs. Since low-quality entrepreneurs are more likely to suffer from the shortage of credit after the termination of the relationships, while high-quality entrepreneurs suffer less, higher quality entrepreneurs have more access to credit during recessions. This is a situation in which the efficiency of credit reallocation improves.

The other perspective is that recessions weaken the efficiency of resource reallocation or result in an inefficient resource reallocation. Some theoretical models suggest that efficiency is reduced or that inefficient reallocations occur for the following two reasons.

The first is due to frictions in the lending market. For example, suppose that frictions, such as asymmetric information, exist between lenders and borrowers and that some firms are unable to borrow even though they are creditworthy. If such financial constraints are somehow related to productivity during a recession this will lead the relationship between productivity and resource reallocation to change during a recession.

Caballero and Hammour (2005) account for frictions in both the labor market and the credit market and find that the efficiency of resource reallocation weakens when frictions exist in the labor market, while in credit markets frictions result in an inefficient allocation.[10] Barlevy (2003) shows that high productivity firms are more likely to face funding constraints during recessions because they have a greater demand for funds. In this case the relationship between productivity and the funding reallocation is inefficient, which is opposite of the relationship in normal times. Osotimehin and Pappadà (2017), similar to Barlevy (2003), also focus on financial constraints. In their model, as the impact of the constraint is pronounced both for high quality firms and low quality firms, the efficiency of resource reallocation weakens but not to the point of becoming inefficient.

[10] Caballero and Hammour (2005) call the state of weakened efficiency in the allocation of resources sclerosis and the state of inefficient allocation scrambling.

The second reason for the reduced efficiency during recessions is a lender's incentive to maintain lending relationships with unviable firms. Dewatripont and Maskin (1995) and Berglöf and Roland (1997) demonstrate that sunk costs create a soft budget constraint problem in which banks provide additional funds to firms that would not normally be productive enough to survive. Bruche and Llobet (2014) point out that banks in financial distress have an incentive to continue lending to firms with low solvency in hopes of a turnaround. The more banks that fall into financial difficulty during a recession the more likely this is to occur.

3.6.2 Efficiency of Credit Reallocation During Recessions: An Empirical Analysis

We have now seen that there are two views on the efficiency of credit reallocation during recessions. One is that efficiency increases and the other is that it decreases, depending on the theoretical model. Because of these conflicting views it is necessary to test which is correct using data.

Using firm-level panel data we first formulate Eq. (3.5) and examine how the efficiency of credit allocation changes over the business cycle.

$$g_{ft} = \alpha + \beta TFP_{ft-1} + \gamma Cycle_t + \delta TFP_{ft-1} \times Cycle_t + \theta X_{ft-1} + \xi Industry_i + \varepsilon_{ft} \quad (3.5)$$

The dependent variable on the left-hand side g_{ft} is the rate of change in interest-bearing debt (sum of loans and bonds) for individual firms, which was previously used to create the measures of credit reallocation. The most important explanatory variables on the right-hand side are TFP_{ft-1}, which is firm-level total factor productivity, and $Cycle_t$, which represents the business cycle.[11] TFP is calculated using the cost-share method. For $Cycle_t$ we use the DI for business conditions (national, all industries) from the Bank of Japan's Tankan survey, as discussed in Sect. 3.5. If the efficiency of credit allocation increases during a recession the coefficient on the interaction term δ is expected to be positive while if efficiency decreases δ will be negative. To examine whether or not the allocation is efficient during recessions rather than simply looking at changes in efficiency it is necessary to examine whether $\beta + \delta Cycle_t$ is positive when the economy is in recession and $Cycle_t$ is negative. If the value of $\beta + \delta Cycle_t$ is positive then a reallocation of credit from firms with low productivity to firms with high productivity is occurring while if $\beta + \delta Cycle_t$ is negative credit is being reallocated from high productivity to low productivity firms.

The control variables in X_{ft-1} include the logarithm of the firm's total assets ($lnAssets_{ft-1}$), the growth rate of sales ($Sales\_growth_{it-1}$), the operating profit to total assets ratio (ROA_{t-1}), and the capital ratio ($Capital\_ratio_{t-1}$).

[11] We would like to thank Young Gak Kim for providing us with the necessary codes to calculate firm-level total factor productivity.

Next, by formulating Eq. (3.6), which does not include an interaction term, we examine how the efficiency of credit allocation in the "lost decade" differs from the preceding and subsequent periods.

$$g_{ft} = \alpha + \beta TFP_{ft-1} + \gamma Cycle_t + \theta X_{ft-1} + \xi Industry_i + \varepsilon_{ft} \tag{3.6}$$

The sample is divided into three periods: the first quarter of FY1980 to the third quarter of FY1990, the fourth quarter of FY1990 to the fourth quarter of FY2001, and the first quarter of FY2002 and later. If is positive during the period corresponding to the "lost decade" (the fourth quarter of FY1990 to the fourth quarter of FY2001) then the allocation of funds can be said to be efficient even during periods of prolonged stagnation. In contrast, if it is positive but smaller in magnitude than in other periods we say that the degree of efficiency is weaker. If β is negative in this period then credit reallocation is inefficient in the sense that the credit moves from more productive firms to less productive firms.

3.6.3 Baseline Estimation Results

Table 3.7 presents the estimation results. Column (1) corresponds to the estimation results of Eq. (3.5), and columns (2) through (4) correspond to the estimation results of Eq. (3.6). In column (1) the coefficients on productivity and the cross term between productivity and business conditions are all positive. The higher productivity is in the previous period the higher the growth rate of interest-bearing debt of that firm. The more positive business sentiment is the greater the impact of productivity on the growth rate of interest-bearing debt.

This means that the positive impact of productivity on the growth rate of debt is lower in recessions than in booms. However, based on the estimated coefficients, $\beta + \delta Cycle_t$ is positive if the DI for business conditions is greater than -20.[12] For most of the analysis period the credit allocation of firms is efficient in the sense that the growth rate of credit is higher for more productive firms than for less productive ones.

There were periods, however, when the DI for business conditions was below -20. In particular, for more than half of the "lost decade" the DI was below -20. Other periods that fall into this category include less than a year in the first half of the 1980s and a year and a half after the collapse of Lehman Brothers in the fall of 2008. During these periods firms' credit allocation was inefficient in the sense that the credit growth rate was lower for more productive firms.

Columns (2) through (4) show that the coefficient on productivity was negative during the "lost decade" and positive before and after. In the 1990s, which includes

---

[12] Based on the coefficient on productivity in column (1) of Table 3.7 and the coefficient on the interaction term between productivity and DI we calculate $-0.00471/0.000239 = -20$.

Table 3.7 Baseline estimation results

Dependent variable: Rate of change in interest-bearing debt				
Estimation method: OLS				
	Entire period	Before the "lost decade"	"Lost decade"	After the "lost decade"
	(1)	(2)	(3)	(4)
$\ln TFP_{t-1}$	0.00471***	0.0160***	−0.00340**	0.00519***
DI	0.000313***	6.33e-05**	0.000297***	4.55e-06
$\ln TFP_{t-1}$*DI	0.000239***			
$\ln Assets_{t-1}$	−0.00104***	−0.000523	−0.00113***	−0.000760***
$Sales\_growth_{t-1}$	0.00343***	0.00163	0.00552***	0.00296***
ROA_{t-1}	−0.409***	−0.365***	−0.408***	−0.514***
$Capital\_ratio_{t-1}$	0.00653***	0.0330***	0.00472**	0.0151***
Constant	−0.000717	0.00694	−0.00130	−0.0166***
Industry FE	Yes	Yes	Yes	Yes
Observations	1,349,175	347,179	484,597	517,399
R-squared	0.002	0.002	0.002	0.002

***, **, and * represent the rejection of the null hypothesis that coefficients are not different from zero at the 1, 5, and 10%, respectively

Notes Figures in the parentheses represent robust standard errors

Source Processed by the author based on Table 4 in Sakai and Uesugi (2024)

Japan's financial crisis, the allocation of funds was inefficient in the sense that funds were shifted from high productivity firms to low productivity firms.

Furthermore, when comparing the 1980s and the period after the 2000s, the coefficient on productivity β, is larger in the 1980s than it is after the 2000s. Thus, efficiency was greater before the "lost decade" than it was after in the sense that the increase in debt was greater in response to the same improvement in productivity.

3.6.4 Estimation Results by Firm Size and Presence of Support from Financial Institutions

The baseline estimation results indicate that there were inefficiencies in the allocation of funds during the "lost decade" of the 1990s. What this does not tell us is why. Theoretically, as noted at the beginning of this section, it could be that productive borrower firms faced financial constraints or it could be that lender financial institutions made forbearance loans in order to avoid the realization of loan losses as a result of the disclosure of non-performing loans.

To determine which of these factors plays a larger role in the inefficient allocation we split the sample into various subsamples and perform estimations for each subsample. First, we split the sample by size, between SMEs which are likely to face financial constraints and large firms which are unlikely to. We also divide the sample between firms that receive financial support from financial institutions and those that do not. If financial constraints are the cause of the inefficient allocation of funds then the coefficient on productivity should be significantly negative in the estimation for SMEs that are more likely to face constraints. On the other hand, if distortions are caused by the motivation of financial institutions then the coefficient on productivity should be negative for firms that receive support from financial institutions. Here we follow Caballero, Hoshi, and Kashyap (2008) to identify the presence of financial support by examining whether the firm is charged an interest rate below the prime interest rate for the most creditworthy companies. Note that Chapter 2 employed this criterion to identify zombie firms. Note also that in the following estimation, which divides the sample by the presence or absence of financial support, the dependent variable is loans from financial institutions, not interest-bearing debt. This change is due to the fact that financial institutions are the main providers of financial support.

Tables 3.8 and 3.9 present the results of the respective estimations. It appears unlikely that the inefficient allocation is due to highly productive firms facing financial constraints; rather, it is due to the provision of forbearance loans by financial institutions. We detail these points in turn.

While the coefficient on productivity in Table 3.8 is significantly negative for large firms during the "lost decade" the coefficient is not significant for SMEs. Although many of the SMEs must have faced credit constraints the coefficient on productivity is not negative in either period for these SMEs. Thus, it is difficult to argue that the inefficient allocation of funds during the "lost decade" of the 1990s was the result of highly productive firms facing financial constraints. What should be noted is that inefficient credit allocation occurred mainly in the 1990s among large firms, those that are less likely to face financial constraints.

Looking at Table 3.9 we find that the coefficient on productivity is negative across many periods for firms receiving financial support while the coefficient is not significantly negative for firms who do not receive support. In the former sample of firms there is a tendency for credit to move from high productivity firms to low productivity firms during the "lost decade" and thereafter, while the inefficient allocation of funds does not occur in the latter group. This indicates that the presence of financial support may result in a distortion in the efficacy of credit allocation.[13]

[13] What is interesting here is that the coefficient on productivity is also significantly negative in column (3) of Table 3.9. This indicates an inefficient allocation of credit among firms that received support even after 2000. This finding differs from the baseline estimates. It remains to be seen what the reasons for, and the implications of, this result are.

Table 3.8 Estimation results by firm size

Dependent variable: Rate of change in Interest-bearing debt

Estimation method: OLS

	Large firms			SMEs		
	Pre "lost decade"	"Lost decade"	Post "lost decade"	Pre "lost decade"	"Lost decade"	Post "lost decade"
	(1)	(2)	(3)	(7)	(8)	(9)
$\ln TFP_{t-1}$	0.0166***	−0.00694***	0.00909***	0.00681	0.000548	0.00186
Number of observations	94,546	183,056	190,068	96,507	98,061	115,571
R-squared	0.003	0.002	0.003	0.003	0.003	0.003

***, **, and * represent the rejection of the null hypothesis that coefficients are not different from zero at the 1, 5, and 10%, respectively. Coefficients on variables other than productivity are omitted
Notes Figures in the parentheses represent robust standard errors
Source Processed by the author based on Table 5 in Sakai and Uesugi (2021)

Table 3.9 Estimation results by the presence of support from financial institutions

Dependent variable: rate of change in loans from financial institutions

Estimation method: OLS

	Firms with financial support			Firms without support		
	Pre "lost decade"	"Lost decade"	Post "lost decade"	Pre "lost decade"	"Lost decade"	Post "lost decade"
	(1)	(2)	(3)	(4)	(5)	(6)
$\ln TFP_{t-1}$	0.0224***	−0.00653***	−0.0165***	0.0123***	−0.000694	0.00618***
Number of observations	38,479	128,090	81,941	292,287	323,230	379,033
R-squared	0.004	0.004	0.003	0.001	0.001	0.002

***, **, and * represent the rejection of the null hypothesis that coefficients are not different from zero at the 1, 5, and 10%, respectively. Coefficients on variables other than productivity are omitted
Notes Figures in the parentheses represent robust standard errors
Source Processed by the author based on Table 6 in Sakai and Uesugi (2021)

3.7 Interpretation of Results: SMEs Do Not Increase Productivity Through Credit Reallocation

Thus far we have separately examined the magnitude and the efficiency of credit reallocation across firms. However, to determine the extent to which the credit reallocation affects the productivity of the firm sector it is necessary to consider them together. The combined analysis will also reveal differences in the nature of the reallocation between large firms and SMEs.

On one hand, an efficient credit reallocation is defined as a state in which productive firms increase their interest-bearing debt. This means that the sensitivity of the growth in interest-bearing debt to productivity is high in the estimations in Sect. 3.6. Specifically, the coefficient on productivity is positive and large. On the other hand, an active reallocation means a large amount of credit reallocation in terms of SUM and EXC. When these two conditions are satisfied credit reallocation in the firm sector leads to an increase in overall productivity.

From this perspective we evaluate the impact of credit reallocation on overall productivity by firm size and time period. Specifically, we divide the sample into large and medium-sized firms and SMEs and examine both the efficiency and size of credit reallocation for many subperiods throughout the period of analysis.

In Fig. 3.2 the vertical axis plots the coefficients on productivity in the credit allocation estimations for subperiods of three years within the period of analysis. Along the horizontal axis we plot the amount of credit reallocation for the same subperiods.

Both the size and efficiency of credit reallocation and the relationship between the two differ considerably across large and medium-sized firms and SMEs. For large and medium-sized firms the variation in efficiency is larger than the amount of credit reallocation. In contrast, for SMEs the variation in the amount of credit reallocation is large while it is difficult to say that allocation is significantly efficient.

When we examine the change throughout the period, for large and medium-sized firms the efficiency of credit reallocation was high in the 1980s and the amount of credit reallocation increased towards the end of the 1980s. However, in the 1990s both the degree of efficiency and the amount of reallocation declined sharply. In the late 2000s efficiency recovered while reallocation remained low.

For SMEs the amount of credit reallocation was large in the 1980s, indicating an active interfirm flow of credit, while there was little statistical evidence for the efficiency of credit allocation. In the 1990s reallocation sharply decreased to the level of large and medium-sized firms. It then gradually recovered in the 2000s but again started to decline in the 2010s.

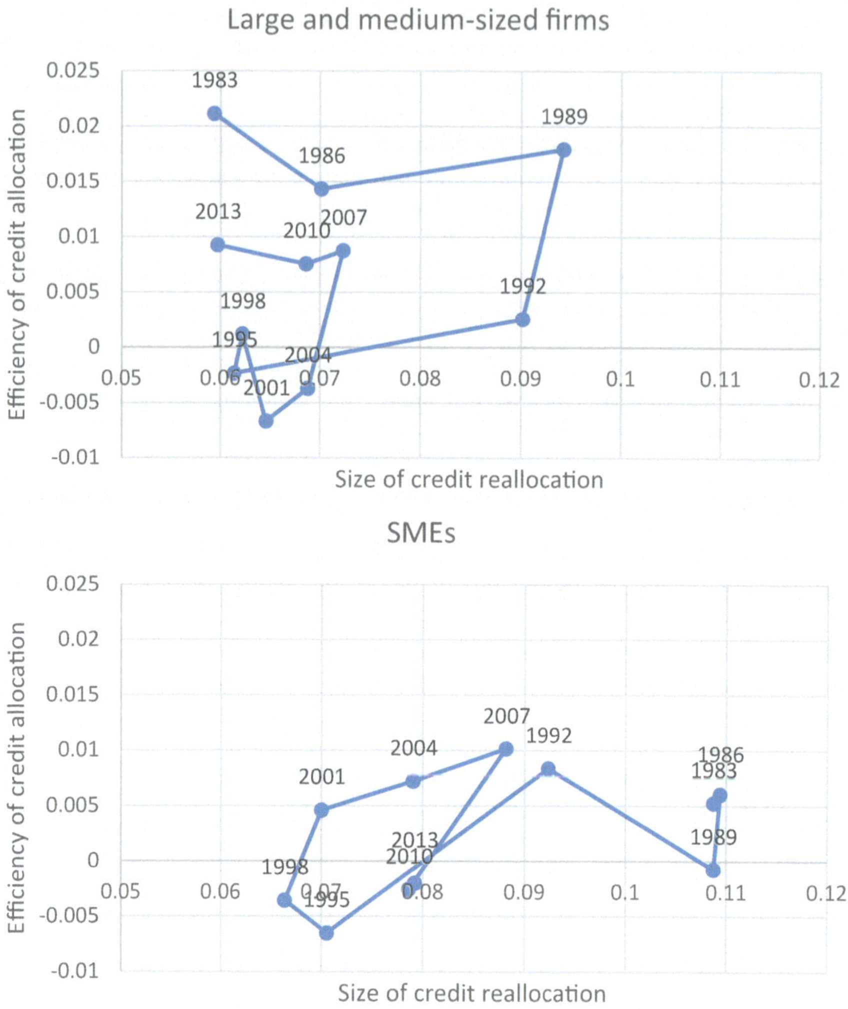

Fig. 3.2 Size of credit reallocation and its efficiency (by firm size) (*Note* For the degree of efficiency, we use the coefficients on productivity in the estimations of Eq. (3.6) for the subsamples of three years, including the year indicated in the figure. *Source* Processed by the author based on Sakai and Uesugi (2021))

In summary, the problems with credit reallocation during the "lost decade" of the 1990s were a decline in efficiency among large and medium-sized firms and a reduction in the amount of credit reallocation among SMEs. Thereafter there was a recovery in both the efficiency and amount of credit reallocation. But this trend has reversed since 2010, indicating the need to closely monitor current trends.

3.8 Summary

In this chapter we focused on interest-bearing debt and loans extended by financial institutions and examined the scale and efficiency of credit reallocation based on firm-level information for varying time periods since the 1980s. Although the scale of credit reallocation is smaller for large firms than for SMEs the reallocation has been generally efficient, with few exceptions such as the 1990s. While the scale of reallocation is larger for SMEs the flow of funds from low-productivity firms to high-productivity firms is unclear. Therefore, it is difficult to say whether SME productivity growth can be attributed to credit reallocation.

As the 2020 White Paper on SMEs states, the labor productivity of SMEs is lower than that of large firms and this gap has been widening in recent years. While there are many ways in which SMEs can improve their productivity,[14] the results of this chapter suggest that there is still room for financial institutions to provide support to SMEs with the aim of improving their productivity.

[14] As the SME Agency (2020) suggests in its analysis, one promising measure for improving labor productivity is for SMEs to raise the capital equipment ratio per employee through aggressive capital investment. However, the SME Agency (2020) also points out that in some labor intensive industries such as accommodation and food services, lifestyle-related services, entertainment, and retail, managerial efforts and the increasing of firm size are not enough to substantially increase their productivity (page 106).

Chapter 4
Interregional Allocation of Funds for Financial Institutions and Its Efficiency

Abstract We develop a new indicator for the interregional allocation of funds through loans and deposits by financial institutions within a country. Using information on loans and deposits held by each financial institution branch we measure the extent to which deposits move between regions to facilitate lending. We then analyze trends in the allocation of funds among regions, including cross-border lending, and examine the efficiency of these allocations. For the interregional flow of funds, deposits collected within a prefecture are most frequently used for loans in that prefecture. On the other hand, some of the deposits collected in a prefecture are used for loans in other prefectures, especially in Tokyo, and the degree of cross-border flows varies greatly from prefecture to prefecture. Recent changes indicate that deposit inflows from rural regions to Tokyo have begun to decline while the flow of funds within the same prefecture has increased. Regarding the determinants of the interregional allocation of funds there is a negative relationship between productivity and the flow of funds, with deposits to be provided as loans moving from productivity-increasing regions to productivity-decreasing regions. The cost of producing information required to lend to remote regions may be a possible cause of this inefficiency.

Keywords Interregional flow of funds via loans and deposits · Lending across prefectural borders · Concentration of banking activities in Tokyo · Deposit coefficient matrix · Deposit inflow matrix · Productivity

---

Supplementary Information The online version contains supplementary material for Supplementary Tables 1 and 2 available at https://doi.org/10.1007/978-981-96-3193-3_4.

I. Uesugi, *The Economics of SME Finance*, Advances in Japanese Business and Economics 36, https://doi.org/10.1007/978-981-96-3193-3_4

4.1 Introduction: Interregional Flow of Funds via Loans and Deposits

In Chapter 3 we examined trends in the reallocation of funds among firms and the efficiency of that reallocation, based on changes in interest-bearing debt held by individual firms. When considering the efficiency of the allocation, however, it is also necessary to take a regional perspective into account. In some regions the demand for funds by firms exceeds their supply in the form of deposits collected from households and other sources while in other regions the demand falls short of the supply. In addition, the transfer of funds between regions which fills these gaps may be efficient or inefficient.

4.1.1 Financial Institutions Fill the Interregional Gap Between Supply of and Demand for Funds

This chapter focuses on the role of deposit-taking financial institutions as fillers of the gap between supply of and demand for funds in a region. Financial institutions play an important role in converting deposits into loans of varying degrees of maturity and liquidity. Many of these financial institutions have a wide network of branches and play an important role in bridging the gap between the supply of and demand for funds in their respective regions by converting deposits into loans across regions.

An example of such cross-regional asset conversion is “cross border lending” by regional financial institutions, which is said to have increased in recent years. This is also called “out-of-prefecture lending” and refers to lending by regional financial institutions in prefectures other than where their headquarters are located. Since business activity in metropolitan areas is generally more active than in regional areas the demand for funds is also higher in metropolitan areas. In order to respond to these regional differences in demand regional financial institutions often open branches in metropolitan areas outside of their “home” region to engage in cross-border lending.

Unlike Shinkin banks and credit cooperatives, whose business areas are defined in their institutional statute, regional banks or banks that are more sizable face few regulatory constraints on their lending behavior, such as the location of their branch offices. Regulations governing the location of bank branches have been eased over time. In FY2002 the government changed branch location regulations from a permit system to a notification system. Sugiyama (2020) notes that the percentage of cross-border branch openings by regional financial institutions increased sharply after FY2002 and that many of these branches were opened in metropolitan areas such as Osaka, Tokyo, Aichi, and Kanagawa. Perhaps due in part to these cross-border branch openings, a newspaper report indicated that the share of outstanding loans to non-local prefectures to overall loans continued to rise throughout the 2010s, reaching 35% at the end of March 2018.[1]

In Japan regional differences have manifested in the increasing concentration of economic activities in Tokyo. Even by international standards Japan is unique in terms of the concentrated population in the Tokyo metropolitan area. It is not only that the concentration is high but that it is continuously rising. This is true of business activities as well. For instance, the headquarters of large firms are highly concentrated in the Tokyo area.[2] Cross-border lending to Tokyo can be considered a reflection of this concentration of both population and economic activity in Tokyo.

4.1.2 Paucity of Analyses on the Actual Status of Cross-Border Lending

There are few empirical studies, however, which detail the actual state of cross-border lending in Japan. One of the few exceptions that examines trends in cross-border lending by regional banks and second-tier regional banks is Ozaki et al. (2019). They describe how the share and growth rate of loans, the number of branches, and loan interest rates differ across regions based on detailed bank lending data collected by the Bank of Japan and classified by region. According to their analysis the share of loans at branches located in the same region as the head office declined from the 2000s until the late 2010s, while the share at branches in Tokyo increased moderately until the mid-2010s. The share of loans at branches in other regions also increased moderately over this period. Tsuruta (2021) uses information on credit-guaranteed loans by prefecture and financial institution to compare the volume of credit-guaranteed loans and credit risk in the prefecture where the head office is located to those in other regions.[3]

Gilje, Loutskina, and Strahan (2016) focus on the shale gas production boom in the U.S. and examine banks' interregional asset transformation from deposits to

---

[1] Nihon Keizai Shimbun, June 14, 2018 morning edition, "Regional Banks' Cross-Border Lending at its Highest."

[2] Reference materials for the final report in the materials for the Round Table Discussion on the Long-term Perspective of the National Land by Ministry of Land, Infrastructure, Transport and Tourism, March 11, 2021.

[3] Kano and Tsutsui (2003) examined whether lending markets are integrated or fragmented across prefectural administrative boundaries by comparing loan interest rates. They found that the loan markets of regional banks are connected across prefectural borders while those of Shinkin banks are fragmented. The geographic scope of the loan and deposit markets will be discussed in Chapter 10 which focuses on the market concentration. Other studies that focus on the physical distance between financial institutions and firms, rather than simply on whether funds cross boundaries, and examine the effect of this distance on lending conditions and bank-firm relationships are Degryse and Ongena (2005), Petersen and Rajan (2002), Agarwal and Hauswald (2010), Nguyen (2019), and Ono et al. (2016) among many others.

loans. They measure the effects of an exogenous and localized increase in deposits for banks on the lending behavior of these banks. More specifically, they find that banks with branches in areas where deposits have surged due to the fracking boom have increased their lending in other regions. Wang (2021) shows that lower oil prices affect banks' lending behavior in the U.S., through reduced deposits with banks that have branches in shale gas extraction areas.

There are few studies worldwide, however, that provide a complete picture of cross-regional asset transformation by financial institutions. Aguirregabiria et al. (2020) use county-level data in the U.S. to measure the gap between deposits and loans at each bank in their sample and then analyze whether the gap is determined by the branch network, market power, and/or economies of scope of banking operations. However, due to data limitations this study does not comprehensively capture the flow of funds between regions via deposits and loans. Kalemli-Ozcan et al. (2010) examine the determinants of the interregional flow of funds by extending the scope of analysis to overall regional savings-investment balances, not limited to those intermediated by financial institutions. Using information on gross regional product and aggregate income at the U.S. state level they show that reallocation of funds occur to fill differences in productivity growth rates across regions. However, even here, the net flow of funds per region is calculated from the gap between income and production and does not capture the gross flow of funds between regions.

4.1.3 Importance of Understanding Trends in the Interregional Flow of Funds Through Loans and Deposits

This chapter uses data on loan and deposit balances at the financial institution branch level to quantify the extent to which deposits collected by financial institutions within a region are used for loans in its own region and other regions. The data is from the Financial Services Agency and has never been used for research before. The data will be summed for financial institutions to examine the trends in and the efficiency of the flow of funds between regions via loans and deposits. To the author's knowledge, this is the first attempt of its kind, not only in Japan but in other countries as well.

In addition to the channel in which funds flow across regions within a financial institution, several other channels need to be considered when accounting for interregional fund allocation. One route is for financial institutions in different locations to exchange funds with one another in the interbank market. Another route for funds to flow outside of a particular region is when households purchase stocks or corporate bonds instead of holding bank deposits. Additionally, if financial institutions that accept deposits invest in government bonds rather than lending to other regions, it would be difficult for us to identify the region to which the deposits move.

Despite the above qualifications, the interregional flow of funds via loans and deposits are quantitatively important. According to the Bank of Japan's Flow of Funds statistics as of the end of March 2021 Japanese households held 956 trillion yen in deposits out of 1,968 trillion yen in financial assets, while their holdings of stocks and bonds were only about one-third, or 321 trillion yen. Depository institutions accepted deposits totaling 1,634 trillion yen, not only from households but also from other entities, and extended 821 trillion yen in the form of loans. The outstanding balance in the call loan and bill market, which reflects the extent of interbank transactions of short-term funds, was only 15 trillion yen. Given these figures, financial institutions' loans and deposits play a significant role in the allocation of funds between regions in terms of volume.

4.1.4 Procedures to Construct the Indicator

To quantify the interregional flow of funds by financial institutions through loans and deposits we take the following steps. Each financial institution has branches in various regions, accepting deposits and loans. Since financial institutions are not concerned about the region from which they receive deposits upon extending loans we assume that deposits accepted by a bank's branches across regions are collected at its head office and then distributed as loans to each branch proportional to the branch's share of deposits. Thus, the flow of deposits to a branch used for loans by all branches and the headquarters can be viewed as the flow of funds across branches and headquarters of a bank.

While on the balance sheets of individual financial institutions the sum of deposits and other funding coincides with the sum of loans and other assets, the volumes of deposits and loans at each branch do not necessarily match. Some branches attract more deposits than loans and conversely some branches have more loans than deposits. Depending on the direction and magnitude of this gap there will be a transfer of funds within a financial institution from branches with a large amount of deposits to branches with a large amount of loans.

By aggregating the flow of funds from a financial institution's branch network to the regional units in which the institution operates it is possible to determine how and to what extent the institution contributes to the allocation of funds among regions through its own loans and deposits. The larger the branch network and the larger the gap between deposits and loans at each branch the more active the flow of funds between regions.

Furthermore, the interregional allocation of funds measured for each financial institution is summed for all financial institutions. As a result we create an interregional flow of funds indicator that covers almost all deposit-taking financial institutions in Japan. This will enable us to better understand the flow of funds between regions and evaluate their efficiency.[4]

---

[4] Each country's central bank publishes Flow of Funds statistics to quantify what financial instruments are held by banks and other financial intermediaries, households, nonfinancial corporations, and governments as assets and liabilities on their balance sheets. In recent years, central banks

4.2 Overview of Results

The indicator of the interregional flow of funds in Japan via loans and deposits for each year from 2005 to 2019 shows that the majority of deposits collected in a prefecture are used for loans within the same prefecture but that the extent differs substantially across regions, indicating a considerably active interregional flow of funds. While the flow of funds between Tokyo and other regions is very large in both directions the amount of deposits collected in the regions and used for loans in Tokyo is greater than the amount of deposits collected in Tokyo and used for loans in the regions, indicating a net inflow of deposits for loans in Tokyo.

Looking at changes in the magnitude of fund allocation for financial institutions of all categories it is clear that the last few years have seen a decline in deposit inflows for loans from the regions to Tokyo and a relative increase in the flow of funds within each prefecture. This finding is the opposite of that of Ozaki et al. (2019) who solely focus on regional and second-regional banks. The difference in the findings indicates that regional banks encourage the flow of funds towards Tokyo while large banks increase their lending in the areas where they collect deposits.

Japan's declining birthrate and aging population is expected to have a significant impact on the future direction of the allocation of funds via loans and deposits between the regions and Tokyo. Fukuda and Okumura (2021) assume that the ratio of the elderly, who withdraw their savings, relative to the middle-aged, determines the savings rate in a region. If this is the case then the savings rate will decline significantly in regions where the ratio of elderly citizens is increasing and the direction of the flow of funds between Tokyo and these regions may be reversed.

The analysis examining the determinants of the allocation of funds across regions reveals three key points. First, when we control for interregional fixed effects we find a tendency for funds to flow to regions with lower labor and capital productivity, a result that is opposite of the findings of Kalemli-Ozcan et al. (2010) which examined the efficiency of capital flows among U.S. states without controlling for such fixed effects. The results suggest the presence of factors that result in this inefficiency such as the informational friction for borrowers located in remote areas.

Second, funds tend to flow from regions where land prices, which are also a profitability indicator for real estate-related lending, are declining to those where they are rising. Since the asset price bubble burst in the early 1990s real estate prices in Japan have been on a long-term downward trend and the share of real estate used as collateral for loans has been declining. Nevertheless, development of the real estate market continues to have a significant impact on the allocation of funds among regions through loans and deposits.

---

have not only kept track of the balance sheets of each of these sectors but have also aggregated and published inter-sectoral exchanges for several financial instruments. Konno (2014) explains the state of development of intersectoral flow of funds statistics by comparing Japan with other countries. In contrast to these "From whom to whom" indicators this section presents "From where to where" indicators that extend the flow of funds to interregional interactions, although it focuses only on the flow of funds through loans and deposits of deposit-taking financial institutions.

Third, funds tend to flow from regions with a high loan market concentration to regions with a low concentration in terms of the loan amount outstanding.[5] If a more concentrated market is more oligopolistic and can charge higher lending rates then funds should flow from relatively less concentrated regions to more concentrated regions. In practice, however, the opposite has occurred. Financial institutions are reducing their loans in regions of higher market concentration perhaps because they expect small gains from entering these markets.

The chapter proceeds as follows. Section 4.3 describes the methodology for measuring the interregional allocation of funds via loans and deposits. Section 4.4 outlines the methodology for examining the determinants of the interregional flow of funds. Section 4.5 describes the data. Section 4.6 describes the characteristics of the interregional flow of funds indicators and how they change over time. Section 4.7 discusses the determinants of the interregional flow indicators. Section 4.8 concludes the chapter.

4.3 Construction of an Interregional Flow of Funds Indicator via Loans and Deposits

4.3.1 Definition

Here we detail how we calculate the interregional funds flow indicator of deposit-taking financial institutions. A depository financial institution (hereafter referred to as a "bank") i collects deposits D_{ij} in region j and lends $L_{ij'}$ in region j'. In this analysis the unit of the region is the prefecture. Although the administrative divisions, prefectures, do not necessarily correspond to the scope of the loan and deposit markets, we follow previous studies (e.g., Uchida and Tsutsui, 2005; Kano and Tsutsui, 2003) and use prefectures as the geographical criterion for the definition of the loan and deposit market.

On the balance sheet of bank i the sum of total lending and non-lending asset management operations in all prefectures equals the sum of total deposits plus non-depository funding in all prefectures as shown in (4.1). To account for non-deposit funding and non-lending asset management operations we add another row of "other funding measures" and another column of "other invested assets" so that total deposits and total loans match for each bank.[6]

[5] Concentration increases when the number of financial institutions present in the market is smaller or when the more institutions have an outsized market share. See the factor decomposition of concentration in Sect. 10.6 in Chapter 10.

[6] If Bank i's total loans across regions are smaller than its total deposits across regions the difference between the two (the amount by which deposits exceed loans) is recorded in "Other invested assets." If the direction of the inequality is opposite then the difference between the two (the amount by which loans exceed deposits) is recorded in "Other funding measures."

$$D_i = \sum_j D_{ij}, L_i = \sum_{j'} L_{ij'}, D_i = L_i \tag{4.1}$$

The prefecture j in which deposits are collected and the prefecture j' in which loans are extended may be the same or they may differ. When a bank opens branches and collects deposits and lends in different prefectures the amount of deposits collected within a given prefecture need not equal the amount of loans provided in that prefecture. For this reason banks move funds across prefectures to adjust for differences in deposits and loans within a prefecture. In other words, within the bank deposits collected in one prefecture are allocated to loans there and in other prefectures.

In addition, deposits may be collected from multiple prefectures to cover the loans made in one prefecture. We define the portion of loans made by bank i in prefecture j' financed by deposits collected in prefecture j as in formula (4.2):

$$\frac{D_{ij}}{D_i} \times L_{ij'} \tag{4.2}$$

It denotes the amount of deposits that bank i allocates from prefecture j to prefecture j' to cover its loans in prefecture j'. We assume that: (a) loans in each prefecture are not primarily financed by deposits in that prefecture; and (b) to finance lending in prefecture j', deposits in prefecture j and in prefecture j' are provided in proportion to their share of total deposits in bank i. Based on these assumptions bank i can finance its loans in prefecture j' not only with deposits from the same prefecture but also with deposits from other prefectures.[7]

We apply this procedure to all the banks in the country and sum the result across all the banks. As a result the proportion of loans in prefecture j' financed by deposits in prefecture j is represented as follows:

$$\sum_i \frac{D_{ij}}{D_i} \times L_{ij'} = L_{j'} \times \sum_i \frac{D_{ij}}{D_i} \times \frac{L_{ij'}}{L_{j'}} \tag{4.3}$$

On the left-hand side of the equation is the amount of loans in prefecture j' financed by deposits in prefecture j. The second part of the right-hand side is the ratio of loans in prefecture j' financed by deposits in prefecture j to the total amount of loans in the prefecture j'.

[7] One alternative approach is not to make assumption (a) and to first use deposits in the prefecture for loans in that prefecture. Uesugi, Hiraga et al. (2021a) provide a numerical example of offsetting loans and deposits within a prefecture and a calculation based on actual data. However, it is natural to assume that financial institutions allocate their total deposits they collect from all the prefectures for loans in all the prefectures, regardless of the prefectures in which they initially collect deposits. Therefore, in the following analysis we assume both (a) and (b).

4.3.2 Numerical Example

To clarify the flow of funds indicator we work through a simple hypothetical example in which four banks in four prefectures in Shikoku have deposit and loan balances as shown in Table 4.1. We show how each of formulas (4.4) and (4.5) result in concrete figures in the example:

$$\sum_i \frac{D_{ij}}{D_i} \times L_{ij'} \quad \text{The amount of bank loans in prefecture j}' \text{ financed by deposits collected in prefecture j} \tag{4.4}$$

$$\sum_i \frac{D_{ij}}{D_i} \times \frac{L_{ij'}}{L_{j'}} \quad \text{The share of bank loans in prefecture j}' \text{ financed by deposits collected in prefecture j} \tag{4.5}$$

We call (4.4) the "deposit inflow matrix" and (4.5) the "deposit coefficient matrix." In Table 4.2 prefecture *j*'s share of total deposits for each bank is shown as a matrix in a left-middle box, while bank i's share of total loans in each prefecture is shown as a matrix in a right-upper box. The deposit coefficient matrix, which is calculated as a result of the multiplication between these two matrices, is shown in the right-middle box. By multiplying by $L_{j'}$ we show the deposit inflow matrix in the right-bottom box.

If we look horizontally (across each row) at the deposit inflow matrix we see how the deposits collected in a particular prefecture are used for loans and other invested assets in each prefecture. In the example the deposits of 2,000 units collected in Tokushima prefecture are allocated to loans of 727 units in Tokushima, loans of 182 units in each of the other three prefectures, and other invested assets of 727 units.

Table 4.1 Numerical example of loans and deposits held by banks in regions

Loans	Bank A	Bank B	Bank C	Bank D	Deposits	Bank A	Bank B	Bank C	Bank D
Tokushima	800	100	200	100	Tokushima	2,000	0	0	0
Kagawa	200	700	400	100	Kagawa	200	1,700	600	0
Ehime	200	300	800	100	Ehime	0	100	2,000	0
Kochi	200	100	200	700	Kochi	0	0	0	1,500
Other invested assets	800	600	1,000	500	Other funding measures	0	0	0	0
Total	2,200	1,800	2,600	1,500	Total	2,200	1,800	2,600	1,500

Source Uesugi, Hiraga et al. (2021a)

Table 4.2 Deposit inflow matrix and deposit coefficient matrix based on a numerical example

						Tokushima	Kagawa	Ehime	Kochi	Other invested assets
					Bank A	0.667	0.143	0.143	0.167	0.276
					Bank B	0.083	0.500	0.214	0.083	0.207
					Bank C	0.167	0.286	0.571	0.167	0.345
					Bank D	0.083	0.071	0.071	0.583	0.172
	Bank A	Bank B	Bank C	Bank D		Tokushima	Kagawa	Ehime	Kochi	Other invested assets
Tokushima	0.909	0	0	0	Tokushima	0.606	0.130	0.130	0.152	0.251
Kagawa	0.091	0.944	0.231	0	Kagawa	0.178	0.551	0.347	0.132	0.300
Ehime	0	0.056	0.769	0	Ehime	0.133	0.248	0.451	0.133	0.277
Kochi	0	0	0	1.000	Kochi	0.083	0.071	0.071	0.583	0.172
Other funding measures	0	0	0	0	Other funding measures	0	0	0	0	0
					Total loans	1,200	1,400	1,400	1,200	2,900
						Tokushima	Kagawa	Ehime	Kochi	Other invested assets
					Tokushima	727	182	182	182	727
					Kagawa	213	772	486	159	870
					Ehime	159	347	632	159	803
					Kochi	100	100	100	700	500
					Other funding measures	0	0	0	0	0

Source Uesugi, Hiraga et al. (2021a)

By looking vertically at the deposit inflow matrix we can see how deposits collected in each prefecture are used for loans in each prefecture. In this example, out of the loans of 1,200 units made in Tokushima Prefecture 727 units are financed by deposits from Tokushima, and 213, 159, and 100 units are financed by deposits from Kagawa, Ehime, and Kochi, respectively.

Looking horizontally at the deposit coefficient matrix we see how the share of deposits collected in a prefecture are used for loans in each prefecture. For instance, deposits in Tokushima account for 61% of loans in Tokushima, and 13%, 13%, and 15% of loans in Kagawa, Ehime, and Kochi, respectively. If we instead look down each column of the matrix (vertically) we see how much of a prefecture's loans are accounted for by deposits from each prefecture. Deposits collected from Tokushima, Kagawa, Ehime, and Kochi account for 61%, 18%, 13%, and 8% of Tokushima's loans, respectively. The sum of these percentages is 100%.

4.4 Examining the Determinants of the Interregional Flow of Funds

In the previous section we developed an indicator of the flow of funds between regions via loans and deposits of financial institutions. In this section we present a framework for analyzing the determinants of this indicator.[8] The value of the flow of funds indicator is determined by factors related to the demand for and supply of funds in prefecture j, where deposits are collected, and in prefecture j', where loans are extended.

It is important to note that our dependent variable measuring the interregional flow of funds is based on deposits and loans and does not consider other non-lending invested assets and non-deposit funding measures. In terms of the deposit coefficient matrix and the deposit inflow matrix (the matrices in the right-middle and right-bottom boxes in the hypothetical example in Table 4.2) we do not use the information in the bottom row and the rightmost column. This is because it is difficult to identify the location of other invested assets and the location of non-depository procurement so that the bottom row and the rightmost column do not provide useful information on the movement of funds between regions. In this study we assume that financial institutions' decisions on the interregional allocation of deposits and loans are made separately from choices between lending and non-lending asset management and between deposits and non-depository fund procurement. We develop an

[8] The analytical framework presented below differs from that in Uesugi, Hiraga, et al. (2021a) in several aspects including the definition of the dependent variable, the explanatory variable representing productivity, and the use of year fixed effects. Note that these revisions are made to produce more accurate estimation results and that the results presented in Sect. 4.7 of this chapter differ in several ways from those in Uesugi, Hiraga, et al. (2021a).

estimation framework for the area in which we are able to identify the prefectures in which deposits are collected and loans are made.[9]

The magnitude of the flow of funds between regions, which we employ as the dependent variable, is defined as follows:

$$Flow_{jj't} \equiv \left(\sum_i \frac{D_{ijt}}{D_{it}} \times L_{ij't} - \sum_i \frac{D_{ij't}}{D_{it}} \times L_{ijt}\right) / \left(0.5 * \left(\sum_i D_{ijt} + \sum_i D_{ij't}\right)\right) \tag{4.6}$$

This is calculated by measuring the amount of deposits flowing from prefecture j to j' for lending and the amount of deposits flowing from prefecture j' to j for lending, subtracting the latter from the former and then dividing by the average of deposits collected in the two prefectures j and j'. The net amount of funds moving from prefecture j to j' is calculated and then standardized by the average deposit amount in both prefectures. This indicates the proportion of funds transferred from prefecture j to j' relative to the total amount of deposits collected in both prefectures.

To analyze the determinants of the interregional flow of funds we estimate the following equation where the flow of funds from prefecture j to j' is the dependent variable:

$$\begin{aligned} Flow_{jj't} &= \alpha + \beta_1 Diff\_Performance_{jj't-1} + \beta_2 Diff\_Stability_{jj't-1} \\ &\quad + \beta_3 Diff\_HHI^L_{jj't-1} + \beta_4 Diff\_HHI^D_{jj't-1} + \beta_5 Diff\_LandPrice_{jj't-1} \\ &\quad + \delta_{jj'} + \mu_t + \varepsilon_{jj't} \end{aligned} \tag{4.7}$$

We use values in the prefecture j' and prefecture j for the following variables: productivity and firm profitability (Performance); firm stability (Stability); loan and deposit market concentration (HHI_L, HHI _D); and land prices (Land price).[10]

"Diff_" indicates that the value of prefecture j' is subtracted from the value of prefecture j. "t" denotes the year. The variable for productivity, Performance, is an important factor in assessing the efficiency of the flow of funds. If lending is allocated according to the level of productivity, i.e., if collected deposits are allocated as loans from low productivity regions to high productivity regions, then the coefficient β_1 will be positive and the flow of funds via loans and deposits by financial institutions is efficient. Studies on the efficiency of resource allocation, such as Foster et al. (2001), examine whether the factors necessary for production are allocated efficiently or not.

[9] Non-deposit funding measures and non-lending asset investment are important to the management of financial institutions. In particular, with regard to the management of funds other than loans their share in the collected deposits continues to rise. We will discuss the impact of the non-lending asset investment on the interregional flow of funds and the importance of examining the efficiency of such investment in the final section.

[10] The Herfindahl–Hirschman Index (HHI) is obtained by summing the square of each firm's share of the market. For more information see Chapter 10.

We often judge the efficiency of fund allocation among regions by examining the inflow of funds from low-productivity regions to high-productivity regions, based on the same idea as in Foster et al. (2001) which examined whether high-productivity firms increase employment and sales relative to low-productivity firms.

The variable measuring the stability of firm management, Stability, captures the regional risk in the firm sector. Even if the productivity and profitability of firms located in a prefecture is lower than in other prefectures, if firms are operationally stable and have a low risk of bankruptcy, banks may extend more loans to this prefecture. Therefore, we use the capital adequacy ratio of firms to measure bankruptcy risk. If funds are flowing to prefectures with high business stability then the coefficient β_2 should be positive.

The variable HHI is used to examine whether funds flow to regions with a higher concentration in the loan and deposit markets. Prefectures with a high concentration in the market for lending may have large interest margins due to weak competition among financial institutions. Financial institutions that observe such a situation may try to increase their lending in that prefecture. In this case the coefficient β_3 will be positive. However, if high concentration is the result of low loan demand and few financial institutions entering the market then financial institutions may instead reduce lending in that prefecture. In this case β_3 is negative.

We take a similar approach to the market for deposits. A high level of concentration in the deposit market could result in low deposit rates. A financial institution may attempt to take advantage of this situation by collecting as many deposits as possible in that prefecture and increasing the outflow of funds. In this case the coefficient β_4 is negative. However, if high concentration is the result of many financial institutions exiting the market, due to low deposit demand, then the deposits that financial institutions collect in that region may decrease. In this case β_4 is positive.

The land price variable, LandPrice, represents the demand for real estate-related lending. During the asset price bubble in the late 1980s Japanese financial institutions not only rapidly increased their lending to construction, real estate, non-banks, and other parties related to the real estate market but also widely extended loans secured by real estate, mainly to small and medium-sized enterprises (SMEs).[11] Such real estate-related lending was often conducted in prefectures where expectations of rising real estate prices were high and this is believed to have led to further increases in real estate prices. After the collapse of the bubble economy the ratio of real estate and other collateral provided by firms to financial institutions declined because of the prolonged decline in real estate prices and because the government encouraged financial institutions to promote lending that did not rely on real estate or other collateral.[12] In recent years, however, financial institutions have increased their housing loans and, in particular, regional financial institutions have increased

---

[11] An analysis by Ono et al. (2021) identifies trends in real estate-related lending during this period.

[12] In the Small and Medium Enterprise Agency's Basic Survey of Small and Medium Enterprises, which provides population estimates of annual trends for SMEs in Japan, the percentage of firms that provide physical collateral for loans to their main bank has declined from over 50% in the 2005 survey to just under 30% in 2019. This is shown in Fig. 9.1 in Chapter 9.

their lending to individuals and privately established asset management firms for the rental real estate industry (Bank of Japan, 2016), among other real estate-related lending activities. If more funds are flowing to prefectures with higher land prices the coefficient β_5 can be expected to be positive.

4.5 Data

This section describes the data used in the analysis. We use data on the outstanding amount of loans and deposits by branch of Japanese financial institutions to create the interregional flow of funds indicator. The data is from the Financial Services Agency (FSA) and is as of March 31 for every year from 2005 to 2019. The financial institutions analyzed in this chapter are city banks, trust banks, other banks, regional banks, second-tier regional banks, Shinkin banks, credit cooperatives, and foreign banks.[13] While the original data is at the branch level, for the purposes of this analysis the data is aggregated at the prefectural level. The results of the HHI calculations are presented in Chapter 10.

To analyze the determinants of the flow of funds we use the Regional-Level Japan Industrial Productivity Database (R-JIP) jointly reported by the Research Institute of Economy, Trade and Industry (RIETI) and Institute of Economic Research of Hitotsubashi University, the Basic Survey of Business Activities reported by the Ministry of Economy, Trade and Industry (METI), and the Prefectural Accounts reported by the Cabinet Office (CAO). The purpose of the R-JIP data is to capture differences in the productivity and industrial structure across prefectures in Japan. It measures nominal and real value added, the real capital stock, and labor hours at the prefecture-industry level, allowing us to measure capital and labor productivity by prefecture. The most recent version of the R-JIP database is limited to the year 2012 and recent information on productivity at the regional level is unavailable. Therefore, we use gross prefectural product per worker through 2019 from the prefectural accounts as an alternative indicator to measure labor productivity in a prefecture. The Basic Survey of Business Activities contains data on profit margins and capital adequacy ratios of firms aggregated at the prefectural level, which we use as indicators of firm performance and business stability, respectively.

The final explanatory variable, real estate prices by prefecture, is the logarithm of the average appraised land price for all purposes by prefecture as indicated by the official land price index published by the Ministry of Land, Infrastructure, Transport and Tourism. We display the list of variables based on these data sources and used in the analysis in Table 4.3.

[13] Deposit-taking financial institutions included in the FSA data but not included in this analysis are the prefectural federations of credit agricultural cooperatives, credit fishery cooperatives, Japan Post Bank, Shoko Chukin Bank, Norinchukin Bank, JA Bank, JF Marine Bank, Japan Federation of Labor Banks, and labor banks. On the other hand, not included in the FSA data are government-affiliated financial institutions other than Shoko Chukin Bank. These government-affiliated financial institutions do not accept deposits.

Table 4.3 Variables employed for the estimation of the determinants of interregional flow of funds

Category of Variables	Variables	Definition	Sources	Period
Flow	Net fund flow ratio	Eq. (4.6)	Calculated by Uesugi et al. (2021) based on the data provided by the Financial Services Agency	2005–2019
Performance	Capital productivity	Real value added/real capital stock	R-JIP by the RIETI and Hitotsubashi University	2005–2012
	Labor productivity	Real value added/ labor input	R-JIP by the RIETI and Hitotsubashi University	2005–2012
	Labor productivity2	Real prefectural gross products/ Number of workers	Gross prefectural products by the Cabinet Office	2005–2019
	Operational profit ratio	Operational profit/ total assets	Basic Survey of Firm Acticities by the Ministry of Economy and Industry	2005–2019
Stability	Capital adequacy ratio	Net worth/total assets	Basic Survey of Firm Acticities by the Ministry of Economy and Industry	2005–2019
HHI	Loan market HHI and Deposit market HHI	See Chapter 10	Calculated by Uesugi et al. (2021) based on the data provided by the Financial Services Agency	2005–2019
LandPrice	Land prices	Appraised value of land for all purposes averaged for each prefecture	Public Notice of Land Prices by the Ministry of Land, Construction, Transportantion, and Tourism	2005–2019

4.6 Characteristics of and Trends in the Interregional Flow of Funds

4.6.1 Indicator of Interregional Flow of Funds as of 2019

Among the indicators of the flow of funds between regions for each year from 2005 to 2019 in Japan we present the deposit coefficient matrix for 2019 in Supplementary Table 1.[14] The matrix shows how deposits and others collected in each of the 47

[14] Supplementary Tables 1 and 2 are presented as an appendix to Uesugi, Hiraga, et al. (2021a), published as a discussion paper by the Financial Research Center of the FSA.

prefectures are allocated to each prefecture as loans and others.[15] The numbers listed in the matrix are the percentage of deposits in a given prefecture that are distributed as loans in each prefecture. The largest 10% are bold and italic, the next 40% are numbered only, and the smallest 50% are left blank.

There are three takeaways from this table. First, lending within a prefecture is most often financed by deposits collected in that prefecture, with the values along the diagonal being the largest. However, there is significant variation across the prefectures. Second, although not as large as the diagonal elements, the surrounding values are also relatively large, indicating many financial transactions between neighboring prefectures. Third, Tokyo not only provides many deposits to finance lending in other prefectures but also accepts many deposits from other prefectures to finance lending in Tokyo. A similar trend, albeit to a lesser degree, is also observed for Osaka.

To illustrate the first two points in more detail, Figure 4.1 arranges the values along the diagonal of Supplementary Table 1 (the ratio of deposits used for loans in one's own prefecture to all the loans extend in the prefecture) from largest (95% in Okinawa) to smallest (36% in Osaka). It is apparent that there are substantial differences across prefectures. The prefectures on the left side of the figure, those with the highest percentages, are geographically isolated (Okinawa and Hokkaido) and/or are large in area (Hokkaido, Nagano, Niigata, and Akita), while those on the right tend to be located in metropolitan areas (Tokyo, Osaka, Aichi, Hyogo, and Kanagawa) or small in area (Kagawa).

We can, to some extent, control for the effect of geographic size on this ratio by calculating the ratio including deposits received from neighboring prefectures. In Figure 4.1 the ratio is calculated by including deposits not only from the "home" prefecture but also from neighboring prefectures that are geographically adjacent.[16] Prefectures where deposits from neighboring prefectures are used more frequently for lending include Shimane, Tottori, Saga, and Gifu. These prefectures and their adjacent prefectures have many branches of the same banks, indicating the strong financial ties between these neighboring prefectures.

When deposits from neighboring prefectures are included, in addition to those from the home prefecture, the inter-prefectural difference in the ratio of loans covered by deposits shrinks. However, the ratio remains low in prefectures located in large metropolitan areas such as Tokyo, Aichi, Hyogo, and Osaka. These prefectures are home to many branches of large banks and regional banks with head offices in far-flung locations, and many of the remote deposits collected by these financial institutions are used for lending.

Taking a closer look at the third finding, that Tokyo not only provides a large amount of deposits to finance lending in other prefectures but also receives many deposits from other prefectures to finance lending in Tokyo, Supplementary Table 2 displays a deposit inflow matrix that measures the amount of funds moving between

[15] Included in the "others" of "deposits and others" and "loans and others." are other non-deposit funding measures and other non-lending invested assets, respectively. The information is shown in the bottom row and rightmost column of Supplementary Tables 1 and 2.

[16] Prefectures that are contiguous by land are defined as neighboring prefectures.

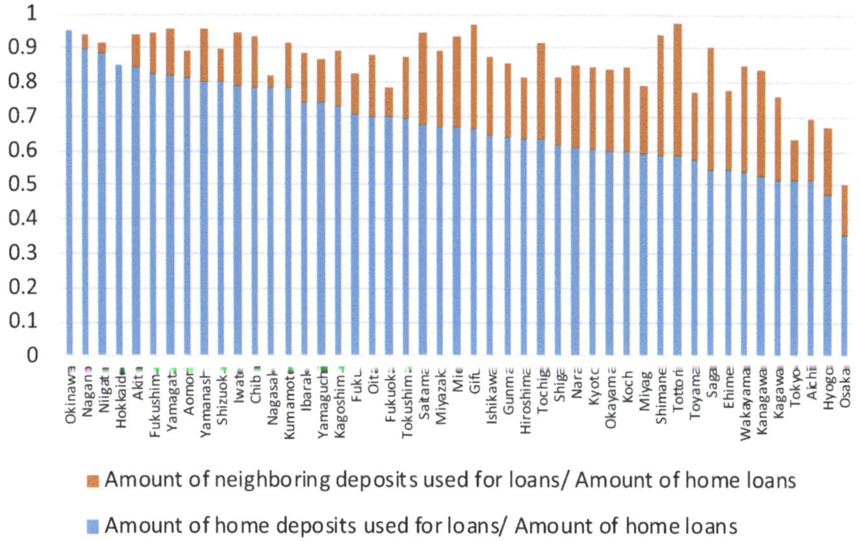

Fig. 4.1 Share of own and neighboring prefectures' deposit used for loans in a prefecture (*Source* Processed by the author based on Uesugi, Hiraga et al. (2021a))

regions. The magnitudes of all matrix elements are standardized by the amount of deposits collected in Hokkaido and used for lending in Hokkaido in 2005, whose value is set to 100. As in Supplementary Table 1, the top 10% of values are bold and italic, the next 40% are numbered only, and the bottom 50% are left blank.

Most of the values in the column showing the volume of deposits flowing in from other prefectures for lending in Tokyo are in bold and italic while only about half of those in the row showing the volume of deposits flowing out from Tokyo for lending in other prefectures are shaded. As can be seen from the Tokyo row in Supplementary Table 1 the flow of funds from Tokyo to the other prefectures accounts for a large share of lending in each region. However, a comparison of the magnitude of the figures in the rows and columns for Tokyo in Supplementary Table 2 shows that the flow of funds from other prefectures to Tokyo is larger than from Tokyo to other prefectures. The net result is an inflow of funds into Tokyo from the rest of the country.

Figure 4.2 shows, by prefecture, how much of the deposits collected in the "home" prefecture flows to Tokyo to facilitate lending. By simultaneously measuring the percentage of deposits that flow out to other prefectures, it is possible to show the share of deposits that flow to Tokyo and the share of deposits that flow to prefectures other than Tokyo.

The prefectures with the highest outflow ratios to Tokyo are those belonging to large metropolitan areas such as Osaka, Aichi, and Hyogo and neighboring prefectures such as Kanagawa, Chiba, Saitama, and Yamanashi. The prefectures with higher outflows to Tokyo than to other prefectures are located mostly in eastern Japan

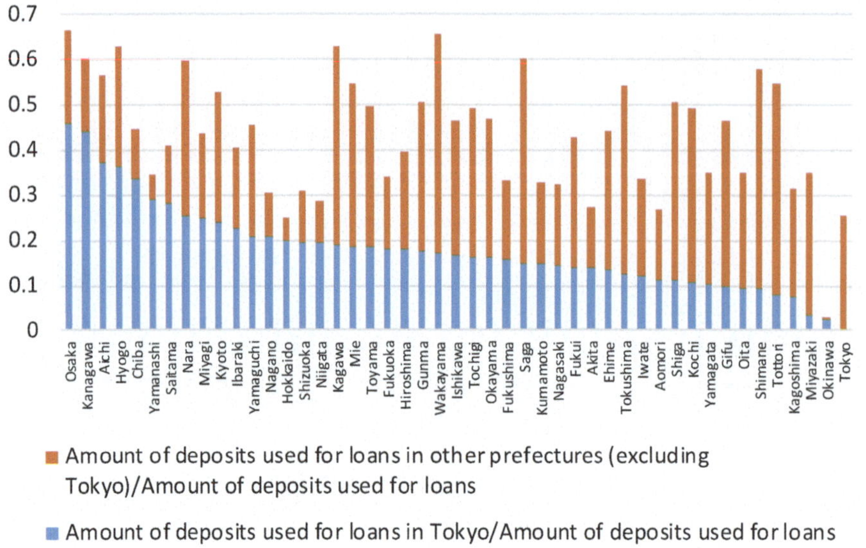

Fig. 4.2 Share of deposit outflow from a prefecture used for loans in Tokyo or other prefectures (*Source* Processed by the author based on Uesugi, Hiraga et al. (2021a))

(Miyagi, Nagano, Shizuoka, Niigata, among others). The extent of inflow of funds into Tokyo is not uniform across the country but it is larger from metropolitan areas other than Tokyo and from prefectures in eastern Japan, mainly in the vicinity of Tokyo.

4.6.2 *Changes from 2005 to 2019*

So far we have focused only on the flow of funds in 2019, the end of the analysis period and immediately preceding the COVID-19 pandemic. Next we focus on changes during the analysis period. Ozaki et al. (2019), one of the few studies to examine Japanese cross-border lending, find that regional banks experienced a relative decline in lending in their home region while lending within Tokyo consistently increased.

Do we obtain the same results when we account for large banks, Shinkin banks, and credit cooperatives in addition to regional banks? In this analysis we focus on the share of deposits in each prefecture that flowed out of the home prefecture to Tokyo and other prefectures and the share that remained in the home prefecture and were used for lending. We aggregate each of these shares across the prefectures and examine changes over time.

Looking at Figure 4.3 we see that the results are the opposite to what was found by Ozaki et al. (2019). First, the share of deposits used for lending within a prefecture has been increasing. Second, the share of deposits used for lending in Tokyo increased

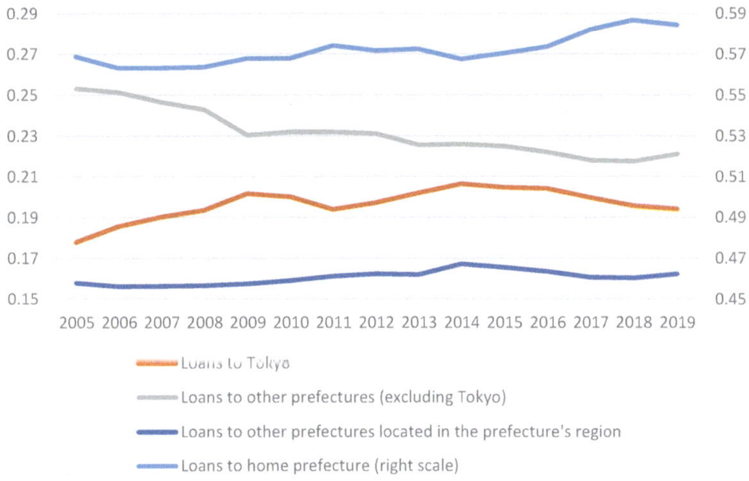

Fig. 4.3 Destination of deposits for loans (excluding other invested assets) collected in home prefecture (*Source* Processed by the author based on Uesugi, Hiraga et al. (2021a))

until around 2014, after which it began to decline. Third, the share of deposits used for lending in other prefectures outside of Tokyo has been declining over the entire period.

Contrary to regional banks, which continue to increase their cross-border lending to Tokyo while reducing their lending in the areas in which their head office is located, other financial institutions, especially large city banks, may instead be increasing lending in areas where the deposits are collected and reducing the transfer of funds to other areas, including Tokyo. Thus, when accounting for all financial institutions, the allocation of funds through lending and deposits no longer moves in the direction of Tokyo.

4.7 Determinants of the Interregional Flow of Funds

In this section we examine which factors are the primary determinants of the interregional flow of funds. Specifically, we estimate equation (4.7) using panel data. Table 4.4 displays the descriptive statistics of the variables included in the estimations. It should be noted that the variables obtained from the R-JIP, which was published only up to 2012, have a limited number of observations.

Based on the deposit inflow matrix, the net flow of funds across prefectures results in a maximum inflow of 6 trillion yen and a minimum of -11 trillion yen. The net funds flow rate, with the deposit amount as the denominator, shows a maximum of about 4% and a minimum of –7%.

Table 4.4 Descriptive statistics

	Number of observations	Mean	Standard deviation	Min	Max
Net fund flow ratio	15,134	–0.0002	0.0045	–0.0685	0.0431
Net fund flow amount (yen)	15,134	–2.58E+10	5.02E+11	–1.07E+13	6.02E+12
Amount of flow from j' to j (yen)	15,134	1.19E+11	9.20E+11	5,233,439	2.37E+13
Amount of flow from j to j' (yen)	15,134	9.34E+10	5.84E+11	5,632,002	1.51E+13
Difference in operating profit ratio	15,134	0.0021	0.0227	–0.1124	0.1051
Difference in capital productivity	8,648	–0.0045	0.0884	–0.4228	0.3899
Difference in labor productivity	8,648	–0.1602	0.8171	–3.5692	3.3874
Difference in labor productivity2	15,134	–0.2891	1.3078	–5.3788	5.4496
Difference in capital adequacy ratio	15,134	0.0038	0.1325	–0.6448	0.5119
Difference in loan market HHI	15,134	0.0164	0.0986	–0.3028	0.3213
Difference in deposit market HHI	15,134	0.0289	0.1145	–0.3113	0.3619
Difference in logged land price	15,134	0.0597	0.8584	–3.3791	3.7173
Operating profit ratio	15,134	0.0400	0.0182	–0.0469	0.1180
Capital productivity	8,648	0.4078	0.0586	0.2713	0.7162
Labor productivity	8,648	4.2462	0.6270	3.2082	6.9995
Labor productivity2	15,134	7.1589	0.9332	5.5610	11.1767
Capital adequacy ratio	15,134	0.3882	0.1011	–0.0072	0.7092
Loan market HHI	15,134	0.2292	0.0707	0.0486	0.3700
Deposit market HHI	15,134	0.2538	0.0823	0.0869	0.4640
Logged land price	15,134	11.2242	0.5108	10.1306	13.8479

Source Tabulated by the author based on the data used in Uesugi, Hiraga et al. (2021a)

Table 4.5 shows the estimation results using the fixed effects model in Eq. (4.7).[17] There are four alternative variables that measure the productivity and profitability of firms in the region, represented as $Diff\_Performance_{jj't-1}$ in this equation, so we use one of each. We include the following variables in all estimations: the capital adequacy ratios, which measures business stability, concentration in the loan and deposit markets, and land prices, which are important for real estate-related lending.

4.7.1 Estimation Results

Among the coefficients that indicate the impact of firms' profit margins and productivity on interregional flows, the coefficient on the difference in operating profit margins is positive and significant in column 1. This implies that more deposits flow as loans from prefectures with lower profit margins to prefectures with higher profit margins.

In contrast, in columns 3 through 6 the coefficients on the differences in capital and labor productivity are all negative and significant. Funds move from prefectures with higher productivity to prefectures with lower productivity. The coefficient on the difference in the capital adequacy ratio, which measures the stability of firm management in the region, is also significantly negative in some estimates, although it is marginal. From these results, we may say that there exists a flow of funds to riskier regions.

Note that these results are about the relationship between the average productivity of a prefecture and the direction of the allocation of funds across the regions. We do not know the productivity of individual firms that each financial institution lends to within the region nor do we know to what types of firms each of the cross-border banks and local banks extend loans to. The recipients of these interregional loans may be local firms with high productivity and low risk, while local financial institutions may be responsible for lending to low-quality, high-risk firms. Conversely, since financial institutions that engage in interregional lending are latecomers to the market they may be forced to lend to low-quality, high-risk firms as a result of local financial institutions securing the high-quality firms.

Although limited to credit-guaranteed loans Tsuruta (2021) obtains results suggesting the latter: using SME loan data at the prefecture-financial institution level he shows that the subrogation rate of financial institutions which lend outside the prefecture of where their headquarters are located exceeds that of those which lend within the headquartered prefecture. This suggests that the credit risk of firms who

[17] In selecting the fixed effects model the Breusch-Pagan test is applied between the pooled OLS and the random effects model and the Hausman test between the random and fixed effects models.

Table 4.5 Baseline estimation results

Fixed effect model						
Dependent variable: Net fund flow ratio						
	(1)	(2)	(3)	(4)	(5)	(6)
Difference in operating profit ratio	0.00155***	0.000763				
Difference in capital productivity			–0.00156***			
Difference in labor productivity				–5.51e-05*		
Difference in labor productivity2					–4.78e-05*	–0.000115***
Difference in logged land price	0.000269***	0.00101***	0.000844***	0.000966***	0.000231***	0.000885***
Difference in capital adequacy ratio	–0.000296*	–0.000329*	–0.000204	–0.000242	–0.000191	–0.000252
Difference in loan market HHI	–0.00460***	–0.00516***	–0.00540***	–0.00519***	–0.00455***	–0.00485***
Difference in deposit market HHI	–0.000197	0.00220**	0.00247**	0.00225**	7.87e-05	0.00240**
Constant	–3.77e-05	–0.000141***	–0.000132***	–0.000144***	–5.40e-05	–0.000173***
Year FE	Yes	Yes	Yes	Yes	Yes	Yes
Interregional FE	Yes	Yes	Yes	Yes	Yes	Yes
NOB	15,134	8,648	8,648	8,648	15,134	8,648
R^2	0.010	0.021	0.024	0.021	0.010	0.022

Source Estimated by the author based on the data used in Uesugi, Hiraga et al. (2021a)

Notes Explanatory variables are lagged by one period (year). ***, **, and * represent statistical significance at 1%, 5%, and 10%, respectively. Figures in parentheses represent standard errors

engage in interregional lending is higher than the credit risk of financial institutions who lend locally.

The coefficient on the difference in land prices between prefectures is consistently positive and significant in all the estimations. This suggests that deposits are flowing in as loans from regions where land prices are relatively low to prefectures where land prices are high. On the other hand, the coefficient on the HHI difference in the loan market is negative and significant in all estimations. A high HHI indicates that there is either a small number of financial institutions in the loan market or a situation where the share of loans among financial institutions is uneven and concentrated among the top financial institutions. As we will show in Chapter 10, a high HHI implies a low degree of competition and a high markup under certain assumptions. If it means that large interest margins can be earned then financial institutions may be more aggressive in their lending and deposits may flow in as loans from other regions. In reality, however, this has not happened and deposits have flowed out to other regions. The high concentration in the lending market at the prefectural level in Japan may represent a situation where few financial institutions enter the market due to limited demand.

4.7.2 Which Explanatory Variables Are Strongly Related to Net Flow of Funds?

The estimates above reveal the relationship between various factors such as productivity, the level of market concentration, and the direction of the flow of funds. Which of these factors are the most important determinants and most closely related to the interregional flow of funds among financial institutions via loans and deposits?

Using the estimation results in Table 4.5 and the standard deviation information for each variable shown in Table 4.4, we calculate the extent to which a change in the explanatory variable impacts the increase or decrease in the flow of funds. We multiply the one standard deviation change in the explanatory variable by the coefficient obtained from the estimation. We then divide this by the standard deviation of the dependent variable. The larger the absolute value of this ratio the greater the impact on the dependent variable. The results are presented in Table 4.6.

We find that the difference in land prices and the concentration in the loan market are strongly related to the dependent variables. Profit margins and productivity, on the other hand, do not have a substantial impact.

For land prices a one standard deviation increase in the difference between high and low land prices (86% in this case) would result in an increase in inflows equivalent to a maximum of 20% of the one standard deviation change in net capital flows. This suggests that the interregional flow of funds is quite sensitive to profitability in the real estate market.

Table 4.6 Impact of a one-standard deviation increase in explanatory variables on the net fund flow ratio

Explanatory variables	Coefficients		Standard deviations	Change in the net fund flow ratio in response to one standard deviation of an explanatory variable		Ratio to one standard deviation of net fund flow ratio	
	Max	Min		Max	Min	Max	Min
Difference in operating profit ratio	0.0016	0.00076	0.023	3.5E-05	1.7E-05	0.8%	0.4%
Difference in capital productivity	−0.0016		0.088	−1.4E-04		−3.1%	
Difference in labor productivity	−5.51E-05		0.817	−4.5E-05		−1.0%	
Difference in labor productivity2	−4.78E-05	−1.15E-04	1.308	−6.3E-05	−1.5E-04	−1.4%	−3.4%
Difference in logged land price	0.00101	0.0002	0.858	8.7E-04	2.0E-04	19.4%	4.4%
Difference in capital adequacy ratio	−0.0002	−0.0003	0.132	−2.5E-05	−4.4E-05	−0.6%	−1.0%
Difference in loan market HHI	−0.0046	−0.0054	0.099	−4.5E-04	−5.3E-04	−10.0%	−11.9%
Difference in deposit market HHI	0.0025	−0.0002	0.115	2.8E-04	−2.3E-05	6.3%	−0.5%

Source Calculated by the author
Note Coefficients are from Table 4.5 and standard deviations are from Table 4.4

For the loan market HHI, when relative market concentration of a prefecture increases the outflow of funds increases by about 10% of one standard deviation of the net funds flow. The result indicates that the decline in loan demand in a prefecture may have resulted in the higher loan market concentration and the increasing outflow of deposits from the prefecture.

4.7.3 What Are the Sources of the Inefficient Interregional Allocation of Funds?

Based on the estimates in Table 4.5 financial institutions' deposits are allocated as loans from regions with higher capital and labor productivity to regions with lower productivity. Why does this inefficient allocation occur? Although it is difficult to identify the precise causes we propose several possible sources of the inefficiency by repeating our estimation for different subsamples by time and region.

We first split the sample into two periods, 2005–2011 and 2012–2019. The estimation results are presented in Table 4.7. Here we use labor productivity indicators based on prefectural accounts for which we have a sufficient number of observations over both periods. We also show estimates for profit margin indicators based on the Basic Survey of Business Activities, which is an indicator of firm performance.

The coefficient on the labor productivity difference is negative for the first half of the sample but is positive for the second half. The coefficient on the difference in operating profit margin is insignificant for the first half but is positive and significant for the second half. This suggests that the interregional allocation of funds has become more efficient over time.

Table 4.8 presents the estimation results when the sample is split by region. First are the estimates that focus on the flow of funds only across prefectures located in each of the non-metropolitan regions, such as Hokkaido/Tohoku, Chugoku, Shikoku, and Kyushu/Okinawa. We consider the efficiency of fund allocation among prefectures belonging to each region. In all cases the coefficient on the difference in labor productivity is positive and significant, while the coefficient on the difference in capital productivity is insignificant. The coefficient on the difference in the operating profit is marginally positive and significant. The coefficient on the difference

Table 4.7 Estimation results (by period)

Fixed effects model				
Dependent variable: Net fund flow ratio				
	2005–2011		2012–2019	
	(1)	(2)	(3)	(4)
Difference in operating profit ratio	–0.000985		0.00121**	
Difference in labor productivity2		–0.000141***		8.62e-05**
Year FE	Yes	Yes	Yes	Yes
Interregional FE	Yes	Yes	Yes	Yes
NOB	6,486	6,486	8,648	8,648
R^2	0.031	0.032	0.003	0.003

Source Estimated by the author based on the data used in Uesugi, Hiraga et al. (2021a)
Notes Explanatory variables are lagged by one period (year). ***, **, and * represent statistical significance at 1%, 5%, and 10%, respectively. Figures in parentheses represent standard errors. Results for estimates for other variables are omitted

in labor productivity, which was negative in the estimation for the entire sample, is now positive.

We next focus on the flow of funds between metropolitan areas such as Tokyo, Osaka, and Aichi versus other regions. The results are shown in Table 4.9. As can be seen from the deposit coefficient matrix in Supplementary Table 1 and the deposit inflow matrix in Supplementary Table 2, a large amount of funds moves between metropolitan areas and other regions and they have a large weight in the economy. The estimation results in Table 4.9 are quite different from those in Table 4.8, with significant negative coefficients on both capital productivity and labor productivity. Only the coefficient on the difference in operating margin is marginally positive and significant.

What is interesting about these subsample estimates is the difference between the flow of funds between metropolitan areas and the rest of the country and the flow of funds within regional areas. The former is inefficient, with funds flowing to areas where firms are less productive, while the latter is efficient, with funds flowing to areas where productivity is higher. Because of the greater distance, and higher transaction and monitoring costs between metropolitan and rural areas than within rural areas alone, it is possible that banks, on average, are unable to lend to areas with more productive firms.

Table 4.8 Estimation results (flow of fund within a region)

Fixed effects model				
Dependent variable: Net fund flow ratio				
	Flow of funds among prefectures in a non-metropolitan region			
	(1)	(3)	(4)	(5)
Difference in operating profit ratio	0.00950*			
Difference in capital productivity		–0.00141		
Difference in labor productivity			0.000789***	
Difference in labor productivity2				0.000613*
Year FE	Yes	Yes	Yes	Yes
Interregional FE	Yes	Yes	Yes	Yes
NOB	910	520	520	910
R^2	0.079	0.077	0.091	0.079

Source Estimated by the author based on the data used in Uesugi, Hiraga et al. (2021a)
Notes Explanatory variables are lagged by one period (year). ***, **, and * represent statistical significance at 1%, 5%, and 10%, respectively. Figures in parentheses represent standard errors. Results for estimates for other variables are omitted

Table 4.9 Estimation results (flow of funds between metropolitan areas and other areas)

Fixed effects model				
Dependent variable: Net fund flow ratio				
	Flow of funds originated from or destined to Tokyo, Osaka, and Aichi			
	(1)	(3)	(4)	(5)
Difference in operating profit ratio	0.00492*			
Difference in capital productivity		–0.00612***		
Difference in labor productivity			–0.000629***	
Difference in labor productivity2				–0.000347***
Year FE	Yes	Yes	Yes	Yes
Interregional FE	Yes	Yes	Yes	Yes
NOB	1,890	1,080	1,080	1,890
R^2	0.023	0.105	0.098	0.027

Source Estimated by the author based on the data used in Uesugi, Hiraga et al. (2021a)
Notes Explanatory variables are lagged by one period (year). ***, **, and * represent statistical significance at 1%, 5%, and 10%, respectively. Figures in parentheses represent standard errors. Results for estimates for other variables are omitted

4.8 Summary

In this chapter, based on loan and deposit information available at the financial institution branch level, data which has not been analyzed previously, we have examined trends in the interregional flow of funds as well as its determinants. We are interested in the amount of interregional lending undertaken by financial institutions, the extent of the concentration of funds in Tokyo, and the efficiency of these interregional flow of funds in terms of productivity.

The results of the empirical analysis do not indicate that there has been an increase in the amount of interregional lending, in that the percentage of deposits collected in a prefecture and lent out within that prefecture has been rising, nor does it appear that these flows have led to an increasing concentration of funds in Tokyo as the share of deposits going to Tokyo has actually shown a decline in recent years. These trends are largely a reflection of the behavior of megabanks and other large banks and are the opposite of the behavior of regional banks.

Given that the proportion of elderly people who withdraw their savings will further increase in rural areas the current pattern of deposits being collected in rural areas and flowing into Tokyo and other large cities as loans may change significantly in the future. The declining extent of deposits in rural areas flowing into metropolitan areas as loans may reflect future demographic changes in Japan's metropolitan and rural areas.

In terms of the efficiency of the interregional allocation of funds we observed a tendency for deposits to flow as loans from regions with higher productivity to regions with lower productivity. However, when we disaggregate by time and region we find that there is an efficient flow of funds between prefectures located in each of the

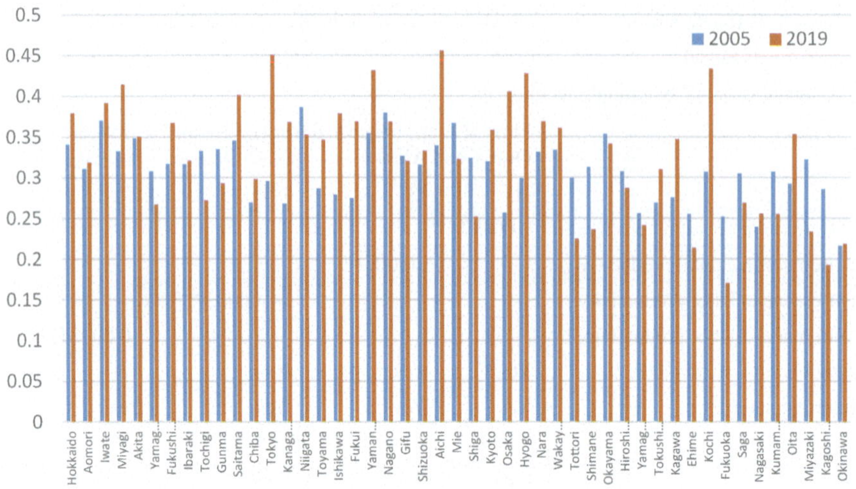

Fig. 4.4 Share of other invested assets to total deposit amount in each prefecture (*Source* Processed by the author based on the data used in Uesugi, Hiraga et al. (2021a))

rural regions. For further analysis we need data on individual firm-bank relationships and firm performance to clarify what precisely results in an efficient interregional allocation of funds.

Lastly, an important point which has not been made in this chapter is the management of assets other than loans at financial institutions. So far our analysis has focused on the portion of deposits collected in each prefecture that is used for lending in each prefecture. However, there is also a substantial amount of funds in "other invested assets," which is shown in the right-most column of the deposit coefficient matrix (Supplementary Table 1) and the deposit inflow matrix (Supplementary Table 2). The ratio of other assets to deposits is rising, reflecting the sluggish demand for loans in Japan overall. In Figure 4.4, which shows the ratio of "other invested assets" to total deposits by prefecture, it is clear that not only has the ratio increased but the increase from 2005 to 2019 tends to be greater in Tokyo, Osaka, and Hyogo prefectures, which are part of metropolitan areas.[18]

To accurately assess whether the deposits received by financial institutions from the various regions are being managed efficiently the performance of assets that are funded by "other invested assets" as well as loans to various regions is important. It is very difficult to determine, however, what the assets held in this category are.[19] An analysis of the interregional flow of funds indicator including the behavior of this "other invested assets" category is an issue for the future.

[18] One financial institution that is not included in the analysis of the interregional flow of funds indicator in this chapter but that manages its collected deposits as assets other than loans to the region is the Japan Post Bank.

[19] For example, if the financial institution holds Japanese government bonds as other invested assets it is necessary to evaluate the performance of the Japanese government's overall activities.

Chapter 5
Government Involvement in SME Finance, Current Situation and Theoretical Background

Abstract It has been pointed out that SME policies in Japan are more comprehensive and detailed than in other countries. In addition, large-scale financial support measures are invoked in response to shocks such as financial crises and the COVID-19 pandemic. We focus on government involvement in SME finance which constitutes a major part of SME policies. Then we provide an overview of the current situation and the theoretical background that justifies the need for such involvement. Specifically, we examine credit guarantees and government financial institutions, play an important role in extending loans to SMEs. We use a simple theoretical model to evaluate which of these does a better job of enhancing social welfare through lending and investment. The results show that credit guarantees are associated with higher social welfare than direct lending by government-affiliated financial institutions. However, the model's predictions are inconsistent in some respects with the data on how firms actually use these support measures. This suggests the need for more detailed empirical analysis of credit guarantees and direct lending by government financial institutions, respectively.

Keywords SME policy · Government intervention · Credit guarantees · Government-affiliated financial institutions · Direct lending · Small and Medium Enterprise Agency · Financial Services Agency · Government risk bearing · Asymmetric information · Countervailing power

5.1 Introduction: Reasons for Government Involvement in SME Financing

Borrowing by firms may not be adequately facilitated by private financial institutions alone. During recessions the supply of funds decreases because the private sector is unable to bear the credit risk of the firms to which it lends. Especially when the borrowers are SMEs, financial institutions may be hesitant to lend because they do not know the quality and behavior of these firms. As a result more firms may be unable to borrow even though they are ready to pay interest rates commensurate

I. Uesugi, *The Economics of SME Finance*, Advances in Japanese Business and Economics 36, https://doi.org/10.1007/978-981-96-3193-3_5

with credit risk. At this point the government sector could intervene to alleviate the undersupply of funds to SMEs.

This chapter, the first of Part 2 of this book, looks at government involvement in SME finance and covers three issues. First, we summarize and characterize government involvement in SME finance. SME finance policy in Japan consists of three categories (policy pillars): (1) direct provision of funds, such as loans, by government financial institutions; (2) indirect support for the provision of funds by private financial institutions, such as credit guarantees; and (3) development of institutional measures to achieve specific policy objectives such as business revitalization. Various entities are involved including the Small and Medium Enterprise Agency, the Financial Services Agency, and the Bank of Japan. (1) and (2) are used on a large scale to provide financial support in the event of major shocks such as the COVID-19 pandemic. In recent years policies to promote specific objectives such as business restructuring and the promotion of lending that is not overly dependent on personal guarantees have become increasingly important.

The second issue is the theoretical relevance of government involvement in SME financing. The most frequently cited reason for intervention has to do with the government's ability to bear risk. The generally accepted theory is that the government bears the burden of risks that the private sector cannot, particularly during a crisis. A second oft cited justification for intervention is the presence of asymmetric information between SMEs and lenders. In this case information problems are mitigated by the government's information production function and promotion of competition in the lending market through the existence of government financial institutions. On the other hand, there exists some justifications, such as term conversion, which have become less relevant as the financial market develops over time.

Third, we compare the two major policy programs: credit guarantees and direct lending by government-affiliated financial institutions. Each plays a major part in policy pillars (1) and (2) and provided 36 trillion yen and 16 trillion yen (as of the end of June 2021), respectively, during the recent COVID-19 pandemic. However, despite the fact that both of them are large in size and share the common feature of risk-taking by the government there has been a paucity of theoretical and empirical evidence comparing these two policy schemes. Based on a simple theoretical model we would expect that credit-guaranteed lending, where the government assumes losses in the event of a default, would have a greater effect on borrowing and investment by high-risk firms than direct lending which simply offers uniformly lower interest rates.

A simple tabulation of the data to examine whether the theoretical predictions hold true reveals that relatively high-risk firms use credit guarantees and somewhat less risky firms use direct lending. On the other hand, we do not find that credit guarantees have greater impact than direct lending on borrowers' leverage and tangible assets. In this and subsequent chapters we examine the effects of credit guarantees and direct lending in more detail and consider the reasons for the differences between theory and data.

The remainder of this chapter proceeds as follows. Section 5.2 presents an overview of the current state of government involvement in SME finance. Section 5.3

summarizes previous discussions on the relevance of policy involvement. Section 5.4 focuses on credit guarantees and direct lending by government-affiliated financial institutions, both of which play a large quantitative role in SME finance policy. We then make theoretical predictions regarding which types of firms would prefer either one of the policy measures to the other and how the amount of firms' borrowing and investment would change in the presence of each of the measures. Section 5.5 examines whether the theoretical predictions are supported by firm survey data in Japan. Section 5.6 provides a summary of the chapter.

5.2 Current State of Government Involvement

The Small and Medium Enterprise Agency (SMEA), a subsidiary administrative body of the Ministry of Economy, Trade and Industry (METI), is primarily responsible for SME finance policies. The policies aim to facilitate the provision of funds to SMEs by underwriting corporate credit risks that the private sector has difficulty handling. The 2021 edition of their SME policy guidebook issued by SMEA (2021) is massive, with its 344 pages covering the SME policies they offer and illustrating the detailed and complex nature of SME financing policies.[1] Among the support measures to facilitate the supply of funds there are direct measures such as loans by government-affiliated financial institutions and investments by the SME Investment & Consultation Companies. Also, there are indirect measures that include the provision of guarantees for loans extended by private financial institutions, investments in private funds that purchase equities of venture business, and support for the securitization of SME loan claims.

On the other hand, there are measures that do not necessarily aim for increasing the supply of funds but instead develop institutional arrangements to help SMEs grow and revitalize their businesses. Examples include the promotion of the Guideline for Managers' Personal Guarantees which provides guidelines for loans that do not require personal guarantees by management, and support for SMEs' business revitalization through the SME Revitalization Support Council.[2]

---

[1] Muramoto (2015) praised these support measures for SMEs as being comprehensive and meticulously organized and being excellent templates for other Asian countries to follow. The author once gave a series of lectures to SME policymakers in ASEAN countries on the preparation of the SME White Paper and the current state of SME finance in Japan, and their response was that "Japan's SME policies are organized and multi-faceted, which make them difficult to transplant.".

[2] Nakata (2013), who details SME policies from 1980 to 2000, lists the major policy areas on the financial side as being the facilitation of private SME financing, the inducement of private financing through the credit enhancement system, loans by three government-affiliated SME finance institutions, loans from the fund for advanced management and the fund for promoting modernization, SME capacity building fund, prefecture-level institutional loans, and direct investment by the SME Investment & Consultation Companies. As Muramoto (2015) points out, the policies during this period are characterized by the following feature: the first half of the period focused on direct lending by government-affiliated financial institutions while in the second half the importance of promoting private-sector lending through credit guarantees increased.

Public involvement in SME finance is not limited to the SMEA. Financial supervision by the FSA and monetary policy by the Bank of Japan have also influenced SME financing through the behavior of financial institutions. An example from the 2000s is the "Action Program on Strengthening Relationship Banking Functions" formulated by the FSA in 2003 which aimed to revitalize SME finance through the promotion of relationship banking by regional financial institutions.[3] The name was later changed to the “Action Program on Strengthening Community-based Banking Functions.” Since the 2007 revision of the Comprehensive Supervisory Guidelines for Small and Regional Financial Institutions the FSA has committed itself to promoting community-based financing and relationship banking. Additional efforts by the FSA to encourage SME financing include the Financial Function Strengthening Act, intended to revitalize regional finance through financial institutions that have enhanced their capital position through the injection of public funds, and the SME Financing Facilitation Act, implemented to support SMEs that faced cash-flow difficulties during the Global Financial Crisis. The Bank of Japan has also encouraged an increase in corporate lending through special operations to facilitate corporate financing, in which funds are lent to banks with the private-sector corporate debt being pledged as collateral.

Local governments have also taken measures to encourage the supply of funds to SMEs. The most prominent and sizable measure is known as “institutional financing.” The institutional financing is mainly related to the credit guarantee programs set up by the central government whereby local governments provide subsidies to private financial institutions, which enables SMEs to receive credit guaranteed loans with reduced interest rates and credit guarantee fees.

5.2.1 Classification of Government Involvement

In Figure 5.1 we categorize the support measures as follows: direct financing, such as loans by government financial institutions; indirect measures to promote financing, such as loan guarantees by credit guarantee corporations; and development of institutional arrangements to realize specific policy objectives.

---

[3] The financial administration of the Japanese government before the 2000s treated the provision of funds to SMEs as special. A prominent example of this is the postwar development of mutual banks (later converted to second regional banks), Shinkin banks, and credit cooperatives as financial institutions for SMEs under the specialized financial institution system (Nishimura, 2011, p. 56).

1. Direct financing

Direct loans (including subordinated loans) by government-affiliated financial institutions

Japan Finance Corporation (Small and Medium Enterprise Business Division, National Life Business Division, Agriculture, Forestry and Fisheries Business Division)

Shoko Chukin Bank

Okinawa Development Finance Corporation

Organization for Small and Medium Enterprise and Regional Innovation

Investment by Small and Medium Business Investment & Consultation Companies and others

Small and Medium Business Investment & Consultation Companies in Tokyo, Osaka, and Nagoya

2. Indirect measures to promote financing

Credit Guarantees

Credit Guarantee Corporations

Institutional financing to support credit guarantees

Local governments in prefectures and municipalities

Investment in private funds

Organization for Small & Medium Enterprises and Regional Innovation, Japan

Support for securitization of loan receivables

Japan Finance Corporation

Injection of public funds into financial institutions, Market operation for corporate financial assistance and others

Financial Services Agency, Bank of Japan

3. Development of institutional arrangement to realize specific policy objectives for SME financing

Guidelines on Managers' Personal Guarantees

Small and Medium Enterprise Revitalization Support Councils

Supervisory Guidelines for Regional Financial Institutions

SME Financing Facilitation Act (from December 4, 2009 to March 31, 2013)

Fig. 5.1 Government involvement in SME financing (*Note* Credit guarantees are subject to insurance underwriting by the Insurance Division of the Japan Finance Corporation. *Source* Prepared by the author based on Small and Medium Enterprise Agency (2021), Muramoto (2015), and Yabushita and Bushimata (2006))

5.2.1.1 Direct Supply of Funds Such as Loans by Government-Affiliated Financial Institutions

First, there are measures in which government-related institutions, such as government-affiliated financial institutions and independent administrative agencies, directly provide loans and equity investments. The largest of these, in terms of volume, is direct lending by two government-affiliated financial institutions: Japan Finance Corporation (JFC) and Shoko Chukin Bank.[4] There are, however, differences between the two. JFC consists of three divisions: Small and Medium Enterprise Business Unit, National Life Business Unit, and Agriculture, Forestry, and Fisheries Business Unit with the first two lending mainly to SMEs. As of March 31, 2020, the National Life Unit had lent to 880,000 clients with an average loan balance of 7 million yen while the SME Unit had lent to 44,000 clients with an average loan amount of 80 million yen.[5] Many of the loans are what are called special loans for specific policy purposes such as safety nets, environmental conservation and energy saving measures, and disaster recovery. In addition, JFC does not collect deposits but instead raises the funds necessary for lending by borrowing from the Fiscal Investment and Loan Program (FILP) and issuing its own FILP agency bonds.[6]

Shoko Chukin, which lends to SME associations and their stakeholder members, is positioned as a government-affiliated financial institution for SMEs because the government holds a large number of shares. However, it differs from other government-affiliated financial institutions in that it does not provide special loans for policy purposes, with the exception of some crisis-response loans, and accepts deposits. It also provides bills discounting and overdrafts.[7]

[4] The Okinawa Development Finance Corporation conducts operations equivalent to those of the Japan Finance Corporation, the Japan Housing Finance Agency, and the Welfare and Medical Service Agency in Okinawa Prefecture, in addition to its own operations to address unique policy issues. The Organization for Small & Medium Enterprises and Regional Innovation, Japan (SMRJ) provides direct loans at low or no interest to finance the development of industrial parks and other facilities. SME Investment & Consultation Companies were established under the SME Investment & Consultation Company Act to provide a long-term stable supply of funds to growth-oriented venture companies, SMEs, and medium-sized enterprises, and to support the stabilization of management and corporate growth while enhancing equity capital without necessarily seeking a stock listing.

[5] By the end of March 2021, when the impact of the COVID-19 pandemic became more apparent, the average loan amount increased significantly to 10 million yen and 105 million yen for the National Life Unit and Small and Medium Enterprises Unit, respectively. However, there has been no change in the order regarding the average loan size by the two units.

[6] The effects of these loans made by the SME Unit will be discussed in Chapters 7 through 9.

[7] In the Bank of Japan's Flow of Funds statistics the Japan Finance Corporation is classified in the category of "government-affiliated financial institutions" while the Shoko Chukin Bank is classified in the category of "small and medium-sized enterprise financial institutions" to which Shinkin banks and credit cooperatives belong.

5.2.1.2 Indirect Support for Financing Provided by Private Financial Institutions

The second set of support measures does not involve government agencies directly supplying funds to SMEs but includes guarantees for loans extended by private financial institutions, investments in funds managed by private venture capitalists, and guarantees for securitized products composed of loans made by private financial institutions. Through these measures private financial institutions are expected to increase the supply of funds to SMEs in the form of loans and equity investments. The largest amount of funds supplied by private institutions through these indirect support measures are credit-guaranteed loans involving the 51 credit guarantee corporations nationwide.[8]

Institutional lending overlaps to a large extent with credit guarantee lending but differs in that local governments are involved.[9] When private financial institutions provide loans with credit guarantees local governments give these financial institutions substantial subsidies used for credit guaranteed loans at lower interest rates and lower guarantee fee rates than usual. The most recent example of these institutional loans is the so-called "zero-zero" which are interest-free and unsecured loans which were offered from May 2020 to the end of March 2021 as part of the financial support measures during the COVID-19 pandemic.

Note that the injection of public funds into financial institutions will impact the behavior of financial institutions by improving their capital adequacy ratios. Among other things, an increase in lending capacity could lead to an increase in lending, including lending to SMEs.[10]

5.2.1.3 Institutional Development for Specific Policy Objectives

The third set of policy measures includes a variety of schemes designed to achieve specific policy objectives such as the survival, growth, and revitalization of SMEs. Although it is difficult to quantify the impact of the introduction of these programs in the form of an increase or decrease in the amount of loans they may have a

---

[8] The scheme and effects of credit guarantees are discussed in Chapter 6.

[9] Since individual municipalities provide their own institutional loan programs and the existence and extent of disclosure on these institutional loans vary greatly among credit guarantee corporations and municipalities, it is very difficult to obtain a complete picture of the institutional loans in terms of size and performance. Fukazawa (2007) is one of the few examples of an attempt to grasp it.

[10] In Japan there are several studies that examine whether the injection of funds into financial institutions, under several different legal frameworks since the late 1990s, has increased lending, including to SMEs. See Osada (2010), Kondo (2018), Nagata (2017), Giannetti and Simonov (2013), Montgomery and Shimizutani (2009), and Nakashima (2016). These studies find that loans by the financial institution that received injections did not necessarily increase. We can further interpret that an increase in lending to SMEs is the result of an SME lending target which is set in the business restructuring plan submitted at the time of the capital injection.

significant impact on the efficiency of SME financing. In addition, several policy measures, although few in number, have been the subject of researchers' analysis.

As explained in Chapter 2, the SME Financing Facilitation Act was designed to support SMEs that had fallen into a financial crisis due to the rapid deterioration of business conditions caused by the Global Financial Crisis and to impose on financial institutions the need to respond to applications to modify the terms of existing loans.

The Guidelines on Managers' Personal Guarantees are designed to help financial institutions lend without excessive reliance on personal guarantees by identifying cases in which a personal guarantee by a manager is not required or in which a manager who has provided a large personal guarantee can retain certain assets when a company enters into judicial liquidation or private liquidation proceedings. The purpose is to reduce the adverse effects of personal guarantees and to encourage drastic business development and early business rehabilitation.

Since the application of the Guidelines began in February 2014 the percentage of loans that do not require personal guarantees has gradually increased, reaching more than a quarter of new SME loans in the first half of FY2020. The first group of measures, direct lending by government-affiliated financial institutions, was also changed to be in line with the government's direction, by granting a number of loans without requiring personal guarantees.[11]

Now that we have provided a brief overview of each of these types of interventions there are three points to be made about government involvement in SME finance in Japan.

5.2.2 Direct Lending by Government Financial Institutions and Credit Guarantees Are Quantitatively Important

First, among the government's support measures for SME financing, direct lending by government financial institutions (first group) and credit guarantees (second group) are the largest in value terms. However, despite their similarity, in that the government sector bears the credit risk, they coexist and are provided by separate institutions.[12]

In light of this it is important to evaluate the effects of the two policy measures from an economic perspective. Therefore, this chapter first develops a simple model of the economic effects of direct government lending and credit guarantees, focusing on the difference between the two in terms of how the government bears the risk. Then, in Chapter 6 and what follows we present the results of our analysis of the

---

[11] This institutional change had interesting results that were unanticipated by researchers. We discuss this issue in Chapter 9.

[12] According to Nemoto (2015), government financial institutions for SMEs in western countries, with the exception of the United States, often provide credit guarantees, equity support, and direct lending in the same organization.

effects of credit guarantees and direct lending by government financial institutions, using firm-level and loan-level data.

5.2.3 *In the Event of a Major Shock Massive Measures Are Taken*

Second, the government has responded to major macroeconomic shocks, such as the crisis caused by COVID-19, by massively expanding some of their support measures. The government intervenes because crises impede SME's cash flow and their ability to borrow from financial institutions. In particular, the use of credit guarantees expanded rapidly in the 1990s, during the recession following the collapse of the bubble economy, and special measures, namely special guarantees and emergency guarantees, were put in place during the Japanese financial crisis and the Global Financial Crisis in the late 1990s and late 2000s, respectively. Safety net lending by government-affiliated financial institutions was also provided on a smaller but still substantial scale.

In response to the COVID-19 pandemic, which began in early 2020, the government provided interest-free and unsecured loans through both the credit guarantee scheme and direct lending if certain requirements were met. This was in response to concerns of a significant reduction in in-person contacts and an unprecedented drop in the level of economic activity following the declaration of the state of emergency in April 2020. It turned out to be an unprecedentedly generous measure. According to Uesugi, Ono et al. (2021) the interval between the time of application and the receipt of funds was about one to two months. Except for the initial period when the program was launched, the provision of funds appears to have been relatively smooth.

5.2.4 *Measures Related to Business Revitalization, Survival, and Exit Are Becoming Increasingly Important*

Third, there has been an increase in the importance of the various measures intended to address the financing problems faced by SMEs, beyond a mere increase in the supply of funds. In particular, an area of focus has been the choice between firm survival/exit and business revitalization. Several measures have been undertaken, including the establishment of the SME Revitalization Support Council and the Regional Economy Vitalization Corporation of Japan and the enactment and enforcement of the SME Financing Facilitation Act.

While it is estimated that 300,000 to 400,000 SMEs have changed the terms and conditions of their loans since the Facilitation Act came into effect, a survey of firms reveals that more than half of them have received a deferral of the repayment period and only a limited number have received more drastic treatment such as a principal reduction or a debt-for-debt swap (DDS) (see Table 2.4 in Chapter 2). In contrast, as many as 16,000 firms that were eligible for support from the SME Revitalization Support Council have formulated and implemented plans, including not only debt rescheduling but also management and asset restructuring to revitalize their businesses.

These measures are expected to increase corporate value by forgiving debt and improving management. They also help to solve the problem of debt overhang whereby new lending is discouraged because banks do not want their borrower firms' cash flow to be used to repay existing loans. These measures are also important from the perspective of reallocating funds from low-productivity firms to high-productivity firms, as discussed in Chapter 3. The JFC and the credit guarantee corporations, which are mainly responsible for measures in the first and second group of support measures, are also expected to play an important role for the efficient choice between business revitalization, survival, and exit.

However, the effects of government measures for business revitalization have not yet been quantitatively examined. For example, there is not enough data available to know how many of the firms that changed the terms and conditions of their loans were able to survive, what the determinants of this success was, and how many firms remained in the market without finding a way to improve their business, even though they had taken advantage of these support measures.

In the following sections we will closely examine the first and the second point. In other words, we will focus on credit guarantees and direct lending by government-affiliated financial institutions, the two most important measures in terms of increasing the supply of funds to SMEs, and evaluate the effectiveness of these measures based on a theoretical framework.

5.3 Theoretical Relevance of Government Involvement to Support Financing

Government involvement in SME financing is necessary when private financial institutions alone cannot provide funds to positive Net Present Value (NPV) firms. When is this the case? Iwamoto (2001) cited countervailing power, information production, maturity transformation, externalities, risk burden, and asymmetric information as reasons why government intervention in loan markets is justified. Based on his discussion, we will examine the validity of these reasons in the following order: risk burden, asymmetric information, information production, and countervailing power.[13]

[13] It may be possible to state that the government sector provides better maturity transformation than private financial institutions when we compare the differences in the duration of funding and lending at government-affiliated financial institutions with those at private-sector financial institutions. Government-affiliated financial institutions procure funds by borrowings from the Fiscal Loan Fund, government-backed bonds, and FILP agency bonds. Repayment terms range from 2 to

5.3.1 Risk Burden

First, we consider the government's burden of risk. The private sector has a limited capacity to bear the credit risk of its lenders, i.e., to bear the loss in the event of a loan default. In contrast, when the government bears the credit risk undertaken by private lenders the ultimate bearer of this burden is the taxpayer and thus the default risk can be spread widely among the public. Because of this the government is able to bear greater credit risk than the private sector alone. We can assume that the government's ability to bear risk becomes more important when the credit risk of borrowers increases significantly or when the private sector's ability to bear credit risk declines. When the economy is in recession and the probability of corporate bankruptcy increases the credit risk of borrowers increases. When this risk rises to a level that private financial institutions are unable to bear alone the need for government intervention arises. Even if the economy is not in a slump, if the health of private financial institutions declines to a point where they are no longer able to bear the credit risk of their borrowers then the government will have a role to play.[14]

This function of government risk-bearing is particularly important for loans to SMEs, including start-ups, which usually have weak ties to private financial institutions, and is the most common argument used to justify government involvement in SME lending.

5.3.2 Asymmetric Information

Second, we consider the role that the government plays in the lending market in the presence of asymmetric information. When an information asymmetry exists between lenders and borrowers, i.e., lenders do not possess information about borrowers, the result is credit rationing in which borrowers are unable to obtain the

---

15 years depending on the type of liabilities. Because debt repayment periods are longer than those of private financial institutions, which are funded mainly by deposits, it is thought that maturity conversion, one of the functions of financial institutions, enables them to lend for longer periods than private financial institutions. However, due to the development of derivative products and other instruments private financial institutions are now able to appropriately manage interest rate risk through ALM (Asset Liability Management) and to the extent that they are able to do so are able to provide long-term loans in the same manner as government financial institutions. Therefore, it is difficult to argue that government-affiliated financial institutions are necessary for long-term lending. Regarding externalities, even if a project has externalities it should be shown why direct lending or credit guarantees by the government, rather than subsidies, are necessary to implement the project. Just because there is an externality does not mean that the government should be involved in the lending market in the form of direct lending or credit guarantees.

[14] It is often shown that the growth rate of outstanding loans of government financial institutions increases relative to that of private financial institutions when the economy is facing a crisis. As an example, see the Ministry of Finance, "Exchange of Opinions between Relevant Ministries and Private Financial Institutions on Policy Financing," document for the eighth meeting, https://www.mof.go.jp/financial_system/fiscal_finance/torikumi/siryou200929.pdf

necessary funds despite their ability to pay. In situations where such credit rationing occurs the government provides direct loans, credit guarantees, and interest subsidies, thereby satisfying the demand for more funds and increasing the amount of borrowing. As a result we expect an increase in social welfare. Stiglitz and Weiss (1981), Mankiw (1986), and Gale (1990, 1991) are examples of studies that find the mechanisms in which government involvement improves welfare in the presence of asymmetric information.

Theoretical models of loan markets under asymmetric information, however, do not always justify government intervention. Some models suggest that when there is overinvestment by firms in equilibrium, government intervention makes lending even more inefficient by providing loans at lower interest rates (De Meza and Webb, 1987). Once it is known that the government will provide credit guarantees a moral hazard problem arises in which riskier projects are selected (Chaney and Thakor, 1985). Providing credit guarantees to firms that cannot borrow in a separating equilibrium increases the incentive for lower quality firms to use guaranteed loans and results in more severe credit rationing (Smith and Stutzer, 1989). It should be noted that whether government intervention improves economy-wide welfare may vary depending on loan market conditions, the form of government involvement, and the nature of the firms receiving support.

5.3.3 Information Production

Third, we consider the possibility that the information produced by the government sector is superior to that produced by the private sector. It is possible that the information produced by the government sector may have value unavailable to the private sector. This has been used as justification for direct lending by government financial institutions, among other types of government involvement. In the case of credit guarantees the information-producing function of credit guarantee corporations has received less attention because financial institutions are responsible for screening and monitoring the firms to which they lend. The role of credit guarantee corporations is limited and the human resource constraints on these corporations are more severe than those on the financial institutions that actually provide the loans.

In the presence of asymmetric information the government sector may be able to resolve the issue by intervening in the credit market. Specifically, the government, through their own screening and monitoring, may be better informed on the quality of borrowers and credit risk, information which is not available to private financial institutions.[15] There is also a possibility that the lending decisions of government financial institutions will be interpreted as signals reflecting the policy intentions of the government sector, and private financial institutions will follow suit. One study which takes this view is that of Higano (1986) who focuses on loans that are in

[15] Ikeo (1998) points out that through the process of government activities it may obtain information that is unavailable to private financial institutions.

line with government policy objectives and extended by the then Japan Development Bank (now the Development Bank of Japan). He argues that the lending by the government-affiliated financial institution sends a signal to private financial institutions that recipients of these loans are low risk which encourages lending to these firms by private institutions. He labeled the function of the government bank the "Cowbell effect."

In response to the argument that screening and monitoring by government-affiliated financial institutions generates more useful information than that of private financial institutions, some have pointed out that there may be no information in the lending of government-affiliated financial institutions beyond that which is indicative of government policy objectives. This is based on the fact that most government-affiliated financial institutions only lend without accepting deposits. Private-sector financial institutions are able to evaluate borrowers' performance and credit risk through the movement of funds in their deposit accounts but most of the government-affiliated financial institutions, which are unable to do so, are inferior to private-sector financial institutions in terms of information production.

Uchida (2016) empirically clarified the advantages to and differences in the information production functions between government financial institutions and private financial institutions. He finds that while private financial institutions generally have superior information production functions there are areas in which government-affiliated financial institutions produce superior information. Here we focus on firms that borrow from the Japan Finance Corporation Small and Medium Enterprise Business Unit (hereafter referred to as "JFC-SME") and firms that borrow from private financial institutions identified through a questionnaire survey of SMEs. We then compare the results of a five-stage scale rating which measures the degree to which government financial institutions and private financial institutions understand the various attributes of the firms.

Table 5.1 shows that the difference between the means of the five-stage ratings is negative for many of the attributes. This indicates that private financial institutions place more emphasis on these firm characteristics when making loans than the JFC-SME. In particular, private financial institutions, relative to the JFC-SME, place more importance on types of information that are not quantified, such as "qualifications of the representative" and "trust relationship with the loan officer." The reason why private financial institutions produce better information in more areas may be due to their physical proximity to borrower firms and the frequency of their interaction. Table 5.1 shows that the average distance from the firm to the private financial institution branch with which it does business is 7 kilometers, which is smaller than the average distance of 33 kilometers to the JFC-SMEs' branches. Reflecting this proximity, the number of annual contacts between financial institutions and firms is also significantly higher for the private financial institutions, than for the JFC-SME.

There are a small number of areas, however, in which government financial institutions produce more information. For instance, in two areas, "business plans" and "on site monitoring of factories and stores," the difference in the five-stage ratings is

Table 5.1 Extent to which financial institutions place importance on each item when making loans

	(1)	(2)	(3)	
	JFC-SME	Private financial institutions	JFC-SME—Private FIs	
	Mean	Mean	Mean	*p*-value
Industry	3.297	3.386	−0.046	0.132
Firm size	3.363	**3.527**	**−0.143**	0.000***
Business base (customers and products)	**3.795**	**3.938**	**−0.153**	0.000***
Business plan	**4.027**	**3.85**	**0.17**	0.000***
On site monitoring of factories and stores	3.179	3.047	**0.1**	0.003***
Profitability	**4.155**	**4.288**	**−0.156**	0.000***
Financial Stability	**4.041**	**4.165**	**−0.139**	0.000***
Physical collateral	**3.739**	**3.649**	−0.058	0.182
Capacity of guarantors	3.258	3.328	**−0.121**	0.000***
Credit guarantees	2.54	3.159	**-0.69**	0.000***
Characteristics of CEOs	**3.729**	**3.82**	**−0.126**	0.000***
Assets held by firms and CEOs	3.342	**3.604**	**−0.285**	0.000***
Main bank status	2.722	**3.647**	**−0.86**	0.000***
Duration of transaction years	3.089	3.401	**−0.248**	0.000***
Disclosure of the firm's financial status	**3.938**	**3.984**	−0.041	0.115
Relationship with loan officers	3.393	**3.584**	**−0.17**	0.000***
Behavior of other financial institutions	3.129	**3.567**	**−0.474**	0.000***
Reputation from tax consultants or public certified accountants	2.635	2.834	**−0.073**	0.000***
Number of transaction years with the bank		36.328		

(continued)

Table 5.1 (continued)

	(1)	(2)	(3)	
Physical distance to the bank (kilometers)	32.693	7.09	26.775	0.000***
Number of contacts per year	5.01	49.12	−42.889	0.000***

Notes Firms state the extent to which they think that each of the JFC-SME and the private financial institutions consider the issue as important. They choose from the scale of 1–5 in which 5 means that "the bank considers the issue as very important" and 1 means that "the bank gives no consideration." Columns (1) and (2) summarize the answers from all the responding firms, while column (3) limits the sample to those that answer about both of JFC-SME and private financial institutions. Figures equal to 3.5 or larger are shown in bold

positive . Although the frequency of contact with firms is low it is clear that the JFC-SME, which provides many loans for capital investment, produces more information related to these items.

In sum, the amount of information produced on borrower firms by private financial institutions exceeds that of government financial institutions. Since the degree of information production, which mitigates asymmetric information, is greater at private financial institutions than at government-affiliated financial institutions, government involvement in the lending market is not justified in terms of information production. On the other hand, government-affiliated financial institutions' traditional focus on information production related to equipment financing is more intensive than that of private financial institutions. This suggests that government-affiliated financial institutions can provide differentiated services from private financial institutions in this area. Creating such an area of superiority over private sector financial institutions is necessary to highlight information production as the raison d'etre of government financial institutions.

5.3.4 Countervailing Power

Next we examine countervailing power. There is a fear that private financial institutions placed in a competition-restrictive environment may become inefficient in terms of their management. In this case the existence of a government-affiliated financial institution would increase the degree of competition in the market and ensure the efficiency of management, a concept known as "countervailing power." The idea of countervailing power itself has been presented in the past (Kaizuka, 1981). In fact, in the recent case of a merger between financial institutions in Nagasaki Prefecture there were concerns about the creation of a competition-restrictive environment. However, many of the customers of the merging financial institutions had business relationships with government-affiliated financial institutions. The overlap in lending between government-affiliated financial institutions and their lending counterparties may be seen as a form of competitive pressure on private financial institutions.[16] However, some studies, such as Ikeo (1998), contend that policies to promote competition among private-sector financial institutions should be implemented regardless of the existence of government-affiliated financial institutions, and that it makes no sense to argue that government financial institutions should exist to promote competition in the private sector.

Nakata and Adachi (2006a), in support of countervailing power, attempt to empirically clarify the possibility that the presence of government-affiliated financial institutions promotes the managerial efficiency of private financial institutions and competition between them. Specifically, they use prefecture-level data on loan rates to calculate their respective deviations from the national average. After decomposing these deviations into factors, including the monopolistic behavior of lenders and the cost inefficiency of lenders, they obtain positive coefficients on these factors in estimations where the share of government financial institutions' loans to SMEs is the dependent variable. This suggests that the role of government-affiliated financial institutions is larger in prefectures with a greater degree of lending market oligopoly and more financial institution inefficiency. However, the results do not confirm the countervailing power hypothesis, that is, that the larger role of government financial institutions increases the managerial efficiency of private financial institutions.

The above discussion of countervailing power assumes that private financial institutions and government-affiliated financial institutions have a substitutive relationship and that the actions of government-affiliated financial institutions affect the lending of private financial institutions. However, if government-affiliated financial institutions are competing on a different playing field from private financial institutions and the degree of substitution is low it will be difficult for government-affiliated financial institutions to become a competing force for private financial institutions. The degree of substitution in lending by both parties will be examined again in Chapter 8.

So far we have reviewed arguments regarding the need for government involvement in SME lending but there are also arguments pointing to "government failures" where government involvement instead undermines the efficiency of the lending market. While private financial institutions may inefficiently allocate funds in the lending market governments can also fail to allocate funds efficiently for other reasons. An example of this is the potential for an inefficient allocation of funds due to political connections.

[16] Naoyuki Yoshino and Naoki Ohgo, "The Merger of Regional Banks in a Declining Population: Examining the Impact of the Merger of the Juhachi and Shinwa Banks" (Kinyu Zaisei Jijo, October 24, 2016) examined firms located in municipalities in Nagasaki prefecture where the two banks were in competition at the time the merger was under review by the government. The percentage of firms that did business with both banks ranged from 1 to 8% while the percentage of firms that did business with one of the merged banks plus the JFC ranged from 15 to 33%.

5.4 Effects of Credit Guarantees and Government Lending Through Risk-Bearing

When discussing the reasons justifying government involvement in financial markets in the previous section there are a variety of policy instruments that can play a role. Even if we narrow our focus to the main instruments of involvement, credit guarantees and government lending, some reasons apply to both while others apply only to government lending.

Correcting the undersupply of loans due to asymmetric information through government risk-bearing is what both credit guarantees and government-affiliated financial institution lending are expected to do. This is because both perform similar functions of assuming the credit risk of firms.

The discussion of information production is applicable to government financial institution lending because it focuses on the process of making credit decisions and monitoring. However, since credit guarantee corporations are not in charge of credit decisions and monitoring as banks are the information production argument does not apply to credit guarantees. In addition, the concept of countervailing power against oligopoly or other types of imperfect competition by private financial institutions applies to lending by government-affiliated financial institutions. Credit guarantees cannot be a countervailing force against lending by private financial institutions because credit guarantee corporations do not themselves lend.

This section focuses on the risk-bearing functions of both credit guarantees and government lending and uses a simple theoretical framework to discuss what effect each has on the economy through risk-bearing.

5.4.1 Different Ways of Risk-Bearing Between Credit Guarentees and Government Loans

Whether through credit guarantees or direct lending by government financial institutions, the need to bear risk is a justification for government involvement. However, even if the government bears the risk of the borrower firm and transfers it to the public the manner in which it bears the risk differs between credit guarantees and direct lending and therefore the effects on the economy will reveal themselves differently.

Credit guarantees are a method in which the government shoulders a certain percentage of the debt owed by a borrower firm to a private financial institution. Only in the case of insolvency does the government pay the financial institution, with the public at large bearing the cost of the guarantee. Alternatively, direct lending by government-affiliated financial institutions is a method in which the government raises funds at a lower interest rate than private-sector financial institutions and lends to firms at a low interest rate with the deficits and costs of delinquent loans being shared by the public. In the former case of credit guarantees the government bears the credit risk of firms that are prone to insolvency while in the latter case of direct lending the government bears the credit risk through lower interest rates on the entire portfolio lent by private financial institutions.

Intuitively, these two programs should have differing effects on the different attributes of lenders but what will be the overall effect on the total volume of lending and investment in the corporate sector? To clarify this we use the theoretical framework of Doi (2005), a modified version of the model of Li (1998), to show, with numerical examples, which types of firms obtain greater benefits from credit guarantees and direct lending by government-affiliated financial institutions. The difference between our analysis here and that of Doi (2005) is that we not only evaluate whether credit guarantees or direct lending are more efficient but also discuss which types of firms, firms with different credit risk and initial endowments, increase their borrowing and investment more from one of the policy instruments than from the other.

5.4.2 Model Structure[17]

This is a two-period model in which individuals choose whether to be entrepreneurs or workers. In the model there are only private financial institutions and there is no government intervention in the lending market, nor taxation to finance government activities. Individuals maximize their utility over the two periods. In the first period they decide how much to consume and save based on a given asset and in the second period they choose whether to become entrepreneurs or workers. If they choose to be workers they receive a fixed wage and an income equal to the savings they made in the previous period multiplied by a fixed interest rate from which they can consume and earn utility. If they choose to be an entrepreneur they will use the capital obtained from their business, i.e., investment, to engage in productive activities. Entrepreneurs have a certain probability of succeeding in their businesses and producing output but if they fail they do not get any output.

Entrepreneurs are divided into two groups depending on whether or not they have enough savings to invest. If their savings are insufficient for the required investment they borrow from financial institutions. If their savings are more than necessary they will invest and earn a fixed rate of interest on the excess funds.[18] With borrowing entrepreneurs default (become insolvent) if their business fails whereas entrepreneurs who do not borrow do not default even if their business fails.

Private financial institutions finance and lend to entrepreneurs at a fixed rate of interest. If the entrepreneur succeeds the financial institution receives repayment of the loan but if the business fails it suffers a loss equal to the monitoring costs.[19] The monitoring costs consist of a portion of the loan amount and a fixed amount. The

[17] More details of the model are provided in the Appendix at the end of the chapter.

[18] What Li (1998) did not assume, but what Doi (2005) corrected, is the existence of entrepreneurs who save.

[19] Li (1998) describes this cost as the "overhead" cost that private financial institutions must pay upon the bankruptcy of an entrepreneur.

financial institution sets the repayment amount so that the cost of financing equals the income from the loan minus the monitoring costs associated with the entrepreneur's default. Here we assume that the success probability of the entrepreneur is known to the financial institution so the interest rate and repayment amount are commensurate with the probability of success of each entrepreneur. Individuals compare the expected utility of being a worker, an entrepreneur who borrows, or an entrepreneur who does not borrow, and then choose the occupation with the highest expected utility over the two periods.

In the model credit rationing does not occur because financial institutions set interest rates with prior knowledge of borrowers' attributes. In other words, the economy is efficient without policy interventions and interventions reduce welfare since there is no market failure due to asymmetric information. It is therefore impossible for government intervention to eliminate the problem of underinvestment because there is none. Instead the model allows us to observe how entrepreneurs' borrowing and investment behavior changes by focusing on risk-bearing by the government which is the most frequently indicated reason for government involvement. It also allows us to compare how different types of interventions reveal the differing effects of risk-bearing.

The expenditures made and revenues earned by financial institutions in the model are represented by the left and right sides of Eq. (5.1) below, respectively. Both are assumed to be equal so that there are neither profits nor losses. How financial institutions break even depends largely on the presence or absence of government intervention and the types of intervention. With no intervention whatsoever, the equation is as follows:

$$(\rho + \varepsilon)b_i = p_i x_i - (1 - p_i)(\beta + \gamma b_i) \tag{5.1}$$

$\rho + \varepsilon$ is the cost of funding per unit for private financial institutions and b_i is the amount of lending to firm i. Their product represents the cost of lending to firm i. ε can also be viewed as the cost of handling deposits. p_i is the probability that firm i will succeed, x_i is the payment (= interest + principal) required by the financial institution lending to firm i, and $\beta + \gamma b_i$ is the financial institution's monitoring cost to confirm if firm i fails.

5.4.3 Government Intervention in the Loan Market: Credit Guarantees

We now consider the case of government intervention in the lending market. We assume two types of intervention which are most commonly used in Japan: credit guarantees and direct lending by government-affiliated financial institutions. First, we consider credit guarantees. We assume that the government sector pays a certain percentage of defaulted loans extended by private financial institutions and that this payment amount is collected equally from all individuals in the model through taxation. In the actual Japanese credit guarantee system firms that use loans with credit guarantees pay guarantee fees to the credit guarantee corporations which in turn provide reinsurance to the credit insurance division of the Japan Finance Corporation (JFC), while the government's investment in the credit insurance division is borne by the public. However, the guarantee fees paid by firms is discarded in the model and the entire financial burden of credit guarantees is shared by the public (as a result, it may be the case that the demand for borrowing and investment by firms receiving loans with credit guarantees is greater than the demand without a guarantee fee).

The conditions that must be met for private financial institutions to lend using credit guarantees are as follows:

$$(\rho + \varepsilon)b_i = p_i x_i + (1 - p_i)\eta x_i - (1 - p_i)(\beta + \gamma b_i) \tag{5.2}$$

Compared to the case without government intervention, $(1 - p_i)\eta x_i$ is added to the right-hand side of the equation. This means that even if a firm fails the government will subrogate the financial institution for the proportion η of the amount scheduled to be repaid. This allows financial institutions to lend more aggressively than they otherwise would in the absence of government intervention. For instance, they can lend more at lower interest rates. However, to finance this government spending a lump-sum tax is imposed on workers and entrepreneurs.

5.4.4 Government Intervention in the Loan Market: Direct Lending by Government Financial Institutions

Next we consider the case in which government financial institutions lend directly. While private financial institutions lend on the same terms regardless of government intervention now there are additionally government financial institutions in the market. These government-affiliated financial institutions obtain funds at a lower cost than private-sector financial institutions and lend at a flat interest rate with no interest margin.[20] Government-affiliated financial institutions are assumed to lend only a portion of their private-sector lending, as a complement to lending by private-sector financial institutions. Government-affiliated financial institutions that lend in this manner do not earn interest margins but are prone to losses because they bear the monitoring costs that would be required if a borrower becomes insolvent, with the deficit being covered by government subsidies.

The reality is that Japanese government-affiliated financial institutions have generally operated according to this setup. In procurement, through government-guaranteed bonds, they are able to take advantage of the creditworthiness of the

[20] As discussed in Section 5.2 JFC raises funds not through deposits but through borrowing from the FILP or through FILP agency bonds.

government to secure funds at lower interest rates, and often apply a uniform interest rate when lending, regardless of the credit risk of the borrowing firms.[21] In addition, in keeping with the objective of complementing the private sector, government-affiliated financial institutions strive to avoid being the largest lender to firms. Finally, balance-of-payments subsidies are disbursed by the government to these financial institutions.[22]

The conditions that must be met for private and government financial institutions to lend in this setting, respectively, are as follows:

Private Financial Institutions:

$$(\rho + \varepsilon)b_i = p_i x_i - (1 - p_i)(\beta + \gamma b_i) \tag{5.3}$$

Government-affiliated financial institutions:

$$\rho z B = \overline{p}\rho z B - (1 - \overline{p})(\beta + \gamma z B) + \tau N \tag{5.4}$$

Loan terms for private financial institutions are the same as in the absence of government intervention, with individual terms set for each borrower. For the loan terms of government financial institutions z is the ratio of the amount of lending by government financial institutions to the amount of lending by private financial institutions, B is the total amount of lending by private financial institutions, $\overline{p}$ is the average probability of business success for the borrower firm, τ is the lump-sum tax rate imposed by the government, and N is the number of individuals in the model.

5.4.5 Comparison of the Effectiveness of Credit Guarantees and Direct Government Financial Institution Lending

We now examine the following issues resulting from individuals' optimization behavior: the choice between being a worker, an entrepreneur who borrows, and an entrepreneur who does not borrow; the amount borrowed and invested; individuals' total utility and social welfare. We compare these across the three cases: the case without intervention; the case with credit guarantees; and the case with direct

[21] It is the case, however, that this uniform setting of the interest rate has been partially changed in recent years. For example, in August 2008, the JFC-SME (formerly the Japan Finance Corporation for Small and Medium Enterprise) decided to introduce a flexible lending rate scheme, which had previously been almost fixed, depending on credit risk. See Chapter 8 for a discussion of the extent to which this institutional change has altered the demand for borrowing from government-affiliated financial institutions.

[22] There have been some changes in policy framework on this point in recent years. For example, with the introduction of risk-adjusted interest rates, the JFC-SME (formerly the Japan Finance Corporation for Small and Medium Enterprise) has switched from receiving subsidies from the government, for the difference between the income and expenditure of its entire loan portfolio, to receiving subsidies for the difference in interest rates of individual loan products.

lending. We examine the impact of credit guarantees and government-affiliated financial institution lending on borrowing, investment, and social welfare. To make the comparisons between the different types of government intervention comparable we equate the amount of lump sum tax across the programs.[23]

Figure 5.2 compares how an individual's occupational choice in the model is determined by the level of initial assets (measured on the horizontal axis) and the probability of business success (measured on the vertical axis), where W represents Workers, EB represents Borrowing Entrepreneurs, and EN represents Non-borrowing Entrepreneurs.

The figure displays the occupational choice behavior of individuals. If the probability of success is low it is rational for an individual to choose to be a worker with a stable income. This is consistent with a large portion of individuals with the lowest probability of success choosing to be a worker instead of choosing to be an entrepreneur. Conversely, it is rational to choose to be an entrepreneur when the probability of success is high. It is also the case that if the level of initial assets is high there is no need to borrow because investment can be financed by assets alone but if initial assets are low it is necessary to borrow to finance investment and operate the business.

The choice between being a worker or an entrepreneur is affected by government intervention in the loan market. Credit guarantees effectively lower the interest rate paid for borrowing from private financial institutions. Also, in the case of direct lending, the interest rates paid to government financial institutions are lower than those paid to the private sector because of the lower funding costs and the fact that the burden of default is borne by all individuals rather than the individual borrower. Therefore, for both credit guarantees and direct lending by government financial institutions it is more rational for an individual to choose to be an entrepreneur who borrows, which is especially true for credit guarantees.

5.4.6 Borrowing and Investment Will Increase with Either Intervention

Thus, government intervention not only increases the number of entrepreneurs who borrow but also increases the amount of borrowing by individual entrepreneurs and the amount of investment they undertake with borrowing and their own funds, relative to the absence of intervention. Figure 5.3 shows this visually. The hump on the far left of the figure is higher, which means that the amount of borrowing and investment increases, particularly for the individuals that, in the absence of government

[23] The distribution of model parameters and individual parameters are presented in the Appendix of this chapter.

No intervention

	Amount of assets									
Success probability	0.1	0.2	0.4	0.5	0.6	0.7	0.9	1.0	1.5	2.0
0.4	W	W	W	W	W	W	W	W	W	W
0.5	W	W	EN	EN	EN	EN	EN	EN	EN	EN
0.5	EB	EB	EB	EN	EN	EN	EN	EN	EN	EN
0.6	EB	EB	EB	EB	EN	EN	EN	EN	EN	EN
0.6	EB	EB	EB	EB	EB	EN	EN	EN	EN	EN
0.7	EB	EB	EB	EB	EB	EB	EN	EN	EN	EN
0.7	EB	EB	EB	EB	EB	EB	EB	EN	EN	EN
0.8	EB	EB	EB	EB	EB	EB	EB	EB	EN	EN
0.8	EB	EB	EB	EB	EB	EB	EB	EB	EN	EN
0.9	EB	EB	EB	EB	EB	EB	EB	EB	EB	EN

Credit guarantees

	Amount of assets									
Success probability	0.1	0.2	0.4	0.5	0.6	0.7	0.9	1.0	1.5	2.0
0.4	EB	EB	W	W	W	W	W	W	W	W
0.5	EB	EB	EB	W	W	EN	EN	EN	EN	EN
0.5	EB	EB	EB	EB	EB	EB	EN	EN	EN	EN
0.6	EB	EB	EB	EB	EB	EB	EN	EN	EN	EN
0.6	EB	EB	EB	EB	EB	EB	EB	EN	EN	EN
0.7	EB	EB	EB	EB	EB	EB	EB	EB	EN	EN
0.7	EB	EB	EB	EB	EB	EB	EB	EB	EN	EN
0.8	EB	EB	EB	EB	EB	EB	EB	EB	EN	EN
0.8	EB	EB	EB	EB	EB	EB	EB	EB	EB	EN
0.9	EB	EB	EB	EB	EB	EB	EB	EB	EB	EN

Direct lending

	Amount of assets									
Success probability	0.1	0.2	0.4	0.5	0.6	0.7	0.9	1.0	1.5	2.0
0.4	W	W	W	W	W	W	W	W	W	W
0.5	EB	EB	W	W	EN	EN	EN	EN	EN	EN
0.5	EB	EB	EB	EB	EN	EN	EN	EN	EN	EN
0.6	EB	EB	EB	EB	EB	EN	EN	EN	EN	EN
0.6	EB	EB	EB	EB	EB	EB	EN	EN	EN	EN
0.7	EB	EB	EB	EB	EB	EB	EB	EN	EN	EN
0.7	EB	EB	EB	EB	EB	EB	EB	EB	EN	EN
0.8	EB	EB	EB	EB	EB	EB	EB	EB	EN	EN
0.8	EB	EB	EB	EB	EB	EB	EB	EB	EN	EN
0.9	EB	EB	EB	EB	EB	EB	EB	EB	EB	EN

Fig. 5.2 Results of individuals' occupational choice in the model (*Source* Calculation by the author)

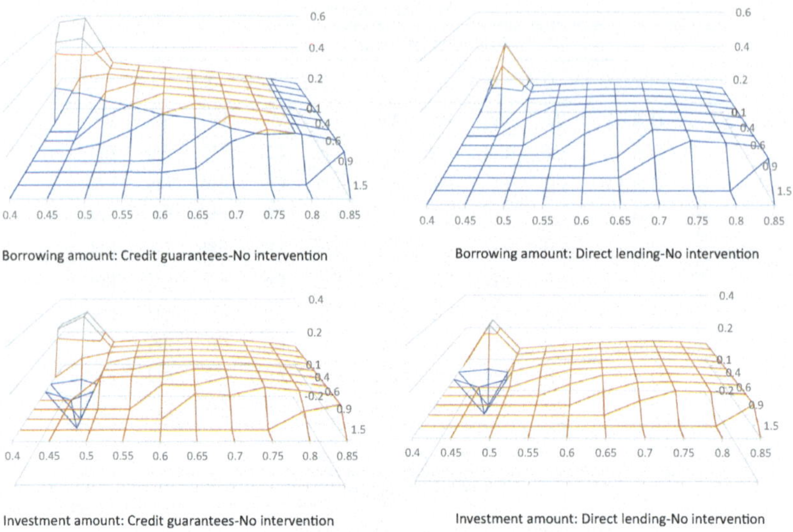

Fig. 5.3 Change in the borrowing and investment in the model (*Notes* The vertical axis shows the difference between the amount of borrowing and investment with and without the intervention of credit guarantees or direct lending, respectively. The horizontal axis represents the probability of success and the depth axis represents the amount of initial asset holdings. *Source* Calculation by the author)

intervention, would otherwise have chosen to be workers because of their low probability of business success and few assets, and also for the individuals who would have invested without borrowing.[24]

What credit guarantees and direct lending have in common is that entrepreneurs with fewer initial assets are likely to borrow and invest more. However, there are differences as to which type of individuals are affected and the degree to which borrowing and investment increases for these individuals. With credit guarantees the increase in borrowing and investment is greater in the low success probability group and decreases as the probability of success increases. In the case of direct lending the increase in the amount of borrowing and investment is generally smaller than in the case of credit guarantees. The increase in borrowing and investment is sizable at low success probabilities as in the case of credit guarantees but this does not diminish as the probability of success increases, which is different from what we see with credit guarantees. These features are due to the uniform interest rates charged by the government-affiliated institutions.[25]

[24] The declining areas (troughs) in the investment figure indicate that individuals who chose to be non-borrowing entrepreneurs in the absence of government intervention now choose to be non-investment workers as a result of government intervention.

[25] Note that when assets held in the initial period are large the amount of borrowing and investment increases as non-borrowing entrepreneurs turn into borrowing entrepreneurs because the required level of investment rises as the probability of success increases.

In this model we consider individuals who make the choice of whether to be a worker or an entrepreneur and, if an entrepreneur, whether to borrow or not borrow funds. After determining what each individual chooses we calculate the utility of individuals in each category and measure by how much utility increases or decreases with government intervention. Figure 5.4 shows the results of this comparison.

For both programs government intervention increases utility for individuals that begin with the smallest amount of initial assets. If we compare credit guarantees and direct lending credit guarantees increase utility in the low probability of success category, while direct lending increases utility in the high probability of success category. Credit guarantees have a comparative advantage in providing funds to entrepreneurs with a low probability of success while direct lending has a comparative advantage in providing funds to entrepreneurs with a slightly higher probability of

Credit guarantees - no inverventio

		Amount of assets									
		0.1	0.2	0.4	0.5	0.6	0.7	0.9	1	1.5	2
Success probability	0.4	-0.017	-0.042	-0.045	-0.045	-0.045	-0.045	-0.045	-0.045	-0.045	-0.045
	0.45	0.025	0.004	-0.044	-0.054	-0.054	-0.045	-0.045	-0.045	-0.045	-0.045
	0.5	0.059	0.038	-0.004	-0.053	-0.069	-0.086	-0.045	-0.045	-0.045	-0.045
	0.55	0.056	0.039	0.004	-0.014	-0.056	-0.070	-0.045	-0.045	-0.045	-0.045
	0.6	0.054	0.039	0.010	-0.004	-0.019	-0.056	-0.077	-0.045	-0.045	-0.045
	0.65	0.051	0.039	0.015	0.003	-0.009	-0.021	-0.062	-0.071	-0.045	-0.045
	0.7	0.046	0.037	0.017	0.008	-0.002	-0.012	-0.031	-0.057	-0.045	-0.045
	0.75	0.039	0.032	0.017	0.009	0.002	-0.006	-0.021	-0.029	-0.045	-0.045
	0.8	0.030	0.024	0.013	0.007	0.001	-0.005	-0.016	-0.022	-0.059	-0.045
	0.85	0.017	0.013	0.005	0.001	-0.003	-0.007	-0.016	-0.020	-0.040	-0.045

Direct lending - no intervention

		Amount of assets									
		0.1	0.2	0.4	0.5	0.6	0.7	0.9	1	1.5	2
Success probability	0.4	-0.045	-0.045	-0.045	-0.045	-0.045	-0.045	-0.045	-0.045	-0.045	-0.045
	0.45	-0.034	-0.042	-0.054	-0.054	-0.045	-0.045	-0.045	-0.045	-0.045	-0.045
	0.5	0.009	-0.003	-0.027	-0.067	-0.045	-0.045	-0.045	-0.045	-0.045	-0.045
	0.55	0.014	0.003	-0.019	-0.030	-0.065	-0.045	-0.045	-0.045	-0.045	-0.045
	0.6	0.018	0.008	-0.011	-0.020	-0.030	-0.062	-0.045	-0.045	-0.045	-0.045
	0.65	0.022	0.013	-0.004	-0.012	-0.021	-0.029	-0.063	-0.045	-0.045	-0.045
	0.7	0.023	0.016	0.002	-0.006	-0.013	-0.020	-0.035	-0.058	-0.045	-0.045
	0.75	0.023	0.017	0.005	-0.001	-0.008	-0.014	-0.026	-0.032	-0.045	-0.045
	0.8	0.019	0.014	0.005	0.000	-0.005	-0.010	-0.020	-0.025	-0.045	-0.045
	0.85	0.012	0.008	0.001	-0.003	-0.007	-0.010	-0.018	-0.021	-0.040	-0.045

Fig. 5.4 Change in individuals' utility in the model (*Notes* Each panel shows the difference in the individual's utility level with and without the intervention. The higher the number the darker the shadow, with the smallest shown in white. *Source* Calculation by the author)

success. Furthermore, credit guarantees generally increase utility to a greater degree than direct lending.

5.4.7 Credit Guarantees, Which Provide a Greater Degree of Support for High-Risk Firms, Increase Social Welfare More Than Direct Lending

The preceding results can be aggregated to the level of the entire economy to examine how economy-wide borrowing, investment, and social welfare change with and without government intervention, and whether this is dependent on the type of intervention. Here, social welfare is calculated by applying the same weights to the utility levels obtained for each category regardless of the amount of initial assets or the probability of business success. The results are presented in Table 5.2. We also include the degree of government intervention, i.e., the percentage of lending by government-affiliated financial institutions and the percentage of credit guarantees.

> The aggregate results reveal that borrowing and investment are higher with government intervention than without. The difference is greater in the case of credit guarantees than direct lending. As the previous results by the success probability indicate, the difference between the two is due to how the government sector bears the credit risk of entrepreneurs.

With credit guarantees the government bears the credit risk of the entrepreneur in the form of a payment in lieu of a certain percentage of the entrepreneur's failure and insolvency. The new term $(1-p_i)\eta x_i$ added to Eq. (5.2) from Eq. (5.1) increases the incentive for financial institutions to provide loans with credit guarantees to entrepreneurs who have a low probability of business success, i.e., high credit risk. These high credit risk entrepreneurs have traditionally not been able to borrow or invest sufficiently because of the high interest rates that they were being charged. The credit guarantee greatly improves the financing situation of these entrepreneurs,

Table 5.2 Social welfare, borrowing amount, and investment amount

	Amount of borrowing	Amount of investment	Social welfare	Ratio of direct lending by the government to total loans by private financial institutions	Ratio of guaranteed amount to total loan amount
Credit guarantees	0.4148	0.7034	1.7542		0.1550
Direct lending	0.3619	0.6666	1.7470	0.1497	
No intervention	0.2641	0.6099	1.7734		

Source Calculation by the author

who had relatively low levels of borrowing and investment, and leads to a significant increase in their overall borrowing and investment.

Direct lending by government financial institutions similarly offers lower interest rates to entrepreneurs but in a very different manner. Eq. (5.4) shows that government financial institutions are able to offer lower interest rates to borrowers because they use their creditworthiness to procure funds at lower interest rates and pass this directly on to the borrower entrepreneur without adding an interest margin. The key difference between credit guarantees and direct lending is in the way the interest rate is applied. Direct lending does not focus on entrepreneurs with high credit risk, but instead applies to a certain percentage (z) of the loans extended by private financial institutions. As a result entrepreneurs with a low probability of success, whose demand for borrowing and investment would be greatly increased by the lower interest rate, do not receive as large of a benefit as they would from a credit guarantee, and so their overall borrowing and investment do not increase as much as they would from a credit guarantee. The reason why social welfare is lower with direct lending than with credit guarantees is due to the fact that the amount of borrowing and investment does not increase by as much.

5.4.8 Issues in Comparing Credit Guarantees and Government Financial Institutions

The theoretical model demonstrates that there is a difference between credit guarantees and direct lending in terms of the extent to which they stimulate borrowing and investment by entrepreneurs. Credit guarantees provide better conditions for lending to those with higher credit risk than direct lending, resulting in a larger increase in lending and investment and higher social welfare.[26]

Should direct lending by government financial institutions be substituted for credit guarantees? We do not believe that this is necessarily the case and several perspectives not previously presented should be considered.

The first issue is how to evaluate the effect of interest rate reductions on firms with a low probability of business success. For firms that have a low probability of success and a high likelihood of falling behind on their debt repayment a reduction in interest rates can significantly increase borrowing and investment. However, these firms may also have projects of low value and may not be viable in the long run. The question is whether the effect of increased borrowing and investment by these firms can be considered an increase in social welfare in the same way that an increase in

---

[26] Doi (2005) conducted a social welfare comparison that included interest subsidies in addition to credit guarantees and direct lending and obtained results similar to those found in this chapter. Doi (2005) then points out that the benefits of direct lending are not significant unless private financial institutions are oligopolistic and there is a distortion in the interest rates. He noted that it is desirable to shift the emphasis to the provision of credit guarantees rather than direct lending by government financial institutions.

borrowing and investment by good firms, those with a high probability of business success, would be.

In Japan, how to deal with zombie firms that have difficulty surviving without support from financial institutions has been a longstanding policy issue, as discussed in Chapter 2. Whether the increase in social welfare is looked upon positively depends on whether the increase in investment and borrowing through credit-guaranteed loans is occurring in viable, though low-quality, firms or in zombie firms that would have difficulty surviving without support.

The second question is whether it is actually the case that firms who use credit-guaranteed loans experience lower borrowing rates and consequently increase their borrowing and investment, as predicted by the theory. Eq. (5.2) assumes that interest rates will decrease (x will be smaller) and the amount of loans will increase (b will be larger) to the extent that financial institutions receive subrogation payments. Whether or not this actually happens in reality, however, depends on the amount of bargaining power between private financial institutions and firms. It is possible that corporate borrowing costs will fall as the theory assumes or that private financial institutions will gain rents without interest rates falling. In contrast, the interest rate on direct loans by government financial institutions is determined by the term and type of loan, plus (currently) the credit rating of the firm, and there is no room for negotiation between the government financial institution and the firm.

5.5 What Are the Actual Effects of Credit Guarantees and Direct Lending by Government Financial Institutions?

In this section we examine the second point mentioned at the end of the previous section, namely, whether the borrowing interest rate is actually lower for firms that use credit-guaranteed loans, as predicted by theory, and whether the amount of borrowing and investment increases as a result. We do this by presenting results based on actual firm survey data.

5.5.1 Examination Using Firm Survey Data

In February 2008 the Research Institute of Economy, Trade and Industry (RIETI) conducted a survey of firms titled "Survey of Transactions with Firms and Financial Institutions." A summary of the survey, which also covered an additional follow-up survey conducted in February 2009, at the time of the global financial crisis, is presented in Uesugi et al. (2009).

Questionnaires were sent to 17,018 firms nationwide, mostly SMEs, and responses were received from 6,124 firms, or 36% of the total. Designed to identify the structural characteristics of SME finance, the survey asked firms about the terms and conditions of their trade credit transactions, the different roles played by the firms' major financial institutions, including main banks, and the government's involvement in the loan market.

The survey included a question on the use of credit-guaranteed loans and loans from government-affiliated financial institutions at the time of the survey. Specifically, firms were asked to respond to these two financing methods from the following options: 1. use them; 2. have no current balance but have used them; 3. would like to use them in the future; 4. know about them but have not used them; and 5. do not know about them. Firms that responded 1 or 2 were considered to be using each measure, respectively, and their attributes were compared. In the survey, there are 1203 firms that use or have used credit guarantees and 1282 firms that use or have used direct lending from government financial institutions. For these two groups we test two hypotheses implied by the theoretical analysis in Section 5.4.

Hypothesis 1 Firms that use credit guarantees are most likely to be in the higher credit risk category. Firms that use direct loans from government financial institutions are more likely to be in the lower credit risk category.

Hypothesis 2 Firms that use credit guarantees borrow more and have more tangible assets than firms that use direct loans from government financial institutions.

Hypothesis 1 and Hypothesis 2 are derived from the results shown in Figures 5.4 and 5.3, respectively. If the theoretical argument is correct credit-guaranteed loans should be used mainly by firms in the highest credit risk category and there should be more lower risk firms using direct loans. In addition, firms that use credit-guaranteed loans should borrow and invest more than firms that use direct lending, and the difference should be more pronounced for riskier firms.

We use the credit score, which is researched and assigned by one of the major credit research companies in Japan, Tokyo Shoko Research, to measure credit risk. The credit score ranges between 0 and 100 and is based on several firm characteristics such as creditworthiness and growth potential. The results testing Hypothesis 1 are shown in Figure 5.5.

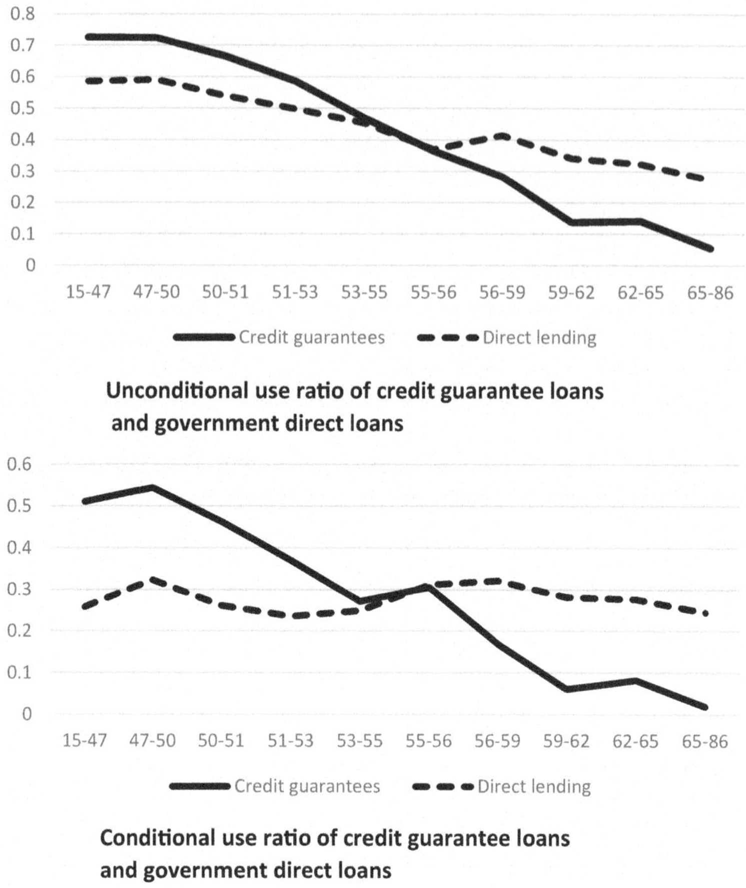

Fig. 5.5 Use ratio of credit guaranteed loans and direct loans by the government-affiliated financial institutions (by credit score category) (*Notes* The vertical axis indicates the use rate and the horizontal axis indicates the credit score, divided into 10 categories. The solid line indicates the use rate of credit guaranteed loans and the dotted line indicates the use rate of direct loans by government financial institutions. The denominator in the left panel is the number of firms that responded to this question. The right panel shows the use ratio of guaranteed loans among firms that do not use direct loans (solid line) and the use ratio of direct loans among firms that do not use guaranteed loans (dotted line). *Source* Processed by the author based on Uesugi et al. (2009))

5.5.2 *Results*

As predicted by the theory, the use rate of credit guarantees is higher for firms in the lower credit categories and decreases as the credit score increases. In other words, firms with higher credit risk make more use of credit guarantees. While we observe the same negative correlation between the use rate of direct loans and the credit score the correlation is much weaker than for credit guarantees. In particular, looking at the use ratio of direct loans for firms that do not use credit guarantees the highest use ratios are seen for firms with credit scores in the ranges of 47–50 and 56–59. This indicates that relatively low risk firms tend to use direct loans. In summary, we obtain consistent results with Hypothesis 1: firms use both credit-guaranteed loans and direct loans by government financial institutions according to their credit risk.

We next test Hypothesis 2. If the hypothesis is correct firms that use credit guarantees should have more tangible fixed assets and a larger loan amount outstanding than firms that use direct loans. In particular, we would expect this to be more pronounced for firms with higher credit risk. However, Figure 5.6 shows that these expectations do not seem to hold.

Looking at the borrowing ratios in the left panel of the figure the difference between the solid line and the dotted line is small and the solid line is not necessarily always higher than the dotted line. Just because a firm uses credit guarantees does

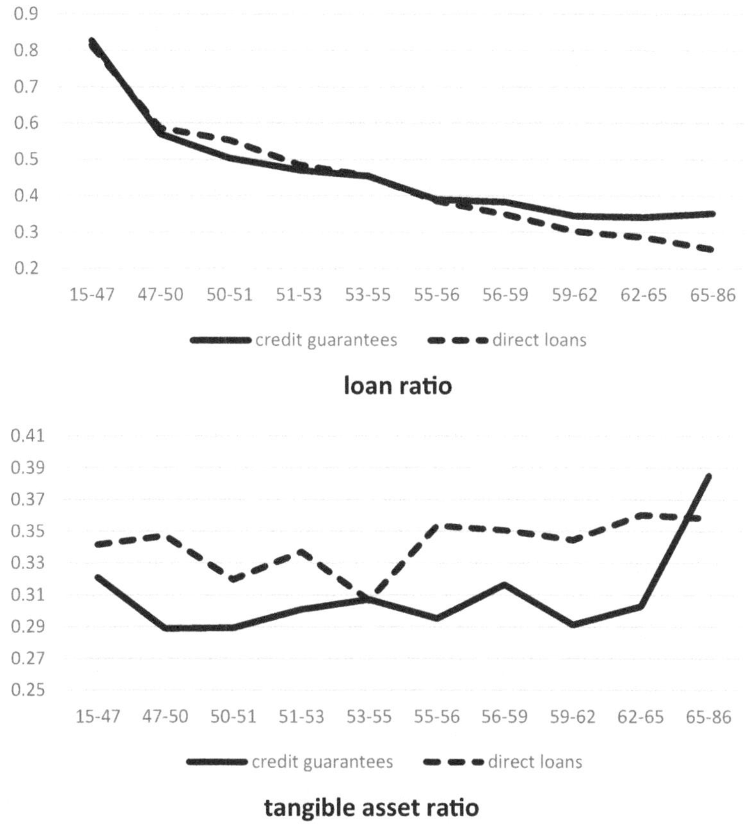

Fig. 5.6 Borrowing ratio and tangible fixed asset ratio (*Notes* The vertical axis is the ratio and the horizontal axis is the credit rating, divided into 10 categories. The solid line indicates the figures for firms using credit guaranteed loans and the dotted line indicates the figures for firms using direct loans. *Source* Processed by the author based on Uesugi et al. (2009))

not mean that it has a larger outstanding loan balance than a firm that uses direct lending.

The tangible fixed asset ratio in the right panel reflects the trend in firm capital investment. Again, the solid line is not necessarily above the dotted line and, in fact, the dotted line is above the solid line in most areas. The firms that use loans from government financial institutions seem to have larger demand for capital expenditures, resulting in a higher tangible fixed asset ratio.

Looking at the results Hypothesis 2 does not hold. The theoretical model predicted that the interest rate on credit guaranteed loans would decline by a larger margin because private financial institutions would not have to bear the credit risk of their borrowers and that the financing and investment environment should improve as a result. However, while we do not directly compare interest rates the borrowing ratios of firms using credit guarantees are about the same as firms using direct lending, and the tangible fixed asset ratio, which reflects capital investment, is rather low for firms using credit guarantees.

Of course, the results here only look at the relationship between the use of credit guarantees and government lending, and firm attributes at a given point in time, and does not control for other factors, including the amount of assets, making it difficult to discuss the causal effects of credit guarantees and direct lending on firm behavior. The results do show, however, that the reality differs from the theoretical predictions, which focuses on the government's ability to bear the credit risk of firms. It is clear that a more careful empirical analysis, one that takes into account factors not considered here, is needed.

5.6 Summary

This chapter provides an overview of government policy involvement in SME finance, discusses the theoretical justification of this involvement, and then compares credit guarantees and direct lending by government financial institutions, which are the two largest policy measures in terms of scale. However, the utilization of the two support measures as predicted by the theoretical model and the impact of these measures on borrowing and capital investment differs in several aspects from the actual data. In the following chapters we will clarify what happens to firms that use credit guarantees and what happens to firms that use direct lending from government financial institutions through empirical analysis using firm-level or loan-level data.

Appendix: Model Setup Based on Li (1998) and Doi (2005)

We set up a two-period model in which individual i chooses whether to be a borrowing entrepreneur, a non-borrowing entrepreneur, or a worker. Individuals maximize the following lifetime utility:

$$U_i = \frac{(c_{i1})^{1-\alpha}}{1-\alpha} + \delta c_{i2}\ \alpha > 0, \alpha \neq 1, \delta > 0$$

where U denotes the utility of individual i and c_{i1} and c_{i2} denote the individual's consumption in the first and second periods, respectively. α is a parameter. In the first period individuals consume their initial assets (w_i) minus the savings (s_i) they carry over to the next period.

$$c_{i1} = w_i - s_i$$

Individuals in the second period have different levels of utility depending on whether they are workers, entrepreneurs who borrow, or entrepreneurs who do not borrow. Workers consume with fixed income (q) and gross earnings from savings (ρ).

$$c_{i2} = q + \rho s_i$$

The borrowing entrepreneurs make an investment in capital (k_i) and borrow the difference between the required amount of capital and savings (b_i). They use the capital to carry out production activities and, with a certain probability (p), succeed and obtain a product ($\Gamma(k_i)^a$) to repay their borrowing (x_i). On the other hand, with probability ($1-p_i$) the project fails and they earn nothing, making the borrowing non-repayable.

$$c_{i2} = p_i\Gamma(k_i)^a - p_i x_i$$

The non-borrowing entrepreneurs invest (k_i) in capital and save the surplus (s_i -k_i). They use the capital to carry out production activities and, with a certain probability (p_i), succeed and obtain a product ($\Gamma(k_i)^a$). With probability ($1-p_i$) they fail and obtain nothing from the production activity. But they still consume because they have gross earnings (ρ) from savings.

$$c_{i2} = p_i\Gamma(k_i)^a + \rho(s_i - k_i)$$

Under the above constraints and the bank's break-even conditions presented in the text we solve the utility maximization problem as a worker (w), an entrepreneur who borrows (EB), and an entrepreneur who does not borrow (EN) to obtain the optimal lifetime utility levels U_w*, U_{eb}*, and U_{en}* for each occupation, and then choose the occupation that provides the maximum level.

In making occupational choices specific values of the model's parameters must be given to obtain the optimal lifetime utility level. It is also necessary to set the distribution of the probability of business success and the amount of endowed assets in the initial period. The parameters and the distribution are shown in below and in Table 5.3.

Table 5.3 Table for the distribution of success probability of a firm and its assets

plw	0.1	0.2	0.4	0.5	0.6	0.7	0.8	1	1.5	2
0.4	0.01	0.01	0.01	0.01	0.01	0.01	0.01	0.01	0.01	0.01
0.45	0.01	0.01	0.01	0.01	0.01	0.01	0.01	0.01	0.01	0.01
0.5	0.01	0.01	0.01	0.01	0.01	0.01	0.01	0.01	0.01	0.01
0.55	0.01	0.01	0.01	0.01	0.01	0.01	0.01	0.01	0.01	0.01
0.6	0.01	0.01	0.01	0.01	0.01	0.01	0.01	0.01	0.01	0.01
0.65	0.01	0.01	0.01	0.01	0.01	0.01	0.01	0.01	0.01	0.01
0.7	0.01	0.01	0.01	0.01	0.01	0.01	0.01	0.01	0.01	0.01
0.75	0.01	0.01	0.01	0.01	0.01	0.01	0.01	0.01	0.01	0.01
0.8	0.01	0.01	0.01	0.01	0.01	0.01	0.01	0.01	0.01	0.01
0.85	0.01	0.01	0.01	0.01	0.01	0.01	0.01	0.01	0.01	0.01

Note The horizontal axis indicates the asset level and the vertical axis indicates the probability of business success

Parameters $\alpha = 0.25$, $\mathrm{a} = 2/3, \delta = 1.5, \Gamma = 2$, $\mathrm{q} = 0.1, \rho = 1.01, \beta = 0.04, \varepsilon = 0.005, \gamma = 0.05, \tau = 0.03$

Chapter 6
The Impact of Credit Guarantees on SME Finance

Abstract Credit guarantees have both positive effects, such as encouraging borrowing and investment by small and medium-sized enterprises (SMEs) by taking on risks that private financial institutions cannot bear alone, and negative effects, such as less non-credit guaranteed loans which reduces monitoring and increases moral hazard. By analyzing the large-scale credit guarantee programs implemented during the past two economic crises in Japan we observe the following: (1) guaranteed loans are used by high credit risk firms with positive book values; (2) the increase in credit-guaranteed loans exceeds the decrease in non-credit guaranteed lending, improving the financing environment for firms; and (3) there is no improvement in the subsequent performance of firms receiving guaranteed loans. Following the implementation of each of the programs, the government has made institutional revisions in order to strengthen the involvement of financial institutions and credit guarantee corporations with the firms receiving guaranteed loans. As such, it is important to understand what impact these measures will have on the performance of these firms.

Keywords Credit guarantee corporation · Special credit guarantee program · Emergency credit guarantee program · Non-credit guaranteed loans · Credit-guaranteed loans · Moral hazard · Shared responsibility system

6.1 Introduction: Factors to Consider in the Effects of Credit Guarantees

In Chapter 5 we mentioned risk-taking as one of the reasons for government intervention in the lending market and showed that credit guarantees play a significant role in lending to particularly high-risk firms. We based this on simple theoretical models and numerical calculations. The model showed that credit guarantees could increase social welfare more than direct lending by lowering interest rates for high-risk firms and increasing the demand for credit.

I. Uesugi, *The Economics of SME Finance*, Advances in Japanese Business and Economics 36, https://doi.org/10.1007/978-981-96-3193-3_6

Then we empirically compared firms that used credit guarantees to those that used direct government lending. We found that while it is true that guarantees are used by higher-risk firms, credit guarantee user firms do not borrow more than firms that use direct lending. Further, in terms of capital investment, the ratio of tangible fixed assets is higher for direct lending users. These results run counter to existing theoretical predictions and may be due to previously unconsidered factors.

The prior theoretical analyses do not explicitly consider the fact that credit guarantees are a mechanism by which the government bears all losses on loan defaults, that loans are ultimately provided by private financial institutions, and that these institutions themselves bear credit risk when engaging in non-credit guaranteed lending.[1] Furthermore, information asymmetries between the government and private financial institutions and between private financial institutions and firms are not part of the model discussed in Chapter 5. Taking these factors into account, the existence of credit guarantees seems to affect the behavior of private financial institutions in the following two ways.[2]

First, private financial institutions maximize their profits by selectively using both guaranteed lending and non-credit guaranteed lending, the latter of which carries credit risk. If they expect that providing credit-guaranteed loans will increase their profits more than non-credit guaranteed lending they may reduce non-credit guaranteed lending and increase credit-guaranteed lending, resulting in a smaller than expected increase in total lending.

In particular, financial institutions are likely to reduce non-credit guaranteed lending and increase credit-guaranteed lending to firms expected to be high credit risks. Private financial institutions often build close relationships with borrowing firms and can obtain private information, including credit risk, which is not available to the government sector. Financial institutions then use this information to choose between non-guaranteed lending and guaranteed lending.

Second, the presence of credit guarantees reduces the amount of credit risk borne by private financial institutions which may lead them to neglect the screening and monitoring they would have engaged in had they extended a traditional loan. In a situation where there are information asymmetries between borrowing firms and financial institutions the reduction in monitoring may lead firms to slacken their management efforts or make riskier investments, potentially worsening their performance.

[1] In practice, among government-affiliated financial institutions, Shoko Chukin Bank uses credit guarantees but its share of credit guarantees is small. Therefore, in what follows we will refer to "private financial institutions that use credit guarantees."

[2] Attention should also be paid to the attributes of credit guarantee corporations which are public institutions that provide credit guarantees. In Sect. 6.6 we examine this point by including variables related to credit guarantee corporations in the estimations.

6.2 Focusing on Two Large-Scale Credit Guarantee Programs Implemented in the Past

In this chapter we account for the effect of the government bearing the risk of borrowing firms through credit guarantees, the effect of financial institutions substituting credit guaranteed lending for non-guaranteed lending, and the effect of changes in the behavior of borrowing firms. In the empirical analysis we focus on two credit guarantee programs, the Special Credit Guarantee Program and the Emergency Credit Guarantee Program. At the time of implementation each were implemented at unprecedented scales.

The Special Guarantee Program was implemented in response to the financial crisis in Japan in the late 1990s which was caused by non-performing loans in financial institutions. The Emergency Credit Guarantee Program was implemented in response to the global financial crisis that began with the collapse of Lehman Brothers in the fall of 2008. As shown in Table 6.1, both programs provided a massive amount of credit guarantees. The background of each program is as follows:

6.2.1 Special Credit Guarantee Program (October 1998 to March 2001)

Throughout the 1990s the Japanese economy experienced a prolonged period of stagnation and the government frequently used the credit guarantee program as a means of stimulating the economy. As a result the share of such loans to the total amount of loans made to SMEs increased. The important factor in this trend was the Special Credit Guarantee Program for financial stability. The purpose of this program was to alleviate the severe credit crunch faced by SMEs in the Japanese economy which had been brought about by the financial crisis. The financial crisis began in the fall of 1997, precipitated by the collapse of major financial institutions such as Hokkaido Takushoku Bank and Yamaichi Securities due to the worsening non-performing loan problem. At the time the guarantee ratio for general credit guarantees was 100%, meaning the guarantee ratio for special guarantees was also 100%.

In addition, firms using special guarantees were less likely to provide collateral or third-party guarantees than those using regular credit guarantees. Moreover, the scale of such special guarantees was unprecedented. A limit of 20 trillion yen was established at the time of the program's introduction and was subsequently increased to 30 trillion yen in 1999.

Another feature of the program was how lenient the criteria were for granting guarantees. Credit guarantees were provided as long as there were no so-called negative list items such as substantial negative net worth that threatened the continuation of

Table 6.1 Overview of the Special Credit Guarantee Program and the Emergency Credit Guarantee Program

	Special Credit Guarantee Program (Financial Stability Special Guarantee Program)	Emergency Credit Guarantee Program
Period	October 1, 1998 to March 31, 2001	October 31, 2008 to March 31, 2011
Purpose	The purpose is to supply necessary business funds to SMEs having difficulty in raising funds due to changes in the financial environment, through loans with credit guarantee corporations, and thereby contribute to the development of SMEs	The purpose is to create a business environment whereby SMEs in almost all industries can raise the necessary business funds promptly, through as simple a procedure as possible, under the current severe economic conditions triggered by international financial instability, and thereby contribute to the business development of SMEs
Guarantee Target	(Municipal certification) SMEs who are having difficulty in raising necessary business funds due to changes in the financial environment (Guarantee examination) Excluding those who engage in window-dressing, violent illegal acts, and those who have fallen into a substantial negative net worth	(Municipal certification) SMEs with a profit rate of −3% or more compared to the same period of the previous year in the last three months
Guarantee Ratio	100% guarantee	100% guarantee
Guarantee Period	(Equipment loans) Within 7 years (Working capital loans) Within 5 years	Within 10 years
Guarantee Limit	30 trillion yen	36 trillion yen
Actual amount of guarantees used	28.9 trillion yen	27.1 trillion yen

Source Created by the author based on materials from the Small and Medium Enterprise Agency

the business, tax delinquency, default, or falsification of financial statements. Needless to say, the acceptance rate was extremely high.[3] As a result, the total amount of guarantees granted during the period reached approximately 1.7 million cases

[3] In its annual audit report the Board of Audit (1999) reports the results of the inspection of the Special Credit Guarantee Program and shows the number and the amount of applications for and acceptances by the program in 1998, the first fiscal year of the program. There were 818,000 applications for ¥16.9 trillion, out of which 754,000 applications for ¥14.4 trillion were approved. As a result, the acceptance rate was 92% in terms of the number of applications and 85% in terms of the applied loan amount.

and ¥28.9 trillion, substantially increasing the balance of Japan's credit guarantee program as a whole.

There were two major criticisms of the program. The first was the possibility of substituting between credit-guaranteed loans and non-guaranteed loans. The credit guarantee corporations, in principle, prohibited using new credit-guaranteed loans to apply to the collection of existing claims of the financial institution in question, a practice called "old debt transfer." This is because the purpose of providing credit guarantees is to facilitate the financing of SMEs, not the collection of claims by financial institutions. However, since the credit guarantee corporations have no means of regulating the actions of financial institutions there has been a persistent suspicion that financial institutions are engaging in "old debt transfers": financial institutions lending to businesses in distress and to those with low capital ratios, that want to increase their own capital ratios by reducing their risk-weighted assets, had more motivation to engage in such behavior. The more "old debt transfers" that occur the less improvement there is in the financing environment for SMEs.

Second, there was the possibility of moral hazard in borrower firms. For example, there were newspaper reports that "funds borrowed using special credit guarantees for working capital were used for stock investments" (Nikkei Financial Newspaper, February 16, 2000) and "a firm went bankrupt within a month of obtaining a special credit guaranteed loan" (Nihon Keizai Shimbun, January 11, 1999, morning edition, page 27). Such moral hazards may have led to poor corporate performance and defaults.

As of the end of October 2005 the Credit Guarantee Corporations had made subrogation payments of ¥2.3 trillion to financial institutions that provided special guaranteed loans. A large portion of this repayment was covered by the reinsurance arranged by the credit guarantee corporations in advance, and the deficit in the reinsurance sector was ultimately covered by government capital injections, a cost ultimately borne by the public.

6.2.2 Emergency Credit Guarantee Program (October 2008 to March 2011)

Ten years after the crisis of the late 1990s and early 2000s a global financial crisis occurred in the fall of 2008. In Japan this crisis and the subsequent severe recession is referred to as the "Lehman Shock" of September 2008. In order to mitigate the negative impact of this shock on economic activity governments around the world implemented cash flow support measures, such as tax cuts and trade promotion measures, for businesses. Of these various measures credit guarantees were the most frequently used. According to the OECD (2009), 19 of the 23 member countries (at the time) introduced or expanded credit guarantee systems in response to the global financial crisis.

Japan's credit guarantee system, which in principle had provided 100% coverage, introduced a liability sharing system in October 2007 whereby loan-providing financial institutions would also bear a portion of the loan amount and interest payments in the case that a borrowing firm was unable to repay. In response to the global financial crisis, however, the government implemented an emergency guarantee program with a 100% guarantee ratio at the end of October 2008. In addition to the 100% credit guarantee the emergency measure included a credit guarantee fee of 0.75% to 0.8% (compared to 0.45% to 1.9% for regular credit guarantees, with an average of 1.15%) and a risk weight of 0% under the Basel II Accord (compared to a 10% risk weight for regular credit guarantee-backed loans), favorable conditions for both borrower firms and financial institutions.

The 100% guarantee and the fact that borrower firms were not required to provide collateral were features of both the Special Credit Guarantee Program and the Emergency Credit Guarantee Program. One difference between the programs was that the screening process for granting guarantees was stricter under the Emergency Guarantee Program. While the Special Guarantee Program provided guarantees as long as the firm did not fall on the "negative list" the Emergency Guarantee Program did not adopt this type of guarantee acceptance mechanism. On the other hand, the emergency guarantees had larger limits on the amount and duration of use than the special guarantees.

In both cases the actual amount of guaranteed loans exceeded 10% of the entire amount of loans outstanding to SMEs at the time. These programs, implemented in response to crises, were large enough in scale that they had the potential to substantially affect the lending market, positively or negatively. Moreover, while similar in scale and implemented in response to crises that occurred 10 years apart the background of the two programs differed in that the first was triggered by the problem of non-performing loans in financial institutions and the second by the decline in real demand due to the global economic contraction. Additionally, the determining factors and effects may have been different. This chapter will empirically clarify these points.

6.3 Overview of Results

An analysis of the data reveals the following points regarding the impact of credit guarantees on the financing of SMEs. First, the prime factor determining the use of either of the large-scale credit guarantee programs is credit risk: high credit risk firms tend to use these programs more often. This result, predicted in Chapter 5, indicates that the provision of credit guarantees helps with cash flow and particularly the cash flow of high-risk firms.

Beyond credit risk, however, the characteristics of the firms making use of the guarantee programs differ depending on which program we are considering, with these differences reflecting the differing environments faced by the financial institutions. For instance, the tendency for firms with low capital ratios to use the program during the Special Guarantee period weakened during the Emergency Guarantee period. At the end of the 1990s the non-performing loan problem of some major banks was severe and these banks were more likely to use government risk-sharing measures than other banks. In addition, during the Special Guarantee period firms with weaker relationships with financial institutions were also more likely to use the program. This is in contrast to the Emergency Guarantee period when firms with closer relationships were more likely to use it.

Both programs were successful in improving the financing environment for firms. The increase in borrowing, especially in the long term, is greater for program-using firms and the increase in the tangible fixed asset ratio is greater for Special Guarantee-using firms. Not only did these programs improve the financing of individual firms but they also had a positive effect on maintaining the stability of the financial system.

On the flip side there is evidence that these programs may have worsened the financing environment for SMEs. In the case of special guarantees the interest rate firms are charged for using the program increases rather than decreases. And the extent of an increase in the loan ratio is smaller for firms that transacted with financial institutions that faced with their own financial difficulties. Even with the emergency guarantees the extent of an increase in the loan ratio is smaller for firms that obtain the guarantee through their main bank, which has abundant information on borrower firms, than for firms that obtain the guarantee through an institution other than their main bank.

If we consider the effects on firms' ex-post performance it is difficult to make a direct comparison of these programs because the measurement periods differ. But, the probability of program user firms falling into financial distress increases more than that of non-users in the case of the Special Credit Guarantee Program. Further, firms that use the program through main banks do experience a decrease in sales and a decline in credit scores in the case of the Emergency Credit Guarantee Program although the decrease in profit margin is not necessarily large.[4] The reasons for the lack of improvement in these performance measures are due to a reduction in monitoring by financial institutions and the weakening of the requirement that firms pledge collateral or personal guarantees.

The remainder of this chapter proceeds as follows. Section 6.4 provides a theoretical overview of the impact of credit guarantees on firms. Section 6.5 presents the results of the empirical examination, focusing on the Special Guarantee Program, and Sect. 6.6 on the Emergency Guarantee Program. Section 6.7 discusses the changes in the credit guarantee system made after the implementation of the Special Guarantee Program and their subsequent effects. Section 6.8 concludes the chapter.

---

[4] The result explained in this chapter that "the use of special credit guarantees does not necessarily improve performance" is different from Uesugi et al. (2006) and Uesugi (2008, a chapter included in Watanabe and Uesugi, 2008). These articles found that the improvement in ROA is greater for special credit guarantee user firms than for non-user firms. However, after changing the estimation method and adding additional explanatory variables, Uesugi et al. (2010) found that the performance of guarantee user firms deteriorated not only in terms of profitability variables but also in terms of dummy variables regarding financial distress. I apologize for the inconsistency between these studies and I would like readers to use results in this chapter and in Uesugi et al. (2010) hereafter.

6.4 Credit Guarantee Scheme and Its Impact on Firms

In this section we lay out the framework of the credit guarantee system in Japan and discuss the theoretical impact of credit guarantees on borrower firms.

6.4.1 Framework of the Credit Enhancement Scheme, Including the Credit Guarantee Scheme

The Japanese credit guarantee scheme consists of three main entities: SMEs, financial institutions, and credit guarantee corporations. This works in conjunction with a credit insurance system where the credit guarantee corporations are reinsured by the Japan Finance Corporation. These two systems are collectively referred to as the credit enhancement system. The right half of Fig. 6.1 shows the credit guarantee system while the left half shows the credit insurance system.

When SMEs borrow from financial institutions credit guarantee corporations serve as public guarantors. The corporation receives credit guarantee fees and, in the event of a loan default, makes a subrogation payment to the financial institution. Credit guarantee corporations receive donations and contributions from local governments to compensate for bearing the risks associated with credit guarantee operations.

All loans guaranteed by credit guarantee corporations are partially covered by the credit insurance based on the SME Credit Insurance Act. The credit guarantee

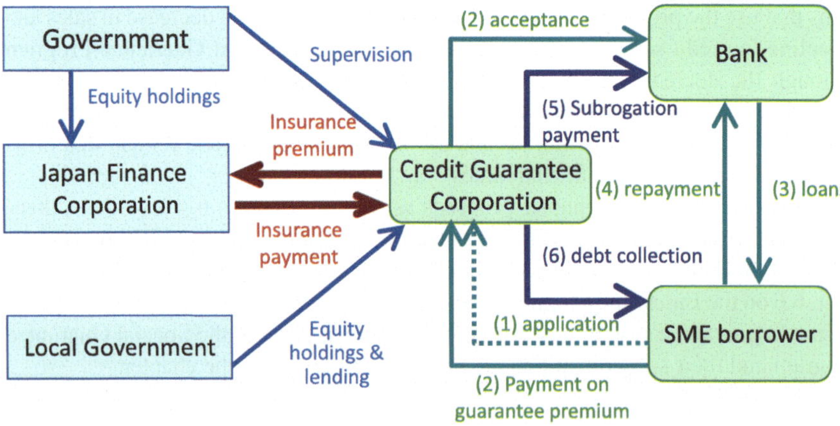

Fig. 6.1 The credit enhancement (credit guarantees and credit insurance) scheme (*Notes* [1] Applications for credit guarantees are often filed by financial institutions as agents. [2] The credit guarantee premium was fixed before 2006 but flexible according to the categories of firm credit risk after 2007. It was fixed for the special credit guarantee and the emergency credit guarantee programs. [5] Subrogation payment and [6] debt collection occur when a borrower SME is unable to repay the debt)

corporations pay insurance premiums to the Japan Finance Corporation (JFC) for the coverage. When subrogation occurs a certain portion of the amount is paid by the JFC to the guarantee corporation. After the subrogation and insurance payment process the credit guarantee corporation reimburses the JFC a portion of the insurance payment, proportional to the insurance coverage ratio, once the corporation recovers subrogated payments from the defaulted SMEs.

The expectation is that because of this dual system of credit guarantees and credit insurance financial institutions will be more willing to lend to SMEs and thus facilitate their financing needs.

In addition, using this credit guarantee system, local governments such as prefectures and municipalities are able to provide financing support measures through subsidized credit guaranteed loans, as explained in Chapter 5. They either subsidize firms' interest payments or their payment of credit guarantee fees. A substantial portion of the funds delivered by the large-scale credit guarantee program implemented in response to the COVID-19 pandemic comes through these subsidized loans. Approximately 23 trillion yen has been provided by private financial institutions on a virtually interest-free and unsecured basis from its inception on May 1, 2020, through to the end of March 2021.

6.4.2 Theoretical Underpinnings on the Impact of Credit Guarantees

There are two perspectives on the impact of credit guarantees on firms: how the firm's financing environment changes and how the firm's performance changes.

6.4.2.1 Changes in the Financing Environment 1: Effects Through Risk Sharing Under Asymmetric Information

The model discussed in Chapter 5 did not account for asymmetric information between firms and financial institutions. In this case the level of lending is optimal without government interventions. Even if the government bears risk through credit guarantees, which would increase a firms' borrowing and investment, it would reduce social welfare. If we account for asymmetric information, however, the lending level in the absence of government intervention is sub-optimal and there exists the possibility of increasing social welfare through government credit guarantees.

Asymmetric information between borrowers and lenders, depending on the attributes and behavior of borrowing firms, may result in credit rationing and the under-supply of loans (Stiglitz and Weiss, 1981; Mankiw, 1986; Gale, 1990, 1991; Innes, 1991). In the absence of government intervention loan market equilibrium is inefficient in the sense that projects with positive net present value (NPV) are not implemented. The provision of credit guarantees, however, can reduce lending rates, alleviating the problem of credit rationing and the under-supply of loans, which results in the implementation of projects with positive NPV.

6.4.2.2 Changes in the Financing Environment 2: Substitution of Guaranteed Loans for Non-Guaranteed Loans by Financial Institutions

Another factor not considered in the discussion of risk sharing is that financial institutions provide both credit-guaranteed loans and non-credit-guaranteed loans to firms. When the government bears the credit risk of firms through credit guarantees the question arises as to how financial institutions treat their own non-guaranteed loans in which they themselves bear the risk. Does a bank's total lending increase or decrease?

If the guarantee ratio is not 100% the provision of credit guarantees by a financial institution will lead to a reduction in non-guaranteed lending in order to keep the expected losses arising from loan defaults constant.

The risk weight used for calculating regulatory risk-weighted assets is also smaller for guaranteed loans than for non-guaranteed loans. Therefore, for financial institutions that aim to keep their amount of risk-weighted assets constant it is necessary to reduce non-guaranteed lending in response to the increase in guaranteed lending, as long as the risk weight of credit-guaranteed loans is not 0%.

In the two large-scale credit guarantee programs considered here, however, the guarantee ratio is 100%, so financial institutions do not bear the credit risk of borrowing firms. In addition, the risk weight of credit-guaranteed loans adopted in the Basel Accords is often 0%.[5] In such an environment there is not much need to reduce non-guaranteed lending so long as the credit risk and risk-weighted assets of the firms they underwrite are kept constant.

However, financial institutions that are vulnerable to regulatory and market pressures, such as those with low capital adequacy ratios, may significantly reduce the amount of non-guaranteed, but positive NPV, loans during severe recessions while increasing the amount of guaranteed loans. These vulnerable financial institutions use credit guarantees to strengthen their capital position and relieve regulatory pressures (Diamond, 2001).

The discussion thus far has suggested that guaranteed loans and non-guaranteed loans are substitutes. In contrast, Wilcox and Yasuda (2019) make the argument that these two can instead be complements.

After formulating that banks maximize profits by choosing the amount of non guaranteed lending and risk they theoretically demonstrate that, under certain conditions, guaranteed loans and non-guaranteed loans are complements. First, they show

[5] At the time of Basel II the risk weight was set to 0% for loans with a 100% guarantee (following the notice of the overall change in the criteria for the appropriate level of bank capital in accordance with the bank's asset holdings that were stipulated in the Ministry of Finance's Notice Number 55 on March 31, 1993. The Ministry's notice was based on Article 14-2 of the Banking Act (Law Number 59 in 1981)).

that the existence of guaranteed loans increases the risk-taking of financial institutions. They then predict that if the recovery rate is low and the amount of non-guaranteed loans is small relative to net worth credit guarantees will have a pump priming effect, resulting in an increase in non-guaranteed loans.[6]

6.4.2.3 Changes in the Financing Environment 3: Substitution of Guaranteed Loans for Non-Guaranteed Loans Within a Firm

As discussed above, when considering the loan portfolio held by financial institutions credit guarantees usually improve the financing environment for borrowers as a whole by increasing the total amount of both guaranteed and non-guaranteed loans. This argument, however, only applies to a bank's overall loan portfolio. In other words, the financing environment faced by individual SMEs may differ. There is a possibility that non-guaranteed loans will decrease by an equivalent amount, or more, as the increase in guaranteed loans. Vogel and Adams (1997) argue this from a practitioners' perspective without providing a theoretical model. What are the characteristics of firms that experience a decline in non-guaranteed loans that is greater than the increase in guaranteed loans?

First, the soundness of the financial institutions with which the firm transacts plays an important role. Financial institutions that are constrained by capital adequacy regulations are likely to increase guaranteed loans while reducing non-guaranteed loans in order to keep their risk-weighted assets constant, leading to a clear substitutive relationship. In addition, financial institutions with a greater need to strengthen their financial position are expected to reduce their non-guaranteed loans to low quality firms, relative to high quality firms. In other words they will make an effort to minimize the expected loss they may incur on their loan claims.

The "closeness" of the transaction relationship between financial institutions and firms also affects the degree of substitution between these loans. There are two dimensions to this. If the transaction relationship between the financial institution and the firm is close the financial institution is said to be engaging in relationship lending. As defined by Diamond (2001), a financial institution that provides relationship lending is a "lender who can make larger payments to borrowers in the future based on knowledge about the borrower." In the case of relationship lending it is expected that the degree of substitution between the two types of loans will be small as the financial institution will not reduce non-guaranteed loans even while increasing guaranteed loans, given the expectation of future payments.

However, even if the relationship with firms is close the financial institution may not necessarily engage in relationship lending. Financial institutions may exploit the

[6] Wilcox and Yasuda (2019) also conducted an empirical analysis using bank-level data and found a complementary relationship between credit-guaranteed lending and non-credit guaranteed lending (Table 3). The complementary relationship is found by dividing the sample between banks that use a lot of guaranteed loans and those that use relatively few. Note, however, that the number of banks in the latter category is relatively small (Table 4).

information they have about the borrower based on a close relationship to significantly reduce non-guaranteed loans to firms they know to be risky while increasing guaranteed loans. In this case the degree of substitution between the two types of loans is expected to be large.

6.4.2.4 Impact on Ex-Post Performance of Firms 1: Investment Promotion Effect

The effects of risk-sharing under asymmetric information also affects the firms' ex-post performance. If credit is rationed and loans are under-supplied due to asymmetric information about the attributes and behavior of borrowing firms, and the government sector takes on the credit risk of firms through the credit guarantee system, this lowers lending interest rates and alleviates the loan supply problem. As a result firms implement projects with positive NPV, improving their performance.[7]

Even when these investment effects do occur, however, it is difficult to predict an increase in profitability, such as in ROA. Firms are expected to implement projects with higher profitability first and the additional projects carried out by obtaining credit-guaranteed loans are likely to be of lower quality than those that have already been implemented.

6.4.2.5 Impact on Ex-Post Performance of Firms 2: Moral Hazard Effect

The effects of government credit guarantees on firms are not all positive. Unlike with non-guaranteed lending private financial institutions may neglect ex-post monitoring of borrower firms as the amount of risk they bear decreases due to the credit guarantee. Particularly when the guarantee ratio is 100%, the reduction in monitoring is expected to be even larger. Further, if collateral is not required by the guaranteed loan contract there is a high possibility of a moral hazard in the sense that the borrower firm is less likely to exert managerial effort, as shown by Boot, Thakor and Udell (1991), and that the firm is more likely to undertake risky investments, as shown by Stulz and Johnson (1985).

[7] On the other hand, as deMeza and Webb (1987) show, there can be excessive investment by firms in equilibrium under asymmetric information. In this case the introduction of credit guarantees further increases excess investment, lowering economic welfare.

6.5 Examination of the Effects of the Special Credit Guarantee Program

In the next two sections we empirically examine the theoretical predictions presented in Chapter 5. We begin by discussing the Special Credit Guarantee Program which was implemented for about two and a half years beginning in 1998.

6.5.1 *Empirical Approach*

In analyzing the effect of the use of special guaranteed loans it is not sufficient to simply compare firms that use the special guarantee with those that do not since the use of the special guarantee is not random but is instead determined by factors that also affect the ex-post performance of firms. For example, suppose there are two types of firms: firms with limited resources that have few investment opportunities and cannot borrow funds without collateral and firms with abundant, high-quality investment opportunities that can borrow funds without paying a guarantee fee. Since the firms that have difficulties in obtaining funding are more likely to need credit guarantees they will use them, while the firms that have no difficulties in obtaining funding will not. However, since the former group have fewer promising investment projects than the latter the investment stimulus effect of using special guarantees is underestimated.

To eliminate this selection bias we use propensity score matching estimation. The method is as follows.

i First, a probit model is used to estimate the determinants of the use of special guarantees in year t based on the variables in year $t-1$. Firms that use special guarantees are the treatment group. Propensity scores are assigned to each of the firms in the estimation. The propensity score e(·) is defined by the following equation:

$$e(X_{t-1}) \equiv \Pr(SCG_t = 1|X_{t-1}), \tag{6.1}$$

where X_{t-1} represents the variables related to firm and financial institution attributes in year $t-1$.

ii Next a k-nearest neighbor matching algorithm is used to match the treatment group firms with the control group firms. In other words, for each treatment group firm that used the special guarantee the k non-user firms with the closest propensity score are selected as the control group. In the following analysis we set $k = 5$.[8] The propensity scores for matching treatment group firms and control group firms are recorded in the same year.

iii Finally, the variables related to the ex-post performance of the selected treatment and control group firms are arranged from year $t - 1$ to year $t + i$. Here, we set $i = 0, 1, 2, 3, 4$.[9]

6.5.2 Data

A firm-level panel data set, which consists of several sources, is created for the analysis. The most important data source is the Survey of the Financial Environment (hereafter, SFE) conducted primarily by the Small and Medium Enterprise Agency from 2001 to 2005. The SFE questionnaires were mailed to approximately 15,000 firms with a response rate of about 50%. The recipient firms were selected from the corporate database held by Tokyo Shoko Research. The information obtained from this database was added to data from the SFE for the period 1998–2005. Information on the capital adequacy ratios of financial institutions was obtained from the Nikkei Financial QUEST Database and databases on Shinkin banks and credit cooperatives for the period 1998–2000.

There are several advantages to using this data. First, it allows us to identify not only the use or non-use of special credit guarantees but also the approximate timing of their use. Second, the data cover a period of six years, allowing us to capture both the short-term effects, such as the improved financing environment due to special guarantees, and medium-term performance effects, such as profitability and bankruptcy. Third, we have information on borrowing firms and the financial institutions that extend loans to these firms. This allows us to determine how the financial condition of the financial institutions affects the effectiveness of the credit guarantee.

6.5.3 Hypotheses to Be Tested

Based on the theoretical framework presented in Sect. 6.4 we formulate three hypotheses regarding the effects of special credit guarantees. Hypotheses 1 and 2 are related to financing.

---

[8] k can be set arbitrarily. There are alternative matching methods other than the nearest neighbor matching, including kernel matching and matching with radius. However, results are qualitatively the same across the different matching methods.

[9] In addition to the above steps we implement balance tests between the treatment and control groups.

Hypothesis 1 (Financing Availability)
The availability of loans increases for firms that use credit guarantees. This is especially true for firms transacting with financial institutions with low capital adequacy ratios.

Hypothesis 2 (Substitution between credit guaranteed loans and non-guaranteed loans)
Since non-guaranteed loans decrease as guaranteed loans increase, the extent of the improvement in the financing environment due to the use of credit guarantees is limited. The improvement in loan availability for firms transacting with financial institutions with low capital adequacy ratios is smaller than for firms transacting with financial institutions with high capital adequacy ratios.

The next hypothesis, Hypothesis 3, concerns firm performance. It is divided into a and b, expecting positive and negative effects on firm performance, respectively.

Hypothesis 3 (a) (Investment Promotion Hypothesis)
Ex-post performance improves for firms using credit guarantees because they are able to implement positive NPV projects.

Hypothesis 3 (b) (Moral Hazard Hypothesis)
Firms using credit guarantees are more likely to face moral hazard and thus lower profit margins and an increased likelihood of falling into financial distress.

6.5.4 Results on the Determinants of the Use of the Special Credit Guarantee Program

First, we present the results of the probit model calculating the propensity score on the left side of Eq. (6.1). This allows us to determine which firms with what attributes use special credit guarantees. The estimation equation is as follows

$$\Pr(\mathrm{SCG_t} = 1|\mathrm{X_{t-1}}) = \Phi\begin{pmatrix} \beta_0 + \beta_1\mathrm{Availability_{t-1}} + \beta_2\mathrm{Allocation_{t-1}} \\ + \beta_3\mathrm{Performance_{t-1}} + \beta_4\mathrm{General_{t-1}} \\ + \beta_5\mathrm{Bank_{t-1}} + \beta_6\mathrm{Relationship_{t-1}} \end{pmatrix} \tag{6.2}$$

Since the use of a special credit guarantee is determined by both firms and financial institutions we include the attributes of each as explanatory variables. The dependent variable is the use or non-use of special credit guarantees in year t. The X_{t-1} variables are divided into six groups: availability of financing for the firm (Availability); allocation of assets held by the firm such as tangible assets and cash and deposits (Allocation); performance of the firm (Performance); general attributes of the firm such as industry, size, and age of the firm (General); attributes of the financial institutions the firm transacts with (Bank); and the relationship between the firm and its financial institutions (Relationship).

The estimation results are shown in Table 6.2. The coefficients on the loan ratio, long term and short term loan ratio, and the interest rate are all positive and significant. Firms that are more dependent on loans, especially long-term loans, and those facing higher interest rates tend to use special credit guarantees. On the other hand the coefficients on cash and deposits, working capital, and tangible fixed assets are all negative and significant. Firms with more liquid assets and tangible fixed assets are less likely to use special credit guarantees. The interest rate coverage coefficient is significantly negative. This indicates that firms with high profitability and profit margins that significantly exceed their interest expenses are not likely to use special credit guarantees.

In cases of firms' financial distress the sign of the coefficient reverses depending on the indicator. The coefficient on the dummy variable for interest coverage falling below a certain level is positive and significant, indicating that firms with profits falling below interest payments make more use of special guarantees. In contrast, the coefficient on the negative net worth dummy is negative and significant, reflecting the criterion that special guarantees are not allowed to be used in cases of significant negative net worth.

Looking at the number of years of transactions with financial institutions (significant negative coefficient) and the number of financial institutions that the firm transacts with (significant positive coefficient), special credit guarantees are more often used by firms that do not have close relationships with financial institutions.

We next examine the impact of the attributes of the financial institutions that the firm transacts with. The probability of using a special credit guarantee increases for firms that transact with financial institutions with low capital adequacy ratios. However, the coefficient on the capital adequacy ratio of financial institutions and on the interaction of the capital ratio and the dummy for regional financial institutions are similar in size but opposite in sign. We interpret this to mean that the capital ratio of regional financial institutions has no significant impact on the use of the special credit guarantee.

In the late 1990s and early 2000s there was often a concern about whether the major banks satisfied the required 8% capital adequacy ratio. As a result these banks had a stronger incentive to use the special credit guarantee program than other banks. On the other hand regional financial institutions who were relatively less concerned about their financial soundness were not concerned about the use of the program to improve their financial soundness.[10]

[10] The difference between major banks and regional financial institutions is believed to have been influenced by the different attitude of the government towards the handling of non-performing loans. The government injected public funds into major banks in 1998 and 1999 but was heavily criticized that the timing of these public fund injections was too late or the amount was too small. In 2002 the government established the Financial Revitalization Program, aiming to reduce non-performing loans at major banks. As a result of these policies major banks in the late 1990s and early 2000s continued to face strong pressure to reduce non-performing loans and maintain a certain level of the capital ratio. In contrast, for regional financial institutions the "Action Program for Strengthening the Function of Relationship Banking" was formulated in March 2003, aiming to handle non-performing loans through different measures than those required of major banks. The pressure

Table 6.2 Estimation results on the determinants of the use of special credit guarantees

Estimation method: Probit model	
Dependent variable: *SCG* (Dummy for the use of Special Credit Guarantees)	
	Coefficients
Availability	
LOANRATIO	1.555***
MATURITY	0.318***
RATE	5.885***
Allocation	
CASH	−0.741***
WCAP	−0.523***
FCAP	−1.009***
Performance	
ICOVER	−0.005***
CAP_NG	−0.315***
ICOVER_SM	0.194***
General	
Ln EMP	−0.097***
Ln CAPITAL	−0.163***
Ln AGE	0.084**
YEAR1999	0.770***
YEAR2000	0.261***
Bank	
BANKCAP	−6.933***
REGIONAL	−0.757***
*REGIONAL*BANKCAP*	5.689**
Relationship	
Ln RELYEAR	−0.123***
NUMBANK	0.030***
CONSTANT	0.945**
Industry Dummies	Yes
N	10,046
Pseudo R-sq	0.176
Log Likelihood	−4208.360

Source Processed by the author based on Table 4 in Uesugi et al. (2010)

Notes ***, **, and * respectively represent a statistical significance at the 1%, 5%, and 10% level. Dependent variable is measured in year t while explanatory variables are measured in year t−1

6.5.5 Results on the Effects of the Use of the Special Credit Guarantee Program

Next we examine the impact of the use of the special guarantee program on firms. Firms that used special credit guarantees make up the treatment group while firms that did not use special guarantees, but were selected based on the propensity scores calculated by the probit model, make up the control group. We then calculate changes in loan availability, asset and fund allocation, and performance for the treatment and control groups and compare the changes across the two groups. Since the guarantee program was offered in years 1999, 2000, and 2001 $t-1$ indicates the year before each of these respective years and we examine the changes from year $t-1$ to years t up to $t+4$.

For example, the treatment effect for the loan ratio (LOANRATIO) is represented by the following Eq. (6.3) below. First, for each of the special credit guarantee user firms (treatment group) and non-user firms matched to the treatment group (control group) we calculate the difference as follows:

$$\Delta LOANRATIO_{t+i}^{j} = LOANRATIO_{t+i}^{j} - LOANRATIO_{t-1}^{j} \tag{6.3}$$

where $j = \{\text{treatment group, control group}\}$ and $i = \{0, 1, 2, 3, 4\}$. Next, we subtract the calculated difference for the control group from the calculated difference from the treatment group. In other words we calculate the difference-in-differences (DID) to obtain the treatment effect.

$$\Delta^2 LOANRATIO_{t+i} = \Delta LOANRATIO_{t+i}^{\text{Treatment}} - \Delta LOANRATIO_{t+i}^{\text{Control}} \tag{6.4}$$

The results of the treatment effect estimation are shown in Table 6.3. The columns for the treatment and control groups show the level of each variable and the difference between the values for t + i and t − 1 corresponds to Eq. (6.3). DID shows the treatment effect which corresponds to Eq. (6.4). There are several notable findings.

Consistent with Hypothesis 1 there is an improvement in loan availability among firms using the special credit guarantee program. The increase in the loan ratio for guarantee user firms was 1.8 percentage points higher in the year the program was used than for non-users. The largest treatment effect is seen in the fourth year with a difference of 2.9 percentage points. This is due to an increase in the long-term loan ratio. These results indicate that, in general, the loan ratio increases more for special credit guarantee users than it does for non-users. In contrast, the results are not consistent with Hypothesis 2. The positive treatment effect in the loan ratio indicates that the decline in non-guaranteed loans, if any, is no greater than that of the increase in guaranteed loans. Note, however, that some aspects of the financial environment faced by credit guarantee users actually deteriorate rather than improve.

exerted by the government on regional financial institutions to reduce their non-performing loans was weaker than what was faced by the major banks.

Table 6.3 Estimation results for the treatment effect of special credit guarantees (base case)

		Treatment	Control	DID			Treatment	Control	DID
LOANRATIO	*t−1*	0.499	0.498		*ROA*	*t−1*	0.015	0.013	
	t	0.515	0.496	0.018***		*t*	0.014	0.016	−0.004***
	t + 1	0.509	0.490	0.019***		*t + 1*	0.013	0.020	−0.004***
	t + 2	0.502	0.479	0.020***		*t + 2*	0.013	0.022	−0.005***
	t + 3	0.504	0.472	0.028***		*t + 3*	0.019	0.019	−0.002
	t + 4	0.494	0.463	0.029***		*t + 4*	0.023	0.020	−0.001
LONGRATIO	*t−1*	0.317	0.318		*p(DEFAULT = 1)*				
	t	0.342	0.323	0.019***					
	t + 1	0.336	0.318	0.018***		*t + 1*	0.001	0.000	0.001
	t + 2	0.325	0.308	0.016***		*t + 2*	0.005	0.002	0.003**
	t + 3	0.326	0.309	0.014***		*t + 3*	0.025	0.010	0.016***
	t + 4	0.320	0.303	0.013***		*t + 4*	0.019	0.017	0.001
RATE	*t−1*	0.030	0.030		*p(CAP_NG = 1)*	*t−1*	0.075	0.069	
	t	0.029	0.028	0.001**		*t*	0.081	0.076	−0.001
	t + 1	0.028	0.027	0.002***		*t + 1*	0.087	0.080	0.000
	t + 2	0.028	0.026	0.002***		*t + 2*	0.075	0.070	0.004
	t + 3	0.027	0.025	0.003***		*t + 3*	0.080	0.070	0.011*
	t + 4	0.027	0.025	0.003***		*t + 4*	0.073	0.058	0.025***

(continued)

Table 6.3 (continued)

		Treatment	Control	DID			Treatment	Control	DID
FCAP	*t−1*	0.298	0.302		*p(ICOVER_SM = 1)*	*t−1*	0.493	0.497	
	t	0.300	0.300	0.004***		*t*	0.494	0.435	0.063***
	t + 1	0.302	0.301	0.005**		*t + 1*	0.436	0.397	0.044***
	t + 2	0.304	0.305	0.002		*t + 2*	0.426	0.376	0.051***
	t + 3	0.314	0.313	0.001		*t + 3*	0.422	0.387	0.036**
	t + 4	0.311	0.316	−0.002		*t + 4*	0.376	0.364	0.023

Source Processed by the author based on Table 5 in Uesugi et al. (2010)
Notes ***, **, and * respectively represent a statistical significance at the 1%, 5%, and 10% level. Treatment effects for each variable are presented in the column of DID. For example, treatment effects for the loan ratio are defined as $(LOANRATIO_{t+i}^{Treatment} - LOANRATIO_{t}^{Treatment}) - (LOANRATIO_{t+i}^{Control} - LOANRATIO_{t}^{Control})$.
Treatment effects for defaults are defined in a different formula: $p(DEFAULT = 1)_{t+i}^{Treatment} - p(DEFAULT = 1)_{t}^{Control}$. The number of observations differs for the different number of years after the use of the program due to the sample attrition

For instance, the interest rate increases more for special credit guarantee users than for non-users. This increase is 0.1 percentage point in the first year and 0.3 percentage point in the fourth year. The tangible fixed asset ratio increases by more for special credit guarantee users up to the year $t + 1$. It is possible that the improved financial environment due to the use of credit guarantees facilitates firms' capital investment.

In terms of the impact on ex-post firm performance it is more likely that special guarantee users experience a decline in profitability and an increase in the probability of financial distress. The operating profit ratio falls by about 0.5 percentage point more for users than non-users in the second year following the guarantee program. It is then insignificant thereafter. However, the decline in profitability does not necessarily mean deteriorating performance. Since total loans and tangible fixed properties both increase more for guarantee user firms than for non-users we may interpret the decline in profitability to be the result of an increase in assets rather than a decrease in profits.[11]

On the other hand the probability of falling into financial distress, such as a default, in which the firm incurs significant costs, tends to be higher for credit guarantee users. The proportion of firms with interest coverage below 1, where profits are less than interest payments, rises the most in the year following the use of the guarantee before gradually decreasing. Subsequently, this spills over to other financial distress indicators. In addition to the increased probability of negative net worth from the third to the fourth year the probability of default for users also exceeds that of non-users by 1.6 percentage points through the third year. In light of Hypotheses 3(a) and 3(b), which discuss the impact of special credit guarantees on firm performance, the results are somewhat consistent with Hypothesis 3(a) in that investment in tangible fixed assets initially increases. However, other results are evidence of a moral hazard which is consistent with Hypothesis 3(b) in that not only does the profit margin decline but the probability of insolvency and default increases after the use of the credit guarantee program. On balance, Hypothesis 3(b) is more likely to be in line with the estimation results than Hypothesis 3(a).[12]

---

[11] The results here differ from the findings of Uesugi et al. (2006) and Uesugi (2008) which showed a larger increase in operating profit margin. Changing the estimation method and adding explanatory variables when calculating propensity scores to make the matching more accurate in the first stage may have led to this.

[12] The moral hazard hypothesis predicts that firms will change their ex-post behavior by neglecting management efforts and/or investing in risky assets. On the other hand, the deterioration in ex-post performance observed in this study may be due to adverse selection where firms' hidden attributes, such as riskiness, are realized in their ex-post performance. In general it is difficult to empirically distinguish between the two mechanisms. However, in the DID estimation process we control for time-invariant firm characteristics by taking differences over time. Therefore, it is plausible to say that we control for the factors that potentially cause adverse selection.

6.5.6 The Impact of the Financial Condition of the Financial Institutions on the Treatment Effect

In the estimation discussed previously we obtained results consistent with Hypothesis 1. In this subsection we examine whether the hypothesis still holds when the soundness of the financial institution is accounted for. That is, whether the degree of improvement in the financing environment is greater or less for firms that transact with financial institutions with low capital ratios.

If Hypothesis 1 is correct firms transacting with financial institutions that are constrained by low capital ratios will see a larger increase in loan ratios because these financial institutions make full use of the credit guarantee program to boost their lending activities. If, on the other hand, Hypothesis 2 holds, firms transacting with financial institutions that have low capital ratios will see a smaller increase in the loan ratio as these financial institutions attempt to substitute credit guaranteed loans for non credit-guaranteed loans.

To examine which one of these hypotheses holds we split the sample into two groups based on the type of financial institutions (major banks or regional financial institutions) and measure the treatment effect within each subsample. There are three reasons why major banks were more likely to be constrained by capital ratios. First, because major banks engaged in international operations they were, at the time, subject to the 8% capital adequacy regulation based on the Basel Agreement. In contrast, most regional financial institutions did not engage in international operations and were thus subject to a more lenient 4% capital ratio regulation. Second, all major banks received injections of public funds during the Japan's financial crisis in the late 1990s. Third, even after receiving public funds, it might have been the case that the capital ratio for major banks were actually lower than officially published figures because the amount of public funds used was small relative to their potential non-performing loans.

The first two columns in Table 6.4 show the estimation results for the major banks and regional financial institutions, respectively. Here the variable is limited to the long-term loan ratio in order to compare Hypothesis 1 and 2. It is notable that the increase in the ratio of long-term loans continues to increase for firms transacting with regional financial institutions, while the increase in the ratio diminishes over time for firms transacting with large major banks.

We next divide the firms transacting with major banks and regional financial institutions into four groups based on the respective financial institutions' capital ratio and measure the treatment effect.

The results are presented in the third through sixth columns of Table 6.4. For firms transacting with major banks belonging to the lowest capital adequacy ratio category the treatment effect, (i.e., the increase in the long-term loan ratio for the special credit guarantee users) is significantly positive in year *t*. After that initial year, however, the effect is no longer significant. In contrast, for firms that transact with major banks in the highest capital adequacy ratio category the increase in the long-term loans ratio is unchanged over the period.

Table 6.4 Estimation results for the treatment effect of special credit guarantees (by type of financial institutions and their capital ratio)

		DID	DID	DID	DID	DID	DID
		Major banks	Regional financial institutions	Major banks		Regional financial institutions	
				Capital ratio		Capital ratio	
				First quartile (min)	Fourth quartile (max)	First quartile (min)	Fourth quartile (max)
LONGRATIO	*t*	0.015***	0.021***	0.020***	0.015*	0.027***	0.019***
	t + *1*	0.012**	0.022***	0.003	0.033***	0.027***	0.032***
	t + 2	0.009	0.021***	−0.006	0.035***	0.040***	0.023***
	t + *3*	0.018**	0.017***	0.006	0.037**	0.017	0.021**
	t + *4*	0.009	0.015***	−0.012	0.045***	0.023*	0.025**

Source Processed by the author based on Table 6 in Uesugi, Sakai, and Yamashiro (2010)
Note ***, **, and * respectively represent a statistical significance at the 1%, 5%, and 10% level

For regional financial institutions we do not find any difference in the persistence of the treatment effect depending on the capital adequacy ratio. The increase in the long-term loan ratio for special guarantee users does not depend on the level of the capital ratio of regional financial institutions that the firms transacts with.

In summary the results are generally consistent with Hypothesis 1, although we do find that the effect of the increased borrowing is not necessarily sustained for firms borrowing from major banks. While both the loan ratio and the long-term loan ratio increase initially after the use of the special guarantee program this effect tends to decline over time. This is especially the case for the long-term loan ratio. This trend was stronger for firms transacting with major banks with low capital adequacy ratios.

Since we cannot distinguish between credit-guaranteed and non-credit guaranteed loans in the breakdown of borrowing we do not know the extent of substitution between the two. The results of the subsample analysis, however, are consistent with Hypothesis 2 (substitution hypothesis), that financial institutions facing capital adequacy constraints are more likely to limit the increase in the loan amount outstanding by substituting non-guaranteed loans with guaranteed loans.[13]

[13] Wilcox and Yasuda (2019) employ bank-level panel data instead of the firm-level data used in this chapter to examine the substitutability/complementarity between guaranteed loans and non-guaranteed loans in Japan in the late 1990s and early 2000s. They, in contrast to our results here, find a complementary relationship between guaranteed loans and non-guaranteed loans, while the relationship becomes substitutive for banks that have already extended many credit guaranteed loans.

6.5.7 The Impact of Firm Equity on the Treatment Effect

In this subsection we examine how the treatment effect differs depending on the level of net worth held by the credit guarantee program users. We expect that credit guarantee user firms with more equity capital are less likely to suffer from moral hazards since they have much to lose in the case of default and that, as a result, their performance improves.

For this purpose we measure the treatment effect after dividing the sample into four parts depending on the firm's capital adequacy ratio in year t−1. The results are presented in Table 6.5. It is clear that the effect of the use of special credit guarantees differs significantly depending on borrower firms' capital ratio. The loan ratio of firms that use the special credit guarantee program increased across all capital ratio categories. The type of assets that increase with the improvement in loan availability, however, does depend on the level of the ex-ante capital ratio. Specifically, the tangible fixed asset ratio increases for guarantee users with low capital ratios while the opposite (i.e., the fixed asset ratio decreases) is true for users with high equity capital ratios.

This asset allocation behavior which is dependent on the firm's equity capital position does affect its ex-post performance. There is a clear decline in the performance of special guarantee users with low capital ratios. They experience larger declines in operating profits, a larger probability of the interest coverage ratio being less than 1, and a larger likelihood of default. In contrast, there is no deterioration in ex-post performance for users with high capital ratios. By holding more cash and deposits instead of making capital expenditures these firms avoided risk-taking that would have worsened their performance.[14]

6.5.8 Summary of the Determinants and Effects of the Special Credit Guarantee Program

The 30 trillion yen special guarantee program was established to alleviate the credit crunch that occurred during the Japanese financial crisis. It did have the effect of easing the financial constraints faced by firms which in turn resulted in an increase in capital investment for a short period after the use of the program.

The results, however, run contrary to the simple prediction that loan availability would improve once the government assumed firms' credit risk by 100% and imposed lenient conditions for the use of the program. Interest rates paid by firms using the special guarantee program rose rather than fell and firms transacting with financial

It is an important future task to examine whether banks that simultaneously employ guaranteed and non-guaranteed loans increase these loans to the same firm or whether these banks provide each of these two types of loans to different firms.

[14] Although not shown in Table 6.5 the results show that the cash deposit ratio decreases for firms with the lowest capital ratio and that it increases for firms with the highest capital ratio.

Table 6.5 Estimation results for the treatment effect of special credit guarantees (by borrower firms' capital ratio)

		DID	DID Firm capital ratio	DID	DID
		First quartile (min)	Second quartile	Third quartile	Fourth quartile (max)
LOANRATIO	*t*	0.013***	0.015***	0.025***	0.031***
	t + 1	0.011**	0.017***	0.024***	0.034***
	t + 2	0.028***	0.016***	0.026***	0.028**
	t + 3	0.043***	0.013**	0.037***	0.037***
	t + 4	0.048***	0.009	0.030***	0.039***
FCAP	*t*	0.006***	0.002	0.001	−0.002
	t + 1	0.007**	0.004	−0.002	−0.005
	t + 2	0.004	0.007*	−0.008	−0.016**
	t + 3	0.001	0.014***	0.004	−0.013*
	t + 4	−0.004	0.007	0.003	−0.018**
ROA	*t*	−0.006***	−0.001	−0.005*	−0.006
	t + 1	−0.006***	0.000	−0.008**	−0.004
	t + 2	−0.010***	−0.003	−0.009**	−0.003
	t + 3	−0.007***	0.001	−0.003	−0.004
	t + 4	−0.007**	0.003	0.000	0.000
p(DEFAULT = 1)	*t + 1*	0.002	0.001	0.000	0.000
	t + 2	0.004	0.002	0.002	0.000
	t + 3	0.021***	0.013**	0.007	0.000
	t + 4	0.004	0.002	0.000	0.002
p(ICOVER_SM = 1)	*t*	0.080***	0.036*	0.080	0.033
	t + 1	0.060**	0.058**	0.035	−0.006
	t + 2	0.109***	0.060**	−0.003	−0.017
	t + 3	0.059**	0.048*	0.028	0.003
	t + 4	0.057*	0.036	0.011	−0.072

Source Processed by the author based on Table 8 in Uesugi et al. (2010)
Note ***, **, and * respectively represent a statistical significance at the 1%, 5%, and 10% level

institutions with weak capital positions experienced smaller increases in the loan ratio. Furthermore, although the results are not shown here there is a tendency for financial institutions to reduce the frequency of monitoring and to require less collateral or personal guarantees from firms that borrow only with credit guarantees. These factors may have resulted in poorer ex-post performance for firms that used special credit guarantees.

This is because private financial institutions make their credit decisions based on their own profit maximization motives considering the presence of the guarantee program. In order for credit guarantees to have the desired effect it is essential to design a system based on an understanding of the behavioral patterns of the private financial institutions.

This brings up the next question: when the government offers credit guarantees to firms and financial institutions what effect does the relationship between the financial institution and the firm have on the use and effectiveness of credit guarantees? With this in mind the next section will discuss the determinants and effects of emergency guarantees which were once again implemented on a massive scale with the onset of the global financial crisis, exactly 10 years after the Special Credit Guarantee Program.

6.6 Examination of the Effects of the Emergency Credit Guarantee Program

We examine the effects of the Emergency Credit Guarantee Program which was in place for two and a half years starting at the end of October 2008.

6.6.1 Empirical Approach

To investigate the effects of loans backed by the emergency credit guarantees we use the same propensity score matching method used in the analysis of the special credit guarantee. The difference here, however, is that a kernel matching algorithm, which changes the weights of non-user firms according to the distance based on propensity scores, is used to match non-user firms with firms that used emergency credit guarantees. Further, due to data limitations, the examination of firms' ex post performance is limited to the period from year t to $t + 1$.

6.6.2 Data

While we created a firm-level panel data for the examination of the special credit guarantee in the previous section here we construct a panel dataset at the firm-financial institution relationship level. The most important data source for this dataset is the Firm and Financial Institution Transaction Survey conducted by the Research Institute of Economy, Trade and Industry (RIETI) in February 2008 and the Firm and Financial Institution Transaction Survey under the Financial Crisis conducted in

February 2009, hereinafter referred to as the 2008 RIETI Survey and the 2009 RIETI Survey, respectively.

In the 2008 RIETI Survey questionnaires were sent to 17,018 firms to identify their relationships with financial institutions, including their main banks, and the terms and conditions of their trade credit transactions. The survey was sent to firms that had previously responded to the Surveys of Financial Environment used in the previous chapter and implemented by the Small and Medium Enterprise Agency Survey. There were 6124 responding firms, a response rate of 36%. In the 2009 RIETI Survey questionnaires were sent to 5979 of the firms that had responded to the 2008 RIETI survey, excluding those that had defaulted, and responses were received from 69% of them, or 4103 firms. The aim of the survey was to clarify the financial environment faced by these firms during and after the global financial crisis.

The surveys asked about the use of credit guarantees, the amount of credit guaranteed loans, the outstanding balance of loans, and the relationship between these firms and their financial institutions. In particular, the 2009 RIETI Survey asks specifically about the use of the emergency guarantee program. Based on this information we construct a panel dataset at the firm-financial institution relationship level.

Both of these surveys are useful in several respects for examining the effects of emergency credit guarantees. First, they identify the financial institutions with which each responding firm has the most and second most amount of outstanding loans, allowing us to examine the impact of the financial condition of these institutions on firms' financing. The survey also asks about the financial institutions that firms consider to be their main banks. In the dataset used here 89% of firms indicated that the financial institution with which they held their largest outstanding loan balance was their main bank. By identifying the financial institutions with large outstanding loan balances and those acknowledged by firms as main banks it is possible to distinguish between main banks and non-main banks in the analysis.

Second, the surveys allow us to know the use and loan amount of emergency credit guarantee-backed loans for each financial institution with which the respondent firms have a transactional relationship. In addition, we have information on the outstanding loan balance of firms in 2008, before the global financial crisis, and in 2009, during the crisis, separately for loans backed by the emergency credit guarantee program and other loans not backed by the program. These other loans include loans backed by the general credit guarantee scheme and loans without credit guarantees. We are thus not only able to determine the amount of emergency credit guaranteed loans obtained by firms but also the extent to which their outstanding balance of other loans has changed from 2008 to 2009.

In addition to the RIETI surveys we use several other data sources. First, we use firms' financial information from the Tokyo Shoko Research database. To get an accurate picture of pre-crisis financial conditions, firms for which information is available only prior to January 2008 are excluded from the analysis. Second, information on the financial status of the main bank and other financial institutions for firms are obtained from the Nikkei Financial QUEST Database. If a financial institution is not available in the database we supplement our data set with information published by the Financial Services Agency and by the individual financial institutions themselves. Credit cooperatives and other financial institutions for which the necessary information is not available are excluded from the dataset. Third, to calculate the share of financial institutions in a region we use data on the number of branches from the Japan Financial Directory of the Japan Financial News Service. Information on credit guarantee corporations providing emergency guarantees in each region is then obtained from their respective disclosure information.

As a result of the sample selection process we construct a panel dataset with firm-financial institution relationships as the unit of observation. We further limit the dataset to include relationships that contain information on the dependent and explanatory variables.[15] The result is a dataset of 2499 transaction relationships. The number of individual firms included is 1732. Of these, 1502 observations are for the relationship between firms and their main banks, and 997 observations are for the relationship between firms and financial institutions other than their main banks.

6.6.3 Hypotheses to Be Tested

The impact of the use of emergency credit guarantees on firm financing and performance can be either positive or negative. On the positive side government risk-taking may improve firms' loan availability resulting in an increase in their capital investment, which we found in the previous section. On the negative side the government behavior may reduce financial institutions' incentive to monitor borrower firms which leads to deteriorating firm performance. Hypothesis 1 encompasses both of these possibilities:

Hypothesis 1 (Effects of credit guarantees)
The availability of funds increases for firms that use credit guarantees. However, the ex-post performance of these firms worsens because of problems with overinvestment and moral hazards.

Using characteristics of the relationship between firms and their main bank, and between firms and other financial institutions, we construct a hypothesis based on how these relationships affect the effectiveness of credit guarantees. A number of studies have examined the relationship between firms and financial institutions, focusing on its potential to eliminate information asymmetries and improve the availability of funds for small and young firms (Angelini et al., 1998; Cole, 1998; Jiangli et al., 2008; Petersen and Rajan, 1994). Previous studies, however, have rarely examined the role

[15] The variables with the most missing values are the names of the main banks and non-main banks and the characteristics of relationships between firms and financial institutions. To check for the presence of selection bias due to missing values we compared the 2371 firms with information on sales, number of employees, profits, and sales-to-profit ratio with those that are excluded from the sample due to missing information. There are no significant differences between the two in these variables, suggesting that the degree of selection bias due to missing variable information is small.

of relationships in improving firms' loan availability and ex-post performance, when the government provides credit guarantees, a measure which aims to improve the availability of funds for SMEs. There are two conflicting possibilities.

The first focuses on the negative aspects of the relationship. Financial institutions may use the information they have accumulated about borrowing firms through their relationship to differentiate between credit-guaranteed loans and non-guaranteed loans for their own benefit. In this case the relationship between the firm and the financial institution reduces the effectiveness of the credit guarantee.

It has long been known that financial institutions, which extend loans based on proprietary information about firms, may have conflicts of interest with the investors who supply funds to these firms. Take, for example, the relationship between financial institutions and general investors who purchase corporate bonds. In this case the financial institution has an incentive to underwrite corporate bonds issued by low-quality firms and sell them to external investors, while at the same time reducing its existing lending to these firms.[16]

Something similar may occur with credit guarantees. It is possible that financial institutions transfer risk to the government by increasing guaranteed loans to low quality firms while at the same time reducing non-guaranteed loans to these firms. The more information the main bank has the more likely it is to take actions that reduce the effectiveness of guaranteed loans.

The second possibility focuses on the positive aspects of the firm-bank relationship. In this case financial institutions utilize the information obtained through relationships and use credit guarantees as one tool to help borrower firms that are in temporary financial distress. Here guaranteed loans and non-guaranteed loans are complements and credit guarantees improve the financing environment for firms. The main bank, which has a close relationship with the firm and interacts with it on a daily basis, is more likely to use this proprietary information to help in the case of temporary distress. To summarize, there are two contrasting predictions in the following hypothesis.

Hypothesis 2 (Effects of a main bank relationship and credit guarantees)
If the main bank uses its information advantage to identify low-quality firms and substitutes guaranteed loans for non-guaranteed loans, transferring credit risk to the credit guarantee system, the improvement in loan availability for firms using credit guarantees is limited and their ex-post performance will decline. On the other hand,

[16] There are studies that examine the relationship between commercial banks and their subsidiaries' underwriting business and security prices. They focus on the possibility of conflicts of interest between commercial banks and external investors in the United States and Japan by employing historical events as an exogenous driver for these conflicts. The historical events include the introduction of the Glass-Steagall Act (Kroszner and Rajan, 1994, 1997; Puri, 1996) and the Gramm-Leach-Bliley Act (Gande, Puri, Saunders, and Walters, 1997) in the US, and the Financial System Reform Act in Japan that allowed banks to enter the securities business through securities subsidiaries (Hamao and Hoshi, 2000; Kang and Liu, 2007).

if the main bank uses its information advantage to assist firms in temporary financial distress it will use guaranteed loans as part of that support. In this case the firm's loan availability and its ex-post will improve.

6.6.4 Results on the Determinants of the Use of the Emergency Credit Guarantee Program

As with the examination of special credit guarantees we present the estimation results of the probit model with the use or non-use of the emergency credit guarantees as the dependent variable. The explanatory variables are grouped as follows: use of regular credit guarantees; firm attributes; financial institution attributes; the relationship between the firm and their financial institutions; attributes of the credit guarantee corporation; and local economic conditions. The main difference in these estimations as compared to those estimating the determinants of the use of the special guarantee program is the inclusion of variables related to the attributes of the credit guarantee corporations themselves.

There were 52 credit guarantee corporations in Japan at the time the emergency guarantees were introduced, located in each of the prefectures and several ordinance-designated and other cities.[17] The credit guarantee corporations decide whether to provide guarantees upon receiving applications from firms or financial institutions. Although the accepted guarantees are reinsured by the credit insurance division of the Japan Finance Corporation (JFC) the guarantee corporation's own financial performance would be harmed if there were many subrogation payments. Therefore, we should expect the financial health of the corporation itself to influence whether or not the emergency credit guarantee is granted. The relationship between the credit guarantee corporation and the financial institution making the application may also affect the acceptance of the guarantee. For example, if many of the board members of the credit guarantee corporation are from regional financial institutions the credit guarantee corporation may approve guarantees more quickly because they are familiar with the background of the financial institution's guarantee application.

Table 6.6 presents the estimation results. We begin by examining the results for all transaction relationships between firms and their financial institutions, including those involving firms' main banks. There are four key findings.

First, the coefficient on the loan ratio is positive and significant, the coefficient on credit scores is negative and significant, and the coefficient on the negative net worth dummy is negative and significant. While firms with higher credit risk tend to use emergency guarantees this may reflect the fact that firms whose financial condition has deteriorated to the point of negative net worth are less likely to be approved for

[17] The ordinance-designated cities and other cities were Yokohama, Kawasaki, Nagoya, Gifu, and Osaka. Among them, the Osaka City Credit Guarantee Corporation merged with the Osaka Prefecture Small and Medium Enterprise Credit Guarantee Corporation in 2014 to become the Osaka Credit Guarantee Corporation.

Table 6.6 Estimation results on the determinants of the use of emergency credit guarantees

Estimation method: Probit model Dependent variable: ECG_DUM	Entire sample Coeff.	Relationships with main bank Coeff.	Relationships with non-main bank Coeff.
Characteristics of credit guarantees			
RCG_DUM	0.623***	0.697***	0.407**
Firm characteristics			
LOAN_ENQUIRY	−0.459**	0.199**	−0.345*
SHARPERATIO	−0.043	−0.029	−0.081
SCORE	−0.035***	−0.043***	−0.010
CAPRATIO_NG	−0.603***	−0.579***	−0.859*
LOANRATIO	0.771***	0.773***	0.778**
lnSALES	−0.079**	−0.090**	−0.029
lnFIRMAGE	−0.078	−0.064	−0.133
Bank characteristics			
B_REGIONAL	−3.268***	−2.476*	−4.040***
B_REGIONAL*BIS	0.296***	0.240**	0.342**
BIS	−0.293***	−0.234**	−0.340***
BANKSHARE	0.821*	0.774	0.592
HHI	−1.606*	−1.027	−4.166**
Characteristics of bank-firm relationship			
B_MAIN*ENQUIRY	0.674***		
B_MAIN	0.636***		
B_CONTACT	−0.067**	−0.041	−0.154**
Characteristics of credit guarantee corporations and local economic conditions			
CGC_NETWORTH	2.369	5.390	−6.927
CGC_BOARD	1.060*	2.337***	−2.074*
LOCAL_CONDITION	0.000	0.007	−0.027
constant	3.468***	4.154**	3.640
Industry dummies	yes	yes	yes
Number of Observations	2499	1502	992
Log likelihood	−786.3189	−599.93684	−160.93293

Source Processed by the author based on Table 5 in Ono et al. (2013)
Note ***, **, and * respectively represent a statistical significance at the 1%, 5%, and 10% level

the emergency credit guarantee. In addition, the sales level coefficient is negative and significant, indicating that smaller firms are more likely to use emergency guarantees.

Second, looking at the attributes of the financial institutions with which firms transact the probability of using the emergency credit guarantee program increases for firms that transact with financial institutions with low capital ratios. However, this holds only for the relationships with large banks and not for those that involve regional financial institutions.

Third, emergency guarantees are more likely to be provided through the relationships that involve main banks rather than those that involve non-main banks. In addition, the guarantees are more likely to be provided through the relationships that involve frequent interactions between firms and financial institutions.

Fourth, looking at the attributes of the credit guarantee corporations, a positive but marginally significant coefficient is obtained on the number of directors coming from financial institutions.

The above results are similar to those found in the previous section on the determinants of the use of special credit guarantees, although there are differences. First, the use of credit guarantees declines when firms become insolvent, a result common to the use of both special and emergency guarantees. However, the absolute value of the coefficient on the negative net worth dummy is smaller in the estimates pertaining to special credit guarantees, indicating that the extent to which insolvent firms are discouraged from using credit guarantees is more apparent for the emergency credit guarantee program. This may reflect the fact that the screening process was more rigorous when granting emergency credit guarantees than special credit guarantees.

Next, results for both guarantee programs show negative and significant coefficients on the capital ratio of the major banks but insignificant coefficients on the capital ratio of regional financial institutions. On the other hand, the absolute value of the negative coefficient for major banks is smaller for emergency credit guarantees than for special credit guarantees, indicating that the positive effect of low bank capital ratios on the use of credit guarantees is weaker for the emergency credit guarantees. Based on this finding we infer that the extent to which the soundness of financial institutions affected the firms' financing environment was stronger during the Japanese financial crisis in the late 1990s and early 2000s than in the subsequent period.

Further, the relationship between firms and financial institutions has the opposite impact on the probability of using an emergency credit guarantee versus a special credit guarantee. In the case of emergency guarantees the probability of using credit guarantees increases for firms that have more frequent interactions with financial institutions. This indicates that the closer the relationship between the two the more the emergency guarantee is used. The opposite holds for special guarantees: credit guarantees were used more frequently in cases where the relationship between the two was not close. In particular, the probability of using credit guarantees is lower for firms that have transacted with financial institutions for many years and for those that have a small number of financial institutions with which they transact.[18]

We next divide the sample into a sample that includes main bank relationships and a sample that includes other financial institution relationships and apply the same probit model to estimate the determinants of the use of emergency credit guarantees. The results for these two subsamples differ from those for the full sample in two respects.

First, the coefficient on the dummy variable for firms applying for loans from financial institutions changes in sign across subsamples.[19] In the main bank relationship subsample firms that applied for loans are more likely to use emergency credit guarantees while in the other financial institution relationship subsample firms that did not apply are more likely to have a higher use rate of guarantees. Since applying for a loan implies that firms have a demand for funds, firms with a stronger demand for funds use emergency guaranteed loans via their main bank.

Second, regarding the attributes of the credit guarantee corporation it is only for the main bank relationship sample that the coefficient on the ratio of board members from financial institutions is positive. The result may indicate that a dominant bank in a region exerts its bargaining power over a credit guarantee corporation to have credit guaranteed loans for its customer firms only when the bank serves as their main bank.

6.6.5 Results on the Effects of the Use of the Emergency Credit Guarantee Program

We next examine the impact of the use of emergency credit guarantees on firms. The methodology we follow is the same as in the previous section but the unit of analysis is the firm-financial institution relationship rather than the firm alone. The treatment group includes the firm-financial institution relationships that used emergency credit guarantees while the control group includes the relationships that did not use guarantees but were "closer" to the treatment group in terms of propensity scores as calculated by the probit model. For each group we examine changes in financing, asset allocation, and performance from 2008 (year t) to 2009 (year $t+1$). We then estimate the treatment effect (DID) by comparing the change between the two groups.

Table 6.7 presents the results of the estimation. The changes from year t to year $t+1$ for the treatment and control groups are in the "treatment group" and "control

[18] Whether this will continue to hold into the future is an important issue considering the crucial role played by the relationship between firms and financial institutions in the funding environment.

[19] The term "loan applications" here refers to a firm's applications for short-term loans in the previous year, which can be guaranteed or non-guaranteed. Even when the firm do not take initiative on short-term loans, financial institutions may encourage the firm to obtain the emergency credit guarantee loans.

group" columns, respectively. The "DID" column contains the treatment effect which is simply the difference between the two groups.

Panel (a), which covers the entire sample, reveals that the treatment effect is significant and positive for all variables related to financing. The increase in the

Table 6.7 Estimation results for the treatment effect of emergency credit guarantees

(a) Entire sample			
Variables	Treatment	Control	DID
ECG_LOAN_RATIO	0.103	0.000	0.103***
dB_LOAN_RATIO	0.050	0.000	0.050***
dB_TLOAN_RATIO	0.042	0.000	0.042***
dROA	−0.020	−0.005	−0.015
dSALESRATIO	−0.141	−0.012	−0.128***
dCOSTRATIO	−0.120	−0.007	−0.113***
dSCORE	−1.132	−0.497	−0.635***
dRATE	−0.003	−0.001	−0.002
(b) Firm-main bank relationships			
Variables	Treatment	Control	DID
ECG_LOAN_RATIO	0.107	0.000	0.107***
dB_LOAN_RATIO	0.049	−0.001	0.050***
dB_TLOAN_RATIO	0.044	0.002	0.042***
dROA	−0.020	−0.005	−0.016
dSALESRATIO	−0.151	−0.015	−0.136***
dCOSTRATIO	−0.131	−0.011	−0.120***
dSCORE	−1.140	−0.507	−0.633***
dRATE	−0.002	−0.001	−0.001
(c) Firm-non-main bank relationships			
Variables	Treatment	Control	DID
ECG_LOAN_RATIO	0.072	0.000	0.072***
dB_LOAN_RATIO	0.057	0.003	0.054***
dB_TLOAN_RATIO	0.023	0.011	0.012
dROA	−0.021	−0.020	−0.002
dSALESRATIO	−0.074	−0.055	−0.018
dCOSTRATIO	−0.053	−0.036	−0.017
dSCORE	−1.069	−0.961	−0.108
dRATE	−0.011	0.000	−0.011

Source Processed by the author based on Table 6 in Ono, Uesugi, and Yasuda (2013)

Note ***, **, and * respectively represent a statistical significance at the 1%, 5%, and 10% level

amount of outstanding loans in the treatment group significantly exceeds the increase in the control group due to the loans being backed by the emergency credit guarantees.

The use of loans backed by emergency credit guarantees amounts to 10.3% of total assets for the firms in the treatment group. For these firms the increase in loans from the financial institution in the relationship exceeds the increase in loans from the financial institution in the control group by 5.0% of total assets. The increase in overall loans for firms in the treatment group also exceeds the increase in the overall loan amount by 4.2% of total assets of firms in the control group.

There are two notable findings. First, the increase in the amount of loans from the financial institution in the relationship falls by about half for firms that used emergency credit guarantees because of a reduction in "other loans" from the financial institution. "Other loans" refers to non-guaranteed loans made by financial institutions. Second, the outstanding amount of loans from other financial institutions that do not provide loans backed by emergency credit guarantees also declines slightly. Given these points, the financing environment improves for firms that use emergency credit guaranteed loans, although the effect is substantially reduced by the decrease in non-guaranteed loans. These results are consistent with the first half of Hypothesis 1.

Although results are not shown in the table we also estimate the impact on tangible fixed assets, number of employees, and cash and deposits to examine how firms use the funds they obtained. We find no significant treatment effects for these variables. Next, looking at the firm performance, the decline in the sales to asset ratio, the operating expenses to asset ratio, and credit score were significantly larger for the treatment group than the control group. The decline in both the sales ratio and the operating expense ratio in the treatment group is considerably larger than in the control group, at 12.8% and 11.3% of total assets, respectively. The decline in credit scores in the treatment group is about 0.6 point larger than in the control group. Although we obtain insignificant estimates for operating profit the significant decline in both sales and expenses indicates a significant decline in performance for firms using emergency credit guarantees. These results are consistent with the second part of Hypothesis 1 in that improvements in the financing environment do not lead to the implementation of positive present value projects or to an improvement in firm performance.

We now turn our attention to panel (b) which focuses on the firms' relationships with their main banks. It is clear that there is substitution between loans backed by emergency credit guarantees and non-guaranteed loans within the same financial institution as observed in panel (a). In addition, the ex-post decline in firm performance is almost the same as the decline we see in panel (a). These results suggest that main banks, which are better informed through their long-term relationships with firms, use this information to provide emergency guaranteed loans to firms that they expect to experience weaker performance while at the same time reducing non-guaranteed loans. This is consistent with the prediction in Hypothesis 2.

Finally, we look at the results of the treatment effect in panel (c) which focuses on the firms' relationship with a financial institution other than the main bank. The results are quite different from what we find in panel (b). First, unlike what we see in panels

(a) and (b), the increase in emergency guaranteed loans is only partially offset by a decrease in other loans from the financial institution. The use of emergency credit guaranteed loans results in an increase in loans equivalent to 7.2% of total assets for firms in the treatment group. The increase in the loan amount from the same financial institution in the treatment group still substantially exceeds the increase in the control group, by 5.4% of total assets. The extent to which the increase in emergency guaranteed loans is offset by the decrease in other loans is limited to 1.8% of total assets (=7.2%–5.4%). This is smaller than the 5.7% of total assets (=10.7%–5.0%) in the main bank case.[20]

Based on these results we now evaluate the plausibility of our hypotheses. Regarding Hypothesis 1, firms' financial conditions improved substantially. However, tangible fixed assets did not increase significantly and sales fell by more than operating expenses for firms that use emergency guaranteed loans. This suggests that emergency credit guarantees induced moral hazards rather than eased firms' financial constraints to encourage the implementation of projects with positive net present value. All of these are consistent with the hypothesis. For Hypothesis 2 the substitution between emergency guarantee loans and non-guaranteed loans as well as the deterioration in ex-post performance is more evident for firms that use emergency guarantees through their main bank than for those that use guarantees through non-main bank relationships. This suggests that main banks, which have abundant information on borrower firms, use this knowledge to provide guaranteed loans to relatively riskier firms. This is consistent with the first half of Hypothesis 2.

6.6.6 Summary of the Determinants and Effects of the Emergency Guarantee Program

Ten years after the special credit guarantee program the emergency credit guarantee program was introduced in response to the global financial crisis triggered by the Lehman shock. Like the special credit guarantee the emergency credit guarantee tends to be used more by firms with high credit risk. There are several differences, however. First, firms transacting with low capitalized major banks make less use of credit guarantees under the emergency credit guarantee program than for the special credit guarantee program. Second, firms that have close relationships with their main bank are more likely to use the emergency guarantee program while the opposite is true for the special credit guarantee program.

In terms of the effects of credit guarantees, like the special guarantee they do improve the firms' financing environment. However, the extent of the increase in loans

[20] However, it is necessary to interpret the insignificant treatment effect for loans from all banks. In this regard the probit model estimation results, which show that non-main bank financial institutions provide emergency credit guarantee loans when firms do not apply for the loans, are important. Not applying for loans means that the firm has a small demand for loans. Even if loans from all the financial institutions did not increase the firm may have undertaken necessary investments.

for firms that use the guarantee program via their main bank, which has abundant information on borrower firms, is limited as compared to firms that use the guarantee via other financial institutions. In addition, the decline in performance in terms of sales growth and credit scores is greater for firms that use emergency credit guarantees through their main bank. Main banks substitute guaranteed loans for non-guaranteed loans for firms whose performance is expected to decline sharply. They do this rather than increase their own non-guaranteed loans to help borrowers cope with the financial crisis.[21]

6.7 Changes in the Credit Guarantee System and Their Impact

At the beginning of this chapter we pointed to the possibility that the credit guarantee system does not have the desired effect posited in the previous chapter because of the incentives and behavior of financial institutions that provide loans backed by credit guarantees.

In the credit guarantee system the role of the government is limited to providing loan guarantees for SMEs, and without financial institutions that actually provide the loans the SMEs will not be able to obtain funds. On the other hand, financial institutions aim to maximize their own profits and as a result their behavior may run counter to the original policy objective of the credit guarantee system. An example of this is the substitution of credit guaranteed loans for non-guaranteed loans for risky, but viable, borrower firms. Another example is the lack of monitoring by financial institutions of firms that receive guaranteed loans which leads to the deterioration in the performance of these firms. Financial institutions that provide guaranteed loans are less likely to monitor borrowers than those that provide non-guaranteed loans since expected losses from firm defaults are small when the loans are guaranteed. The difficulty in properly designing a credit guarantee system lies in achieving the goal of improving the firms' financing environment while at the same time providing financial institutions with an incentive to participate in the system.

The problem in the credit guarantee system had been recognized by the Japanese government. In the 20 years since the end of the special guarantee program, interspersed with the emergency guarantee program, the government reformed the system twice: first from 2005 to 2007 and later from 2016 to 2018.

[21] Note, however, that the examination here is limited to a short period of time following the introduction of the program. Therefore, it is not clear whether treatment firms eventually went bankrupt due to financial difficulties.

6.7.1 Institutional Changes in the First Reform from 2005 to 2007

The first reform involved the introduction of risk-based guarantee fees in 2006 and full introduction of partial guarantees in the year 2007. Until then, all credit guarantees in Japan, with a few exceptions, covered 100% of the debt. With a 100% guarantee financial institutions offering guaranteed loans were not required to assume any firm credit risk at all. For this reason a June 2005 report by a subcommittee established by the Small and Medium Enterprise Agency to study the credit guarantee system noted that "There is a strong concern that SMEs that borrow only with guaranteed loans are less likely to receive proper monitoring and to establish close relationships with lenders than are SMEs that receive non-guaranteed loans (See Summary III. Current Status of Credit Enhancement System (5) Changes in the Lending Attitude of Financial Institutions)." The report then recommended that "it is necessary for guarantee corporations and financial institutions to share responsibility appropriately, for financial institutions to provide loans responsibly as lenders, and for both to work together to continuously assess the managerial motivation of SMEs and provide appropriate support to SMEs with respect to i) loan execution and ii) support for management and revitalization after the loan has been extended. (See IV Issues and Measures for Reviewing the Credit Enhancement System, 2(1))." Based on this recommendation the government introduced a responsibility-sharing system in 2007 under which guarantee corporations take on 80% of the realized loss from defaulted guaranteed loans while financial institutions take on 20%.

In addition, guarantee fee rates had previously been uniformly set to ensure equality among regions. In the case of the special credit guarantee program, described in Sect. 6.5, the credit guarantee corporations set a uniform but lower than usual guarantee fee rate. The subcommittee, however, was concerned about the presence of adverse selection in setting a uniform fee rate. They pointed out that "Since the current guarantee fee structure is uniform for SMEs, the system is structured so that SMEs in good business conditions bear a relatively high guarantee fee. On the other hand, the lack of flexibility in guarantee fees makes it difficult to provide guarantees to SMEs that start or revitalize businesses, or to SMEs that have considerably increased their credit risk. (See IV Challenges of Reviewing the Credit Enhancement System and Countermeasures 1(2)(iii))." In response to this point the subcommittee recommended that "Credit guarantee corporations should restructure the system to make it fair and flexible, and to be able to provide credit guarantees to a wider range of SMEs under appropriate conditions by quantitatively and qualitatively measuring the SMEs' creditworthiness and establishing a guarantee fee structure that appropriately takes the creditworthiness into account (Ibid.)." Based on this recommendation the credit guarantee corporations reformed the guarantee fee structure so that the guarantee fee rate would be lower for low-risk firms and higher for high-risk firms. The fee rate is determined according to the nine categories of firms' creditworthiness that is calculated from the financial statement information.

What were the effects of changes to the credit guarantee system during this period? The responsibility-sharing system seems, to some extent, to have alleviated the problem of poor performance of firms using credit guarantees due to financial institutions' negligence in screening and monitoring. Saito and Tsuruta (2018), using bank-level data, examine 100% guarantees and 80% guarantees under the responsibility-sharing system lending and find that subrogation rates are lower for the latter, even after controlling for a variety of factors.

At the time of the change there were concerns that the lower guarantee coverage would narrow the range of firms to which financial institutions provided guaranteed loans and that firms that had previously received guaranteed loans might face increased difficulty in obtaining funds.[22] In reality, however, there has been no evidence of tighter financing conditions for Japanese SMEs since 2007.

Judging from the above the changes to the credit guarantee system that require financial institutions to bear a greater share of credit risk have helped to change the behavior of financial institutions in a direction consistent with the original purpose of credit guarantees, as seen in the decline in the subrogation payment rate for the portion subject to the responsibility-sharing system.

6.7.2 Institutional Changes in the Second Reform from 2016 to 2018

The second reform included the introduction of a framework in which credit guarantee corporations would need to consider both non-guaranteed and guaranteed loans when providing credit guarantees and a reclassification of the types of loans eligible for a 100% guarantee.[23]

Behind the former change was the criticism that by simply focusing on adjusting the amount of risk borne by financial institutions the credit guarantee system did not lead to the meaningful support for borrower firms. In discussions within the government an example was given in which there was no main bank for firms that relied exclusively on credit-guaranteed loans. When the firms' business condition deteriorated there was no effective support provided by creditors for the firms' recovery because the absence of a main bank led to a coordination failure among the creditor financial institutions. In a contrasting example firms receiving a mix of guaranteed

[22] See "Summary of Opinions on the Draft Report of the Subcommittee on the Future of Credit Enhancement System and the Replies by the Subcommittee." https://www.chusho.meti.go.jp/kinyu/2005/download/050623publiccomment.torimatome.pdf (accessed May 29, 2021).

[23] As a result of the restructuring of the system the government introduced a new credit guarantee program with 100% coverage to cope with future large-scale economic crises as a new safety net measure. It also increased the limit of the 100% credit guarantees for startup firms and micro businesses that face severe financial constraints. It also reduced the guarantee coverage from 100 to 80% for a certain type of safety net credit guarantees (safety net credit guarantee type No. 5). There were many other changes including management support by credit guarantee corporations.

and non-guaranteed loans saw their performance improve.[24] This suggests that in order for financial institutions to fully support borrower firms it is important to have a mix of credit guaranteed loans in which financial institutions partially bear the credit risk and non-guaranteed loans in which financial institutions fully bear the credit risk.

Based on these findings one of the key points of the system reform was to focus not only on the guarantee coverage ratio but also on the amount of financial institutions' risk burden when viewed as the sum of guaranteed and non-guaranteed loans. After the reform credit guarantee corporations are required to publicly report the amount of non-guaranteed loans extended by financial institutions to firms requesting credit guarantees. For each financial institution and prefecture the number and amount of non-guaranteed loans are published every six months, making transparent the amount of non-guaranteed loans financial institutions are extending to firms to which they are also providing credit guaranteed loans.

However, even if credit guarantee corporations take into account the existence and amount of non-guaranteed loans when approving guarantees this does not mean that they set a quantitative target for the volume of non-guaranteed lending to firms for which they provide credit guarantees. Even if the objective of the policy is to increase the amount of non-guaranteed loans it is likely to be achieved through the interaction between credit guarantee corporations and financial institutions, or peer pressure, through the public release of information.

It is not yet clear what effect increasing non-guaranteed lending will have on the performance of firms using credit guarantees, as not much time has passed since the system change. However, Yamori (2021) and Ono (2019) use newly published data to examine the determinants of the percentage of loans with credit guarantees and the relationship between the percentage of loans with credit guarantees and the subrogation rate of guaranteed loans. Some estimates by Ono (2019) show that a higher percentage of non-guaranteed loans also results in a lower subrogation ratio for that financial institution. This suggests that the mere presence of non-guaranteed loans provides an incentive for financial institutions to properly screen and manage their claims, even for loans backed by credit guarantees. Whether this is truly the case, and whether it leads to improvements in firm performance during normal times as well as a reduction in firm bankruptcies as indicated by the subrogation ratio, is an issue that needs to be examined in order to evaluate whether credit guarantees are functioning effectively.

[24] See Figure 3 in the report "Towards the Establishment of a Sustainable Credit Enhancement System to Support the Development of SMEs and Micro Businesses" (December 20, 2016) reported by the Working Group on Financing of the Subcommittee on Basic Issues in the SME Policy Council.

6.8 Summary

In this chapter we focused on credit guarantees as a form of government intervention in the loan market and examined their effects on SME financing. The credit guarantee programs analyzed were contingency programs offered during past severe economic downturns. When viewed as an emergency response it is important to note that large-scale credit guarantees have definitely helped SMEs' financing and maintained the stability of the financial system. This was particularly significant for the Special Guarantee Program at the end of the 1990s when Japan's financial system was on the brink of a crisis.[25]

In response to the COVID-19 pandemic the Japanese government provided large-scale interest-free and unsecured institutional loans combined with subsidies. The mechanism as to how this affected the firm financing environment is similar to what we have seen in the past as it was based on the previous two large-scale programs addressed in this chapter, and contributed to an improvement in firm financing (Uesugi, Ono et al., 2021, 2022; Honda et al., 2023).

A key issue common to these large-scale credit guarantee programs is whether the assistance provided is effective in increasing the viability of firms. The results obtained from the last two programs indicate that firms that have used credit-guaranteed loans have performed more poorly than non-users.

The reforms implemented since the 2000s have increased the level of risk borne by financial institutions for guaranteed loans, required financial institutions to report to credit guarantee corporations on the mix between guaranteed and non-guaranteed loans, and expanded management support provided by guarantee corporations. These changes are intended to encourage private financial institutions and credit guarantee corporations to increase their monitoring of borrowing firms and to enhance their support for these firms. It remains to be seen whether these efforts will lead to improved business conditions for firms using guaranteed loans.

[25] On the other hand, previous research that examined the impact of capital injections into financial institutions during this period, which we referred to in a footnote in Chapter 5, does not necessarily conclude that lending to SMEs increased. What form of intervention is desirable is a future research topic.

Chapter 7
The Impact of Direct Lending by Government Financial Institutions on SME Finance

Abstract Similar to credit guarantees, direct lending by government financial institutions plays a role in bearing firms' credit risk that private financial institutions cannot assume. Using loan-level information of the Japan Finance Corporation's Small and Medium Enterprise Business Unit we conduct an analysis on the determinants and effects of such lending. Regarding the determinants we find that: (1) JFC loans are used by SMEs with high profitability and growth potential but low capital adequacy ratios and thus the government sector bears the credit risk of firms through these JFC loans; and (2) the degree of risk-bearing by government financial institutions through direct lending increases during recessions. Regarding the effects of direct lending we find that: (1) the financing environment has improved for firms using JFC loans, and the phenomenon observed in Chapter 6, in which an increase in loans backed by credit guarantees is offset by a decrease in non-guaranteed loans, is unlikely to occur between JFC loans and loans extended by other financial institutions; (2) tangible fixed assets tend to increase more in JFC loan user firms, and they are more active in capital investment; and (3) the ex-post performance of JFC loan user firms does not improve.

Keywords Japan Finance Corporation Small and Medium Enterprise Business Unit (JFC-SME) · Former Japan Finance Corporation for Small and Medium Enterprise (JASME) · Private-sector squeeze · Cowbell effect

7.1 Introduction: What Are the Advantages and Disadvantages of Lending by Government Financial Institutions?

Chapter 6 examined the effects of credit guarantees on SME financing. In this chapter we focus on direct lending by government financial institutions, an equally important measure of government intervention in Japan, and examine its effects on SME financing and performance.

I. Uesugi, *The Economics of SME Finance*, Advances in Japanese Business and Economics 36, https://doi.org/10.1007/978-981-96-3193-3_7

In general, the notion that government ownership and management of financial institutions facilitate supply of funds to firms is not limited to Japan but is widespread across the world. La Porta et al. (2002) found that in 1995 about 40% of the world's banking sector assets were owned by the public sector. Because of their size, as well as the fact that their operations overlap with those of private sector financial institutions and affect the competitive environment of the lending market, economists, policymakers, and practitioners have questioned the importance and effectiveness of government ownership and management of financial institutions.

According to the theoretical model in Chapter 5, direct lending also has the effect of increasing borrowing and investment by firms with relatively high credit risk through risk bearing by the government. This is because government-affiliated financial institutions lend to SMEs at lower interest rates, through low-interest financing backed by government credit and/or through government subsidies. Compared to credit guarantees, which stimulate borrowing and investment by risky firms by covering default losses, the increase in borrowing and investment through direct lending is moderate. Furthermore, economic welfare is lower with direct lending than with credit guarantees.

However, compared to credit-guaranteed loans, where the actual loan interest rate may vary depending on negotiations between the private financial institution and the firm, the interest rate in direct lending is predetermined based on the term, type of loan, and credit risk of the firm, leaving no room for negotiation.[1] If interest rates are reliably lower with direct lending then underinvestment due to asymmetric information and other factors may be mitigated to a considerable extent.

On the other hand, direct lending can present certain challenges that credit guarantees do not. The first issue is "government failure." When the government sector is involved in lending there are agency problems (Banerjee 1997) arising from the fact that employees within government organizations have different objectives from those of the government, and the emphasis on political objectives, such as maximizing employment and providing benefits to fringe businesses, can undermine economic efficiency (Shleifer and Vishny 1994; Shleifer 1998). If the agency problems associated with government intervention are large relative to the effectiveness of assuming credit risk then direct lending by government financial institutions will be ineffective and difficult to justify.

The second issue is the criticism that comes from private financial institutions that believe the government is "squeezing the private sector." They feel that they are being deprived of lending opportunities when government financial institutions extend loans with low interest rates, taking advantage of subsidies from the government and implicit government guarantees when they procure funds from the market. For private financial institutions the credit guarantee associations that provide credit guarantees are allies, so to speak, who bear the loss of their own loans to SMEs.

[1] However, there has been no actual evidence of whether government interest rates are lower or higher than interest rates charged by private financial institutions when borrower characteristics are controlled for. We report the results on this issue in Chapter 8.

These guarantee corporations are not in competition with the private financial institutions. In contrast, government-affiliated financial institutions which provide lending services are competitors to private-sector financial institutions and are said to use their competitive advantage to "squeeze the private sector."

However, the degree of the private sector squeeze, i.e., the degree to which government-affiliated financial institutions are viewed by private-sector financial institutions as unfair competitors, varies depending on the state of the economy. In times of crisis the risk tolerance of private-sector financial institutions declines and risk-bearing by government-affiliated financial institutions is welcomed. On the other hand, during normal times the need for risk-taking by government-affiliated financial institutions declines because the private sector has sufficient risk tolerance and attitudes of the private financial institutions drastically change.[2]

If, even in normal times, there are some externalities in the investment projects for which government financial institutions lend, and if private financial institutions can benefit from them, the perception of the private sector squeeze will recede. In academic studies of the SME lending market, however, lending externalities by government-affiliated financial institutions have not been the focus of much research.

In light of these issues this chapter analyzes the effects of direct lending by government financial institutions on the financing and performance of SMEs and presents findings on the relationship between lending by the government and by private financial institutions. The subject of the empirical analysis is the lending operations of JFC's Small and Medium Enterprise Business Unit (hereafter, JFC-SME). JFC is a government-affiliated financial institution established in 2008 by merging several existing institutions as part of the consolidation of government-affiliated financial institutions, and JFC-SME is the former Japan Finance Corporation for Small and Medium Enterprise. JFC-SME has provided us with anonymous data on its borrowing customers, allowing us to evaluate the lending done by JFC-SME from various perspectives. All of the research that the author has been involved in, described in this chapter through Chapter 9, is based on the results obtained in the course of these activities in this research project.[3]

7.2 Overview of Results

This chapter analyzes the determinants and effects of direct lending by the JFC-SME. For the determinants we have two findings. First, JFC lending is used by SMEs with high profitability and growth potential but low capital adequacy ratios. Firms with low capital adequacy ratios are considered high risk because of their

---

[2] An example of such criticism is the National Association of Regional Banks (2017). This is the result of a survey conducted by the association in which 64 regional banks, members of the association, responded based on interviews with their customers regarding the actual activities of government-affiliated financial institutions.

[3] Apart from those involving the authors, Yamori (2016), Yamori et al. (2014), Ogura (2018), Uchida (2016), and Sekino and Watanabe (2016) are results related to research projects in the JFC-SME.

increased probability of bankruptcy and this is consistent with the commonly-held belief is that the government bears the credit risk of firms through direct lending. Yet when we narrow our analysis to firms included in the JFC's corporate database, such as previous borrowers and their related companies, we find that the JFC lends to firms with high profitability, capital adequacy ratios, and internal ratings. This indicates that government-affiliated financial institutions, just like private-sector financial institutions, are concerned about firms' creditworthiness and lend to those with high creditworthiness among the firms that demand the JFC's loans.

Second, a comparison of normal times and times of recession reveals that the state of the economy directly affects the determinants of direct loan usage. For example, during the Global Financial Crisis the negative coefficient on the capital adequacy ratio increased and the coefficient on the paid interest rate became positive. In other words, when the economy is weak firms that are less financially sound rely more heavily on public-sector loans, and the level of risk-bearing by government financial institutions increases.

The effect of JFC's direct lending is characterized by the following three points. First, the financing environment has improved for firms using JFC loans. The substitution between credit guaranteed loans and non-guaranteed loans, as seen in Chapter 6, is less likely to occur between JFC lending and lending by other financial institutions. Conversely, the so-called Cowbell effect, in which JFC lending induces lending by other financial institutions, occurs only in certain circumstances.[4]

Second, as the financing environment improves the increase in tangible fixed assets tends to be larger for JFC-utilizing firms, indicating that they are actively engaged in capital investment. With regards to employment the growth rate in the number of employees in JFC loan-user firms tends to be higher than non-user firms. However, for the actual number of employees we generally find no statistically significant positive effect. Thus, lending by the JFC tends to increase the capital stock more than employment.

Third, as far as firm performance such as profit margins is concerned, the effect of JFC lending is not necessarily positive. In particular, not only is the increase in profit margin for JFC user firms smaller than that of non-users but the probability of financial distress, such as deficits or negative net worth, is also higher for JFC users than non-users.

The remainder of this chapter proceeds as follows. Section 7.3 summarizes the previous studies on direct lending. Section 7.4 and subsequent sections present the results of our analysis, focusing on the JFC-SME. After presenting the analytical framework in Sect. 7.4, Sect. 7.5 discusses the determinants of direct lending and Sect. 7.6 analyzes the results on the effects of direct lending. Section 7.7 concludes the chapter.

---

[4] Regarding the substitutive and complementary relationship between JFC loans and loans by other financial institutions for JFC-user firms we measure the relationship more precisely in Chapter 8, focusing on events in which the JFC interest rate changes exogenously.

7.3 Previous Research on Lending by Government Financial Institutions to SMEs

To date research on the role of Japan's government-affiliated financial institutions has mostly focused on the Japan Development Bank (hereafter JDB, now the Development Bank of Japan). Horiuchi and Sui (1993, 1994), Fukuda et al. (1995), Hanazaki and Hachisuka (1997), and Lin et al. (2017), using a dataset focusing on listed firms, have analyzed how the capital investment behavior of firms and the lending behavior of private financial institutions are affected by the JDB lending.

On the other hand, despite their importance and the magnitude of their lending there have been few empirical studies on the role played by government financial institutions for SME financing, mainly due to limited data availability. In recent years, however, several studies have been conducted, including some using firm-level and loan-level data. These studies focus on the determinants of loans that government financial institutions extend and the economic performance of firms and regions where borrowing firms are located. In particular, since the aforementioned research project on the effectiveness of policy finance was established in the JFC-SME it has become possible to conduct a more detailed analysis of the effectiveness of SME lending by government-affiliated financial institutions. In the following sections we look at these various studies, all focused on Japan, in terms of how lending by government financial institutions is determined, what effects are generated by the use of such lending, and how the lending by government financial institutions and private financial institutions relate to one another.[5]

7.3.1 Determinants of Lending by Government Financial Institutions

Nakata and Adachi (2006a) use prefecture-level panel data from the early 2000s to examine the factors determining lending by the former National Life Finance Corporation and the former JASME, both being government-affiliated financial institutions

[5] Empirical studies on the effects of government ownership and management of financial institutions exist in other countries as well. La Porta, Lopez-de Silanes, and Shleifer (2002) found that countries with higher public sector ownership of banking sector assets have lower subsequent financial system development and economic growth. Micco et al. (2007) find that public sector ownership of banks reduces bank performance in developing countries. Sapienza (2004) looked at Italian state banks and showed that their loan interest rates are lower in the southern Italian region where political ties have a strong influence, even after controlling for various factors. She argued that public sector ownership and management of banks distorts the efficiency of the allocation of funds. Alternatively, some studies emphasize the positive aspects of public sector bank ownership and management. Micco and Panizza (2006), using bank data in both developed and developing countries, show that banks owned by the government tend to exhibit more countercyclical lending behavior. Behr, Norden, and Noth (2013) find that German state banks ease firms' borrowing constraints and state that public sector ownership and management of banks have positive economy-wide effects.

for SMEs. They first calculate the deviation of interest rates charged by banks located in each prefecture from the national average and decompose the deviation into several components: those due to the monopolistic behavior of lenders; the cost inefficiency of lenders; agency costs; and the creditworthiness of borrowers. These factors are then used as explanatory variables in an estimation with the share of government lending to SMEs as the dependent variable. The estimation results show that all of the explanatory variables obtain positive coefficients. Interest rates tend to be higher in prefectures with a higher concentration in the lending market, higher fixed costs for banks, and higher creditworthiness of borrowers. Government-affiliated financial institutions lend more in these areas than private financial institutions. Since interest rates are higher in prefectures with a higher concentration, it is possible that the volume of lending in the market is smaller than in the case of perfect competition. The study asserts that by lending to these areas government financial institutions are appropriately allocating scarce resources to "hard-to-borrow" areas.

Ogura (2018) uses loan-level and firm-level data to examine the objectives of JFC-SME in terms of their lending behavior during the period from 2007 to 2011, a period that included the Global Financial Crisis. In his theoretical model the objective function of government financial institutions is set up in two alternative ways: one to maximize the profit of all lenders and the other to maximize their own profit. If the objective function is to maximize the profit of all lenders it is predicted that government financial institutions will lend more to firms that have weaker relationships with private financial institutions when a demand shock occurs.

Based on the theoretical prediction he analyzes JFC-SME's lending to firms with weak relationships with their main banks during the global financial crisis. Specifically, he employs the change in loans per firm-bank to total assets ratio for the dependent variable, and the crisis dummy, post-crisis dummy, main bank lending share, and relationship with the main bank for explanatory variables. Furthermore, he controls for firm-year fixed effects by taking advantage of the characteristics of the data set in which one firm has outstanding loans from multiple financial institutions.

The results show that borrowing from government financial institutions increased after the financial crisis for firms that satisfy one of the following conditions: their main bank was a large bank; the share of their main bank within all the banks they transacted with was small; they changed their main bank; and they had a large number of banks with which they transacted. In other words, when firms increased their demand for liquidity the JFC-SME increased their lending to these firms that had weak relationships with their main bank. This is consistent with the model's prediction that the objective of government financial institutions is to maximize profits for lenders as a whole, not for themselves.

Unlike studies that focus on the economic determinants of government financial institution lending, Imai (2009) focuses instead on political factors. He finds that from 1975 to 1992 lending by government-affiliated financial institutions as a whole, including those to SMEs, reflected the results of elections at the national level.[6]

[6] The government-affiliated financial institutions included in the analysis are: for SMEs (National Finance Corporation and JASME); for large firms (JDB and Export–Import Bank of Japan);

The study constructed several variables including the ruling party's voting share, the length of term of elected representatives, and the difference in the voting share between a winning representative and the runner-up and used them for the estimation. It then found that the longer the terms of elected representatives, and the tighter the election, the larger the amount of per capita lending by government-affiliated financial institutions in the prefecture.

In summary, the results indicate that lending by government-affiliated financial institutions to SMEs tends to be higher in a highly concentrated loan market and during periods of recessions or economic crisis. This can be interpreted as being a result of government-affiliated financial institutions actively taking risks to provide loans in regions and at times when private financial institutions are reluctant to lend. On the other hand, there exists some research that finds a positive impact of regional political interests on the supply of loans by government-affiliated financial institutions.

7.3.2 Effects of Lending by Government Financial Institutions on Firms and Regions

Yasuda (2004) examined how loans by government financial institutions impacted a firm's start-up capital using data from a survey of firms founded between 1989 and 2002. The analysis reveals that lending by government-affiliated financial institutions increased the amount of a firm's start-up capital relative to that of a firm that did not borrow from a financial institution. However, when firms obtained loans from private financial institutions rather than from government-affiliated institutions their start-up capital was even larger. Yasuda (2004) also found that, regardless of the type of financial institution the loan came from more start-up capital promoted subsequent firm growth as measured by the number of employees.

Nemoto, Fukanuma, and Watanabe (2006) examine the specific issue of whether lending by government-affiliated financial institutions promotes firm growth as measured by the number of employees. They base their study on survey data of firms founded after the 1980s through 2003. The results indicate that the growth rate of firms that received loans from government-affiliated financial institutions was lower than that of other firms when they were first established but the effect weakened over time and, from the eighth year after the firm's establishment, loans from government-affiliated financial institutions were more effective in increasing firm growth. It can be inferred that the supply of funds from government-affiliated financial institutions stimulates the medium- to long-term growth of established firms.

---

for housing loans (Japan Housing Finance Corporation); for specific regions (Hokkaido Tohoku Development Corporation and Okinawa Development Finance Corporation); for public corporations (Japan Finance Corporation for Public Enterprises); for agriculture, forestry, and fisheries (Japan Finance Corporation for Agriculture, Forestry, and Fisheries); and for environmental sanitation-related firms (Japan Finance Corporation for Environmental Sanitation).

Imai (2018) examines how the presence of government financial institutions affects the efficiency of investment using prefecture-level cross-sectional data averaged over the period 1975–2000. The analysis first calculates an efficiency index of capital allocation for each prefecture. Using prefectural accounts published by the Cabinet Office he estimates the elasticity of investment to value added for each prefecture where the dependent variable is the growth rate of investment and the explanatory variable is the growth rate of value added. This elasticity measures the extent to which capital moves from industries with declining value added to industries with increasing value added within the same prefecture. Imai (2018) asserts that prefectures with larger elasticity values have more efficient capital allocations. He then performs an estimation using this elasticity index, along with total factor productivity growth rate and investment output ratio as a dependent variable and the share of lending by government-affiliated financial institutions during the same period as an explanatory variable.

The estimation results indicate that prefectures with a higher share of lending by government financial institutions have lower elasticity indices, lower TFP growth rates, and higher investment-output ratios. This suggests that a greater presence of government-affiliated financial institutions leads to an inefficient capital allocation among industries and lower productivity growth. He also presents estimation results that include the political leanings of prefectures measured by the share of votes cast for the ruling Liberal Democratic Party as an instrumental variable.[7]

Sekino and Watanabe (2016) analyze the effects of lending by government-affiliated financial institutions on firm performance during Japan's financial crisis in the late 1990s and 2000s. Using loan-level data from the JASME they focus on the impact of JASME loans made from December 1997 to March 1999 for the period through FY2003. Using the rate of change in lending attributable to the excess equity capital of the banks with which the firms transact as an instrumental variable for lending by the JASME they examine the effect that the amount of lending by the JASME has on the profit margins of the firms.

The results show that lending by JASME has a negative effect on firm performance, as measured by profit margins, for two or three years following the loan, after which the effect becomes insignificant. During Japan's financial crisis lending by JASME offset the decline in lending by private financial institutions as their capital adequacy ratios declined but the effect of this on corporate profit margins was negative rather than positive. The authors interpret this ex-post trend of deteriorating performance as being due to the fact that the JASME dared to lend to firms which were likely to face a financial constraint due to the poor ex-ante performance.

[7] Estimation using this instrumental variable is reasonable if the assumption that political tendencies in a region are not affected by regional economic activity and that political tendencies affect the efficiency of economic activity only through the share of lending by government financial institutions is met.

7.3.3 Relationship Between Government Financial Institutions and Private Financial Institutions

Ogura (2018) showed that during the global financial crisis government-affiliated financial institutions for SMEs increased their lending to firms that had little or no relationship with private financial institutions. This indicates that in an environment where the risk-taking capacity of private financial institutions falls during a crisis lending by government-affiliated financial institutions has a substitutive relationship with private financial institution lending.

What is the relationship between the two types of lending in normal times? The general perception is that government-affiliated financial institutions compete with private financial institutions in the loan market. According to the National Association of Regional Banks (2017) there have been several instances of government-affiliated institutions taking away lending opportunities from private financial institutions. However, a number of clients of government affiliated financial institutions are firms that many private financial institutions do not lend to, such as newly founded small firms. In addition, according to JFC-SME, since FY 2018 it has started taking a more collaborative approach to lending with private financial institutions and has communicated this policy to the firms to which it lends. More recently, government-affiliated financial institutions have also publicly announced that they are actively collaborating with private financial institutions. Tanaka (2018) uses specific examples to illustrate the track record of cooperation between the JFC and private financial institutions, showing that in FY2016 the number of cofinancing loans between the two institutions amounted to 19,671, or 732.2 billion yen.[8]

It is not clear whether the relationship between government-affiliated and private financial institutions is one of competition, as argued by the Japanese Association of Regional Banks, or one of "cooperation and collaboration" as described by the government-affiliated financial institutions themselves. A previous study by Yamori (2016), based on a survey of firms, summarized the views of firms regarding the substitutive/complementary relationship between the two types of financial institutions.

Based on the same firm survey as Uchida (2016) used, Yamori (2016) examined the impact of such borrowing on the relationship with private financial institutions among firms that had borrowed from the JFC. Below are the results of his study.

The study counted the number of firms whose outstanding loan amount borrowed from the most important bank that they transacted with increased as well as the number of firms whose amount decreased when the firms received loans from the JFC-SME. Overall, the number of firms reporting a decrease exceeds the number reporting an increase. This can be interpreted as a decrease in the demand for private financial institution loans from firms that obtained loans from the JFC. The number of firms that responded that the interest rate on loans from their main bank had

[8] The cofinancing here differs from syndicated loans in which multiple financial institutions participate in lending to a firm under a single contract in that JFC and private financial institutions make individual loan contracts with the firm.

decreased also exceeded the number of firms that responded that the interest rate had increased, consistent with the view that the demand for loans from private financial institutions had decreased as a result of the substitution of JFC loans for private institution loans. Overall, the survey responses seem to indicate a substitutive relationship between loans from government financial institutions and loans from private financial institutions.

However, the level of awareness of this substitutive relationship varies depending on the age of the responding firm. For firms founded before 1989 and equal to or more than 24 years old at the time of the survey the number reporting a decrease far exceeds the number reporting an increase, indicating a clear substitution relationship. In contrast, for younger firms founded in 1990 or later these numbers are almost the same and the substitutive relationship is not clear. For these firms, borrowing from the JFC often leads to increased borrowing from the main bank, indicating the presence of the cowbell effect in which JFC lending induces private financial institutions' lending.

It should be noted that this analysis does not explicitly take into account the reasons why firms use government bank loans and it is not clear how long it takes for changes in the amount of loans from main banks to appear after a firm borrows from the government banks. It does seem to be the case, however, that older firms with established relationships with private financial institutions are more likely to substitute between JFC loans and private main bank loans while younger firms are less likely to substitute between the two.

7.4 Examination of the Determinants of Lending by the JFC-SME and the Effects on Firm Performance: A Framework for Analysis

In this section we introduce an analytical framework with which to identify the determinants of lending JFC-SME lending and examine the effects of this lending on firm performance. The data used are anonymous loan-level and firm-level data provided by the JFC-SME which are the same as those used by Ogura (2018) and Sekino and Watanabe (2016). In addition, we use a firm database consisting mainly of SMEs accumulated at the Research Institute of Economy, Trade and Industry (RIETI).

The difference with studies such as those of Ogura (2018) and Sekino and Watanabe (2016) is that instead of focusing solely on the financial crisis of the late 1990s and early 2000s in Japan and the Global Financial Crisis beginning in the fall of 2008 we focus on government financial institutions from the late 1990s to the recent past. The point is to identify long-term trends in the determinants and effects of lending. Another feature that distinguishes our analysis from the previous studies is that we conduct our analysis by not only using data provided by JFC-SME but also by merging the data with panel data on SMEs from a different database.

7.4.1 JFC-SME (Formerly JASME) as one of government-affiliated financial institutions

JFC-SME is a business unit established within Japan Finance Corporation (JFC), one of the government-affiliated financial institutions, and is responsible for lending to SMEs. Article 1 of the Japan Finance Corporation Act, which sets forth the basis for its establishment, states that the JFC shall, with the aim of complementing the financing provided by private financial institutions, assume the function of supporting SME financing and providing financing to deal with damage caused by disruptions to domestic and foreign markets or a major disaster. Prior to October 2008, when the JFC was established through the merger of several government-affiliated financial institutions, the former JASME had been performing almost the same functions as this unit.

There are three types of operations conducted by the JFC-SME: loan operations, securitization support operations, and credit insurance operations, of which the focus here is on loan operations. Table 7.1 shows the number of firms with outstanding loans and balances, as well as the amount of loans per firm, for these lending operations. The average balance of JFC-SME loans per borrower was 136.23 million yen and the median was 64.33 million yen.

Table 7.1 Number and amount of outstanding JFC-SME loans and JFC-SME loan amount per firm

			JFC-SME loan amount outstanding per firm (million yen)					
End of fiscal year	Number of firms that have loan amount outstanding from JFC-SME	Total JFC-SME loan amount outstanding (trillion yen)	Mean	Min	p25	Median	p75	Max
2002	49,262	7.21	146.46	0.02	30.00	78.72	190.00	2096.03
2003	49,860	7.34	147.19	0.01	30.00	79.49	191.51	2103.88
2004	49,663	7.32	147.36	0.03	29.94	79.26	191.52	2073.37
2005	48,538	6.93	142.75	0.08	28.40	75.78	185.88	2592.61
2006	47,291	6.37	134.74	0.04	25.81	70.00	175.01	2540.88
2007	46,073	5.80	125.78	0.02	23.29	63.52	162.00	2464.65
2008	44,832	5.61	125.10	0.02	22.05	61.71	161.11	3201.66
2009	46,571	6.17	132.40	0.08	23.80	65.52	170.03	3091.65
2010	46,717	6.43	137.62	0.01	24.53	67.84	174.88	2989.25
2011	46,958	6.44	137.11	0.08	23.50	65.79	173.83	2886.15
2012	47,234	6.43	136.23	0.05	22.51	64.33	172.08	2851.76

Source Processed by the author based on Table 1 of Uesugi, Uchida, and Mizusugi (2016)

With regard to the lending operations conducted by the JFC-SME Table 7.1 shows changes in the JFC-SME's loan balance, indicating a change in its lending stance. The loan balance began to decline in the early 2000s from 7.34 trillion yen at the end of FY2003 to 5.61 trillion yen at the end of FY2008. The decline in outstanding loans during this period of relatively strong economic growth, prior to the Global Financial Crisis, is attributed to the November 2005 decision by the government's Council on Economic and Fiscal Policy to halve the ratio of outstanding loans provided by the government banks to GDP during FY2008 to achieve a smaller and more efficient government.

Subsequently, however, loan balances have begun to increase. This reflects the importance of government-affiliated financial institutions as funding providers during times of crisis, such as the Lehman shock, the subsequent severe economic recession, and the Great East Japan Earthquake.

7.4.2 Dataset Construction

The data used in the analysis is constructed from two sources: anonymous JFC data provided by JFC-SME and RIETI data collected by Tokyo Shoko Research (TSR), a private credit research firm, which is held by the Research Institute of Economy, Trade and Industry (RIETI). Firms included in the first database are mostly those that borrow from the JFC-SME while the latter mainly includes firms that do not borrow from the government bank. The RIETI data was also used to examine the effects of special and emergency guarantee programs in Chapter 6. The JFC data contains anonymized information on all JFC-SME borrowers and loan contracts, including loan-level information such as contract dates, loan amount, interest rate, loan types since 1995, firm-level financial information since the early 1990s, and firm-level information on JFC-SME's internal ratings for borrower firms since 2002. The data additionally includes information on the loan amount outstanding for the JFC-SME and for other financial institutions at the end of each fiscal year since 2002.

Information pertaining to the time and duration of the contract and the outstanding amount of public finance loans is used to identify when a firm used the JFC-SME and the outstanding amount of loans during that time period. The JFC data also includes information on some firms that have never obtained a JFC loan. Included are firms that submitted financial statement data to JFC at the application stage but did not subsequently obtain a JFC loan, as well as firms that are part of a group of firms that have obtained a JFC loan.[9] This data is considered to include not only firms that demanded and obtained JFC loans but also firms that demanded but were unable to obtain loans.

---

[9] According to the JFC firms applying for loans generally submit financial statements at the time of application, except for newly established firms. However, in the data it is difficult to distinguish between firms that submitted financial statements for borrowing but could not borrow and firms that were included in the JFC database only because their affiliated firms obtained JFC loans and had no demand for loans themselves.

However, the JFC data alone are not sufficient to examine the characteristics of JFC loan user firms. This is because there are firms that did not apply to the JFC in anticipation of rejection even though they had demand for JFC loans and firms that did not need JFC loans at all. Therefore, we employ the RIETI data which includes information on a large number of firms that do not use JFC loans in conjunction with the JFC data.

The RIETI data includes information on more than 20,000 firms that responded to the annual survey on corporate financing conducted by the SME Agency from 2001 to 2003. It should be noted that, unlike the JFC data, the RIETI data does not provide information on the details of loan contracts with financial institutions, outstanding loans from each financial institution, or internal ratings.

A common feature of both data is the relatively small number of microbusinesses included, as compared to the distribution of firm size in Japan. The reason for this is that for the JFC data we do not have information on the borrower firms in the National Life Unit of the same JFC (National Life Finance Corporation before October 2008) which are smaller in size than those in the JFC-SME. For the RIETI data the average firm size is larger than that in the population of firms in Japan since the survey was limited to firms that had a solid business foundation to regularly provide financial statements.

7.4.3 Combining the Datasets

We combine the two datasets by first using the firm attribute information in both the JFC and RIETI data to identify "firms that have used JFC, firms that are included in the JFC data but have not used JFC," and "firms that are included only in the RIETI data and have not used the JFC at all."

Next we construct the panel by matching firms in each fiscal year through the financial data in each dataset. In doing so financial statement items are organized so that the contents of the JFC financial data and the RIETI financial data are the same.

7.4.4 Dataset Size and Summary Statistics

While the data covers the period from 1995 to 2012 we use the period from 1998 to 2012 for our estimations, since the presence of JFC use can be more accurately identified using information in later years.

For the JFC data there are 747,177 observations (number of firm-year observations) for which financial information exists during the estimation period. Not all firms in the dataset obtained JFC loans in all years. Based on JFC loan contract records there are 602,356 firm-years for which JFC loan amount outstanding exists and 144,761 firm-years for which it does not. In order to analyze the determinants and effects of new loans received from the JFC we narrow down the sample to those firms that obtained new loans from the JFC and those that did not. Since ex-post performance is tracked for three years after new loans we define "JFC user firms in year t" as those that did not have a JFC loan contract as of March 31 of year t−1 but had a JFC loan contract as of March 31 of year t. We also define "non-JFC user firms" as those that did not use JFC loans from year t−1 to March 31 of year t+3. For example, if a firm signed a loan contract with the JFC between April 1, 2007 and March 31, 2008 it is treated as a new user of the JFC in 2008.[10]

The number of observations to be analyzed as users and non-users are 47,709 and 79,946, respectively. For firms that use the JFC we also use information on their outstanding JFC loan amount as of March 31 of each year. On the other hand, for the RIETI data, after excluding firms included in the JFC data there are 219,207 firm-year observations for which financial information is available. These are firms that have not used JFC at all and we treat them as "non-JFC users." For the point in time of financial information we adopt the information in year t if the point in time the financial information is recorded is in the period from April 1 in year t − 1 to March 31 in year t. For example, information for the fiscal year ending in June 2007 and information for the fiscal year ending in March 2008 are treated as the financial information in 2008.

From the above we can identify the user/non-user firms in the JFC data and the non-user firms in the RIETI data. We then construct two datasets for analysis, (1) and (2), using the respective firm data. Dataset (1) includes only JFC user and non-JFC user firms from the JFC data, with 127,655 firm-year observations. Dataset (2) includes only RIETI data for non-JFC users while JFC data is used for users, with 266,916 firm-year observations.

While many of the non-JFC user firms in (1) include firms that have a demand for JFC loans the non-JFC user firms in (2) do not provide any financial information to the JFC, and many of them are considered to be firms that do not have demand for JFC loans. The number of observations by year for datasets (1) and (2) is shown in Table 7.2. Even for the smaller dataset (1) there are at least 6,000 records for each year from 1998 to 2011.

7.4.5 *Analytical Framework: Determinants of the Use of JFC Loans*

Similar to the analysis conducted in Chapter 6 we use the framework of estimating treatment effects through propensity score matching. First, we identify the types of firms to which JFC loans are extended.

Examining the characteristics of firms that obtain JFC loans has two implications. First, we compare firm size, industry, region, credit risk, and other attributes of JFC

[10] The Global Financial Crisis triggered by the collapse of Lehman Brothers and the resulting recession was most severe in the fall of 2008 and the first half of 2009 but in this data firms that signed new loan contracts during that period appear as new borrowers in the 2009 to 2010 period.

Table 7.2 Number of observations in datasets (1) and (2)

	Dataset (1)			Dataset (2)		
	Number of JFC user firms	Number of non-JFC user firms	Total number of firms	Number of JFC user firms	Number of non-JFC user firms	Total number of firms
1998	7157	9147	16,304	7157	14,025	21,182
1999	5561	7810	13,371	5561	15,219	20,780
2000	3852	5934	9786	3852	16,663	20,515
2001	3151	5191	8342	3151	17,375	20,526
2002	2835	4989	7824	2835	17,286	20,121
2003	2752	4998	7750	2752	16,408	19,160
2004	3229	4695	7924	3229	15,488	18,717
2005	2591	4710	7301	2591	14,923	17,514
2006	2037	6131	8168	2037	14,044	16,081
2007	1613	5353	6966	1613	14,141	15,754
2008	1621	4967	6588	1621	13,762	15,383
2009	1963	4750	6713	1963	13,484	15,447
2010	4419	4814	9233	4419	13,201	17,620
2011	3227	4823	8050	3227	12,770	15,997
2012	1701	1634	3335	1701	10,418	12,119
Total	47,709	79,946	127,655	47,709	219,207	266,916

Source Processed by the author based on Table 2 of Uesugi, Uchida, and Mizusugi (2016)

user firms with two groups of non-JFC user firms: a group of non-user firms included in the JFC database and those included in an outside database of relatively large Japanese SMEs. This allows us to determine the types of firms that the JFC lends to or the types of firms that are willing to use JFC lending. Second, we can match firms that use JFC loans with firms that do not use them and calculate propensity scores to estimate the treatment effect.

To understand the characteristics of the JFC loan user firms we conduct estimations using a probit model with a dummy variable for the use/non-use of JFC loans as the dependent variable and attributes of the firms as the explanatory variables. For the explanatory variables we employ financial information such as profit margins and capital adequacy ratios, the number of employees, the region in which the firm's headquarters are located, and other attributes, which can be observed from outside JFC. We also employ internal ratings that JFC uses to evaluate firms based on its own information. The estimation equation is shown in Eq. (7.1) below:

$$\Pr(\mathrm{JFC}_t = 1|\mathrm{X}_{t-1}) = \Phi\big(\beta_0 + \beta_1\mathrm{Firm}_{t-1} + \beta_2\mathrm{Rating}_{t-1} + \beta_3\mathrm{Region}_{t-1} + \beta_4\mathrm{Industry}_{t-1}\big) \quad (7.1)$$

where JFC is a dummy variable that takes the value of 1 if the firm is a new recipient of a JFC loan and 0 otherwise; Firm is a vector of variables indicating firm attributes that can be observed externally such as profit margin and firm size; Rating is a variable indicating internal ratings; Region is a variable indicating the region where the firm's headquarters is located; and Industry is a variable indicating the industry to which the firm belongs. These explanatory variables are used for period $t - 1$ which is the period immediately prior to the use of the JFC loan in period t.

What are the signs of estimated coefficients of the explanatory variables? Also, to what extent does the internal rating information, produced independently by the JFC, affect the use of JFC loans? From the JFC's perspective, in order to increase its earnings, it is desirable to have business relationships with firms that are less likely to default on their loans. It is also desirable to extend loans that are secured with valuable assets to minimize the JFC's loss given default. Therefore, we expect that the probability of lending by the JFC will be higher to firms with higher profitability and capital adequacy ratios and firms with more collateral assets such as land. We would then expect that the coefficients on profitability, capital adequacy ratio, and the ratio of land to total assets will all be positive. As for internal ratings, which are independently produced by the JFC, the probability of receiving a JFC loan is expected to be higher for firms with normal credit ratings since their risk of default is lower. So we would expect the coefficient on the internal rating variable to be positive as well. The preference to lend to high-quality firms is universal to all types of financial institutions whether they are government-affiliated or private.

On the flip side, from the borrower's perspective firms with no other means of financing due to high credit risk, a lack of land to be used as collateral, and/or being denied loans from private financial institutions will have a stronger demand for JFC loans. When the loan demand factors become dominant as determinants of the use of JFC loans coefficients on the profit margin, capital adequacy ratio, and land holding ratio are all expected to be negative. When estimating Eq. (7.1) in the reduced form without identifying shocks to demand it is difficult to assume which of the demand side or the supply side is dominant as determinants of the use of JFC loans.

Note, however, that we have two datasets available: dataset (1) consisting only of firm information data held by JFC and dataset (2) in which the JFC data is merged with the RIETI data on non-JFC users. When dataset (1) is used to estimate the use of JFC loans we interpret the coefficients as reflecting the lending attitude of the JFC as the provider of funds since this data is mainly provided by firms that demand to obtain loans from JFC. In contrast, when dataset (2) is used we interpret the estimation results as being influenced by factors on the funding demand side.

Estimating Eq. (7.1) annually over the sample period allows us to track changes in the determinants over time: from the late 1990s to more recent times there have been several major changes in the JFC's lending practices and attitudes. How have these affected the magnitude and sign of the coefficients on the explanatory variables?

As we saw earlier there were several economic crises in the Japanese economy in the past. These include the Japanese financial crisis of the late 1990s and early 2000s, the Global Financial Crisis triggered by the Lehman shock in the fall of 2008, and the severe economic downturn that followed. During each crisis period the JFC provided special loans to firms experiencing temporary cash-flow difficulties due to changes in transaction relationships with financial institutions. The special loans were also provided to firms that experienced a temporary decline in sales or other deterioration in business conditions due to external factors such as changes in the social and economic environment. In these crisis times it is expected that the JFC lends to financially distressed firms more than in normal times as the JFC targets firms in more difficult financial situations in such periods.

7.4.6 Analytical Framework: Ex-Post Performance of Firms Using JFC Loans

In this section we analyze the effect of JFC loans on firm performance. The method of analysis is a matching estimation using propensity scores.

Specifically, we estimate the treatment effect of using JFC loans by calculating the change in firm performance from year t to year t + 3, starting from year t - 1, the year prior to receiving the loan. For the estimation of the treatment effect we compare JFC users (treatment group) and non-users (control group) to calculate the difference in the extent of the change in the performance variables between the two. The important point is that we do not employ all the JFC user firms and non-user firms for estimating the treatment effect: instead we use the results of the probit model estimations to calculate the propensity scores and select non-user firms with similar attributes to the JFC user firms. This removes the bias that ex-ante attribute differences affect ex-post performance through the use/non-use of JFC loans. The treatment effect is shown in Eq. (7.2).

$$\theta_{ATT}^{j} = \mathrm{E}\left(\Delta^{j} Y_{T=1} | p(X), T = 1\right) - E_{p(X)|T=1}\left[\mathrm{E}\left(\Delta^{j} Y_{T=0} | p(X), T = 0\right)\right] \quad (7.2)$$

where θ_{ATT}^{j} represents the average treatment effect, the change in performance from t−1 to t+j (j = 0,1,2,3). T (=0,1) is the treatment dummy variable indicating the presence of new loans by the JFC. $\Delta^{j} Y$ represents the change in the firm performance from t − 1 to t + j. $p(X)$ is the propensity score based on the parameters estimated in Eq. (7.1). E is the expected value and replaced by the mean of the sample.

There are three types of ex-post performance indicators (Y) for which treatment effects are examined: those related to financing, those related to firm behavior, and those related to firm performance. First, focusing on credit availability and firm behavior we examine whether JFC lending eases firms' credit constraints and whether it results in an increase in employment and tangible fixed assets. If we only look at the impact of JFC lending, holding all else constant, it would seem obvious that firms' outstanding borrowings would necessarily increase and that ex-post financing would improve. However, it is rare that firms transact only with the JFC and that they usually have lending relationships with other private financial institutions. Whether these private financial institutions increase or decrease their lending to these firms will determine the direction of change in the firms' overall financial environment. Theoretically, since the JFC lends to firms whose finances are temporarily deteriorating through programs such as safety-net loans there is a substitutive effect of private financial institutions reducing their own loan balances because they consider the credit risk of firms using JFC loans being high. Alternatively, there is a complementary effect of private financial institutions increasing their loans because they consider the firms to which JFC lends as a result of its screening having a high probability of survival. This complementary effect is similar to the so-called "cowbell effect" pointed out by Higano (1986) and Fukuda et al. (1995) where lending by the Japan Development Bank (now the Development Bank of Japan), one of the government-affiliated financial institutions, induces private financial institutions to extend loans.

Second, along with these changes in the financing environment we also observe changes in employment and tangible fixed asset balances. This is to verify if the changes in firms' financing environment does affect their activities on the real side.

Finally, we focus on firm performance, such as profit margins and financial distress, and examine whether performance (or the change in performance) is affected by the JFC lending. If JFC lending eases firms' borrowing constraints and allows them to undertake projects that would have been impossible in the past then the increase in sales and profit margins should reduce the likelihood of financial distress and improve firm performance. However, JFC lending often targets firms that are temporarily experiencing financial difficulties so there is a possibility of a significant deterioration in short-term performance. On the other hand, if politicians intervene in lending decisions and subsequent monitoring, or if there is a lack of incentives to motivate appropriate monitoring by lenders, the performance of firms using JFC loans may deteriorate ex post.

7.5 Results: Determinants of the Use of JFC Loans

The results of the probit model estimation of Eq. (7.1) are presented in this section.[11] The period of estimation is from 2003 to 2011. In order to examine the differences in results across different datasets we implement estimations using only externally observable variables such as corporate financial variables for datasets (1) and (2). For dataset (1) we also conduct estimations with the internal rating variable included.

We implement many probit model estimations with three different dataset/variable combinations for the nine-year period. Hence, we explain the representative estimation results for the year 2008 and then summarize the marginal effects of several explanatory variables for each year and their significance levels.

[11] Uesugi, Uchida, and Mizusugi (2016) also provide estimates for the period from 1998 to 2002. However, since it is generally sufficient to look at the Global Financial Crisis to identify special features of JFC lending during recessions and the estimation period using internal rating data is limited we limit the period for analysis here to 2003 and beyond. The results for 2003–2010 are used to calculate propensity scores and estimate treatment effects.

7.5.1 Determinants of JFC Loan Use in 2008

In Table 7.3 we first review the results of the estimation for 2008 using datasets (1) and (2) without internal ratings for the explanatory variable. There are two main findings.

First, across the different datasets the signs of the coefficients on operating profit ratio, interest payment rate, and sales growth rate are the same. That is, firms with higher profit margins and sales growth rates and firms with lower interest payment rates have a higher probability of using the JFC loans. Second, the signs of the

Table 7.3 Estimation results on the determinants of JFC loan use in 2008

	Dataset (1) without internal ratings	Dataset (1) with internal ratings	Dataset (2) without internal ratings
	Year 2008	Year 2008	Year 2008
	Marginal effects	Marginal effects	Marginal effects
Operating profit ratio	0.767***	−0.823**	0.254***
Capital adequacy ratio	0.280***	−0.102	−0.165***
Interest payment rate	−3.276***	0.223	−0.400**
Land ratio	−0.057	−0.216**	0.095***
Cash deposit ratio	0.965***	0.625***	−0.004
Sales growth rate	0.091***	0.119**	0.067***
ln(Number of employees)	0.006	−0.009	−0.055***
High internal rating dummy		0.956***	
Medium internal rating dummy		0.794***	
Low internal rating dummy		0.259**	
Regional dummies	yes	yes	yes
Industry dummies	yes	yes	yes
Number of observations	3082	2446	10,579
LRchi2(20)	426.190	2453.380	1455.580
Prob > chi2	0.000	0.000	0.000
Pseudo R2	0.102	0.725	0.186
Log likelihood	−1879.787	−465.995	−3180.766

Source Processed by the author based on Table 5 of Uesugi, Uchida, and Mizusugi (2016)
Notes Figures represent the marginal effects of a change in each of the explanatory variables on the probability of the use of JFC loans. ***, **, and * respectively represent a statistical significance at the 1%, 5%, and 10% level

coefficients on the capital adequacy ratio, land holding ratio, cash and deposits ratio, and the number of employees differ depending on the dataset we use. In dataset (1) the probability of using JFC loans is higher for firms with larger capital adequacy ratios and cash and deposit ratios, and the number of employees and the land holding ratio do not significantly affect the probability of using the JFC, while in dataset (2) the opposite is true, that is, the probability of use increases for firms with smaller capital adequacy ratios, less employees, and larger land holding ratios.

In general, firms with high profit margins and growth rates are expected to have a greater demand for funds and as a result financial institutions are aggressive in extending loans to these firms, while firms with substantial cash and deposits and high capital adequacy ratios are considered to have little demand for financing but financial institutions are eager to lend to these low-risk firms. Dataset (1) includes many firms that want to obtain loans from the JFC while dataset (2) includes many firms that do not submit financial statements to the JFC and have no demand for loans. It is therefore likely that the lending attitude of the JFC is the main driver of the estimated results in dataset (1) while it is firms' demand for funds that may drive the results in dataset (2).

Next, looking at the results of the estimation using dataset (1) with the addition of internal credit ratings (the baseline is potential bankruptcy or worse), in the second column of Table 7.3 the effect for the upper-middle internal rating dummy is significantly positive while the effect and significance decrease for the lower rating dummy. This indicates that the JFC is more willing to provide public finance loans to firms with high internal ratings. The sign of the coefficients on the firms' financial variables changes considerably when the internal credit rating variables are not included as explanatory variables. In other words, the effects of operating profit margin, capital adequacy ratio, and paid interest rate, which were significant when internal ratings were not used, either reversed signs or became insignificant when internal ratings were added. This implies that internal ratings contain more information on firms' financial conditions than the variables from financial statements.[12]

7.5.2 Changes in the Determinants of the JFC Loan Use Over Time

Table 7.4 displays the estimated results for several explanatory variables from the probit model for each year from 2003 to 2011. The table shows how the determinants of the JFC loan use have changed over time.

First, the results of the estimation using dataset (1) and without including internal ratings as an explanatory variable implies that the JFC has an accommodative lending

[12] The reasons why the JFC's internal ratings alone do not determine the JFC's lending decision include the following: missing information on borrowers' credit risk by reducing the number of rating categories from the original 12 to 4; and different lending criteria for working capital loans and equipment loans that are included in the dataset.

Table 7.4 Major determinants of JFC loan use for 2003–2011

	2003	2004	2005	2006	2007	2008	2009	2010	2011
	dF/dx	dF/dx	dF/dx	dF/dx	dF/dx	dF/dx	dF/dx	dF/dx	dF/dx
Dataset (1) without internal ratings									
Operating profit ratio	0.725***	0.827***	0.562***	0.925***	0.792***	0.767***	0.947***	0.233**	0.212*
Capital adequacy ratio	0.540***	0.553***	0.412***	0.430***	0.291***	0.280***	0.315***	0.154***	0.144***
Interest payment rate	−3.897***	−6.455***	−4.015***	−3.616***	−2.577***	−3.276***	−1.667***	0.099	−0.865*
Land ratio	0.171***	0.106*	0.117**	0.061	0.047	−0.057	−0.167***	−0.139***	−0.114**
Cash and deposit ratio	1.086***	0.704***	0.865***	0.749***	0.973***	0.965***	0.958***	0.544***	0.553***
Sales growth rate	0.178***	0.223***	0.115***	0.162***	0.198***	0.091***	0.100***	0.014	0.012
ln(number of employees)	0.063***	0.049***	0.040***	0.038***	0.056***	0.006	0.045***	0.086***	0.043***
Dataset (1) with internal ratings									
Operating profit ratio	0.046	0.175	−0.303	−0.417	−0.920***	−0.823**	−0.132	−0.552***	−0.627***
Capital adequacy ratio	0.177***	0.281***	0.016	0.135*	−0.083	−0.102	−0.053	0.004	−0.028
Interest payment rate	−2.146***	−3.375***	−1.276	−0.859	0.489	0.223	2.453**	1.273**	0.554
Land ratio	0.208**	0.175*	0.183**	−0.025	0.026	−0.216**	−0.468***	−0.257***	−0.177***
Cash and deposit ratio	0.533***	0.428***	0.482***	0.288*	0.533***	0.625***	0.432**	0.271***	0.664***
Sales growth rate	0.023	0.109*	0.052	0.082	0.167***	0.119**	−0.042	−0.031**	0.007
ln(number of employees)	0.055***	0.039***	0.016	0.010	0.025*	−0.009	0.014	0.023***	−0.009
Dataset (2) without internal ratings									
Operating profit ratio	0.516***	0.399***	0.447***	0.384***	0.252***	0.254***	0.314***	0.268***	0.425***
Capital adequacy ratio	−0.100***	−0.048***	−0.127***	−0.109***	−0.132***	−0.165***	−0.208***	−0.466***	−0.281***
Interest payment rate	−0.369**	−1.026***	−0.834***	−0.653***	−0.048	−0.400**	−0.350*	0.981***	0.058
Land ratio	0.257***	0.166***	0.213***	0.171***	0.147***	0.095***	0.088***	0.136***	0.062**

(continued)

Table 7.4 (continued)

	2003	2004	2005	2006	2007	2008	2009	2010	2011
	dF/dx	dF/dx	dF/dx	dF/dx	dF/dx	dF/dx	dF/dx	dF/dx	dF/dx
Cash and deposit ratio	−0.065**	−0.090***	−0.038	−0.040*	−0.004	−0.004	−0.040	0.063*	0.038
Sales growth rate	0.031***	0.045***	0.063***	0.041***	0.062***	0.067***	0.118***	0.051***	0.129***
ln(number of employees)	−0.054***	−0.049***	−0.061***	−0.060***	−0.046***	−0.055***	−0.057***	−0.070***	−0.079***

Source Processed by the author based on Table 6 of Uesugi et al. (2016)
Notes Figures represent the marginal effects of a change in each of the explanatory variables on the probability of the use of JFC loans. ***, **, and * respectively represent a statistical significance at 1%, 5%, and 10% level

behavior during recessions. The effect of the operating margin is smaller in both the 2010 and 2011 estimates,[13] which suggests that the JFC lent regardless of firms' profit margins during the severe recession which followed the collapse of Lehman Brothers in the fall of 2008.

We also see this accommodative behavior when we look at the coefficients on the interest payment rate and the sales growth rate in 2010. The estimates are not significantly different from zero, which we interpreted as the JFC focuses less on credit risk, as represented by the paid interest rate, and the growth potential of firms, as represented by the sales growth rate, when making lending decisions.

Next, when internal ratings are included as an explanatory variable we find that the absolute value of the negative estimated effect of the operating profit ratio increased from 2007 to 2011, the effect of the paid interest rate became significantly positive in 2009 and 2010, and the positive and significant effect of the sales growth rate turned negative in 2010. Also, the estimated coefficients' internal ratings for the top and middle-ranked firms became smaller in 2010.

Furthermore, estimation results using dataset (2) reinforces our finding of the accommodative lending behavior during the recession observed in dataset (1). Specifically, the effect of the interest payment rate is significantly positive in 2010 and the negative effect of the capital adequacy ratio is larger. Given that the demand for JFC loans is more apparent in dataset (2) we can assume that firms with a high credit risk, such as those paying high interest rates and having low capital adequacy ratios, are demanding JFC loans and that the JFC is supplying funds to these firms.

It should be noted that the timing of this accommodative lending by the JFC was after the actual recessionary period: the Cabinet Office's business cycle reference date indicates a peak in February 2008 and a trough in March 2009. However, the increased tendency to lend to riskier firms shows up not during the April 2008 to March 2009 period, which we show as 2009 in the estimation results, but during the April 2009 to March 2010 period, which we show as 2010 in the results. In addition, it is not 2009 but rather 2011 when the economy was in an expansionary phase, which provides results closer to the 2010 estimates. There clearly appears to be a time lag before recessions lead to accommodative lending behavior by government financial institutions and a time lag before recoveries lead to the termination of their accommodative lending behavior.

7.6 Results: Effects of the Use of JFC Loans on Firms

In this section we examine the impact of JFC loan use on firms. As in the previous section datasets (1) and (2) are used for the estimations. The estimation period is each of the years 2003–2010, from which we examine firms' ex-post performance up to three years later.

[13] While not shown here the 1998 and 1999 estimates also show that the marginal effects are smaller and less significant than other years.

Since we estimate the treatment effects on ex-post performance at four points in time for each of three different data sets, and there are eight starting years from 2003 to 2010 to measure the effect, the results obtained are too numerous to explain in detail.[14] Therefore, in what follows we present the estimation results for the 2008 sample and report the coefficients and significance levels of the treatment effects from 2003 to 2010, as in Sect. 7.5.

7.6.1 Treatment Effects of JFC Loan Use in 2008

The effects of the JFC loan use, for the case in which loans were first extended in 2008, are shown in Table 7.5. Let us first examine the results for the variables related to financing and firm behavior. For these variables the differences in results across the three datasets are small. Based on the results estimated using dataset (1) without internal ratings included as explanatory variables, we have three main findings.

First, a positive and significant treatment effect is obtained for total loans. For example, in the DID column the treatment effect of the increase in loans due to JFC lending standardized by total assets is 18.7 percentage points, which is statistically significant at the 1% level.[15] The treatment effect from $t - 1$ to $t + 3$ is also more than 20 percentage points for each year. For firms that use the JFC the increase in total loans is larger than for firms that do not use JFC, indicating that their financing environment has improved. These results are qualitatively the same when including internal ratings as explanatory variables and when using dataset (2).

Second, when we examine whether JFC loans or loans from other financial institutions make a larger contribution to the treatment effect on total borrowings JFC loans are far more important. Specifically, the treatment effect of JFC loans from $t - 1$ to $t + 3$ is slightly less than 20 percentage points while the treatment effect of loans other than JFC loans is significant only in $t + 1$ and $t + 2$, and it is much smaller in size in the range of 4 to 8 percentage points.

---

[14] When using 2010 as the base year treatment effects are estimated for three time periods instead of four due to the availability of data.

[15] The treatment effect of 18.7 percentage points is based on figures not shown in the table and calculated as follows. For the treatment group firms that used JFC the increase in total loans was equivalent to 17.7% of total assets in year t. For the control group firms that did not use JFC total loans decreased and the change was equivalent to -1.0% of total assets. The difference between the two groups was 18.7 percentage points.

Table 7.5 Treatment effect of the use of JFC loans in 2008

		Dataset (1) without internal ratings	Dataset (1) with internal ratings	Dataset (2) without internal ratings
		DID	DID	DID
Δtotal loan/assets	t	0.187***	0.169***	0.165***
	t + 1	0.226***	0.219***	0.178***
	t + 2	0.275***	0.273***	0.210***
	t + 3	0.222***	0.274***	0.210***
ΔJFC loan/assets	t	0.172***	0.172***	0.171***
	t + 1	0.185***	0.185***	0.181***
	t + 2	0.193***	0.193***	0.192***
	t + 3	0.199***	0.199***	0.195***
Δnon-JFC loan/assets	t	0.015	−0.003	−0.006
	t + 1	0.041**	0.035**	−0.003
	t + 2	0.082***	0.080***	0.018
	t + 3	0.023	0.075**	0.015
Investment/assets	t	0.145***	0.151***	0.152***
	t + 1	0.197***	0.224***	0.206***
	t + 2	0.248***	0.258***	0.239***
	t + 3	0.190***	0.303***	0.278***
Δln(number of employees)	t	0.043***	0.056	0.033***
	t + 1	0.049**	0.052	0.021*
	t + 2	0.095***	0.024*	0.010
	t + 3	0.078**	0.057*	0.011
Δoperating profit ratio	t	0.001	−0.010***	−0.010***
	t + 1	−0.001	−0.007	−0.011***
	t + 2	0.011**	0.004	−0.007**
	t + 3	−0.002	0.023	−0.007**
Ratio of deficit firms	t	−0.030	0.035**	0.039**
	t + 1	−0.061*	0.029	0.056***
	t + 2	−0.081**	0.097	0.034*
	t + 3	−0.020	−0.070	0.057***
Ratio of negative net worth firms	t	−0.036	−0.106	−0.031***
	t + 1	−0.058*	−0.050	0.004
	t + 2	−0.042	0.028	0.036**
	t + 3	−0.011	−0.046	0.060***
Ratio of defaulted firms	t	−0.020*	0.011	
	t + 1	−0.061***	−0.005	

(continued)

Table 7.5 (continued)

		Dataset (1) without internal ratings	Dataset (1) with internal ratings	Dataset (2) without internal ratings
		DID	DID	DID
	t + 2	−0.046***	0.001	
	t + 3	−0.029**	0.007	

Source Processed by the author based on Table 7 of Uesugi et al. (2016)
Note ***, **, and * respectively represent a statistical significance at 1%, 5%, and 10% level

In fact, what Higano (1986) called the cowbell effect, whereby lending from the JFC induces lending from other sources, is not common.[16] This complementary relationship between the two types of lending is even weaker and statistically insignificant when we use dataset (2).

Third, positive and significant treatment effects are observed for both capital investment and the number of employees. The treatment effect for capital investment ranges from 14 percentage points to 25 percentage points from year t to t + 3, with the ratio of capital investment to total assets for JFC users being significantly higher than for non-users. The treatment effect on the number of employees is similarly positive, ranging from 4 percentage points to 10 percentage points. Again, these results are qualitatively the same when including internal ratings as explanatory variables and when using dataset (2).

We now examine the results for the firm performance variables. For these variables the results differ significantly across the datasets. We first discuss the results estimated without using internal ratings in dataset (1). The treatment effect on the operating profit ratio is positive at 1.1 percentage points in year t+2 while it is insignificant in other years. The treatment effect on the probability of firms' falling into deficit, insolvency, and default is often significantly negative, indicating that the ratio of JFC loan user firms falling into financial distress is significantly lower than that of the control group firms. In general, the JFC loan users experience an ex-post improvement in performance.

However, when internal ratings are included as explanatory variables in the estimations the treatment effect is virtually absent. For instance, the increase in operating profit margin for JFC loan user firms is smaller than for non-users in year t and the ratio of firms in deficit increases. The internal ratings prepared by the JFC contain information on firm credit risk that is not included in reported financial information.

[16] It should be noted that although the results of the treatment effect obtained in this study indicate that the relationship between JFC lending and lending from other sources is complementary the direction of causality assumed by the cowbell effect in which JFC lending induces lending from other sources cannot be identified. For example, if firms' demand for capital investment and working capital increase simultaneously and if JFC lending, which provides long-term funds, and lending from other sources, which provides short-term funds, increase simultaneously a complementary relationship between JFC lending and lending from other sources will be detected in a statistically significant way. In this case, however, there is no cowbell effect whereby government lending activities stimulate lending from other sources.

For this reason, using internal ratings seems to be better able to match the attributes of JFC user and non-user firms and thus estimate the treatment effect more accurately.

Since internal rating information does not exist for the firms in dataset (2) matching is performed without it. The results show that the increase in operating profit margin for user firms is smaller than for non-user firms and the ratio of firms that fall into deficit or insolvency is higher. Based on the above results it cannot be said that the improvement in ex-post performance is greater for firms that use JFC loans than for firms that do not use them.

7.6.2 *Changes in Treatment Effects of JFC Loan Use Over Time*

Here we investigate whether the results of treatment effect for the firms that received JFC loans in 2008 are the same as for other years. We also examine whether the effect of JFC loan use during recessions differs from the effect in normal periods. For dataset (1) we proceed with the estimation that uses internal ratings to more accurately match firms that use and do not use JFC loans and discuss it along with the results using dataset (2). For the time frame with which to measure the ex-post variables we focus on changes to year t+2 which is somewhat representative of the trend over the entire period. Looking at Table 7.6 there are three takeaways.

First, there is a positive and significant treatment effect for total loans in all years, indicating the improvement in credit availability which reflects an increase in JFC loans. In contrast, for non-JFC loans the treatment effect is significant only for a limited number of years but all the significant coefficients are positive.[17] The existence of a substitutive or complementary relationship between JFC loans and other loans is also important in determining whether there is a private-sector squeeze due to government bank lending and whether JFC lending has any informational value and causes the cowbell effect on the lending behavior of private financial institutions. Chapter 8 reexamines this issue using exogenous institutional changes by the JFC.

Second, for firm behavior such as employment and capital investment positive effects from the use of JFC loans are observed for almost all years. More often than not we obtain a positive and significant treatment effect for capital investment more frequently than for employment. The more pronounced increase in the capital stock may be due to the fact that a substantial portion of JFC lending is specifically for capital investment purposes. These positive effects on firm behavior were also weakened temporarily during the global financial crisis as the treatment effect on the number of employees was insignificant in 2008 and 2009.

[17] We occasionally observe negative treatment effects when we widen the timeframe to include years t, t + 1, and t + 3. Even so, such cases are still limited other than an exceptional case of the treatment effect starting in year 2010 through years t and t + 1.

Table 7.6 Treatment effect of the use of JFC loans: 2003–2011

	2003	2004	2005	2006	2007	2008	2009	2010
	DID	DID	DID	DID	DID	DID	DID	DID
Dataset (1) with internal ratings								
Δtotal loan/assets	0.261***	0.319***	0.186***	0.162*	0.409***	0.273***	0.211***	0.233***
ΔJFC loan/assets	0.204***	0.207***	0.217***	0.217***	0.239***	0.193***	0.203***	0.139***
Δnon-JFC loan/assets	0.057	0.112***	−0.031	−0.055	0.171***	0.080**	0.008	0.093***
Investment/assets	0.255***	0.262***	0.200***	0.128	0.418***	0.258***	0.176***	0.137***
Δln(number of employees)	0.128***	0.146***	0.064	0.164***	0.137**	0.024	0.068	0.135***
Δoperating profit ratio	0.005	0.011	−0.008	0.005	−0.009	0.004	0.014	0.001
Ratio of deficit firms	−0.064	−0.078	−0.008	0.034	0.049	0.097	−0.177**	−0.038
Ratio of negative net worth firms	−0.064	−0.015	0.017	0.030	0.015	0.028	−0.020	−0.052
Ratio of defaulted firms	−0.014	−0.014	−0.004	0.005***	−0.014	0.001	0.001	
Dataset (2) without internal ratings								
Δtotal loan/assets	0.193***	0.208***	0.225***	0.288***	0.309***	0.210***	0.215***	0.159***
ΔJFC loan/assets	0.202***	0.203***	0.214***	0.213***	0.234***	0.192***	0.197***	0.139***
Δnon-JFC loan/assets	−0.009	0.004	0.011	0.075***	0.074***	0.018	0.018	0.019
Investment/assets	0.248***	0.288***	0.293***	0.366***	0.375***	0.239***	0.252***	0.141***
Δln(number of employees)	0.047***	0.036***	0.060***	0.067***	0.045***	0.010	0.014	0.030**
Δoperating profit ratio	−0.003*	−0.005**	−0.002	−0.004*	−0.009***	−0.007**	−0.002	−0.005**
Ratio of deficit firms	0.017	0.047***	0.015	0.037**	0.038**	0.034*	0.014	0.032**
Ratio of negative net worth firms	−0.001	0.019**	0.024***	0.030***	0.036***	0.036**	0.027**	0.039***

Source Processed by the author based on Table 8 of Uesugi et al. (2016)
Note Treatment effect from year t − 1 to t + 2. ***, **, and * respectively represent a statistical significance at 1%, 5%, and 10% level

Finally, we obtain very different results for profit margins and the ratio of firms in financial crisis depending on the use of datasets (1) and (2), which was also the case when we examined 2008. When treatment effects are calculated using dataset (1) with internal ratings for matching, the results of treatment effects are mostly statistically insignificant. On the other hand, the treatment effects using dataset (2) show a smaller increase in terms of profit margins for the JFC loan users than for non-users and a higher likelihood of falling into the deficit and insolvent status for the JFC loan users than for non-users. Based on these results there is little evidence to say that the extent of improvement in ex-post performance is greater for firms that use JFC loans than for non-user firms.

7.7 Summary

There has been almost no analysis of the determinants and effects of lending by government financial institutions to SMEs from an economic perspective due to a lack of data. Private-sector financial institutions generally have two views on government financial institution lending: "government financial institutions are completely different from us" and "they squeeze out profits from private financial institutions in the same lending market." The current analysis has revealed that these two views coexist in that there are similarities and differences between government and private financial institutions. For this purpose, it is useful to examine the determinants and effects of loans by the JFC-SME which constitutes a major part of the government bank loans.

Loans by the JFC are extended to SMEs with high profitability and growth potential but low capital adequacy ratios. Low capital adequacy ratios represent high credit risk through the increased probability of bankruptcy. The JFC appears to be more willing to bear the credit risk of firms with high leverage than private financial institutions and in this respect the JFC's behavior differs from that of private financial institutions. On the other hand, the JFC assigns internal credit ratings to firms that applied for loans and lends to high-quality firms. In this respect its lending practices do not differ much from private-sector financial institutions.

Compared to credit-guaranteed loans, which are widely used by private-sector financial institutions and whose role in the financing environment was analyzed in Chapter 6, government-affiliated financial institution lending is similar in that it actively bears the credit risk of firms but there are also some clear differences. First, an increase in lending by government-affiliated financial institutions does not necessarily result in a decrease in lending by private financial institutions; there may be a simultaneous increase in lending by private financial institutions. This is different from the case where an increase in credit-guaranteed loans is offset by a decrease in private-sector loans, which has important implications for the financing of SMEs that rely on these loans.

The second difference is the impact on real activity, such as increased capital investment, among firms that used government financial institution loans. This is in contrast to the analysis in Chapter 6 on the effects of special credit guarantees where the positive effects on capital investment disappeared relatively quickly. While this may reflect the fact that the SMEs analyzed in this study have obtained the JFC loans for the capital investment it may also be a strength of the government bank loans relative to loans with credit guarantees.

The size of the lending operations of the government-affiliated financial institutions in this analysis ranges from 6 trillion yen to 7 trillion yen.[18] In addition to the government-affiliated financial institutions included here there are also the National Life Unit of the JFC and the Shoko Chukin Bank, both of which are engaged in lending to SMEs.[19] In the future it will be necessary to discuss what role the credit guarantee system and government-affiliated financial institutions should play in the government's involvement in the lending market, taking into account these other government-affiliated financial institutions.

[18] The loan amount outstanding increased substantially in response to the COVID-19 pandemic, with the outstanding loan balance exceeding 8 trillion yen as of March 31, 2021.

[19] Dore et al. (2021) examine the program of Small Business Management Improvement Loans (Marukei Loans) provided by the National Life Unit of the JFC, which is low-interest and requires no collateral or personal guarantees.

Chapter 8
Do Government Financial Institutions Squeeze Profits from Private Financial Institutions?

Abstract We examine whether government-affiliated financial institution lending substitutes for private-sector lending through low interest rates. We first find that loan interest rates offered by government-affiliated financial institutions are lower than those of the private sector. We then focus on an exogenous institutional change in which a government-affiliated financial institution introduced a risk-adjusted loan interest rate scheme and decreased interest rates for creditworthy firms. If a substitutive relationship between the government and the private sector lending exists then this institutional change should have resulted in creditworthy firms being more dependent on government loans than less creditworthy firms. We find that the change in the JFC's interest rate structure did not result in private-sector lending to creditworthy firms being replaced by the JFC lending. Specifically, not only is the increase in borrowing from the JFC larger for creditworthy firms than for less-creditworthy firms but also the increase in borrowing from the private sector is larger for these creditworthy firms. As a result the extent of an increase in the dependence on JFC borrowing (i.e., the ratio of borrowing from the JFC to borrowing from the private sector) is not larger for creditworthy firms than for less creditworthy firms.

Keywords Pressure on the private financial institutions · Risk-adjusted interest rates · Substitutive and complementary relationships · Co-Financing · Interest rates charged by government financial institutions · Interest rates charged by private financial institutions

8.1 Introduction: Importance of Verifying Substitutive and Complementary Relationships Due to Differences in Interest Rates

Chapter 7 empirically clarifies the determinants and effects of lending by the JFC Small and Medium Enterprises Unit (JFC-SME) which is one of the major government-affiliated financial institutions. The main debate about the impact of direct lending by government-affiliated financial institutions on the firm financing

I. Uesugi, *The Economics of SME Finance*, Advances in Japanese Business and Economics 36, https://doi.org/10.1007/978-981-96-3193-3_8

environment is if it has a substitutive relationship with private financial institutions or if it has a complementary relationship, which is referred to as the cowbell effect or the priming effect. In times of crises a substitutive relationship is not considered a problem because the risk-taking function of the private sector deteriorates, however, in normal times when the private sector has the capacity for risk-taking it is viewed as problematic because of the competitive squeeze put on private financial institutions.[1]

In Chapter 7 we compare JFC-borrower firms to firms that did not borrow from the JFC but had similar prior attributes and examine whether borrowing from other financial institutions has increased more for these JFC user firms. We find that even among JFC-borrower firms borrowing from other sources did not necessarily fall. However, we did not specify the reasons for the new use of government loans by the treatment group firms.

From the standpoint of private financial institutions it is important to understand the reasons behind the increase in the government bank lending. When these financial institutions insist on the presence of the private-sector squeeze they are concerned with a situation in which borrowing from government banks is preferred to that from the private sector because of the favorable lending terms offered by government-affiliated financial institutions, even when the demand for borrowing remains constant.

The level of loan interest rates is what private-sector financial institutions pay most attention to as their concern is with the difference between their lending conditions and those of their counterparts. As the Japanese economy continues to stagnate and the low interest rate environment due to significant monetary easing has persisted it has become increasingly difficult for private-sector financial institutions to earn sufficient profits from their loans. One reason for this is the low interest rate for long-term loans offered by government-affiliated financial institutions. Specifically, low interest rates offered by government financial institutions have reduced the demand for loans from private-sector financial institutions which charge relatively high interest rates. Alternatively, private financial institutions have been forced to lower their loan rates to compete with the rates offered by government-affiliated financial institutions. In this case, the setting of interest rates by government-affiliated financial institutions distorts the competitive environment in the loan market.

An example of an argument that focuses on the levels of interest rates is provided by the Regional Banks Association of Japan (2017) which is also discussed in Chapter 7. A total of 64 member regional banks in the association responded to a questionnaire survey based on interviews with their customers regarding the actual activities of government financial institutions. As shown in Figure 8.1, the average offered interest rate for government financial institutions as a whole is reported to be lower than that of regional banks, especially for creditworthy firms.[2]

---

[1] Ogura (2018) and Sekino and Watanabe (2014) have shown the existence of a substitutive relationship between the government and private financial institutions in emergency times.

[2] In addition, examples of problems related to government financial institutions include "deprivation of lending opportunities for private banks (substitute for loans extended by private banks)," "problematic sales activities," "interest rate reductions," "shouldering the loans extended by financial institutions," and "uncooperative attitude toward firms that undertake restructuring.".

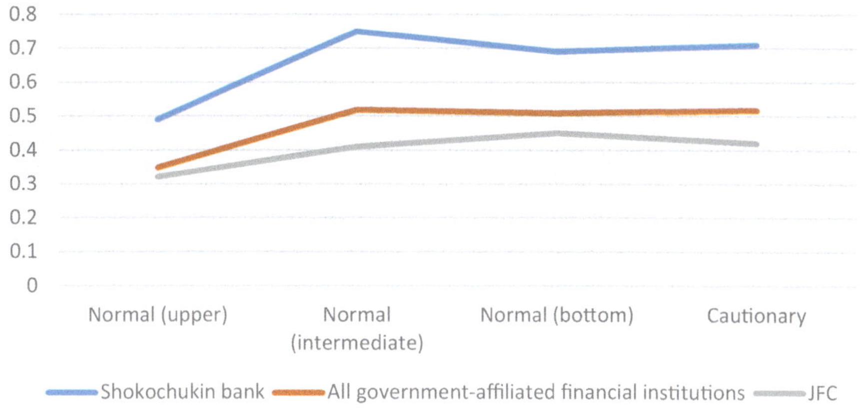

Fig. 8.1 Average offered loan interest rates by the government-affiliated financial institutions (*Source* Regional Banks Association of Japan (2017)) (*Note* The interest rates are standardized by the average offered interest rate by private regional banks,which is unity)

However, it is unlikely that this interest rate comparison between the private and the government sector was made under similar circumstances since the report does not indicate what the banks are hearing from borrower firms and how the results of the interviews are summarized into the statistics shown in Figure 8.1. Furthermore, while the report compares interest rates and presents examples it does not quantitatively verify whether there exists the substitution of private financial institution lending by public financial institutions.

A more comprehensive evaluation of the supply of funds by public financial institutions was conducted by the Ministry of Internal Affairs and Communications (2003). The study examined "the development of complementary roles of government financial institutions to private sector finance" and investigated whether government financial institutions play a complementary role to the private sector or whether they have a competitive relationship, using questionnaires and interviews with financial institutions, borrowers, and experts as well as aggregate statistics on the lending volume of each government-affiliated financial institution. However, there are no quantitative examinations on the existence of substitutive relationships using the loan-level data.

This chapter therefore examines whether the assertion that interest rates set by government financial institutions are squeezing lending by private financial institutions is correct by focusing on two points. First, we compare the interest rates of private financial institutions and government financial institutions for loans made to the same firms to determine whether the interest rates of government-affiliated financial institutions are really lower and if so by how much. We then examine whether the loan demand by firms that has been met by private financial institutions is substituted for loans by government financial institutions when an exogenous reduction in interest rates at government financial institutions occurs.

The analysis focuses on the same firms that receive loans from the JFC-SME as in Chapter 7. In particular, it is important to examine the substitution between the JFC-SME and private-sector lenders. Many of the SMEs that receive loans from the other units within the JFC, including the National Life Unit, are relatively small in size, which makes these firms less likely to be eligible for financing by private financial institutions. Under these circumstances it is difficult to criticize the National Life Unit as putting pressure on the private sector. On the other hand, the recipients of loans from the JFC-SME often overlap with those of regional financial institutions and the relationship between the JFC-SME and these private financial institutions can easily become competitive.

We perform the following two analyses. The first analysis uses loan-level data of firms that borrowed from the JFC-SME to estimate and compare the actual interest rates on loans extended by private and public financial institutions to the same firms. This allows for a more accurate comparison of interest rates, controlling for borrower attributes.

The second analysis focuses on the introduction of the risk-adjusted interest rate scheme by the JFC-SME in August 2008. This was a major institutional change in the government loan scheme whereby the interest rate on JFC-SME loans which had previously been fixed regardless of the credit risk of the firm was lowered for creditworthy firms and increased for less creditworthy firms.[3] Borrowers were not informed of this change in advance and only learned of the changes in their interest rates when they communicated with the JFC-SME regarding their lending terms and conditions. In this analysis we consider this an exogenous change in lending rates by a government-affiliated financial institution and examine the impact of this event on private financial institution lending.

8.2 Overview of Results

The main findings of the analyses are as follows. The first shows that the mean and median loan interest rates offered by the JFC-SME are lower than the mean and median loan interest rates offered by other financial institutions, most of which are private financial institutions, for the same firms. This means that even after taking into account the characteristics of the borrowers JFC-SME interest rates are often lower than those of other financial institutions.

[3] This change in the scheme was aimed at enabling government banks to lend to high-risk firms by setting interest rates commensurate with the risk. The introduction of risk-adjusted interest rates was in line with the policy request from the discussions on administrative and fiscal reform at the time, which called for both government and private banks to set interest rates according to credit risk. Specifically, the JFC-SME lowered the interest rate for low-risk borrowers below previous levels while raising the interest rate for high-risk borrowers above previous levels, provided that the overall average interest rate remained unchanged. This institutional change is unique in that it was implemented exogenously regardless of the degree of competition from private financial institutions and the individual circumstances of borrower firms.

The results of the second analysis shows that first, interest rates paid by creditworthy firms to the JFC-SME fell by more than those paid by less creditworthy firms as a result of the introduction of risk-adjusted interest rates. This contrasts with the change in interest rates paid to other financial institutions where there is no difference. This implies that even though the JFC-SME lowered their interest rates for creditworthy firms due to the institutional change other financial institutions have not followed suit.

With regard to the amount of loans the JFC-SME increased their loans to creditworthy firms more than they did to less creditworthy ones. This may be due to the fact that the interest rates paid to the JFC-SME were lowered for firms with low credit risk as a result of the institutional change which increased demand for JFC loans among firms with low credit risk. On the other hand, the decrease in loans from other financial institutions was smaller for creditworthy firms than for less creditworthy firms. As a result there was not a significant difference in the change in the dependence on JFC lending between creditworthy and less creditworthy firms. The Global Financial Crisis occurring at the time of the institutional change led to an overall increase in reliance on JFC loans but the magnitude of this effect was the same for creditworthy and less creditworthy firms. These results are consistent across different sample periods and estimation methods.[4] To summarize, with the introduction of the risk-adjusted interest rate for JFC-SME loans we find no supporting evidence for the substitutive relationships between the government loans and loans by private financial institutions.

The remainder of this chapter is organized as follows. Section 8.3 describes the data used in the analysis. In Section 8.4, based on the loan-level data and financial data from the JFC-SME, we calculate loan interest rates from JFC-SME and those from other financial institutions and compare these two. Section 8.5 focuses on the impact of the introduction of the risk-adjusted interest rate scheme by the JFC-SME on the amount of and the interest rate for JFC-SME loans and those for loans by other financial institutions. It presents an analytical framework and then shows empirical results. Section 8.6 summarizes the chapter.

8.3 Data

The data used in the first analysis comprises the loan contract details for each loan between the JFC-SME and the borrower SME, the annual financial statements of each borrower firm, and the fiscal year end internal rating of each firm by the JFC-SME.[5] The loan contract information includes the amount of the loan, the interest rate,

[4] There are, however, some types of firms for which private bank loans are more likely to be substituted for by the government bank loans, although the results are insignificant. The old firms, whose estimation results are shown in Table 8.4, are an example of such firms.

[5] Information on year-end outstanding loans from the JFC-SME and other private financial institutions for each firm is used to check the validity of these results.

duration, collateral and personal guarantees, the type of loan, repayment frequency, grace period before the start of repayment, and repayment method whether the loan is repaid on an equal principal basis or on an equal principal plus interest basis. Additionally, data about early redemption, delinquency, and rescheduling (change of loan terms) for each firm are used to obtain more accurate calculation results.

In the second analysis, in addition to the interest rate information for each firm obtained in the first analysis, data on firm attributes such as size, age, sales growth rate, profit margin, and industry, as well as information on firm-bank relations, such as the number of financial institutions and the physical distance between the firm and the government financial institutions or private financial institutions, are included.

In principle the analysis is conducted at the firm level. When comparing lending by the two different types of financial institutions only firm-level information is available for lending by other financial institutions although we have information at the loan level for JFC lending. The analysis period is from FY2005 to FY2016, and we use information on loan contracts going back to 1995.[6]

8.4 Analysis of Interest Rates

This section presents the results of the interest rate analysis. Here, we use the loan contract and financial data to calculate the loan interest rates of the JFC-SME and other financial institutions and compare the two. For the sake of simplicity "JFC-SME" and "JFC" are used hereafter to mean the same thing.

8.4.1 Method of Interest Rate Calculation

This section explains how we calculate the lending interest rates of both the JFC and other financial institutions. While loan-level information exists for the JFC's lending rates such data is not available for loan rates by other financial institutions. In order to obtain comparable interest rates between the two we use data held by the JFC to obtain the stock-based interest rates paid by each firm to the JFC and other financial institutions, respectively, for each firm and year.

We use the following four steps to calculate JFC-SME loan rates and other financial institution loan rates:

[6] In this chapter lenders other than the JFC-SME are referred to as "other financial institutions." These "other financial institutions" include not only financial institutions such as private banks, Shinkin banks, credit cooperatives, and government financial institutions other than the JFC-SME but also entities such as CEOs of borrower firms and their relatives. However, most of the firms borrowing from the JFC-SME are relatively large SMEs and the role of lending by the CEOs and their relatives is relatively small.

(i) For each firm determine the amount of interest paid to the JFC for each fiscal year and the principal balance at the end of the fiscal year (March).
(ii) Subtract (i) from the interest expense and discount fee paid on each firm's income statement to determine the interest paid to other financial institutions and other entities for each fiscal year.
(iii) For each firm subtract the outstanding loan amount from the JFC at the end of the fiscal year, obtained in (i), from outstanding loans (= short-term loans + long-term loans + discounted notes), obtained from the balance sheet, to obtain outstanding loans from other financial institutions at the end of the fiscal year.
(iv) For the JFC loan interest rate divide the amount of interest paid to the JFC, which is determined in (i), by the average of outstanding loans at the end of the current and previous fiscal year. For the loan interest rate charged by other financial institutions divide the amount of interest paid to other financial institutions determined in (ii), by the average of outstanding loans by other financial institutions at the end of the current and previous fiscal year determined in (iii).

The JFC interest rate obtained through this process is the "JFC interest rate" and the interest rates of other financial institutions are referred to as the "private financial institution interest rate."[7]

8.4.2 *Comparison of Statistics and the Distribution of Public and Private Interest Rates*

We next compare the JFC and private financial institution interest rates. Table 8.1 displays the mean, standard deviation, and median of both interest rates for the FY 2005 to FY2016 period. In order to avoid arbitrary treatment the interest rates are not trimmed at the top and bottom 1% points, nor are they winsorized.

However, the smaller the value of outstanding loans from other financial institutions (= outstanding loans—outstanding JFC loans) the greater the possibility that the interest rate, which is the interest paid to the private sector divided by outstanding private sector loans, is subject to the measurement errors. Such errors are caused by differences in the timing of the measurement of outstanding interest-bearing liabilities and that of outstanding JFC loans. To minimize the possibility of these errors the analysis is limited to firms and fiscal years in which the ratio of outstanding JFC borrowings to outstanding interest-bearing debt at the end of the previous and current fiscal years is less than 50%.

---

[7] In the calculations attention was paid to the following points: the discrepancy between the month in which firms close their books (often March, but sometimes other months as well) and the month in which the JFC's outstanding loans are recorded (March); consideration of missing information on loan contracts with very long terms of over 10 years that the JFC executed before 1995; and the exclusion of loans with early redemptions, delinquencies, and rescheduling. For details, see Uesugi et al. (2020).

Table 8.1 JFC loan interest rates and PFIs' loan interest rates

FY		Number of observations	Mean	Min	Median	Max	PFIs—JFC (mean)	PFIs—JFC (median)
2005	Interest rate charged by JFC	15,324	0.0163	0.0000	0.0164	0.0474		
	Interest rate charged by PFIs	15,017	0.0218	−0.0205	0.0202	1.0086	0.0055	0.0038
2006	JFC	15,717	0.0162	0.0002	0.0162	0.0899		
	PFIs	15,410	0.0212	−0.0221	0.0194	0.9188	0.0050	0.0033
2007	JFC	15,742	0.0167	0.0000	0.0163	0.0644		
	PFIs	15,462	0.0224	−0.0200	0.0205	2.4794	0.0058	0.0042
2008	JFC	15,600	0.0173	0.0000	0.0169	0.0571		
	PFIs	15,309	0.0226	−0.0210	0.0209	0.7681	0.0053	0.0040
2009	JFC	15,251	0.0177	0.0000	0.0173	0.0992		
	PFIs	14,945	0.0218	−0.0329	0.0199	3.2277	0.0041	0.0026
2010	JFC	15,753	0.0172	0.0000	0.0167	0.0992		
	PFIs	15,479	0.0213	−0.0194	0.0199	1.6298	0.0041	0.0032
2011	JFC	16,342	0.0163	0.0000	0.0157	0.0992		
	PFIs	16,076	0.0200	−0.0143	0.0188	1.0287	0.0036	0.0031
2012	JFC	17,209	0.0154	0.0000	0.0145	0.1024		
	PFIs	16,963	0.0194	−0.0813	0.0182	0.9243	0.0041	0.0037
2013	JFC	18,492	0.0142	0.0000	0.0132	0.0992		
	PFIs	18,268	0.0188	−0.0161	0.0173	1.3323	0.0046	0.0041
2014	JFC	18,954	0.0136	0.0000	0.0120	0.0992		
	PFIs	18,765	0.0180	−0.0235	0.0163	2.5108	0.0044	0.0042
2015	JFC	18,716	0.0129	0.0000	0.0108	0.1201		
	PFIs	18,598	0.0171	−0.0517	0.0150	2.5731	0.0042	0.0042
2016	JFC	19,251	0.0123	0.0000	0.0096	0.0991		
	PFIs	18,755	0.0168	−0.0336	0.0135	15.2154	0.0044	0.0039

Source Processed by the author based on Panel (a) Table 1 in Uesugi et al. (2020)
Notes PFIs stands for private financial institutions. For FY2005 the mean (median) interest rate charged by the JFC is 1.63% (1.64%) while that by PFIs is 2.18% (2.02%)

The first thing that can be noted from this table is that the maximum and minimum interest rates are more extreme for the private financial institutions than for the JFC. The maximum for the JFC interest rate is about 10% in any given year while the minimum is 0%. The maximum for the private sector interest rate is greatest in FY 2016, at 1500%, while the minimum is negative in every year. Because there are raw numbers for the amount of interest payment made to the JFC and the amount outstanding of JFC loans the interest payments to the JFC are never negative, while the maximum interest rate of about 10% corresponds to the rate charged for one of the equity-like loan programs.[8] In contrast, both the numerator and the denominator for the private-sector interest payments are obtained respectively by subtracting the interest payments to the JFC from the entire amount of interest payments and by subtracting the outstanding JFC loan balances from the total loan amount outstanding. Hence, these numerators and denominators may be subject to possible measurement errors in the JFC interest payments and the JFC loan outstanding amount. This is the reason why the minimum private sector interest rate is sometimes negative and its maximum rate is occasionally very large.

If we instead focus on the extent to which the mean value exceeds the median, in each year the mean is about 0.1 to 0.3% points higher for the private-sector interest rates and about 0.0 to 0.3% points higher for the JFC interest rates. These figures indicate that the means of the two interest rates are still comparable despite the very large maximum values of the private-sector interest rates. Therefore, we first compare the JFC and private-sector rates by focusing on the mean and the median.

8.4.3 *After All, JFC Interest Rates are Lower than Private-Sector Interest Rates*

For both the mean and median JFC rates are consistently lower than private sector rates. This ranges from 0.3 to 0.6 % points for the mean and from 0.3 to 0.4 % points for the median. The slightly larger deviation for the average is likely due to the fact that the maximum value of the private-sector interest rate is larger than the maximum value of the JFC interest rate. For the JFC rates, both the average and median interest rates peaked in FY2009 before gradually declining. We observe the same pattern for the private-sector except that the peak occurs a year earlier, in FY2008. Looking at the difference between the private-sector and JFC rates we see that the spread for both the average and median rates is smallest from the late 2000s to the early 2010s, with the difference being slightly larger in the periods before and after.[9]

[8] In the majority of cases where the JFC interest rate is recorded as zero the JFC extended a loan at the end of the fiscal year but the monthly interest payments had yet to begin. On the other hand, the high JFC interest rate of about 10% may be for equity-like loans extended by the JFC.

[9] One of the reasons behind the low JFC interest rates is the presence of loan programs to promote specific government policies. For these loan programs special interest rates are applied which are below the base rate for the JFC.

8.4.4 *Variation in JFC Rates Rose After the Introduction of Risk-Adjusted Interest Rates*

Next we consider the standard deviation of each interest rate. The standard deviation of JFC interest rates gradually increases over the entire sample period. This is due to JFC's introduction, in August 2008, of a risk-adjusted interest rate scheme whereby interest rates, which were previously fixed regardless of credit risk, were now set lower for creditworthy borrowers and higher for less creditworthy borrowers. This institutional change resulted in more interest rate variation across firms. The standard deviation of private-sector interest rates, on the other hand, has always been larger than the standard deviation of JFC rates. Moreover, with the exception of FY 2016, which shows extremely large values, the standard deviation has been rising and falling in short cycles rather than displaying unidirectional changes over time.

Figure 8.2 displays histograms of the JFC and private-sector interest rates for different internal ratings. There are eight rating categories above the possible bankruptcies being displayed, with smaller numbers indicating higher ratings. Both the JFC interest rates and private-sector interest rates are split into 20 segments with an interval of 0.25 percentage points. Firm-fiscal year observations with interest rates above 5% are excluded. Panels A and B respectively represent the two periods before (FY2005 to FY2007) and after (FY2011) the introduction of the risk-adjusted interest rate scheme by the JFC. In both periods, the mode values and the overall distribution of JFC interest rates are to the left of private-sector interest rates, which is consistent with the results in Table 8.1. In addition, the overall distribution of both interest rates shifts to the left in FY2011, as compared to the FY2005 to FY2007 period, indicating interest rates declining in the loan market as a whole.

8.4.5 *The Relationship Between Credit Risk and Interest Rate Levels Has Become Similar Across the Public and Private Financial Institutions*

Although it is difficult to discern in the histograms it is worth noting that the relationship between the mode of JFC interest rates and internal ratings changed after the introduction of risk-adjusted interest rate scheme. In other words, in the Panel A histograms for JFC interest rates from FY2005 to FY2007, the mode was almost the same regardless of the rating. This indicates that during this period the JFC set interest rates almost independently of firm risk. However, this changed in the FY 2011 histogram, with higher ratings (smaller numbers on the graph) leading to lower mode rates. In contrast, in Panel B for private-sector interest rates, the higher the rating, the lower the mode in all of the histograms. The extent of a difference in the most frequent interest rate category across internal ratings is larger for the private sector than for JFC in FY 2011.

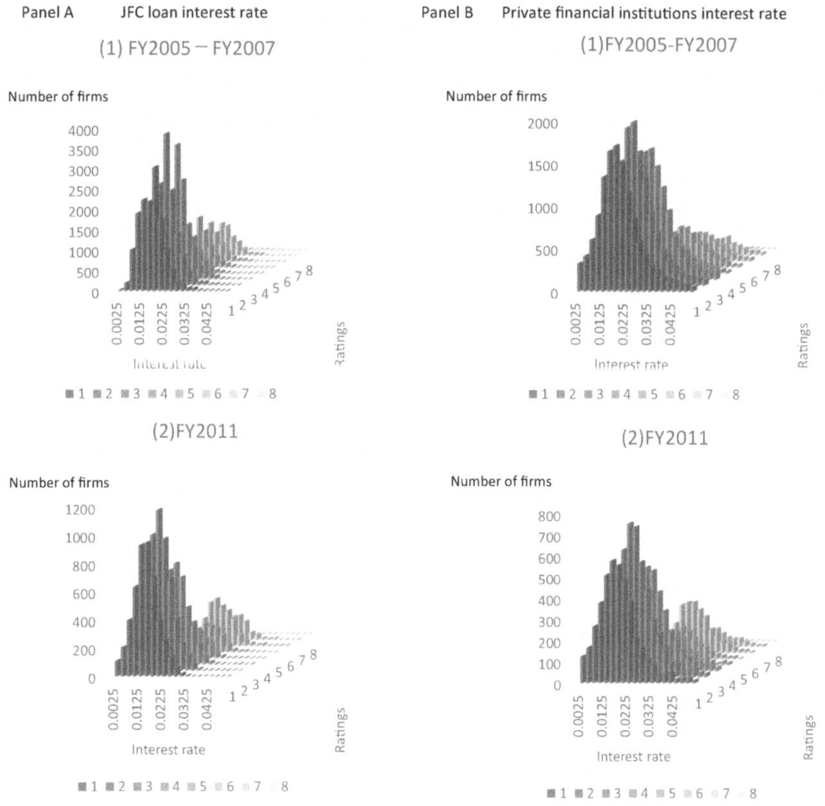

Fig. 8.2 Distribution of JFC interest rates and private financial institutions' loan interest rates (*Source* Figure 3 in Uesugi et al. (2020))

In general, private-sector financial institutions set loan rates commensurate with the credit risk of firms. Even government-affiliated financial institutions cannot set the same interest rates without regard to the degree of credit risk of the firms to which they lend, which was probably the reason for the introduction of the risk-adjusted interest rate scheme in 2008. As a result, the correspondence between credit risk and interest rates for the JFC and the private sector has increased and, thus, private-sector financial institutions may have felt competitive pressure from government-affiliated financial institutions.

8.4.6 *Importance of Examining How Differences in Interest Rates Lead to Substitutive or Complementary Relationships*

So far we have presented and compared statistics pertaining to calculated public- and private-sector interest rates. Interest rates, however, are only one component of the various loan terms and conditions. Individual loans differ in terms of collateral, personal guarantees, duration, purpose of loans, and other conditions. Hence, borrowers choose their loan contracts based not simply on the interest rate but on other factors as well. Therefore, even if the actual interest rate is low this does not necessarily mean that JFC loans substitute for loans by other financial institutions.

Thus, when examining the substitutive or complementary relationship in lending among financial institutions we need more than a simple comparison of interest rates. In the next section we focus on the institutional change of the JFC's introduction of the risk-adjusted interest rate scheme to clarify the details of the change and its resultant impact on the amount of loans. Through this examination we determine whether there has been any substitution in lending among financial institutions as a result of the change in the JFC interest rate.

8.5 Analysis of the Impact of JFC's Risk-Adjusted Interest Rates

Focusing on the introduction of the risk-adjusted interest rate scheme by the JFC-SME in August 2008, we analyze how this exogenous institutional change in JFC interest rates has affected private-sector interest rates as well as loans by both the JFC and other financial institutions. After providing an overview of the institutional changes and our analytical methods we discuss the estimation results.

8.5.1 *Overview of the Institutional Change*

According to the FY2008 Business Report the JFC-SME introduced a scheme whereby loan interest rates were based on the credit risk of the borrower and other factors on August 18, 2008, except for some special loan programs. As a result the JFC's interest rates on new loans to firms with low credit risk and high credit ratings were lower than they had been previously while the JFC's interest rates for firms with high credit risk and low credit ratings were higher. This was a major institutional shift since until July 2008 the JFC-SME's loans had the same interest rates regardless of credit rating as long as the loan term, collateral, and personal guarantees were the same.[10]

This change was introduced by the initiative of the JFC-SME, independent of the firms' demand for funds or the behavior of private financial institutions. The range of changes in interest rates according to the internal credit rating is determined in advance by JFC and depends on the loan period and the availability of collateral and personal guarantees. Additionally, the rate does not vary with the loan amount, the geographic location of the firm, or the negotiations between the firm and the JFC.

The JFC-SME did not disclose the extent of interest rate changes for each rating resulting from the scheme change. Based on the results of our analysis we assume that JFC interest rates decrease for creditworthy firms in the 1–4 rating categories and remain the same or increase for less creditworthy firms in lower rating categories.[11] We then treat the highly rated firms as the treatment group and the other firms as the control group and analyze the effect of the lower interest rate for the creditworthy firms as a result of the scheme change.

This scheme change applied to all firms that use JFC-SME loans, not only to some specific borrowers. Therefore, the criteria for the treatment and control groups could vary depending on the hypothesis we wish to test. For example, if one wants to examine the effect of an increase in JFC interest rates rather than their decrease due to the change in the scheme it is possible to define the treatment group as firms in the lower internal rating categories where JFC interest rates increased and the control group as firms in the intermediate rating categories where JFC interest rates remained almost the same.[12]

8.5.2 Analytical Method

In this section we measure the treatment effect of the scheme change based on the following equation employing each of the JFC interest rate, the private-sector interest rate, the JFC loan amount, and the private-sector loan amount for the dependent

---

[10] Loan interest rates for the JFC are set based on a base interest rate. The base interest rate used to be benchmarked by the long-term prime loan interest rate. However, in order to take into account of the funding costs incurred by the JFC, since FY2006 the base interest rate has been based on the borrowing interest rate of the Fiscal Loan Fund, which is the main funding source for the JFC. Note that this change has been applied to all firms borrowing from the JFC-SME and therefore does not affect the estimated results of the treatment effects.

[11] The validity of this assumption is confirmed by conducting the following estimations. We estimated an equation using the JFC interest rate under secured lending contracts as the dependent variable and using dummy variables for each internal rating as well as the loan term, with the existence of personal guarantees included as explanatory variables. We obtain coefficients on the rating dummy variables before and after the scheme change to detect the dummies whose coefficients declined substantially after the change in the scheme. The estimation results show that the JFC interest rate declined for highly rated firms with ratings of 1 to 4 by more than firms with other ratings after the change.

[12] Uesugi et al. (2020) have the results on this particular point.

variable:

$$Y_{it} = \alpha + \beta_1 Treatment_i + \beta_2 After_t + \beta_3 Treatment_i \times After_t + X_{it-j}\delta + \varepsilon_{it}, \quad (8.1)$$

where t denotes fiscal year 2005 onward. Y_{it} is the dependent variable for the treatment effect and seven variables are used alternately: the JFC interest rate; the private sector interest rate; the JFC loan amount; the JFC loan to total assets ratio; the private sector loan amount; the private sector loan to total assets ratio; and the JFC loan to private sector loan ratio.

$Treatment_i$ is a variable that represents the firms whose interest rates declined as a result of the scheme change, specifically a dummy variable that takes the value 1 if firm *i* remained between rating categories 1 to 4 in FY 2007 and FY 2008, the years before and after the scheme change, and 0 if it remained between rating categories 5 to 8 during the same period. The dummy variable will hereafter be referred to as the "high rating dummy".[13] Firms whose ratings have shifted are excluded from the sample. $After_t$ is a dummy variable that takes a value of 0 if t is before FY2007 and 1 if t is after FY2008. $Treatment_i \times After_t$, the interaction term, will be referred to as the "high rating × after institutional change dummy."

$X_{it\text{-}j}$ is a vector of variables including firm i's attributes and its relationship with its financial institutions in year t−j. Firm attributes include the rate of change in sales in the previous year ($j = 1$), the logarithm of the number of employees, the debt to total assets ratio, the operating profit margin, industry dummies, and the logarithm of firm age in the current year ($j = 0$). In particular, the rate of change in sales is intended to control for a firm's demand for funds. For the relationship with the banks we use the number of financial institutions in the current year ($j = 0$). We also use the physical distance from the JFC-SME's branches, the physical distance from their main bank's branches, and the physical distance from the sub-main bank's branches, all of which are measured as of 2013 ($t-j = 2013$). Of all the variables in X only the firm-bank distance variables are constant over time.

From this estimation we obtain estimates of the vector of coefficients $\alpha, \beta_1, \beta_2, \beta_3$, and δ corresponding to each variable, the most notable of which is β_3. This coefficient measures the magnitude of the change in the dependent variable before and after the scheme change for highly rated firms minus the magnitude of the change for other firms, which is the treatment effect of the scheme change.

For highly rated firms, which belong to the treatment group, a negative treatment effect, which represents a decrease in the JFC interest rate, is expected because the interest rate for obtaining new government bank loans will decrease after the scheme change. As a result the demand for JFC loans will increase and JFC loans are expected to increase to a greater extent after the scheme change than for the other firms in the control group, indicating a positive treatment effect on government bank loans. If JFC lending and private-sector lending have a substitutive relationship we would expect a negative treatment effect. In other words, highly rated firms will decrease

[13] When individual dummy variables were set up for each individual ratings category the relationship between the rating categories and some dependent variables was not linear.

their private-sector borrowing by more than other firms after the program change, and due to the overall decrease in demand private-sector interest rates will decline as well. As a result the ratio of JFC loans divided by private-sector loans is expected to increase more for highly rated firms after the scheme change. Given these points, if there is a substitutive relationship between JFC lending and private sector lending the sign of β_3 for each dependent variable is expected to be as follows:

JFC loan interest rates −
Private financial institution loan interest rates −
JFC loan amount +
JFC loans to total assets ratio +
Private financial institution loan amount−
Private financial institution loans to total assets ratio −
Ratio of JFC loans to private financial institution loans +

In estimating treatment effects the condition of parallel trends must be satisfied (i.e., there is no difference in the way the dependent variable changes between the treatment and control groups prior to the scheme change). Therefore, Figure 8.3 compares the average values of several dependent variables between the treatment and control groups for the FY 2005 to FY 2016 period. As can be seen, there is no clear difference between the movements of the two groups before the institutional change.

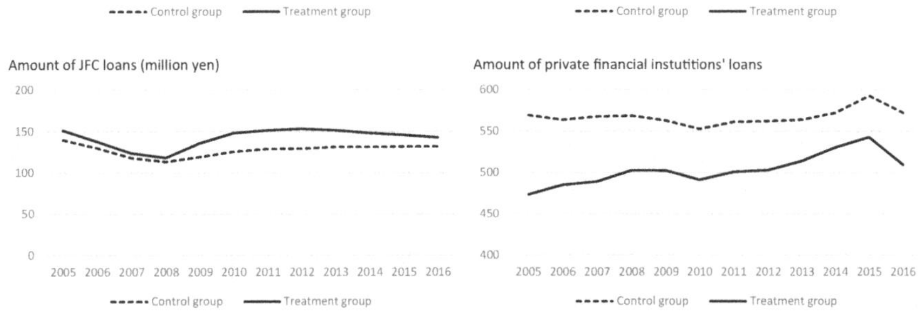

Fig. 8.3 Development of the dependent variables (*Source* Processed by the author based on Figure 4 in Uesugi et al. (2020)) (*Note* The real line represents treatment group firms, while the dotted line represents control group firms. The loan amount is the amount of loan outstanding)

8.5.3 Treatment Effects of Institutional Change: Baseline Estimation Results

Table 8.2 shows the baseline estimation results for each dependent variable in columns 1 through 7. In the baseline estimation the period covered by the estimation is from FY2005 to FY2007 and from FY2009 to FY2011. FY2008 is excluded because during this time the risk-adjusted interest rate scheme was introduced. Therefore, by setting $After_{2008} = 1$ there will be a substantial number of observations that are falsely identified as firms that faced the institutional change even though they actually did not. Another reason to exclude observations in FY 2008 is to circumvent the impact caused by the Global Financial Crisis that was triggered by the collapse of Lehman Brothers in the fall of 2008 and followed by various support measures including the monetary policy. In order to remove the effects of the shocks and support measures it makes sense to exclude 2008 from the analysis.

The treatment effect of the institutional change is represented by β_3 which is the coefficient on the high rating × institutional change dummy ($Treatment_i \times After_t$). First, let us review the coefficients in the estimations where the dependent variable are the interest rates. Since the JFC-SME interest rate on new loans to highly rated firms is expected to fall the JFC interest rate, measured on a stock basis, is also expected to decline. If private financial institutions seek to avoid having their own lending substituted by the JFC lending the private-sector interest rate is also expected to decline. In fact, we find that the coefficient is negative in the JFC interest rate estimation in column (1), which is as expected. The decrease in interest rates is 0.2 percentage points larger for highly rated firms than for other firms, indicating that the JFC offered lower rates to these firms as a result of the scheme change.[14]

However, the coefficient is not significant in the private-sector interest rate estimation in column (2). This indicates that the interest rates of other financial institutions do not follow JFC interest rates in that there is no decline for highly rated firms.

Next we review the results for the loan variables. For JFC loans (loan amount and loan-to-asset ratio) we expect positive coefficients due to the increase in loan demand caused by the decline in the JFC interest rate. In fact, in columns (3) and (4) the coefficients are positive for both the amount of JFC loans and the ratio of JFC loans to total assets. The increase in JFC loans and the increase in the ratio of JFC loans to total assets are larger for highly rated firms by 17 million yen and 0.8 percentage points, respectively, than for other firms after the change in the scheme.[15]

For private-sector lending (loan amount and loan-to-asset ratio) we expect negative coefficients because demand for private-sector lending should decrease if JFC loans substituted for private-sector loans. We do not find this to be the case, however. In

[14] Figure 8.3, which shows the development of the JFC loan interest rates for the treatment and control groups, also indicates a relatively larger decrease in the loan rates for the treatment group than that for the control group, which is consistent with this result.

[15] Figure 8.3, which shows the development of the amount of JFC loans outstanding for the treatment and control groups, also indicates a relatively larger increase for the treatment group than for the control group.

Table 8.2 Baseline estimation results

	Dependent variables						
	(1)	(2)	(3)	(4)	(5)	(6)	(7)
	JFC interest rate	PFI interest rate	JFC loan amount	JFC loan ratio	PFI loan amount	PFI loan ratio	JFC loan to PFI loan ratio
Explanatory variables							
After × Treatment	−0.002***	0.000	16.546***	0.008***	37.493***	−0.001	−0.006
After	0.002***	−0.001***	−0.855	0.002	−43.726***	0.001	0.015*
Treatment	−0.001***	−0.007***	23.095***	0.019***	−34.110***	−0.051***	0.103***
Sales growth	−0.000***	−0.002***	13.410***	0.015***	58.737***	0.027***	−0.044***
ln(number of employees)	−0.001***	−0.000***	71.130***	−0.016***	345.663***	0.012***	−0.086***
Leverage	0.004***	0.000*	156.092***	0.182***	693.472***	0.633***	−0.530***
Operating profit margin	−0.001***	0.008***	100.913***	−0.013	329.638***	−0.076***	0.180***
ln(firm age)	0.000***	−0.000	18.874***	−0.016***	114.226***	0.002	−0.077***
Number of banks a firm transacts with	−0.000	−0.000***	8.882***	−0.018***	116.425***	0.030***	−0.150***
Number of observations	42,919	42,902	95,935	95,672	95,672	95,672	95,614
R-squared	0.123	0.062	0.262	0.209	0.394	0.626	0.098

Source Processed by the author based on Table 2 in Uesugi et al. (2020)
Note ***, **, and * represent the significance level of 1%, 5%, and 10%, respectively

column (5), which shows the results for the amount of loans, the coefficient is positive and significant. The increase in private-sector loans is 37 million yen larger for highly rated firms than it is for other firms after the scheme change. In column (6), which shows the results for the ratio of private-sector loans to total assets, the coefficient is insignificant. Both of these results differ from the expected negative coefficients. Not only is the increase in JFC loans larger for highly rated firms relative to other firms but the increase in private-sector loans is either larger or stays the same.

When the ratio of JFC loans to private loans is used as the dependent variable in the estimation we would expect to obtain a positive coefficient due to an increase in JFC loans coupled with a decrease in private loans. The coefficient in column (7) is insignificant, however, reflecting the results in columns (3) through (6). Highly rated firms have not become particularly more dependent on JFC loans than other firms, even after the scheme change.

8.5.4 Results for the Robustness

In this section we check the robustness of the baseline estimations by examining the coefficients on the interaction term of $Treatment_i \times After_t$ for different sample periods and using different estimation procedures. Table 8.3 displays the estimation results for Eq. (8.1). Row (a) of the table restates the results from the baseline estimation while rows (b) through (k) contain the results using different sample periods. While the period covered by the baseline estimates was FY2005 through FY2011 except for FY2008, rows (b) through (k) present estimates for different periods. These include estimates that add FY2008 to the baseline and estimates that employ the same period of FY2005–FY2007 before the scheme change, but a different year from FY2008 through FY2016 for the period after the scheme change. Among these, the estimates that employ FY2008 for the period after the scheme change (row (c)) shows the largest deviation from the baseline. Here, highly rated firms increased rather than decreased their reliance on private-sector loans. These results may be due to the special circumstances of 2008 when the introduction of the risk-adjusted interest rates coincided with the Global Financial Crisis and various policy support measures were implemented to counter the crisis.

The estimates for the other sample periods do not differ qualitatively from the baseline estimates in that while the JFC interest rate declines there is no significant change in private-sector interest rates and the amount of JFC and private-sector loans significantly increase. Further, the results for the JFC loan ratio are the same as in the baseline estimates in that the coefficient is positive.

In addition to changing the estimation periods we also limit our estimates to firms with fiscal years ending in March. This is to address a possible measurement error due to the different fiscal years of the firms. The results are shown in row (l) and are very similar to the baseline estimation results in row (a). That is, the signs of the significant coefficients are the same and their magnitudes are similar.

Table 8.3 Estimation results for robustness of the baseline

	Dependent variables Estimation methods	JFC interest rate	PFI interest rate	JFC loan amount	JFC loan ratio	PFI loan amount	PFI loan ratio	JFC loan to PFI loan ratio
(a)	Baseline	−0.002***	0.000	16.546***	0.008***	37.493***	−0.001	−0.006
(b)	FY2005–2011	−0.002***	−0.000	10.879***	0.004**	36.984***	0.002	−0.029***
(c)	FY2005–2007 & FY2008	−0.001***	−0.001**	−3.932	−0.004*	34.368***	0.011***	−0.093***
(e)	FY2005–2007 & FY2010	−0.003***	0.000	20.006***	0.009***	32.534***	−0.008**	0.009
(g)	FY2005–2007 & FY2012	−0.004***	0.000	17.205***	0.010***	37.674***	−0.000	0.008
(i)	FY2005–2007 & FY2014	−0.004***	0.001	9.042***	0.002	63.688***	0.016***	−0.060***
(k)	FY2005–2007 & FY2016	−0.004***	0.000	7.260**	−0.001	62.053***	0.021***	−0.097***
(l)	Fiscal year ending in March	−0.003***	0.000	17.234***	0.010***	36.112**	−0.008	0.024
(m)	Firm fixed effects	−0.002***	0.000	15.062***	0.002*	38.548***	−0.010***	−0.007
(n)	Macro economic variables added	−0.002***	0.000	16.513***	0.008***	37.565***	−0.001	−0.006
(o)	Different control group	−0.003***	−0.000	21.683***	0.012***	34.290***	−0.005	0.006

Source Processed by the author based on Table 5 in Uesugi et al. (2020)
Notes Figures in the table represent coefficients on the interaction term of After × Treatment. ***, **, and * represent the significance level of 1%, 5%, and 10%, respectively

We also re-estimate Eq. (8.1) including firm fixed effects. The fixed effects take into account unobservable firm-specific factors that have a constant effect on interest rates and lending over time. The results of this analysis are presented in row (m). Comparing the estimated coefficients with those obtained in the baseline estimation, the sign for the private-sector loan ratio estimation is negative which differs from the insignificant coefficient in the baseline estimation. Except for the estimation, the signs of coefficients for the other estimations are the same as those obtained in the baseline estimation.

As a final robustness check we performed estimations for the treatment group, with comparisons being restricted to those for which the JFC interest rate most likely increased. In the baseline estimation the treatment group consisted of firms in rating categories 1 through 4 for which JFC interest rates were likely to have declined while the control group consisted of firms in lower rating categories. In this case the control group could include firms in rating categories where the JFC interest rate unchanged. Therefore, we estimate the treatment effect by employing firms with credit ratings 1 through 4 as the treatment group and firms with credit ratings 6 through 8 and likely to have faced higher JFC interest rates as the control group. The results (row (o)) show that all the statistically significant coefficients have the same signs as those in our baseline estimates.

8.5.5 *What are the Reasons for No Significant Substitution?*

Given our estimation results the introduction of the risk-adjusted interest rate scheme led to a relative decline in JFC interest rates for highly rated firms, resulting in a larger increase in JFC loans than for other firms. However, the increase in private-sector lending has also been larger for higher rated firms and as a result there has been no increase in the relative dependence on JFC lending. There are two possible reasons why JFC lending has not substituted for private-sector lending despite the decline in JFC interest rates.

The first possibility is that there was demand for loans from highly rated firms that could not be met by the JFC loans. For firms with a large demand for funds JFC loans with relatively low interest rates may not have been sufficient to meet their demand and this may have led them to increase their use of loans from private-sector financial institutions. Despite the estimation attempts to control for firms' loan demand using the sales growth rate this may not be sufficient.

The second possibility is that the nature of JFC lending differs from that of the private sector lending. Using a firm-level survey Uchida (2016) compares the JFC-SME and private financial institutions regarding the areas of expertise and the extent of the expertise. He finds that private sector financial institutions obtain non-financial soft information from their borrower firms more than the JFC. If private financial institutions have close relationships with firms and are better at producing information on borrower firms' credit risk than the JFC borrower firms will not reduce the demand for loans from these private sector banks even if firms are able to obtain JFC loans at low interest rates. In addition, until the late 1990s the JASME (the predecessor of JFC-SME) specialized in long-term, low-interest loans for equipment financing, which most of the private financial institutions did not do. And even at the time of the 2008 scheme change JASME depended on equipment investment loans more than private financial institutions. If the purposes of lending activities are different, in that JFC lending is for capital investment and private sector lending is for working capital, the degree of substitution between the two may be small.[16]

8.5.6 Results of Subsample Estimation

In this subsection we test these two possibilities by dividing the sample. To examine the first possibility of the loan demand size we split the sample by the size and age of a firm. We assume that the larger or younger the firm the less likely it is that JFC loans alone will be sufficient to meet its financing needs. Yamori (2016) examined the percentage of firms that reported a decrease or increase in the borrowing from their main bank when they received loans from the JFC (here including loans from both the national life unit and from the SME unit) and detailed that younger firms were less likely to report a decrease in borrowing from their main bank. We examine whether we obtain similar results here.

To examine the second possibility of the closeness of the firm-bank relationships we divide the sample by the number of financial institutions with which firms transact. We expect that the smaller the number of private financial institutions the closer the firms' relationship with each private bank and as a result we would expect a smaller increase in the JFC loans and a larger increase in the private sector loans. To examine the possibility of different purposes of loans between the JFC and private financial institutions we divide the sample in two according to how funds from the JFC are used between FY2009 and FY2011: firms that used JFC loans for capital investment and firms that used JFC loans for working capital purposes only. We then implement estimations for these subsamples.

The results are presented in Table 8.4. We focus on the coefficients on $Treatment_i \times After_t$ which is the interaction term to measure the treatment effect. First, we show the results when the sample is divided by asset size and firm age. When the dependent variable is the amount of private-sector loans the results differ depending on firm size. The sign of the coefficient is positive for the subsample containing the largest firms but it is insignificant for small firms. This is consistent with the argument that

[16] Another possible reason is that JFC loans have become subordinated in terms of repayment priority during the period of analysis. The JFC-SME has become more aggressive than other financial institutions in providing loans that did not require collateral or personal guarantees. Unsecured loans and loans that do not require personal guarantees are subordinated in the order of repayment in the event of bankruptcy. As a result it may have been the case that private financial institutions are eager to lend to firms that the JFC-SME extends loans to. The introduction and the impact of such loans by the JFC are discussed in Chapter 9.

Table 8.4 Estimation results for the subsample analysis

Dependent variables						
(1)	(2)	(3)	(4)	(5)	(6)	(7)
JFC interest rate	PFI interest rate	JFC loan amount	JFC loan ratio	PFI loan amount	PFI loan ratio	JFC loan to PFI loan ratio
Number of financial institutions that a firm transacts with: 4 or less						
−0.002***	0.001	19.439***	0.019***	−10.150	−0.010	−0.019
Asset size: Less than 520 million yen						
−0.002***	0.000	6.453***	0.015***	−1.124	−0.007	−0.011
Firm age: Less than 45 years old						
−0.002***	−0.000	15.136***	0.007***	42.310***	0.001	−0.015
Purpose of loans: Capital investment						
−0.002***	−0.000	−1.479	−0.011**	53.725*	0.021***	−0.014
Dependent variables						
(8)	(9)	(10)	(11)	(12)	(13)	(14)
JFC interest rate	PFI interest rate	JFC loan amount	JFC loan ratio	PFI loan amount	PFI loan ratio	JFC loan to PFI loan ratio
Number of financial institutions: 5 or more						
−0.003***	−0.000	16.652***	0.007***	40.420***	−0.001	0.001
Asset size: 520 million yen or more						
−0.003***	−0.000	13.869***	0.003	30.721***	0.000	−0.006
Firm age: 45 years or more						
−0.003***	0.001	17.061***	0.009***	22.345	−0.004	0.012
Purpose of loans: Working capital						
−0.002***	0.000	13.034***	0.006***	33.925***	−0.000	−0.024**

Source Processed by the author based on Table 6 of Uesugi et al. (2020)
Note Figures in the table represent coefficients on the interaction term of After × Treatment. ***, **, and * represent the significance level of 1%, 5%, and 10%, respectively

the larger the firm the greater its demand for funds and the more it makes use of private-sector loans to meet the demand that cannot be covered by the JFC loans.

When the sample is split by firm age we find that the sign of the coefficient is positive for the subsample of younger firms but it is insignificant for the subsample of older firms. This is also consistent with the argument that the younger the firm the larger their demand for loans and the more likely it makes use of private-sector loans to meet the demand that cannot be covered by the JFC loans.

When we split the sample by the number of financial institutions we find that the sign of the coefficient is insignificant for the subsample of firms with a small number of bank relationships while it is positive and significant for the subsample with a large number of bank relationships. This is inconsistent with the prior expectation that the smaller the number of a firm's financial institutions the closer the individual relationships, resulting in a large, positive coefficient. However, the number of financial institutions may not be an appropriate indicator for the closeness of the relationships but an indicator for the loan demand. If so, the results are consistent with those we obtained from the subsample analysis by firm size and age.

Finally, when we divide the sample according to the loan type we find that the amount of JFC loans did not increase and that the JFC loan ratio decreased for firms that used JFC loans for capital investment purposes. This contrasts with the increase in both the JFC loan amount and JFC loan ratio for firms using the loans for working capital purposes. We infer that firms demanding funds for capital investment do not increase their amount of JFC borrowing simply because interest rates have declined. The sign of the coefficient on private-sector loans is positive for both loan types. The ratio of private-sector loans increased for firms that borrow for capital investment while the ratio of JFC to private-sector loans decreased for firms that borrow for working capital, indicating that the proportion of private-sector loans is increasing for both types of firms. These results imply that public-sector loans are not substituting for private-sector loans regardless of the purpose of public-sector loans.

To summarize all of the above findings, the most likely reason for the lack of evidence for the substitutive relationship between JFC loans and private sector loans is the firms' sizable demand for loans. Firms not only borrow from the JFC but also from private financial institutions to fulfill their demand for funds.

8.6 Summary

In this chapter we compare loan interest rates charged by the JFC-SME (formerly JASME) with loan interest rates charged by private financial institutions. We then examine the impact of the risk-adjusted interest rates scheme by the JFC on interest rates and lending by the JFC and private financial institutions.

Throughout the analysis period the interest rate on JFC-SME loans was lower, on average, than the private sector interest rate for the same firms. However, examining the impact of an exogenous change in the interest rate charged by the JFC-SME we find no evidence that private-sector loans to highly rated borrowers were replaced by loans from the JFC-SME. Under the low interest rate environment of recent years the firms' financing behavior may have been sensitive to a small difference in interest rates, which is the focus of the Regional Banks Association of Japan (2017). However, the results of this chapter suggest that there has been no hard evidence for the substitutive relationship between the JFC loans and the loans by the private sector.

Government-affiliated financial institutions, especially the JFC-SME, have promoted cooperation and collaboration with private financial institutions as discussed in Tanaka (2018). In particular, from FY2018 onward the JFC has begun to indirectly consult with firms' main bank about co-financing when borrowers have a need for funds, mainly for projects where the loan amount is expected to exceed a certain level.[17] The fact that the JFC's relatively lower loan interest rates to creditworthy borrowers have not been followed by lower private sector loan interest rates, and that the JFC lending has not substituted for private sector lending, may be due in part to this proactive effort on the part of government-affiliated institutions towards cooperation.

It is important to note that the fact that lending by private-sector financial institutions to highly rated firms has not been replaced by lending by government-affiliated institutions does not necessarily evidence for no pressure put on the private sector.

The conclusion as to whether or not a private sector squeeze is occurring depends on the analytical framework we set up. For example, if we start the discussion given the existence of the government financial institutions, like we did in this chapter, we find no evidence for the private sector profit squeeze. However, if one considers that private financial institutions would have benefited from all the lending without the existence of government-affiliated financial institutions in the first place then private-sector pressure does exist.

What this argument says is that as long as the scheme is designed to allow both the government and the private sector to lend to firms in the same lending market then private-sector financial institutions will surely increase their profits if all government-affiliated financial institutions exit the market, and the existence of government-affiliated financial institutions will always put pressure on the private sector. To eliminate this squeeze on the private sector it is necessary to redefine the division of roles between the private and government sectors by allowing, for example, the government sector to lend only to firms that have proven that they are unable to secure funds from private financial institutions.

In addition to the quantitative examination of whether or not firms substitute between the government and private sector lending, which we did in this chapter, there are several future research topics. These include: (1) a quantitative evaluation of the extent to which the government sector is able to bear risk when it engages in operations in areas where the private sector cannot lend; (2) a discussion of the types of lending the private and government sectors are good at; and (3) a discussion of the pros and cons of having the government and private sectors coordinate lending in the same market or lend in separate markets.[18]

[17] According to the JFC-SME there are a certain number of cases where the JFC is consulted by the main bank through the firms to which it lends.

[18] Studies outside of Japan have suggested two polar views: a view that co-financing discourages political intervention to public financial institutions (De Aghion, 1999) and a view that excessive use of co-financing reduces the screening incentives of financial institutions (Arping et al., 2010).

Chapter 9
Is it Possible to Finance SMEs without an Excessive Reliance on Personal Guarantees and Collateral?

Abstract As part of its intervention in SME finance the Japanese government has promoted SME lending that does not overly rely on collateral or personal guarantees. We examine the plausibility of such a policy action. In the early mid-2000s government-affiliated financial institutions introduced a scheme that let firms choose between unsecured and secured loans and between loans that did not require personal guarantees from management and loans that did require such guarantees. What have government-affiliated financial institutions learned? How effective has the scheme been? With regard to personal guarantees it was found that covenants (financial covenants included in a loan contract) may substitute for managerial discipline imposed by personal guarantees. With regard to unsecured lending, firms that previously would not have been able to borrow due to a lack of collateralizable assets increased their borrowing and investment. However, the ex-post performance of firms with collateralizable assets that chose to borrow without collateral deteriorated. When firms' moral hazard is the cause of poor performance a mechanism is needed to curb this behavior when providing unsecured loans.

Keywords Non-Guaranteed loans · Unsecured loans · Guidelines on Management Personal Guarantees · Covenants · Relationship banking

9.1 Introduction: The Government has Promoted Lending Independent of Collateral and Personal Guarantees

As discussed in Chapter 5, an important pillar of government intervention in SME finance is the development of institutions to realize specific policy objectives. One of these policy objectives has been the government's "promotion of lending that is not overly dependent on collateral and personal guarantees."

The government has long advocated "lending without an excessive reliance on personal guarantees and collateral" and in 2003, when the Financial Services Agency's Financial System Council made policy recommendations to strengthen relationship banking functions, it noted that "there is strong concern that the lending

I. Uesugi, *The Economics of SME Finance*, Advances in Japanese Business and Economics 36, https://doi.org/10.1007/978-981-96-3193-3_9

practices of small and regional financial institutions have focused on securing collateral and guarantees, leading to the in sufficient credit risk measurement and monitoring, and weak screening and monitoring capabilities" as well as that "the council hopes a further commitment by small and regional financial institutions to curb the excessive reliance on collateral and personal guarantees." In response to the recommendations the Action Program for Strengthening Relationship Banking released by the Financial Services Agency stated, "From the perspective of promoting loans that emphasize business cash flows and do not overly rely on collateral and guarantees, we request that each financial institution conducts thorough loan reviews and introduces financial covenants and credit scoring models. We also request that financial institutions avoid excessive use of third-party guarantees." The FSA's supervisory guidelines for major banks, as well as for small and regional financial institutions, also stipulate that the main focus of supervision should be the establishment of lending practices that, in principle, do not require guarantees from third parties other than CEOs of the company.

It is clear from the policy recommendations and directions that the policymakers' position was based on the understanding that the inclination toward real estate lending had led financial institutions to neglect screening and monitoring which in turn led to the creation and collapse of the bubble economy and the financial crisis that accompanied the subsequent increase in non-performing loans. The government wanted to reduce the use of collateral and personal guarantees in order to prevent the deterioration of the screening and monitoring capabilities of financial institutions. Additionally, based on the recent recognition that personal guarantees had become an obstacle to business successions, promoting loans without personal guarantees has been recognized as the measure for smooth business successions in the country.[1]

9.1.1 The Use of Third-Party Guarantees and Collateral has Declined Substantially

To what extent have these government policies been adopted by private financial institutions? The first change was in the practice of requiring third-party guarantees, either by unaffiliated family members or friends of the business owner, in addition to personal guarantees by the business owner himself/herself when taking out a loan. Essentially forcing third parties who were not directly involved in the business to become guarantors due to personal relationships was considered to be a major social problem and there were quite a number of cases where these people ended up bearing a heavy social and economic burden due to a subsequent deterioration in the borrower firm's business situation.

[1] The Strategy for Revitalizing Japan, formulated by the government on June 14, 2013, states that the government will reduce the burden of personal guarantees for business owners at the time of business succession through the formulation of guidelines and other measures to exempt personal guarantees.

Since FY 2006 the credit guarantee corporations have prohibited, in principle, the use of a third party other than the owner of the company as a guarantor for any project for which a guarantee application has been submitted. The FSA's supervisory guidelines also state that, in principle, third-party personal guarantees other than by the manager should not be taken. Perhaps reflecting the government's stance, the percentage of third-party personal guarantees has declined substantially.

The next change was in the provision of collateral, mainly real estate. The provision of collateral is not prohibited although the Financial Services Agency's supervisory guidelines for regional financial institutions indicate that excessive reliance on collateral should be eliminated. In recent years, however, competition in the corporate loan market has intensified and interest rate spreads have declined.[2] Cognizant of this increased level of competition in the loan market, private financial institutions might provide loans without collateral as one of the funding measures accompanied by favorable terms and conditions to borrower firms.[3]

In fact, if we look at the percentage of SMEs providing third-party guarantees and collateral to their main banks in the Basic Survey of SMEs we see that there has been a substantial decline beginning in the mid-2000s and continuing to the present period, as shown in Figure 9.1. The share of firms providing third-party guarantees among firms borrowing from their main bank has decreased from 18% in 2005 to 6% in 2019. The share of firms providing collateral slowly declined from over 50% in 2005 to around 40% in 2011, with the downward trend intensifying in the 2010s, while by 2019 it was less than 30%.

9.1.2 *Reliance on Personal Guarantees by the CEOs Themselves Remains High*

On the other hand, the most frequently requested guarantees by financial institutions are personal guarantees provided by the CEOs themselves, which has not decreased over time. Figure 9.1 shows that until recently more than 60% of firms provided personal guarantees when borrowing from their main banks.

This was identified as an obstacle to drastic business development and early rehabilitation efforts by SMEs, and in December 2013 the "Guidelines on Management Personal Guarantees" were published and became effective in February 2014. This set

---

[2] The gradual increase in concentration in Japan's regional loan market since the 2000s as well as the increase in competition and decline in price–cost margins will be discussed in Chapter 10.

[3] Honjo et al. (2019) find results somewhat consistent with this view using firm-level data from the Basic Survey of Small and Medium Enterprises. According to them the ratio of firms that pledge collateral to their main bank is high in Okinawa and Iwate and low in Tokyo and Miyagi. The concentration of the loan market, which will be presented in Chapter 10, shows that it is high in Okinawa and low in Tokyo. Taken together, these two results suggest that firms are more likely to be asked to provide collateral in regions where concentration is high and the degree of competition among financial institutions is moderate.

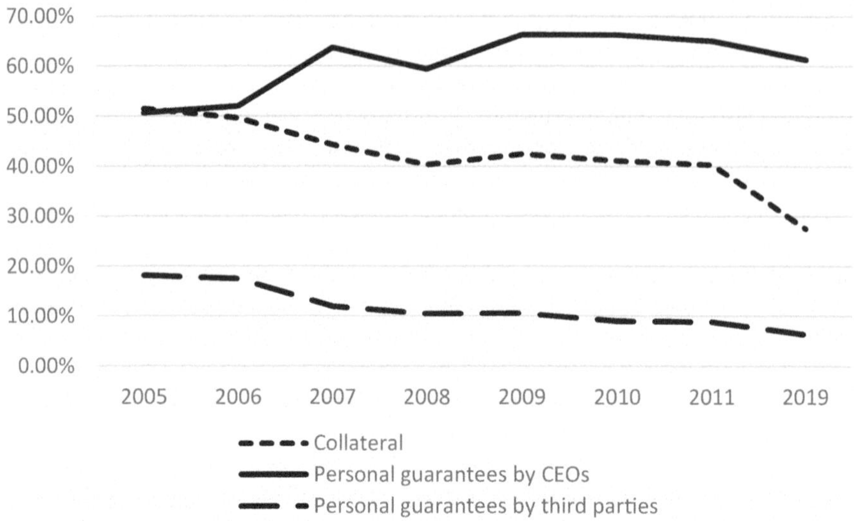

Fig. 9.1 Ratio of SMEs that pledge collateral and personal guarantees to their main banks (*Source* processed by the author based on SME agency "Basic Survey on SMEs") (*Note* Ratio is calculated as the number of firms that pledge collateral/personal guarantees to the total number of firms that obtain loans from their main banks)

voluntary rules for SMEs, CEOs, and financial institutions regarding personal guarantees and it was hoped that this would reduce the number of loans using guarantors to the satisfaction of all parties involved.

Personal guarantees by management are also seen as a disincentive to business succession in SMEs. Would-be successors of a business are reluctant to do so because they recognize the loss if the business they inherit fails and if they have already succeeded obligations for personal guarantees. Nevertheless, until recently there were many cases of pledging so-called double personal guarantees in which a guarantee contract with the new CEO was added without canceling the guarantee contract with the old CEO at the time of business succession.

In order to monitor the progress of the guidelines the FSA obtains reports from private financial institutions nationwide on the number of loans for which personal guarantees are not required and then compiles and publishes these reports on a regular basis. Figure 9.2 shows that the double personal guarantees, which were criticized as an obstacle to business succession, have rapidly been eliminated. On the other hand, the percentage of loans without personal guarantees has been increasing, although the increase has been gradual.[4]

[4] In the first half of FY2020 the ratio of loans without personal guarantees rose by about 5%. However, this increase may be temporary, reflecting the large-scale implementation of funding support measures with favorable terms for borrowers in response to the COVID-19 pandemic.

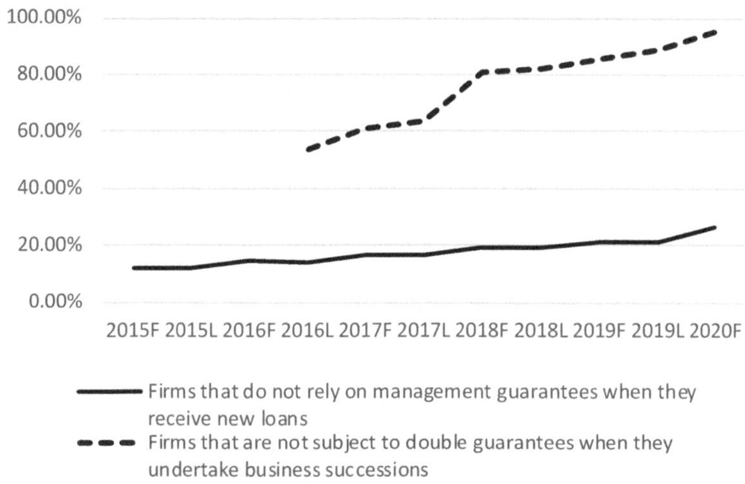

Fig. 9.2 Ratio of number of new loans by private financial institutions that do not require personal guarantees by CEOs (*Source* Processed by the author based on FSA "report on the progress in the use of the guidelines on management personal guarantees") (*Note* 2015F stands for the first half of FY2015 and 2015L stands for the second half of the same fiscal year)

9.2 JFC-SME Introduced Loans that do not Require Collateral or Personal Guarantees

9.2.1 Unsecured Loans

From the mid-2000s to the current period the ratio of loans with collateral or third-party guarantees has declined significantly, although the ratio of loans with personal guarantees by the business managers themselves has remained high. Against this backdrop the JFC-SME (JASME prior to October 2008) has attempted, since the mid-2000s, to make its own loans unsecured and without personal guarantees in order to achieve the government's stated goal.

First, unsecured loans were gradually introduced beginning in FY2005. Initially, the JFC set the interest rate on these loans equal to the secured loan rate plus an extra add-on rate based on the credit risk of the firm and the term of the loan.[5] At this stage

[5] From FY2005 to August 2008 there were two special loan programs that require limited or no collateral: the "unsecured special program" under which the full amount of the loan is unsecured and the "partially unsecured special program" under which a portion of the loan is unsecured. The former is a special program that allows the JFC to provide unsecured loans of up to ¥50 million per borrower who have entered into covenants that include financial covenants deemed appropriate by JFC and whose credit risk is relatively small in light of their financial conditions. Financial covenants were required only up to August 2008. For the unsecured portion of the loan amount a surcharge was added to the interest rate set under each special loan program depending on the credit risk of the borrower and the duration of the loan. Under the "partially unsecured program" it was

there were stricter limits on the amount that could be borrowed on an unsecured basis than on the amount to be borrowed on a secured basis.

A major milestone in the unsecured lending scheme occurred in August 2008 when the JFC raised the maximum amount of unsecured loans available for a firm to the same level as that of secured loans. Since then the use of unsecured loans has increased markedly.[6] In FY2007, before the scheme was changed, unsecured loans (unsecured special program) and partially unsecured loans (partially-unsecured special program) amounted to ¥61.6 billion (6.5% of total JFC-SME loans) and ¥132.3 billion (14.0%), respectively. After August in FY2008, unsecured loans alone amounted to ¥260.9 billion (25.7%). In FY2009, the total amount of unsecured loans soared to 1026.6 billion yen (32.0%), and in FY2011 it was 938.9 billion yen (45.9%), close to half of total JFC-SME lending.

An important aspect of the JFC's provision of unsecured loans is that firms have a choice between loan contracts that are unsecured but have higher interest rates and those that are secured with lower interest rates. Of course, the JFC-SME screens loan applicants. However, the credit review does not depend on a firm's choice between unsecured and secured loans nor does the JFC recommend secured loans to individual firms based on their credit risk.

9.2.2 Non-Guaranteed Loans

Next we discuss loans provided by JFC-SME that do not require a personal guarantee by management (hereafter referred to as "non-guaranteed loans").[7] Table 9.1 provides an overview of non-guaranteed loans and related programs. The JFC introduced a scheme for non-guaranteed loans in 2004.

This is a non-guaranteed loan contract that is designed for firms with trustworthy CEOs and exempts firms from pledging personal guarantees. Instead, the contract includes a covenant which the JFC deems appropriate, such as the maintenance of positive net worth and prohibition of loans, investments, and guarantees to third parties, and requires an add-on interest rate of 0.3%. Another scheme of guarantor deferral program was also introduced in FY2007 under which loans are made on a non-guaranteed basis, but if the covenants are violated the loan requires personal guarantees to be pledged. Under the program the borrower firm will not incur a guarantee obligation as long as the firm complies with covenant conditions and the add-on interest rate is 0.1%.

---

possible to waive the requirement for collateral up to 75% of the loan amount and up to 80 million yen per loan program. Again, for the portion of the amount exempted from collateral requirements, a surcharge was added to the interest rate based on the credit risk of the borrower and the duration of the loan set by each special loan program.

[6] In October 2008 the JASME became JFC and the unsecured special loan program was taken over by the JFC-SME without change.

[7] Within the JFC-SME non-guaranteed loans are referred to as "guarantor waiver special program.".

Table 9.1 Details of the non-guaranteed loans and deferred guarantor loans by the JFC

	(1)Non-guaranteed loans (former)	(2)Non-guaranteed loans (new)	(3)Guarantor deferral special program (former)	(4)Guarantor deferral special program (new)
	FY2004-January 2014	February 2014-March 2016	FY2007-January 2014	February 2014-March 2016
Eligible Lending Programs	Only for startup development program in FY2004; all direct loans since FY2005	All direct loans	Only for startup development program in FY2007; all direct loans since FY2008	All direct loans
Additional interest rate at time of loan provision	0.3% for all firms	0.0%-0.4% depending on internal rating and collateral	0.1% for all firms	0.0%-0.1% depending on internal rating and collateral
Details of financial covenants (mandatory covenants; optional covenants can be set separately)	Maintenance of net worth, and prohibition of loans, investments, and guarantees to third parties	Prohibition of negative current profit before depreciation for two consecutive years; prohibition of negative net worth	Quarterly business reports; representations and warranties; acceptance of guidance from JFC for management improvement during business distress; restrictions on total compensation amount for directors; restrictions on total dividend amount to shareholders; and prohibition of loans, investments, and guarantees to third parties	Quarterly business reports; representations and warranties; acceptance of guidance from JFC for management improvement during business distress; restrictions on total compensation amount for directors*; restrictions on total dividend amount to shareholders*
Monitoring Frequencies	Annually	Annually	Quarterly	Quarterly

(continued)

Table 9.1 (continued)

	(1)Non-guaranteed loans (former)	(2)Non-guaranteed loans (new)	(3)Guarantor deferral special program (former)	(4)Guarantor deferral special program (new)
Measures to be taken in the event of violation of financial covenants	Call for early redemption	After violation, 0.3% added interest rate until the final due date	Conversion to guaranteed loans and call for early redemption	Conversion to guaranteed loans
Deferral of penalties when covenants are violated (limited to unavoidable cases)	Both mandatory and optional measures can be deferred	Only voluntary measures can be deferred	Both mandatory and optional measures can be deferred	Optional measures can be deferred. Mandatory measures marked by * can be deferred

Source Created by the author based on the information provided by the JFC-SME

The terms and conditions for non-guaranteed loans were drastically changed in February 2014 when the Guidelines for Management Personal Guarantees came into effect. The most significant change was to the interest rate added to non-guaranteed loans. Before the change this add-on interest rate was 0.3% and fixed but after the change it varied depending on the JFC's internal credit rating and other factors. The intention was to make the loans more attractive by lowering the interest rate for high quality borrowers. The terms and conditions for the guarantor deferral program were also changed in February 2014.

Another change to the scheme was implemented in April 2016. After the change firms, other than those that were in deficit for two consecutive years and in negative net worth, could obtain a non-guaranteed loan with no covenants or interest rate surcharges. This was a major change to the framework, from one that allowed firms to choose whether or not to provide personal guarantees to one that did not require personal guarantees at all.[8]

The use of non-guaranteed loans increased moderately through FY2013, but then surged in FY2014, from 96.2 billion yen (4.5% of total JFC-SME loans) and 147.2 billion yen (8.1%) in FY2012 and FY2013, respectively, to 635.6 billion yen (36.5%) in FY2014, more than one-third of total JFC-SME lending.[9] One of the reasons for this is that, in addition to increased public awareness following the establishment

[8] With this institutional change more than 95% of the JFC-SME's new loans are now made without guarantees. This is a major institutional change in and of itself and should be studied further but no analysis has yet been conducted by researchers.

[9] In contrast, the guarantor deferral special program only accounted for 0.1% of total loans in each year and the effect of the scheme change was primarily seen in the increase in the use of non-guaranteed loans.

and application of the Guidelines on Management Personal Guarantees, the additional interest rate burden for using non-guaranteed loans for highly rated firms was lowered. It is believed that many firms that had previously felt that the benefits of using non-guaranteed loans were small relative to the costs now chose non-guaranteed loans due to the smaller additional interest rate burden after the change in the scheme.

An important aspect of the JFC's provision of non-guaranteed loans is that, as in the case of unsecured loans, firms are allowed to choose between non-guaranteed and guaranteed loans from a set of multiple loan terms. In other words, firms that are approved for a JFC loan can choose between a loan contract that is non-guaranteed but has a high interest rate with covenants and a contract that is guaranteed with a low interest rate and no covenants.

The difference from unsecured loans is that covenants are part of the non-guaranteed loan contract. Since penalties such as the withdrawal of loans or higher interest rates may be imposed on firms that fail to comply with covenants, covenants are expected to serve the same function personal guarantees have served in imposing discipline on managerial behavior. In particular, since the change in the scheme in 2014 firms with high internal ratings are no longer subject to higher interest rates even on non-guaranteed loans, meaning these firms will have to choose between non-guaranteed loans with covenants and guaranteed loans without covenants. It is worth examining the extent to which the inclusion of covenants affects firm choice.

9.3 Overview of Results

The use of unsecured and non-guaranteed loans by the JFC-SME increased dramatically around FY2008 and FY2014. This chapter uses data which covers this particular period to examine the determinants of the use of unsecured and non-guaranteed loans and the ex-post effects on firm activity and performance. In this way we analyze what happens when loans are made without requiring collateral or personal guarantees. The findings are useful not only for government-affiliated financial institutions but also for private-sector financial institutions when they consider how to handle personal guarantees and collateral. The key results of the analysis are as follows.

The effect of unsecured lending differs depending on the extent of tangible fixed asset holdings that could serve as collateral. First, firms that had been unable to borrow from the JFC due to a lack of tangible fixed assets were able to obtain JFC loans. These firms not only increased their borrowing but also their investment and sales, indicating that the use of unsecured loans had a positive effect. However, their financial soundness deteriorated, perhaps because of the expansion of their balance sheets as a result of the increased borrowing.

Firms that had collateralizable assets had been able to previously obtain secured loans, so there was no immediate increase in their lending, investment, or sales. Rather, given the option of a secured, low interest rate or an unsecured, high interest rate, there was a clear tendency for firms with higher ex-post credit risk to opt for the unsecured, higher interest rate loan. We do not know whether the ex-post increase in the credit risk of firms that used unsecured loans was due to the fact that their original high risk only became apparent after time had passed (asymmetric information about the firm's ex-ante attributes) or because the unsecured loan resulted in a moral hazard among the firm's managers and worsened their performance (ex-post change in behavior). If it is the former we cannot say that there was a negative impact of the introduction of the scheme since the introduction of unsecured lending did not change the behavior of firms. If it is the latter it is necessary to take measures to curb the moral hazard of firms using unsecured loans.

In the case of non-guaranteed loans, contrary to our prior expectation that firms with higher credit risk would choose non-guaranteed loans even at higher interest rates, lower risk firms with good internal ratings were more likely to choose non-guaranteed loans. Even though the 2014 scheme change eliminated the interest rate differential between non-guaranteed loans with covenants and guaranteed loans without covenants for highly rated firms, the tendency for firms with lower credit risk to choose non-guaranteed loans was unchanged. Allowing firms to choose between the two types of contracts does not result in managers choosing non-guaranteed loans in order to avoid repayment responsibilities in the event of a firm's default. Rather managers who are confident that they can adhere to their loan covenants such as not becoming insolvent choose non-guaranteed loans. There is still much to learn about why firms with high credit risk would choose a covenant-free loan contract at the risk of being required to fulfill a personal guarantee in the event of default. However, the results indicate the possibility that the disciplining function of personal guarantees on corporate management can be substituted by the content of the loan contract which includes covenants.

In summary, the following points can be made about the possibility of SME financing that does not rely on personal guarantees or collateral. While the introduction of unsecured lending has the effect of expanding the financing possibilities for firms that do not have collateral assets it is necessary to address moral hazard among firms that have switched to unsecured lending from secured lending. With regard to the introduction of non-guaranteed loans, if SMEs are of a size that allows financial institutions to monitor the status of covenant adherence because management and the enterprise are separated to some extent it may be possible to replace the disciplining function of a personal guarantee with other measures such as covenants.

The remainder of this chapter proceeds as follows. Section 9.4 discusses the existing literature, both theoretical and empirical, on the role played by collateral and personal guarantees in the lending market. Sections 9.5 and 9.6 present the results of our examination of the determinants and effects of unsecured and non-guaranteed lending. Sections 9.7 and 9.8 interpret the results and summarize the key findings.

9.4 Theoretical Underpinnings and Empirical Findings on the Role of Collateral and Personal Guarantees

Borrowers, firms and their managers, would prefer to avoid providing collateral or personal guarantees because providing either would result in greater losses in the event that the firm defaults on the loan. The government believes that prospective managers who think they have to provide personal guarantees would be hesitant to take over the business or be less willing to take risks due to the size of the loss in the event the business fails. Therefore, the government thinks that the practice of requiring personal guarantees should be stopped.

On the flip side, if financial institutions do not participate in the loan market firms will not be able to raise funds. In particular, under an information asymmetry between borrowers and lenders it is difficult for financial institutions to lend because they do not have the accurate information on borrowers' credit risk. Collateral and personal guarantees are important lending conditions that alleviate the problems associated with such an asymmetry and allow financial institutions to supply funds more actively. Below we summarize the role of collateral and personal guarantees from this perspective.

9.4.1 Collateral and Personal Guarantees Have the Effect of Facilitating Firm Financing

In cases where there is asymmetric information between borrower firms and lender financial institutions, and financial institutions are unwilling to provide sufficient funds to firms, collateral and personal guarantees can alleviate information problems and encourage financial institutions to lend to firms.

First, collateral and personal guarantees have the effect of imposing discipline on managers of borrowing firms and curbing moral hazards.[10] When managers pledge their own assets either as collateral or in the form of personal guarantees they will lose their own assets should the firm go bankrupt. Managers who expect the costs of default to be high are more likely to exert managerial effort and refrain from risky investments in order to avoid default. When such discipline is functioning financial institutions are more likely to lend to firms. Conversely, if personal guarantees and collateral are no longer required the moral hazard of managers will worsen, firm defaults will increase, and financial institutions will be unwilling to lend.

Using data on Japanese SMEs, Ono et al. (2012) found that the profitability of firms that actually began to provide new collateral to their main banks improved, and that this improvement was achieved mainly through cost savings. This is consistent

[10] One theoretical model is Boot et al. (1991). In their model, collateral, like personal guarantees, has the function of curbing managerial moral hazard. However, that is the case when the asset being offered is owned by the individual manager rather than the firm: in other words, when the collateral is external rather than internal to the firm.

with the view that collateral curbs moral hazards. However, no clear improvement in profitability is found in the case of personal guarantees.

There is a viewpoint that, in the presence of asymmetric information regarding the quality of borrower firms, collateral and personal guarantees actually encourage high-quality firms to participate in the market.[11] The argument is that by providing collateral or personal guarantees themselves firms can signal to financial institutions that they are of high quality with a low probability of default, thereby encouraging financial institutions to supply funds. Conversely, if personal guarantees and collateral are uniformly eliminated an adverse selection problem arises where only low quality firms participate in the market and financial institutions are unwilling to lend.

Collateral and personal guarantees are necessary not only to prevent moral hazard and adverse selection but also to make it easier for financial institutions to protect their own loan assets and increase expected profits to lend. With collateral and personal guarantees financial institutions can minimize their losses by selling the assets pledged as collateral or demanding personal guarantees to be executed, in case of borrower firms defaulting. If financial institutions know that they can minimize their losses they can lend aggressively. On the other hand, if the lender expects to incur large losses in the event of default due to the lack of collateral or personal guarantees some financial institutions may hesitate to lend to the borrower.

9.4.2 Collateral and Personal Guarantees do not Necessarily Inhibit Monitoring and Relationships

Collateral and personal guarantees not only affect the lending capacity of financial institutions but also the relationship between financial institutions and firms. In terms of their impact on the screening and monitoring of firms by financial institutions and on the relationship between firms and financial institutions there are two views: one is that they are substitutive and the other is that they are complementary.

The substitutive view is based on the argument that requiring collateral or personal guarantees reduces the potential losses to the financial institution in the event of default, thereby lessening the incentive for screening and monitoring. The view also refers to the argument that a closer firm-bank relationship decreases the extent of information asymmetry which reduces the need for collateral or personal guarantees to be pledged to enhance the banks' willingness to supply credit. In other words, once close relationships are established there is no need for collateral and personal guarantees.[12]

The complementary view is based on several ideas. First, if the value of an asset depends on the degree of monitoring (e.g., accounts receivable) creditors

[11] Theoretical models include Bester (1985) and Besanko and Thakor (1987).

[12] See Manove et al. (2001) for a theoretical study dealing with the relationship between collateral and personal guarantees and incentives for screening and monitoring, and Boot and Thakor (1994) for a study of the relationship between collateral and personal guarantees and relationships.

should monitor the firms, especially the firms' assets that are pledged as collateral. Second, there exists a complementarity if collateral is provided as compensation for information-producing financial institutions in the presence of multiple creditors. Third, as relationships with financial institutions deepen firms are forced to accept tougher borrowing terms such as pledging collateral and personal guarantees because the relationship is irreplaceable for the firms.[13]

Ono and Uesugi (2009) find that firms that provide collateral are more frequently monitored by financial institutions in the sense that they must submit documents to financial institutions more frequently. They also find that the firms that pledge collateral tend to record longer years of transactions with their main banks..

Based on the above theoretical frameworks and the results of previous empirical studies there is a good reason for banks to require firms to pledge collateral and personal guarantees such as prevention of moral hazards and adverse selection in the loan market. Thus, simply increasing unsecured and non-guaranteed lending may cause adverse effects such as increased moral hazard and increased losses for financial institutions. Is it possible to overcome these adverse effects? What measures should be taken to achieve this?

Therefore, in Section 9.5 and the remainder of this chapter we will identify what insights can be gained from the experience of the JFC-SME in their large scale implementation of unsecured and non-guaranteed lending.

9.5 Analysis of the Effects of Unsecured Loans

In this section we identify the attributes of firms that have chosen to borrow on an unsecured basis from the JFC and analyze the consequences of unsecured borrowing. The effect of using unsecured loans differs between firms that do not have sufficient collateralizable assets and would not, previously, have been able to borrow from financial institutions including the JFC and firms that have sufficient collateral assets and are able to choose between unsecured and secured lending.

9.5.1 Analytical Framework: Number of JFC User Firms Before and After the Introduction of Unsecured Loans and the Attributes of These Firms

Prior to the introduction of unsecured lending firms that did not have sufficient collateral assets were either unable to enter into secured loan contracts or, even if they could, faced financial constraints which limited the amount they could borrow. The belief is that the introduction of unsecured lending eased these financial constraints.

[13] Studies that provide a theoretical background for each include Rajan and Winton (1995), Longhofer and Santos (2000), and Sharpe (1990).

This is because the change in the scheme now makes it possible for a bank to take out an unsecured loan or to borrow up to a required amount by entering into an unsecured loan agreement in addition to its existing secured loans.

We specify the following hypotheses for firms that lack collateral assets.

> **Hypothesis 1:** With the introduction of unsecured lending firms that could not previously enter into secured loan contracts with the JFC will begin borrowing from the JFC.

Hypothesis 1 will be tested by determining whether firms that did not possess sufficient collateral assets and were previously unable to obtain the necessary funds from the JFC began borrowing from the JFC as a result of the introduction of unsecured lending. Specifically, we first analyze aggregate statistics on how the number and the attributes of firms using JFC loans changed before and after 2008, when unsecured lending was introduced. Hypothesis 1 predicts that the number of firms borrowing from the JFC will increase as firms that did not previously have a secured loan contract with the JFC enter into a new unsecured loan contract. Next, we use a probit model to estimate whether the introduction of the new scheme has led more firms to obtain unsecured loans than those that would likely not have been able to obtain loans under the secured loan scheme. Hypothesis 1 predicts that firms with lower tangible fixed asset ratios will use unsecured lending more. The estimation equation is presented in Eq. (9.1):

$$\Pr(\text{NonCollateral}_{it} = 1) = \Phi\begin{pmatrix} \beta_0 + \beta_1 FIRM_{\text{it}} + \beta_2 CREDIT_{it} \\ +\beta_3 REGION_{it} + \beta_4 INDUSTRY_{it} \end{pmatrix} \tag{9.1}$$

NonCollateral is a dummy variable that takes the value of 1 if the firm received an unsecured loan from the JFC and 0 otherwise. Pr(·) denotes the probability that the event in parentheses occurs, where the probability that NonCollateral is 1 is represented by Φ and the cumulative density function of the normal distribution takes a value between 0 and 1 depending on the linear combination of the coefficients and explanatory variables.

FIRM is a set of variables indicating observable firm attributes such as profit margin and firm size, *CREDIT* is a variable indicating the JFC's internal credit rating of the firm, *REGION* is a variable indicating the region where the firm's headquarters is located, and *INDUSTRY* is a variable indicating the industry to which the firm belongs. These explanatory variables are contemporaneous with the use of unsecured loans in period *t*, based on data availability.[14]

---

[14] The use of explanatory variables for period t rather than period t-1 reflects the fact that the JFC-SME, in principle, obtains and examines the most recent three fiscal years' financial statement information for firms with which they enter into new transactions. But for internal rating variables information from the period (t-1) prior to the transaction start date (t) is often unavailable.

9.5.2 Analytical Framework: Ex-Post Performance of Firms Using Unsecured Loans

It should be noted that for firms with sufficient collateral assets the introduction of unsecured lending enables them to choose between secured and low interest rate contracts and unsecured and high interest rate loan contracts. We would predict that profit maximizing firms that are less likely to repay their loans and thus more likely to foreclose on the pledged collateral will choose unsecured, higher interest rate loans while firms that are more likely to repay their loans will choose secured and lower interest rate loans. This is a situation of a separating equilibrium between secured, low interest rate loans and unsecured, high interest rate loans depending on the type of borrower, as shown by Bester (1985). In this case, even after controlling for the credit risk observable from the JFC the credit risk of firms choosing to use unsecured loans should exceed that of firms using secured loans. In addition, firms that use unsecured loans are expected to experience a greater deterioration in the ex-post performance, including an increased probability of financial distress, relative to firms that use secured loans.

Boot et al. (1991) theoretically show that the level of firms' managerial effort differs depending on the provision of collateral. In other words, the borrower firms' ex-post managerial effort is lower when collateral is not used. When such moral hazard occurs the ex-post performance of firms receiving unsecured loans is expected to be worse than that of firms using secured loans regardless of the level of collateral assets held ex ante.

In summary, as shown in Hypothesis 2 below, the introduction of unsecured lending is expected to worsen the ex-post performance of firms using unsecured loans as their credit risk exceeds that of firms using secured loans due to firms' self-selection and moral hazard.[15]

Hypothesis 2: The ex-post performance of firms using unsecured loans will be worse than that of firms using secured loans.

We will use the same framework as in Chapters 6 and 7 to test Hypothesis 2, which is to estimate the treatment effect by the propensity score matching. Specifically, the change in firm performance indicators from the time of the loan provision to one and two years after are calculated for firms that use unsecured loans (treatment group firms) and firms that use secured loans and whose propensity score is close to that of the treatment group firms (control group firms). We then calculate the difference between the two and use this to estimate the effect of the treatment of using unsecured loans.

[15] It is difficult to distinguish whether the deterioration in performance among firms using unsecured lending is the result of original firm attributes that surface later or whether it is the result of an ex-post moral hazard among firms due to the lack of collateral. A study that attempts to distinguish between the two is Uchida et al. (2017).

Using the probit model of the Eq. (9.1) as the qualitative selection model the probability (propensity score) of each firm becoming an unsecured borrower is calculated. We select unsecured borrower firms and secured borrower firms with similar propensity scores to unsecured borrowers as the treatment and the control group firms, respectively. We then estimate the treatment effect as shown in Eq. (9.2):

$$\theta_{ATT}^{j} = \mathrm{E}\left(\Delta^{j} Y_{T=1} | p(X), T = 1\right) - E_{p(X)|T=1}\left[\mathrm{E}\left(\Delta^{j} Y_{T=0} | p(X), T = 0\right)\right] \quad (9.2)$$

θ_{ATT}^{j} is the average treatment effect on the change in performance from period t to period t + j (j= 1,2). T (= 0,1) is the abbreviated notation for the treatment variable in Eq. (9.1), indicating the presence of unsecured loans from the JFC. Δ^{j} Y is the change in the firm's performance variable from period t to period t + j. p(X) represents the propensity score obtained from the estimation of Eq. (9.1). E is the expected value and is represented by the sample mean.

Two types of ex-post performance measures (Y) are used to examine treatment effects. First, we use firms' borrowing ratios, interest rates, capital expenditures, and sales to focus on the improvement in the credit availability and the firm behavior after JFC borrowing. By using these variables we can determine whether the JFC's unsecured loans ease the financial constraints faced by firms and whether capital investment and sales increase as a result. Second, we use profit margins and the likelihood of financial distress to assess firm performance. Hypothesis 2 predicts that the sign of the treatment effect should be negative for profit margin and positive for the probability of financial distress.

9.5.3 Results: Number of JFC User Firms Before and After the Introduction of Unsecured Loans and the Attributes of These Firms

To test Hypothesis 1 Table 9.2 shows how the number and attributes of firms using JFC changed before and after 2008 when unsecured loans were introduced. This table displays the average tangible fixed asset ratio (first row) and the number of firms (second row) for each year, separately for firms using secured and unsecured loans.

The number of firms with which the JFC concluded loan contracts increased in FY2009 more than in FY2008, when unsecured lending was introduced. In particular, the majority of the increase is attributed to the increase in unsecured loan users. The increase was more salient in FY2009 than in FY2008 due to several reasons: the cap on unsecured loans was lifted in August FY2008 instead of April at the beginning of the fiscal year; it took some time for firms to be informed of the existence of the new scheme, and there was a surge in the precautionary demand for such types of financing due to the Global Financial Crisis. However, even after FY2010, when the severe recession had receded, more firms signed loan contracts with the JFC than had prior to

Table 9.2 Number of JFC's secured and unsecured loan user firms and their fixed tangible asset ratio

FY	(a) Secured loans	(b) Unsecured loans	Total	Difference((a)-(b))	t-value
2007	0.575		0.575	–	
	7762		7762		
2008	0.577	0.515	0.556	0.062***	15.4
	8039	4172	12211		
2009	0.590	0.509	0.545	0.081***	26.4
	8814	11036	19850		
2010	0.584	0.510	0.540	0.075***	22.8
	7466	10865	18331		
2011	0.581	0.498	0.525	0.084***	23.2
	5668	11483	17151		

Source Processed by the author based on Table 4 of Uesugi et al. (2015a)
Note For FY2007 and FY2008 we exclude firms that obtained unsecured loans with smaller upper limit or partially unsecured loans from the statistics. ***, **, and * represent statistical significance at the 1%, 5%, and 10%, respectively

FY2007, especially for unsecured loans, indicating that the introduction of unsecured loans had a positive effect on increasing the number of lending relationships between the JFC and firms, even excluding the effect of the Global Financial Crisis.

The ratio of tangible fixed assets has been on a downward trend since the introduction of unsecured lending in FY2008. When we consider unsecured borrowers and secured borrowers separately, the tangible fixed asset ratio for the former is not only low but has been declining since FY2008, as has the ratio for all borrowers.

To provide an additional test of Hypothesis 1 Table 9.3 presents the results of the estimation of the determinants of firms' use of unsecured loans using a probit model. The results show marginal effects for each explanatory variable for firms using unsecured loans in FY2009.[16] For internal ratings the probability of choosing unsecured lending is significantly larger for high-risk firms than for low-risk firms and the probability increases as the risk increases to a certain extent. The estimates for the dummy variables for the length of the relationship with the JFC (baseline is for relationship years between one and six) are also significant. The marginal effect for the dummy for new transactions with the JFC is positive while that for long-term relationships with the JFC is negative, indicating that firms that did not previously have a relationship with the JFC are more likely to choose unsecured loans. As for the other firm attributes, leverage ratio, sales, ROA, and the number of financial institutions all have positive and significant marginal effects, while the tangible fixed asset ratio and firm age both have negative and significant effects.

[16] Although the probit model estimation was conducted for FY2008, when the scheme was introduced, we present the results only for FY2009, the year following the introduction, because the full-scale introduction of unsecured lending started in the middle of FY2008 and the results obtained for FY2009 are likely to apply to other years.

Table 9.3 Estimation results for the determinants of unsecured loans

	FY2009
Estimation method: Probit model	Dependent variable: Dummy for the use of unsecured loans
Explanatory variables	Marginal effects
Internal rating 2	0.278***
3	0.437***
4	0.464***
5	0.373***
6	0.474***
7	0.334***
8	0.727**
9	0.881***
Leverage ratio	0.990***
ln(Sales)	0.174***
ROA	0.484**
Fixed tangible asset ratio	−0.911***
Firm age	−0.005***
ln(number of banks)	0.239***
Dummy for number of relationship years (new)	0.776***
Dummy for number of relationship years (7 years or more)	−0.234***
Constant	−1.292***
Industry dummies	Yes
Regional dummies	Yes
Number of observations	13,322
Pseudo R-squared	0.137

Source Processed by the author based on Table 5 (1) of Uesugi et al. (2015a)
Note ***, **, and * represent statistical significance at 1%, 5%, and 10%, respectively. Results for some of the explanatory variables are omitted

In summary, the results of the analysis indicate that firms using unsecured loans had lower tangible fixed asset holdings and higher credit risk than firms using secured loans. They also show that by introducing the unsecured lending scheme the JFC eased credit constraints for a group of new borrower firms that did not have sufficient collateral assets and increased the number of borrowers.

9.5.4 Results: Ex-Post Performance of Firms Using Unsecured Loans

To test Hypothesis 2 a propensity score is calculated using the coefficients estimated by the probit model. The treatment effect is then estimated after selecting the treatment and control group firms. The results are in Table 9.4 which uses the sample of firms using unsecured/secured loans in FY2009. There are three notable results. First, among the loan availability variables we find a positive and significant effect for the leverage ratio. In other words, two years after the use of JFC loans the change in the leverage ratio is larger for firms using unsecured loans than for firms using secured loans by +0.8 to +0.7 percentage points. On the other hand, no significant treatment effect is observed for the interest rate paid.

Second, for the firm's investment ratio the effect is significantly negative after one year but then changes to positive and significant in the next year. Third, for the

Table 9.4 Estimation results for the treatment effect of unsecured loans

		FY2009		
		Treatment	Control	DID
Leverage ratio	t + 1	0.002	−0.006	0.008***
	t + 2	−0.002	−0.008	0.007**
Interest rate	t + 1	0.000	0.000	0.000
	t + 2	−0.002	−0.002	0.000
Capital investment ratio	t + 1	−0.015	0.012	−0.027***
	t + 2	−0.022	−0.035	0.013*
ln(Sales)	t + 1	0.006	−0.008	0.014**
	t + 2	0.023	0.008	0.015**
ROA	t + 1	0.009	0.011	−0.001
	t + 2	0.012	0.012	0.001
Internal rating	t + 1	0.165	0.039	0.126***
	t + 2	0.236	0.046	0.190***
Dummy for negative operating profits	t + 1	−0.075	−0.069	−0.006
	t + 2	−0.088	−0.087	−0.001
Dummy for negative net worth	t + 1	0.019	0.003	0.016***
	t + 2	0.029	0.010	0.019***
Dummy for possible bankruptcy or lower	t + 1	0.027	0.016	0.010***
	t + 2	0.061	0.042	0.019***

Source Processed by the author based on Table 6 (1) of Uesugi et al. (2015a)
Note ***, **, and * represent statistical significance at 1%, 5%, and 10%, respectively

variables on firm performance such as sales, profitability, and the internal ratings we observe a positive and significant effect on sales. However, the increase in internal ratings is larger for unsecured loan users than for secured loan users, implying that the JFC considers that the credit risk of unsecured loan users has increased. We observe deterioration in the performance of firms using unsecured loans also in the variables related to financial distress such as the negative new worth dummy and the dummy for firms in possible bankruptcy. That is, for unsecured borrowers the increase in the probability of insolvency or bankruptcy is larger than for secured borrowers two years after the use of the loan.[17]

9.5.5 Results: Analysis for Firms with Sufficient Collateralizable Assets

Thus far, in the estimations of the treatment effect to test Hypothesis 2 treatment group firms using unsecured loans were compared with control group firms only using secured loans whose propensity scores were close to the treatment group firms. However, the treatment group includes firms that could only choose unsecured loans because they do not have collateralizable assets. Firms without collateral assets are more likely to have faced a credit constraint and the improvement in their ex-post performance is expected to be larger than firms with collateralizable assets. There may be differences among treatment group firms regarding the amount of assets that can be used as collateral which cannot be controlled for by observable variables. In this case the treatment effect may be overestimated due to the increase in borrowing by the treatment group firms that had no collateralizable assets and no excess debt capacity.

To address this issue we limit the analysis to firms that have excess collateralizable assets and are eligible for both unsecured and secured loan contracts. The JFC examines the amount of assets held by a firm that are not subject to first liens for other lenders when it approves for loans to the firm. Using this information we can obtain a more accurate estimation of the treatment effect limiting our analysis to firms whose collateralizable assets exceed the planned loan amount. However, since this information is only available from FY2011 onward this is the starting point of our sample, unlike the previous section where the sample began in FY2009.

The results are presented in Table 9.5. The results differ considerably from the results for the entire sample of firms. For the entire sample we obtain a positive and significant effect on the leverage ratio in the third year after the use of unsecured loans. In contrast, the effect is insignificant when the sample is limited to firms with excess collateral capacity.

---

[17] Uesugi et al. (2016) also report the results of estimating the treatment effect when dividing the sample according to the number of years firms have transacted with the JFC-SME. This additional test shows that the ex-post deterioration in performance due to unsecured loans is larger for firms that are new to the JFC and have a significant degree of asymmetric information.

Table 9.5 Estimation results for the treatment effect of unsecured loans considering capacity for pledging collateral

		FY2011	FY2011
		Entire sample	Firms with excess collateral capacity
		DID	DID
Leverage ratio	t + 1	−0.001	0.001
	t + 2	−0.004*	−0.002
	t + 3	0.006*	0.001
Interest rate	t + 1	0.000	0.000
	t + 2	0.000	0.000
	t + 3	0.000	0.000
Capital investment ratio	t + 1	0.000	0.012
	t + 2	0.023***	0.003
	t + 3	0.020**	0.003
ln(Sales)	t + 1	0.010***	0.006
	t + 2	0.010**	0.006
	t + 3	−0.005	−0.010
ROA	t + 1	0.002**	0.001
	t + 2	0.002	0.001
	t + 3	0.001	0.000
Internal rating	t + 1	0.062*	0.112***
	t + 2	−0.015	0.085*
	t + 3	0.069	0.140*
Dummy for negative operating profits	t + 1	−0.005	0.012
	t + 2	−0.002	0.003
	t + 3	0.001	0.008
Dummy for negative net worth	t + 1	0.000	0.002
	t + 2	−0.004	0.004
	t + 3	0.022***	0.015*
Dummy for possible bankruptcy or lower	t + 1	0.004	0.005
	t + 2	−0.010**	−0.002
	t + 3	0.000	0.011

Source Processed by the author based on Tables 7 and 8 of Uesugi et al. (2016)
Note ***, **, and * represent statistical significance at 1%, 5%, and 10%, respectively

For the firms' investment ratio and sales amount the overall estimates often yield positive and significant effects, with investment and sales increasing with the use of unsecured loans. However, the effect is again insignificant with the restricted sample.

Looking at internal ratings the deterioration in the ratings for firms using unsecured loans is significant throughout the sample period in the restricted sample, which is similar to the overall estimates. However, the probability of financial distress shows mostly no significant treatment effects for the restricted sample.

When we narrow the focus of analysis to firms that have the collateral capacity to meet their borrowing needs and have the ability to choose between secured and unsecured lending, the previously obtained statistically significant positive treatment effects on the leverage ratio, investment ratio, and sales disappear while the negative treatment effect on internal ratings remains unchanged. Firms with excess collateralizable assets have not faced credit constraints in the past and the introduction of unsecured lending does not lead to an increase in borrowing, sales, or investment. On the other hand, if firms are allowed to choose between unsecured and secured lending there will be a larger deterioration in internal ratings either because firms that consider themselves high credit risk choose unsecured lending or because a moral hazard occurs among firms that choose unsecured lending.

9.6 Analysis of the Effects of Non-Guaranteed Loans

In this section we identify the characteristics of firms that borrow without the provision of personal guarantees to the JFC and analyze the effects of the use of non-guaranteed loans on firms.

First, we compare the attributes of firms that use non-guaranteed loans to firms that use guaranteed loans after the change in the scheme. We also estimate how the characteristics of firms that use non-guaranteed loans changes following the start of the application of the Guidelines on Management Personal Guarantees. Second, we analyze how the use of non-guaranteed loans affects firms' financing environment, investment behavior, and performance.

9.6.1 Analytical Framework: Determinants of Firms Using Non-Guaranteed Loans

We describe the methodology used to identify the characteristics of firms that obtain non-guaranteed loans from the JFC. The first possible factor that influences the use of the loans is the credit risk of the borrower. Comparing borrowers with high credit risk to those with low credit risk, the former are more likely to default than the latter and thus the probability that management will incur a guarantee obligation if it chooses to borrow with a guarantor is higher. Therefore, even if they pay a slightly higher interest rate these firms may choose non-guaranteed lending which imposes a smaller personal burden on the manager. However, as shown in Table 9.1, the JFC's non-guaranteed loans require covenants to be included in the loan contract. It is only the relatively well-performing firms that are able to comply with these provisions and firms with greater credit risk may choose secured lending because they do not want to be penalized for failing to comply with the loan covenants.

To examine the impact of credit risk on the choice of non-guaranteed lending we use two different methods of analysis. The first is a cross-tabulation analysis of variables representing borrower characteristics. In the tabulation the sample is divided into two subsamples, one including firms with non-guaranteed loans and the other including firms with guaranteed loans. Descriptive statistics for each variable are then calculated and compared. We then also conduct a difference in the means test between the samples. In the analysis loans to which a guarantor waiver program is applied are defined as "non-guaranteed loans" while "guaranteed loans" are loans to which no guarantor waiver or deferment program is applied.

The second method is a regression analysis on the choice of non-guaranteed loans. In the estimation the dependent variable is whether or not non-guaranteed lending is chosen by the firm and the explanatory variables are the factors that influence that choice. The regression provides a way to determine the characteristics of the borrowers that choose non-guaranteed lending. Because cross-tabulations make comparisons across samples for each single variable they do not allow for controlling for the effect of other factors. In contrast, a regression analysis considers multiple factors simultaneously and thus can more precisely estimate the determinants of choosing non-guaranteed loans. Here we estimate a probit model for non-guaranteed borrowing choice as shown in Eq. (9.3):

$$\Pr(NONGUARANTEE_{it} = 1) = \Phi\begin{pmatrix} \beta_0 + \beta_1 X_{it-1} + \beta_2 REGION_{it-1} \\ +\beta_3 INDUSTRY_{it-1} + \beta_4 YEAR_{it-1} \end{pmatrix} \quad (9.3)$$

NON_GUARANTEE on the left hand side is a dummy variable that takes the value of 1 when non-guaranteed loans are selected and 0 when guaranteed loans are selected. As in the cross tabulation analysis, the regression excludes the guarantor deferral program from the analysis. Only loans to which the guarantor waiver program applies are considered to be "non-guaranteed loans" and only loans in which a guarantor is required are considered to be "guaranteed loans."

The variables included in the explanatory variable vector are as follows. First, dummy variables are created and used for each value from 1 to 12 for the internal rating by the JFC. Specifically, the top rating of 1 is used as the basis for the remaining 11 dummy variables. For this variable values for the same year are used to obtain a sufficient number of observations. Next we include the leverage ratio, ROA, the tangible fixed asset ratio, firm age, the number of financial institutions a firm transacts with, the number of years of relationships with the JFC, and total assets. For the financial variables we use data one year before the estimation period to avoid issues with endogeneity problems. For total assets and firm age logarithmic values are used to account for non-linearity.

As for other explanatory variables we use a dummy variable indicating that the use of loans is for working capital. This is to account for the use of non-guaranteed loans being affected by the purpose of loans. In addition, since we believe that firms that have used non-guaranteed loans in the past are more likely to use them again we use a dummy variable that takes the value of 1 for firms that used non-guaranteed loans t years ago ($t = 1$ to 3). Region, industry, and year dummies are also included.

We also perform estimations accounting for the effect of the change in the JFC-SME non-guaranteed loan program following the application of the Guidelines on Management Personal Guarantees. In other words, we split the sample according to whether the loans were made after February 2014 or not. By comparing the results of both estimations we can examine how the change in the program affected the determinants of the use of non-guaranteed loans.

9.6.2 Analytical Framework: Non-Guaranteed Loans and Firms' Ex-Post Performance

Here we present a framework to analyze how firms' ex-post performance changes when they choose to borrow without personal guarantees. Since personal guarantees play a similar role to collateral in terms of protecting lenders' assets and imposing managerial discipline on borrowers the impact of the use of non-guaranteed loans on ex-post performance is expected to be similar to the impact of the use of unsecured loans. In other words, it is expected that non-guaranteed loans are less effective in providing incentives to borrowers relative to secured loans, which may reduce borrowers' management and repayment efforts. In addition, borrowers with higher credit risk may choose non-guaranteed loans because they fear incurring a guarantee obligation, and in this regard, non-guaranteed loans may lead to more defaults.

On the other hand, it is also important to consider the different characteristics of guarantees and collateral. Personal guarantees, unlike collateral, place a very high personal burden on the guarantor in the event of default and the incentives given to management may be rather strong. On the other hand, the aforementioned effects may be weakened by the fact that it is less certain that personal guarantees recover lenders' assets than do collateral in the event of a default. Furthermore, since covenants are required for the JFC's non-guaranteed loans only high-quality firms that can meet conditions set by the covenants may use these loans. We will clarify how these various factors result in differing performance.

In order to measure the difference in ex-post performance between firms using non-guaranteed loans and those using guaranteed loans we use the same framework throughout this chapter which is to estimate the treatment effect by propensity score matching. Specifically, the change in firm performance indicators from year t when the loan was extended to year t + 1 through year t + 3 is calculated for each of the firms that used non-guaranteed loans (treatment group firms) and those that used guaranteed loans and whose propensity score is close to that of the treatment group firms (control group firms). The difference between the two is calculated and is then used to estimate the effect of the treatment on the use of non-guaranteed loans. However, since data is only available through FY2014, we assume that the treatment effect will be estimated for up to two years following loans made in FY2012, and for up to one year for loans made in FY2013.[18]

Specifically, the probit model in Eq. (9.3) is used as the qualitative selection model and the probability (propensity score) for each firm to become a non-guaranteed borrower is calculated. Then firms using non-guaranteed loans and firms using guaranteed loans with similar propensity scores are selected as treatment and control group firms, respectively, and the treatment effects are estimated as shown in Eq. (9.4):

$$\theta^j_{ATT} = \mathrm{E}\big(\Delta^j Y_{T=1}|p(X), T = 1\big) - E_{p(X)|T=1}\big[\mathrm{E}\big(\Delta^j Y_{T=0}|p(X), T = 0\big)\big] \quad (9.4)$$

θ^j_{ATT} represents the average effect for the treatment group on the change in performance from period t to period t + j ($j = 1, 2, 3$). Except for the fact that the ex-post period of measurement is now three years, the method for calculating the treatment effect is identical to that in Section 9.5, including the variables used as performance indicators.

9.6.3 *Results: Determinants of Firms Using Non-Guaranteed Loans*

9.6.3.1 Cross-Tabulation Analysis

First, Table 9.6 compares descriptive statistics between firms using non-guaranteed loans and those using guaranteed loans. In this table the sample is divided by guarantor status and the number of observations and mean values are shown for each variable. The rightmost column of the table shows the results of the difference-in-means test with a symbol indicating whether the null hypothesis that the means are equal between the two samples is rejected for each variable.

Compared to borrowers with guaranteed loans, borrowers with non-guaranteed loans have smaller JFC internal rating grades (lower credit risk), lower leverage ratios, more sales, lower tangible fixed asset ratios, and shorter relationships with the JFC. They also have a higher return on assets (ROA), albeit the difference is marginal.

This indicates that firms using non-guaranteed loans are generally better performers than firms using guaranteed loans. Earlier we pointed out that firms

[18] We do not perform an ex-post performance analysis for firms that used non-guaranteed loans after the February 2014 scheme change. This is because the data is very limited after February 2014.

Table 9.6 Characteristics of JFC's non-guaranteed and guaranteed loans

Guaranteed/ Non-Guaranteed	Variables	Number of observations	Mean	Mean difference test (H_0:Guaranteed = Non-guaranteed)
Guaranteed	Internal rating	278,547	3.39	1.03***
	Leverage ratio	263,613	0.60	0.11***
	Sales	263,729	2031.45	−1267.57***
	ROA	259,406	0.03	−0.01*
	Fixed tangible asset ratio	263,613	0.55	0.03***
	Firm age	260,630	50.93	0.22
	Number of financial institutions	225,129	5.36	0.02
	Number of relationship years with JFC	263,729	16.60	1.54***
Non-guaranteed	Internal rating	16,570	2.35	
	Leverage ratio	12,184	0.48	
	Sales	12,185	3299.02	
	ROA	11,963	0.04	
	Fixed tangible asset ratio	12,184	0.52	
	Firm age	12,083	50.71	
	Number of financial institutions	10,561	5.35	
	Number of relationship years with JFC	12,185	15.06	

Source Processed by the author based on Table 5 of Uesugi et al. (2018)
Note ***, **, and * represent statistical significance at 1%, 5%, and 10%, respectively

with a higher credit risk may choose non-guaranteed loans over guaranteed loans due to the possibility of incurring a guarantee obligation in the event of default but the results here are the opposite to this expectation. Rather, the results suggest that the JFC's non-guaranteed loans are used by good firms that are willing to accept a contract with covenants.

The finding that blue-chip firms use non-guaranteed loans contrasts with what we found with collateral. For comparison, Table 9.7 shows the results of similar calculations based on the use of unsecured loans. Compared to firms using secured loans firms using unsecured loans have higher JFC internal ratings (higher credit risk), higher leverage ratios, and more sales. They also have higher ROA, lower tangible fixed asset ratios, lower firm age, transact with more financial institutions, and have shorter relationships with the JFC. Comparing Tables 9.6 and 9.7, non-guaranteed firms tend to have better ratings and lower leverage ratios than unsecured firms. In the case of collateral high-risk firms that wish to avoid transferring collateral assets in the event of default choose unsecured lending whereas in the case of guarantees low-risk firms that can comply with covenants choose non-guaranteed loans. These show an interesting contrast in the characteristics of users of non-guaranteed and unsecured loans.

Table 9.7 Characteristics of JFC's unsecured and secured loan users

Secured/Unsecured	Variables	Number of observations	Mean	Mean difference test(H_0:Secured = Unsecured)
Secured	Internal rating	121,448	3.15	−0.29***
	Leverage ratio	112,867	0.57	−0.05***
	Sales	112,908	2034.38	−108.94***
	ROA	111,194	0.02	−0.01***
	Fixed tangible asset ratio	112,867	0.58	0.07***
	Firm age	111,583	54.44	7.21***
	Number of financial institutions	94,767	5.32	−0.17***
	Number of relationship years with JFC	112,908	17.40	2.86***
Unsecured	Internal rating	99,614	3.44	
	Leverage ratio	90,812	0.62	
	Sales	90,815	2143.32	
	ROA	88,755	0.03	
	Fixed tangible asset ratio	90,812	0.51	
	Firm age	89,866	47.23	
	Number of financial institutions	76,248	5.49	
	Number of relationship years with JFC	90,815	14.54	

Source Processed by the author based on Table 6 of Uesugi et al. (2018)
Note ***, **, and * represent statistical significance at 1%, 5%, and 10%, respectively

9.6.3.2 Regression Analysis

Table 9.8 presents the results of the probit model estimation for non-guaranteed loans. The table contains the marginal effect of each explanatory variable on the choice of whether to take out a non-guaranteed loan: in other words how much the probability of choosing a non-guaranteed loan changes when each explanatory variable is increased by one unit. Column 1 shows the results when data for all years are pooled while columns 2 and 3 show the results of the estimation for the two subsamples, before and after the introduction of the Guidelines on Management Personal Guarantees.

The results for the entire sample in column (1) are generally consistent with the results of the cross-tabulations in Table 9.6. First, we see that lower-rated firms are

Table 9.8 Estimation results for the determinants of non-guaranteed loans

Estimation method: probit model Dependent variable: Dummy for non-guaranteed loans	(1) Entire sample	(2) Before the Guidelines	(3) After the Guidelines
Explanatory variables	Marginal effects	Marginal effects	Marginal effects
Internal rating 2	0.000	0.001	−0.046***
3	−0.007***	−0.001	−0.249***
4	−0.009***	−0.001*	−0.294***
5	−0.009***	−0.001*	−0.279***
6	−0.012***	−0.004***	−0.321***
7	−0.010***	−0.004***	−0.271***
8	−0.009***	−0.007***	−0.204***
9	−0.010***	−0.008***	−0.234***
Leverage ratio	−0.027***	−0.022***	−0.185***
ROA	0.013***	0.004	0.786***
Fixed tangible asset ratio	−0.002*	−0.003**	−0.032
ln(Firm age)	−0.002***	−0.002***	−0.016*
Number of banks	0.000*	−0.001***	0.014**
Number of relationship years with JFC	0.000***	−0.001***	−0.001
ln(Total asset)	0.004***	0.003***	0.048***
Dummy for working capital loans	0.002***	0.002***	−0.005
Industry dummies	Yes	Yes	Yes
Regional dummies	Yes	Yes	Yes
Year dummies	Yes	Yes	Yes
Number of obervations	1,93,216	1,80,585	12,492
Pseudo R-squared	0.42	0.38	0.29

Source Processed by the author based on Table 9 of Uesugi et al. (2018)
Note ***, **, and * represent statistical significance at 1%, 5%, and 10%, respectively. Results for several explanatory variables are omitted

less likely to choose non-guaranteed loans while higher-rated firms are more likely to choose non-guaranteed loans. If we look at firm characteristics, younger firms, firms with lower leverage ratios, and firms with higher ROA are more likely to choose non-guaranteed loans. The longer a firm has been doing business with the JFC the larger its assets and the more it is borrowing working capital loans the more likely it is to choose non-guaranteed loans.

Next we examine the differences in the estimation results before and after the change in the scheme. In terms of loan conditions, before the scheme change the range of the surcharge added to a non-guaranteed loan was the same regardless of the JFC's internal rating. In contrast, after the change, the smaller the firm's internal credit rating (a lowering of the credit risk) the smaller the add-on interest rates to the loan, particularly for firms with the smallest internal ratings where the added interest rate surcharge is zero. In column 2 the results are consistent with the explanation that "good firms that are confident of keeping their covenants choose non-guaranteed loans with higher interest rates" rather than with the explanation that "lower quality firms that do not want to provide personal guarantees are accepting covenants and higher interest rates."

In column 3 we see that demand for non-guaranteed loans increased significantly among firms with internal ratings of 1 or 2 because the interest rate surcharge on non-guaranteed loans was reduced to zero for firms with highest credit ratings. However, even with the zero-interest rate surcharge, firms with an internal rating of 1 are more likely to use non-guaranteed loans than firms with a rating of 2. Again, the explanation that "good firms confident in their ability to keep their covenants choose non-guaranteed loans" fits better than the explanation that "low quality firms unwilling to provide personal guarantees accept covenants."

9.6.4 Results: Non-Guaranteed Loans and Firms' Ex-Post Performance

The results of the analysis are presented in Table 9.9. In this table the findings for each of the nine variables measuring firm performance are reported in columns (1) through (9), respectively. The figures in each column represent the difference between the change in the performance variable for the treatment and control groups over a period of one to three years following the receipt of the loan in year t. Given that non-guaranteed loans were not widely used for some time after its introduction we present DID results for non-guaranteed loans after 2009.[19]

First, we examine the performance indicators of ex-post creditworthiness and the probability of financial distress in columns (1) through (4). There tends to be more improvement in internal credit ratings for firms that use non-guaranteed loans in

---

[19] As for the use of non-guaranteed loans prior to FY2008, the results differ from those shown here, especially in FY2005 when the system was introduced. Note, however, that few firms opted for non-guaranteed loans during the period. See Uesugi et al. (2018) for details.

Table 9.9 Results for the treatment effect of non-guaranteed loans

		(1)	(2)	(3)	(4)	(5)	(6)	(7)	(8)	(9)
		Internal rating	Possible bankruptcy or below	Negative operating profits	Negative net worth	ROA	Capital investment ratio	ln(Sales)	Interest rate	Leverage ratio
FY that started non-guaranteed loans		DID	DID	DID	DID	DID	DID	DID	DID	DID
2009	t + 1	−0.160*	0.003	−0.010	0.010	0.000	−0.021	−0.012	0.000	0.003
2009	t + 2	0.127	−0.010	0.045	0.026**	−0.009*	0.010	−0.068***	0.001***	0.005
2009	t + 3	−0.129	−0.003	0.022	0.039***	0.001	0.106	−0.041*	0.001**	0.002
2010	t + 1	0.112	0.016**	0.040	−0.002	−0.009*	0.003	−0.072***	0.000	0.012**
2010	t + 2	0.014	0.024	0.072	0.022	−0.007	0.045	−0.090***	0.000	0.026***
2010	t + 3	−0.193	0.019	−0.021	0.007	0.010*	0.073***	−0.058*	0.000	0.021
2011	t + 1	−0.128	−0.004	0.038	−0.014	−0.005	0.005	−0.019	0.000	−0.011
2011	t + 2	−0.917***	−0.108***	0.042	−0.019	−0.005	−0.011	−0.030	0.001	−0.015
2011	t + 3	−0.063	0.020	−0.020	0.033	−0.003	0.027	−0.079**	0.000	0.026
2012	t + 1	−0.748***	−0.091***	0.028	0.023	−0.006	0.064*	−0.014	0.000	0.004
2012	t + 2	−0.848***	−0.036**	−0.095*	−0.122***	0.030***	0.026	0.069**	0.001	−0.044***
2013	t + 1	−0.126*	−0.012**	−0.020	0.007	0.004*	0.025	0.013	0.000	−0.004

Source Processed by the author based on Table 10 of Uesugi et al. (2018)
Note ***, **, and * represent statistical significance at 1%, 5%, and 10%, respectively

FY2009 and FY2011 onward. There is also improvement in the variables indicating whether a firm is in financial distress. For the dummy variable of a firm being classified as possible bankruptcy status or below, the increase in the percentage of firms falling into this category tends to be smaller from FY2011 onward, with the exception of FY2010. The increase in the probability of falling into deficit is also smaller in FY2012, and the increase in the probability of insolvency is smaller in the same FY2012, while it is larger in FY2009.

In summary, the results indicate that firms using non-guaranteed loans after FY2011, when there was an increase in the use of non-guaranteed loans, show greater improvement in creditworthiness and a larger decline in the probability of experiencing financial distress than firms using guaranteed loans. Theoretically, the use of non-guaranteed loans may worsen ex-post performance due to weak incentives and self-selection by riskier borrowers. However, since the JFC's non-guaranteed loans are subject to covenants, firms confident of adhering to the covenants (i.e., not incurring deficits for two consecutive years and not becoming insolvent) are more likely to choose non-guaranteed loans, and their actual ex-post performance likely reflects this.

Next, columns (5) through (7) show the results for the performance indicators related to firm activity. ROA increased less for non-guaranteed loan users in FY2009 and for a part of FY2010 but has since then increased more than for firms that use guaranteed loans. For the capital investment rate it increased more for non-guaranteed loan users than for firms using guaranteed loans although there were only a few periods when the results were significant. For the sales amount, with the exception of FY2012, the decrease in sales tends to be larger for non-guaranteed borrowers.

Finally, no clear pattern is apparent when looking at the results for financing in columns (8) and (9). Table 9.4, which contains the treatment effects for unsecured lending, shows that the leverage ratio improved as firms that previously did not have sufficient assets to serve as collateral borrowed more. Since personal guarantees, unlike collateral, can be provided upon request the use of non-guaranteed loans does not necessarily mean an improvement in the financing environment.

9.7 Interpretation of Results

In Sections 9.5 and 9.6 we examined the determinants and effects of unsecured and non-guaranteed loans. This section reviews and interprets the results.

9.7.1 Effects of Unsecured Loans

With the introduction of unsecured loans, firms that previously could not borrow from the JFC because they did not have tangible fixed assets that could serve as collateral become new JFC borrowers. Investment and sales for these firms have increased, indicating that the new approach to lending has had a positive effect. At the same time, however, their financial soundness is declining, perhaps because of the expansion in their balance sheets due to the increased borrowing.

Firms that had adequate collateralizable assets to meet their immediate funding needs had already obtained secured loans so there was no immediate increase in their borrowing, investment, or sales.[20] Rather, given the choice between secured and low interest rate loans and unsecured and high interest rate loans, there was a clear tendency for firms with higher ex-post credit risk to opt for the unsecured and high interest rate contract.

It is unclear whether the increase in ex-post credit risk for firms that used unsecured lending was due to the fact that it only became apparent over time that their risk was high to begin with, or whether the unsecured nature of the loans resulted in a moral hazard among firm managers, which worsened performance. If it is the latter then measures need to be taken to curb the moral hazard of firms using unsecured loans.

As shown in Figure 9.1, the ratio of SMEs that provide collateral including real estate collateral has declined substantially in recent years. This can be evaluated positively because firms that do not have sufficient collateral assets are less likely to face a credit constraint if they do not have to pledge collateral for loans. On the other hand, this may be a result of a competitive environment in the loan market. In the face of sluggish demand for funds and intensifying competition among financial institutions the financial institutions do not only lower interest rates but also offer other favorable conditions including no requirement for collateral to attract firms to borrow money. Currently, corporate bankruptcies are at a historically low level and the problem of losses at the time of debt collection is not so serious. However, with the rapid expansion of unsecured lending there is a growing possibility that losses given default at the time of a firm's bankruptcy will increase. In order to address this potential problem it is necessary to curb moral hazards among firms using unsecured lending through monitoring and other means.

9.7.2 *Effects of Non-Guaranteed Loans*

Contrary to our prior expectation that firms with higher credit risk would choose non-guaranteed loans even at higher interest rates, we find that firms with good internal ratings and lower risk tend to choose non-guaranteed loans. Firms with low credit risk choose the loan contract of non-guarantees with covenants and higher interest rates, while firms with high credit risk choose the loan contract of guarantees with no covenants and lower interest rates. Even though the interest rate differential between guaranteed and non-guaranteed loans was eliminated for highly rated

[20] According to the JFC some of these firms plan to use unsecured loans from the JFC and then simultaneously obtain secured loans from private financial institutions in anticipation of future capital needs. For these firms the introduction of unsecured loans from the JFC has eased their anticipated future borrowing constraints.

firms due to the application of the Guidelines on Management Personal Guarantees the tendency that firms with low credit risk chose non-guaranteed loans with covenants remained unchanged. This does not mean that managers who want to avoid execution of personal guarantees when a firm defaults on their loans choose non-guaranteed loans. Rather this implies that managers who are confident of adhering to the covenants choose non-guaranteed loans.

It is unclear why firms place greater emphasis on compliance with covenants rather than on avoiding the execution of personal guarantees. The cost of being required to fulfill personal guarantees should be greater for firms with high credit risk than for firms with low credit risk. The reason why they choose to pledge personal guarantees is puzzling.[21]

Given these reservations, what the results suggest is the possibility that the disciplining function of personal guarantees on firm management can be replaced by the content of loan contracts, including covenants. Of course, personal guarantees and covenants differ in terms of the occasion in and the extent to which firms and their CEOs are affected. A personal guarantee by management is executed when a firm goes bankrupt, and unpaid debt by the firm and monetary and non-monetary expenses related to personal bankruptcies by managers who pledged personal guarantees for the firm's debt are regarded as costs of the personal guarantee. In the case of covenants, penalties, such as calling a loan and a higher interest rate, are triggered when predetermined conditions are violated, such as insolvency or two consecutive years of deficit. Further, it does not require banks to monitor the debt to execute personal guarantees, while monitoring is required for banks to detect violation of covenants to penalize debtors.[22]

---

[21] The costs associated with fulfilling personal guarantees due to corporate insolvency include monetary costs associated with debt repayment and non-monetary costs, such as the emotional distress caused by the personal bankruptcy of the manager. If the costs associated with fulfilling personal guarantees, including these non-monetary costs, are extremely high firms will try to avoid them regardless of whether their credit risk is high or low. In that case firms that can afford to pay higher interest rates (lower credit risk firms) may be able to remove their personal guarantees.

On the other hand, since personal guarantees, unlike collateral, do not specify the assets backing them it may be perceived that the actual financial loss incurred by management is small even if the guarantee is executed in the event of bankruptcy. In such a case the management would likely be more concerned with the plausibility of complying with the covenants rather than with the existence of a personal guarantee. Consistent with this view, evidence from a questionnaire survey of SMEs conducted by Libertas Consulting Incorporated on behalf of the SME Agency, "2012 Report on the Actual Conditions of SMEs Regarding the Personal Guarantee System (Libertas Consulting Inc.)," is available. In the survey there were firms that responded that personal guarantees by management themselves were not necessary. Among these firms, being asked about the extent to which they would be willing to accept an increase in interest rates resulting from the elimination of personal guarantees, the largest number of firms (37%) responded that "elimination of guarantees is unnecessary if interest rates will rise" while the next largest (30%) responded that "an increase of 0.5% or less" would be acceptable. The cost of personal guarantees, as measured by the degree of willingness to pay higher interest rates, is actually small and there may not be a significant difference in the extent of the cost even if credit risk differs.

[22] Regarding the covenants introduced by the JFC in their loan contracts, their cost to financial institutions would be relatively small since the violation of the covenants can be rather easily verified by the JFC by the annual examination of financial statements.

In light of the benefits and costs there seems to be ample room for financial institutions to use covenants as an alternative disciplinary device to personal guarantees. In fact, one of the regional banks has provided about 100 billion yen in loans with covenants although these loans do not necessarily exempt borrowers from pledging personal guarantees. The presence of covenants helps firms to improve the business conditions through the business feasibility assessments by the bank.[23]

9.8 Summary

This chapter examines the SME financing which does not rely on personal guarantees and collateral. This chapter makes it clear that if the function of personal guarantees is to impose discipline on managers then covenants can replace personal guarantees for SMEs that meet certain criteria and it may be possible to break away from the heavy reliance on guaranteed lending. On the other hand, we also see that while unsecured lending would improve the financing environment for firms without adequate collateral assets, it would also make it more difficult to protect lenders' asset values by minimizing losses given a default incurred by financial institutions in the event of bankruptcy. To deal with this problem it would again be necessary to curb the moral hazard among firms which no longer pledge collateral.

There are several other potential benefits of non-guaranteed and unsecured loans that have not been mentioned thus far. One positive effect of non-guaranteed lending is to promote business successions. It has been pointed out that many potential successors are hesitant to take over a business when approached by the previous president because they do not want to succeed the personal guarantees pledged by their predecessors. The spread of non-guaranteed loans may lessen this hesitation and alleviate some of the difficulties in business succession faced by SMEs, which is currently a serious problem in Japan.

An effect of unsecured loans is that by not requiring real estate and other tangible fixed assets as collateral firms may actively invest in assets that are difficult to use as collateral. Previous studies have found that it is easier for firms to raise funds in countries with better legal schemes for movable collateral assets (Calomiris et al., 2017). In Japan unsecured loans from financial institutions are also expected to promote investment in intangible assets.

The issue of collateral and personal guarantees cannot be solved by simply saying that lending without a reliance on collateral and personal guarantees should be encouraged. In order to achieve an efficient flow of funds, while ensuring the supply of funds to SMEs, it is necessary to consider what schemes related to collateral and personal guarantees should be in place. It is important to continue to develop schemes and accumulate knowledge in practice regarding mechanisms to replace

[23] Shizuoka Bank, one of the largest regional banks in Japan, has extensively used covenants for business loans. For an example see "Shizuoka Bank's loans with covenants for business evaluation have become widespread and established" (Kinyu Zaisei Jijo, March 11, 2019).

personal guarantees and to use assets not simply limited to tangible fixed assets as collateral, such as ABL (Asset Based Lending).

Chapter 10
Loan Market Concentration and Firm Financing

Abstract We calculate the level of concentration in the Japanese loan market by region and discuss its relationship to the market power of financial institutions. This is the first study of its kind to comprehensively and accurately measure loan market concentration at a regional level in Japan. We calculate the Herfindahl–Hirschman Index (HHI) for each prefecture and urban employment area and examine the degree and persistence of the increase in the HHI following financial institution mergers, along with factor decomposition. We also examine the impact of concentration on firm interest rates. The major findings are as follows. First, while the nationwide HHI is rising (increasing concentration) it is declining in metropolitan areas, indicating a polarization of the loan market concentration in the country. Second, the HHI is rising not only because of a decline in the number of financial institutions but also because of the greater variation in market share among financial institutions. Third, the loan HHI rises at the time of financial institution mergers but the magnitude of the increase is attenuated over time. Fourth, as the HHI increases firms' borrowing interest rates rise modestly and gradually.

Keywords Concentration · Herfindahl–Hirschman Index (HHI) · Market power · Degree of competition

10.1 Introduction: Concentration of Financial Institutions in the Market is Important for Firm Financing

A common way for SMEs to obtain financing is to borrow from financial institutions. In this case it is important for a firm to know how many financial institutions it can borrow from. The more financial institutions a firm can borrow from the more bargaining power it has and the better terms it can obtain.[1] Since firms tend to transact with financial institution branches located nearby the number of financial institutions

[1] In Japan, it is common for even SMEs to borrow from multiple financial institutions. See Table 4. 4 in Degryse, Kim, and Ongena (2009) for a survey of the number of financial institutions with which firms transact, including firms outside of Japan.

I. Uesugi, *The Economics of SME Finance*, Advances in Japanese Business and Economics 36, https://doi.org/10.1007/978-981-96-3193-3_10

within a certain physical distance from which a firm can borrow determines the firm's financing environment.

From a financial institution's perspective the number of rival financial institutions surrounding its own bank is an important factor in determining the level of interest rates and volume of loans it can offer to businesses. If there are no other rival financial institutions other than the bank market power will increase and monopolistic interest rates can be set. Even if there are many financial institutions in the area, a bank with a large share of the market can set a high interest rate. On the other hand, the more rival financial institutions there are and the more equal the market share among them, the more intense the competition and the lower the interest rate a financial institution can charge.

Variation in the number of banks operating in the loan market and their market share is called concentration and is often expressed as the Herfindahl–Hirschman Index (HHI). This index indicates the market power that a financial institution has in the loan market, under certain assumptions, and is widely used in policymaking related to financial institutions such as merger reviews.

When the Japan Fair Trade Commission (hereafter JFTC) examines a merger or consolidation of financial institutions the extent to which the merger is expected to increase the HHI is an important factor in determining whether to approve the merger. In its "Guidelines to Application of the Antimonopoly Act Concerning Review of Business Combination"the JFTC sets the standard for when a merger would not ordinarily be considered to substantially restrict competition based on the expected degree of increase in HHI and the resulting level of HHI.

For example, in the review of the merger between Shinwa Bank, a wholly owned subsidiary of Fukuoka Financial Group, and The Eighteenth Bank which was announced in 2016 the total share of the two banks in loans to large and medium-sized firms in Nagasaki Prefecture was about 70%, and the HHI increased by 0.24 from an HHI of 0.28 before the merger to 0.52 after the merger. For loans to SMEs the two banks' combined loan share was approximately 75% and the HHI increased by 0.26 from 0.28, meaning the ex-post HHI was expected to be 0.54. Since an examination of HHIs in the loan market for both large and medium-sized firms and for SMEs indicated that the condition of "little likelihood of substantially restricting competition" set by the JFTC was not going to be satisfied, the review proceeded further to collect additional materials to decide on the merger proposal.[2]

In this chapter we calculate the HHI, the level of concentration in the loan market, using data reported by individual financial institution branches to quantify the nature of concentration, including changes over time and the persistence of any changes. This is the first attempt in Japan to analyze the characteristics of local loan markets based on the branch-level loan and deposit data. The impact of financial institution

[2] The results of the review are presented at the following webpage: https://www.jftc.go.jp/houdou/pressrelease/h30/aug/180824.html.

mergers on concentration will also be measured. After conducting these studies we will also examine the impact of loan market concentration on firm borrowing interest rates.[3]

10.1.1 Herfindahl–Hirschman Index

The Herfindahl–Hirschman index (HHI) as a measure of concentration in the loan market is defined by the following equation for the loan market at time t and region r. In this chapter the unit of region r is either a prefecture or an urban employment area (definition to follow).

$$HHI\_Loan_{rt} = \sum_{i=1}^{n} Share\_Loan_{irt}^{2} \tag{10.1}$$

The component is the share of financial institution i in the total loans of all financial institutions in region r at time t, $Share\_Loan_{irt} = {Loan_{irt}}/{\sum_{i=1}^{n} Loan_{irt}}$. Summing the square of this for all institutions n in the market yields HHI_Loan, the HHI in the loan market.[4]

10.1.2 To Date There Has Been no Loan HHI at the Prefectural Level Based on Comprehensive and Accurate Data

In Japan, while HHI in the loan market has been the subject of strong interest to policymakers and has been used to make policy decisions, in the loan and deposit markets in various regions it has never been comprehensively calculated.[5]

Researchers have previously measured the HHI in the loan market but have not been able to do so comprehensively and accurately due to unavailability of data. For

[3] In this chapter we take a closer look at the structure of the loan market, paying particular attention to concentration, and then discuss its impact on borrower firms' financing. Studies that discuss how market structure affects the managerial behavior of financial institutions can be found in Horie (2015) and Horie and Arioka (2021).

[4] HHI_Deposit, the HHI for the deposit market, can be calculated similarly. The results are presented in Uesugi and Hiraga et al. (2021b). The focus in this chapter, however, is to measure concentration in the loan market as it is more meaningful for SME finance. However, we do discuss the HHI for deposits as a point of comparison with the loan market.

[5] In the United States the Federal Deposit Insurance Corporation (FDIC) publishes financial institution deposits aggregated by various geographic units, including zip codes. The FDIC's webpage also allows users to calculate the current HHI for deposits as well as a hypothetical HHI for any combination of banks as a result of a merger. See https://www7.fdic.gov/sod/sodMarketBank.asp?barItem=2 for the Pro-Forma (HHI) Report.

instance, Nakata and Adachi (2006b), Ogura (2012), and Harimaya and Ozaki (2017) all calculated the HHI but needed to make certain assumptions about the loans and total assets of financial institutions, which may have led their calculated values to diverge from the true HHI, because not all loan and deposit amounts by region and financial institution were available. Deviations are due to excluding large banks from the calculations (Nakata and Adachi, 2006b; Harimaya and Ozaki, 2017), with such deviations associated with the assumption that the amount of assets and loans per branch of a financial institution are considered constant (Ogura, 2012; Harimaya and Ozaki, 2017), respectively. In addition, due to further data availability issues these previous studies mainly use prefectures as the unit of analysis and so are not able to determine what the appropriate geographic scope is when examining concentration in the loan market.

We will use the same data used in the analysis in Chapter 4, loan balance data per branch reported by each financial institution to the Financial Services Agency (FSA), to calculate the HHI in the loan market covering large banks, regional banks, Shinkin banks, and credit cooperatives. We first focus on the prefectural level which has been the focus of previous studies. We then also calculate the loan market concentration of cities, towns, and villages that are closely connected in terms of labor mobility and are grouped together as "urban employment areas."

10.2 Overview of Results

In calculating the loan market concentration at both the prefectural and urban employment area levels for the 2005–2019 period we obtain the following key results. First, there is wide variation in concentration among regions. Figure 10.1 shows the HHI by prefecture and by the finer urban employment area on a map of Japan. We see that the HHI is low in metropolitan prefectures and high in rural prefectures and that the level of concentration varies by urban employment area within the same prefecture.

Average loan HHI in the entire country been on an upward trend throughout the period. However, the level of the HHI in some metropolitan prefectures such as Tokyo, Aichi, Osaka, and Hyogo was originally low and has since declined, indicating increased polarization in market concentration. In addition, the increase in the HHI is not only because of a decline in the number of financial institutions but also because of greater heterogeneity of market share among financial institutions.

Loan HHI rises with financial institution mergers but gradually returns to its original level over time. In areas where the original level of market concentration is low the duration of the HHI increase is short, perhaps because other financial institutions increase their lending after the merger.

Looking at the impact of an increase in the HHI on the firm financing environment we find that corporate borrowing interest rates increase, albeit modestly, after an increase in the HHI and the relationship between a higher HHI and greater market power is generally valid. However, an increase in the HHI due to a merger of financial institutions does not result in a significant change in interest rates.

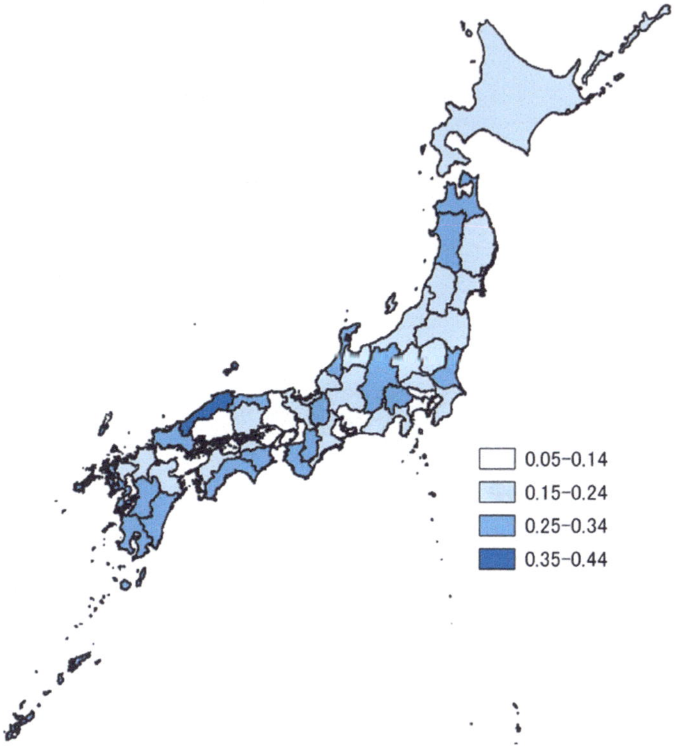

Fig. 10.1 (a) Loan HHI (in 2019, by prefecture, for all financial institutions) (b) Loan HHI (in 2019, by urban employment area including MEA and MCEA, for all financial institutions) (*Note* (a) HHI is higher for darker colors and lower for lighter colors. Financial institutions include those from major banks to credit cooperatives (b) HHI is higher for darker colors and lower for lighter colors. Green represents areas out of urban employment areas. For the explanations about urban employment areas see Sect. 10.4 and 10.5 of this chapter. Financial institutions include those from major banks to credit cooperatives. *Source* Uesugi, Hiraga et al. (2021b))

This chapter proceeds as follows. Section 10.3 describes how the HHI, a measure of market concentration, is conceptually related to market power and competitiveness. Section 10.4 describes the data and discusses the methodology used to calculate the HHI for the loan market. Section 10.5 presents the results of the calculations and notes the developments over time in the loan HHI. Section 10.6 decomposes the loan HHI into two elements: the number of financial institutions and the variation in market share among financial institutions. Sections 10.7 and 10.8 explain the methodology used to calculate how financial institution mergers lead to increases in the HHI and then measure the extent to which the HHI increase is sustained. Section 10.9 examines the relationship between the HHI and interest rates, the borrowing conditions faced by firms. Section 10.10 summarizes the chapter.

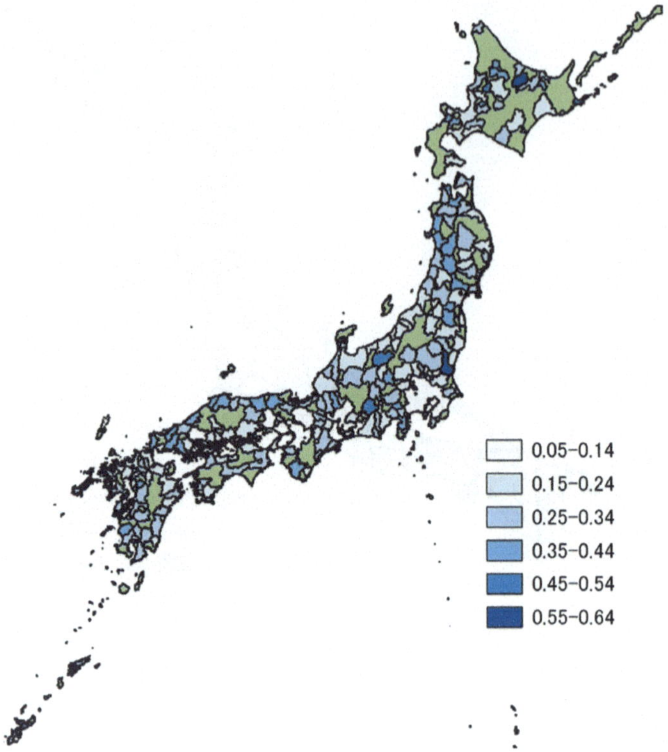

Fig. 10.1 (continued)

10.3 The Relationship Between Concentration and Market Power in the Loan Market

10.3.1 Definition of Market Concentration

The most commonly used measure of market concentration is the Herfindahl–Hirschman Index (HHI), shown in Eq. (10.1). In general, the volume of goods and services traded in a market is used to calculate the share that an individual firm has in the overall market, with the square of this share summed for all firms. Another measure of concentration is the sum of the shares of the three or five firms with the largest market shares, but the HHI is more widely used.

10.3.2 Relationship Between Concentration and Market Power

The purpose of measuring the HHI is to determine the degree of competition in a particular market. When the market is monopolized by one firm and the degree of competition is the lowest the HHI is 1, which is the maximum value. On the other hand, when the market is very competitive, even if some firms earn excess profits, there will be a large number of new entrants which results in more equal shares among many firms and smaller HHIs.

Thus, when considering the HHI at its extremes, monopoly and perfect competition, there appears to be a relationship whereby the HHI becomes smaller as the degree of competition increases. In fact, under certain assumptions, the HHI can be shown to be proportional to the price–cost margin (the degree to which price exceeds marginal cost), which indicates a firm's market power. This point is discussed below.[6]

Consider an industry with m firms producing a single good. As a result of each firm producing only y_j the market as a whole produces $y = \sum_{j=1}^{m} y_j$ goods with a market price of p. The inverse demand function for this good is defined as p(y, z) where z represents the exogenous factors that affect demand. Let $C(y_j, \omega_j)$ be the cost function representing the cost of production for each firm where ω_j is the factor price required for production. In this environment firms maximize profits by

$$\max_{y_j} p(y, z)y_j - C(y_j, \omega_j) \tag{10.2}$$

The first-order condition of the profit maximization problem is

$$p + \frac{\partial p}{\partial y}\frac{\partial y}{\partial y_j}y_j - C'(y_j, \omega_j) = 0 \tag{10.3}$$

We reorganize Eq. (10.3) to obtain the equation for the price cost margin which is the difference between price p and the marginal cost C':

$$\frac{p - C'(y_j, \omega_j)}{p} = \frac{\theta_j}{\varepsilon} \tag{10.4}$$

Here we define $\theta_j \equiv \frac{\partial y}{\partial y_j}\frac{y_j}{y}$, which represents the percentage increase in total market output that would result from a 1% increase in production by firm j. It also represents the degree of competition. If a firm is in a perfectly competitive market $\frac{\partial y}{\partial y_j} = 0$, and θ_j is also zero. If a firm is a monopolist $\theta_j = 1$. If a firm is a Cournot-like oligopolist $\frac{\partial y}{\partial y_j} = 1$ because it believes that other firms do not respond to changes in its own production. Then θ_j is equal to $\frac{y_j}{y}$, that is, the share of one's own production to the

[6] The discussion here is based on Cetorelli (1999).

total market production. Also, $\varepsilon \equiv -\frac{\partial y}{\partial p}\frac{p}{y}(>0)$and represents the price elasticity of demand.[7]

The next step is to add up the price–cost margins obtained for each of the m firms in the market to obtain the market power in that industry. Both sides of Eq. (10.4) are weighted and summed by $\frac{y_j}{y}$, the market share of each firm,

$$\sum_{j=1}^{m}\left[\frac{p-C'\left(y_j,\omega_j\right)}{p}\right]\frac{y_j}{y}=\sum_{j=1}^{m}\frac{\theta_j}{\varepsilon}\frac{y_j}{y} \tag{10.5}$$

The left-hand side of the equation is the average price–cost margin in the industry which is the market power of this industry. This industry-level market power is defined as α. The right-hand side of the equation is rewritten and given the definition $\theta_j \equiv \frac{\partial y}{\partial y_j}\frac{y_j}{y}$. We then obtain the following Eq. (10.6):

$$\alpha=\sum_{j=1}^{m}\frac{1}{\varepsilon}\frac{\partial y}{\partial y_j}\left(\frac{y_j}{y}\right)^2 \tag{10.6}$$

If we make the further assumption that $\frac{\partial y}{\partial y_j}=\gamma\ (>0)$ for all firms then the right-hand side of Eq. (10.6) can be expressed as in Eq. (10.7), the sum of squares of the market share of each firm multiplied by a positive constant $\frac{\gamma}{\varepsilon}$:

$$\alpha=\frac{\gamma}{\varepsilon}\sum_{j=1}^{m}\left(\frac{y_j}{y}\right)^2=\frac{\gamma}{\varepsilon}HHI \tag{10.7}$$

This equation shows that the market power in each industry is positively proportional to HHI, meaning that in industries with higher concentration, as measured by HHI, firms have greater market power in the sense that they earn higher price–cost margins on average.

Based on this theoretical positive relationship between the HHI and the price–cost margin, can we always argue that a higher value of concentration means that a firm is gaining greater market power and more profits?

Equation (10.7) shows that the two are correlated but does not indicate a causal relationship. It is possible that high market concentration allows firms to exercise market power and earn high profits (market power hypothesis) or it is possible that high concentration and high profit margins occur simultaneously as a result of a small number of highly efficient firms that generate high profits and hold a high market share (efficiency hypothesis).

---

[7] This is also called the conduct parameter and indicates the degree of competition in the market. Studies measuring the conduct parameter in the Japanese loan market include Uchida and Tsutsui (2005), Ogura (2020), and Maruyama (2024).

Previous studies on loan and deposit markets in which banks participate focus only on P out of the price–cost margin, (P-MC)/P, to test whether the market power hypothesis or the efficiency hypothesis holds. Since we are talking about banks P corresponds to the loan interest rate in the case of the loan market and the deposit interest rate in the case of the deposit market. In a highly concentrated loan market (deposit market) a bank would have a high loan interest rate (low deposit interest rate) if the market power hypothesis holds, while a bank would have a low loan interest rate (high deposit interest rate) if the efficiency hypothesis holds.

Section 10.9 therefore examines the relationship between interest rates in the loan market (borrowing interest rates from the firms' perspective) and market concentration using prefecture-level panel data for Japan.

10.4 How to Calculate the HHI in the Loan Market

This section describes the methodology used to calculate the HHI for regional loan markets in Japan. We calculate the loan market HHI by both prefecture and urban employment area based on branch-by-branch loan and deposit data which has not been used in previous studies. The data is the same as we used in Chapter 4.[8]

10.4.1 Methodology

The financial institutions included in the data are city banks, trust banks, new forms of banks such as Internet banks, former long-term credit banks, regional banks, second-tier regional banks, Shinkin banks, credit cooperatives, and foreign banks. Government-affiliated financial institutions including the Norinchukin Bank (Norinchukin Bank), the Federation of Credit Agricultural/Fishery Cooperative Associations (JA Shinren, JF Shingyoren), the Shoko Chukin Bank, the Japan Post Bank, the Federation of Labor Banks, labor banks, and agricultural/fishery cooperatives (JA Bank, JF Marine Bank) are not included. These financial institutions are not included either because region-level data is not available or because the financial institutions in question have consolidated their branches across prefectures during the analysis period, and as we want to eliminate any possible effect this consolidation may have on changes in the HHI.

[8] When creating the HHI using this dataset a couple of additional details needed to be taken into consideration. First, the information for each branch reported to the FSA did not include comprehensive information on the city, town, and address of each branch so it was necessary to identify the address of each branch by merging the data with other databases such as Nikkin's Japan Financial Almanac. Second, some of the loan and deposit balances by branch were missing so it was necessary to make some assumptions to supplementary the reported figures. For such details and other points of note see the supplemental discussion in Uesugi, Hiraga, et al. (2021b).

We calculate the HHI in two ways: using all eligible financial institutions and using only regional financial institutions that are below the regional banks. This is because we consider both the loan HHI for firms that are able to borrow from major banks, including megabanks, and the loan HHI for firms that are only able to borrow from regional financial institutions, including regional banks.

The sample period covers all years for which data is available from the FSA, the end of March 2005 to the end of March 2019. We first aggregate the data at the prefectural level, given that most previous studies examine regional loan markets based on the prefecture-level data. In other words, we assume that the regional loan market is defined by prefecture boundaries.

Prefectures, however, are merely administrative units and may differ from the actual geographical area of the loan market.[9] Therefore, as an alternative, and based on economic connections across regions, we also consider urban employment areas, a definition of an urban area proposed by Kanemoto and Tokuoka (2002). An urban employment area is characterized by the degree to which the labor force moves between municipalities during commuting and considers municipalities that are strongly linked to be the same area. If the geographic scope of the loan market is determined by economic ties between regions, as expressed by the closeness of travel to work, then the HHI defined by urban employment areas may be more appropriate than that defined by prefectures.

An urban employment area is a set of municipalities consisting of a central city and surrounding suburban cities that meet the following conditions: (1) within the area there is a central city with a certain level of population in Densely Inhabited Districts (DID) or above; (2) suburban cities are defined as municipalities where 10% or more of the residents commute to the central city; and (3) multiple central cities may exist within the same area. A metropolitan employment area (MEA) is defined as a metropolitan area with a DID population of 50,000 or more in the central city, and a micropolitan employment area (MCEA) is defined as a metropolitan area with a DID population of 10,000 to 50,000.[10] In this study both MEAs and MCEAs will be used as the aggregate unit of metropolitan employment areas.

---

[9] The JFTC's Guidelines for application of the antimonopoly act concerning review of business combination adopt the following approach when determining the scope of the market (referred to as "delineation of a certain area for transactions" in the Guidelines): assume that a firm is a monopoly supplier of a certain commodity in a certain region; then assume that the firm introduces a small but substantial and non-temporary price increase; if the degree of substitution by another commodity or region is limited so that the monopolist firm can increase its profits by raising prices this region is considered to be within the market.

[10] For more information on the classification of urban employment areas see: http://www.csis.u-tokyo.ac.jp/UEA/uea_def.htm.

10.4.2 Remarks When Interpreting the HHI

After identifying the geographic scope of the market the HHI is calculated by aggregating branch-level loans within the market by financial institutions based on the address information of financial institution branches. There are two points to consider when interpreting the results.

First, we assume that lending only occurs within the prefecture or urban employment area where the branches are located. It is natural to assume that financial institutions will lend to firms located in the same region given their physical proximity. Ono et al. (2023), based on a credit research company database containing information on about 3.6 million business relationships between firms and financial institutions, found that the average distance between a firm and its financial institution is 5.5 kilometers and the median distance is 1.6 kilometers. Since the actual distance between a firm and the financial institution with which it does business is small, lending by branches located within a prefecture or urban employment area can be interpreted as being directed to firms located in the same prefecture or urban employment area.[11]

Second, the lending covered here is not limited to loans to firms. Although firms are their largest group of borrowers financial institutions in Japan also lend a substantial amount to households through housing loans and consumer loans as well as local governments.[12] If the ratio of loans to firms, households, and local governments is the same for each financial institution in each region there is no problem in using the obtained HHI as an indicator of the concentration of loans to firms. However, if there are significant differences among regions the results should be interpreted with this in mind.

---

[11] The distance between financial institutions and depositors (here limited to households) also becomes smaller to reduce transaction costs for withdrawing cash. According to NTT Data Management Research Institute (2019), which conducted a survey on the use of deposit-taking financial institutions by individuals, the top three reasons for choosing a main bank are "because the branch is close to home or my neighborhood," "because the bank was designated as a financial institution for receiving salary and other benefits," and "because the institution's ATM is close to home or my neighborhood." Proximity to a branch or ATM plays an important role in individuals' selection of financial institutions for deposit transactions. Although we do not measure the distance between households and financial institutions here, we interpret that deposits at branches are made by residents resided in the same prefecture or in the same urban employment area. The financial institution branch to which households make deposits is affected not only by proximity to their homes but also by the location of their place of employment which makes the payroll transfers. There are some individuals who have deposits at a financial institution branch near their place of work rather than their place of residence due to the establishment of a payroll transfer account. Therefore, it may be preferable to calculate the deposit HHI at the urban employment area level rather than at the prefecture level because the municipality where the individual works and the municipality where they live are likely to be included within the same urban employment area.

[12] Based on the Bank of Japan's Flow of Funds statistics loans to households (housing loans and consumer credit) accounted for 24% of private deposit-taking financial institutions' total outstanding loans (799 trillion yen) as of the end of March 2020. If we consider loans by commercial banks and other financial institutions to local governments as part of municipal debt the share is 6%. The remaining 70% is the share of loans to businesses.

10.5 Measuring HHI in the Loan Market

Below we summarize the results of measuring the loan HHI by region. Four HHI series are obtained by dividing the sample by prefecture and urban employment area, and calculating the HHI for all financial institutions and for regional financial institutions. For individual values, including the HHI for the deposit market, see the appendix tables in Uesugi and Hiraga et al. (2021b).[13]

10.5.1 Loan HHI by Prefecture—Rising but also Increased Polarization

Table 10.1 displays the aggregate results for the HHI when the loan market is defined by prefecture. The table contains the development of the loan HHI for all deposit-taking financial institutions from city banks to credit cooperatives. There are several takeaways.

The average HHI values for the loan market by prefecture are 0.2099 (2005) and 0.2301 (2019). For reference, the average deposit HHIs, in the lower part of the table, are 0.2280 (2005) and 0.2535 (2019). At both points in time the deposit market HHI is larger than the loan market HHI. In both the loan and deposit markets the average value of the HHI, the level of concentration, has been increasing through time.

The HHI values are ordered from smallest to largest and their quantile values are detailed.

There are clear differences in the development of loan HHI at each quantile. The minimum and the 5% quantile values become smaller over time. In contrast, the qu antile values above the median generally increase over time. In prefectures with initially low loan HHIs the level of the HHI has become even lower over time. On the other hand, in prefectures with high initial levels the loan HHI becomes even higher in general with some exceptions. As a result there is a polarization in the level of loan HHIs. In contrast, the deposit HHI tends to rise across all quantiles and no polarization is observed.

This is also evident when examining histograms which show the distribution of the HHI for loans and deposits by year. Figure 10.2 compares the distribution of the loan HHI in 2005 and 2019. Compared to 2005 the four prefectures with the lowest HHI in 2019 (Aichi, Osaka, Hyogo, and Tokyo) have moved further away from the other prefectures. We do not observe the same polarization in the HHI distribution for deposits.

It is clear that the loan market is divided into regions where the number of competing banks with similar market shares is increasing and regions where it is decreasing. On the other hand, we do not observe such polarization in the deposit

[13] This is an appendix to Uesugi and Hiraga et al. (2021b) published as a discussion paper by the Financial Research Center of the Financial Services Agency.

Table 10.1 Development of loan HHI and deposit HHI (all financial institutions, by prefecture)

Year (end of March)	Mean	Min	p5	Median	p95	Max
Loan HHI						
2005	0.2099	0.0716	0.0845	0.2188	0.3153	0.3353
2006	0.2093	0.0800	0.0894	0.2216	0.3104	0.3250
2007	0.2125	0.0724	0.0848	0.2296	0.3119	0.3305
2008	0.2149	0.0683	0.0831	0.2192	0.3110	0.3257
2009	0.2179	0.0545	0.0939	0.2284	0.3113	0.3232
2010	0.2196	0.0538	0.0908	0.2192	0.3157	0.3262
2011	0.2215	0.0505	0.0870	0.2202	0.3103	0.3293
2012	0.2221	0.0505	0.0876	0.2189	0.3104	0.3366
2013	0.2244	0.0501	0.0873	0.2219	0.3137	0.3366
2014	0.2252	0.0522	0.0894	0.2271	0.3172	0.3421
2015	0.2260	0.0512	0.0881	0.2280	0.3151	0.3469
2016	0.2272	0.0503	0.0867	0.2288	0.3177	0.3490
2017	0.2287	0.0501	0.0811	0.2294	0.3315	0.3618
2018	0.2296	0.0486	0.0761	0.2299	0.3301	0.3700
2019	0.2301	0.0505	0.0747	0.2329	0.3462	0.3674
(Reference) Deposit HHI						
2005	0.2280	0.0869	0.0941	0.2426	0.3339	0.4263
2019	0.2535	0.1027	0.1183	0.2643	0.3622	0.4684

Source Uesugi, Hiraga, et al. (2021b)

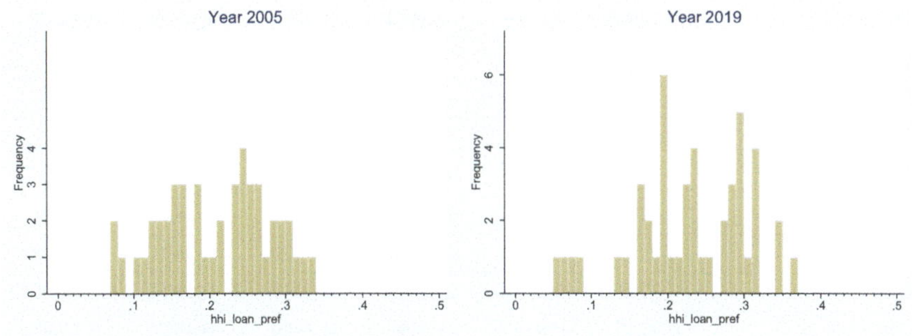

Fig. 10.2 Distribution of loan HHI and deposit HHI (all financial institutions, by prefecture) (*Source* Uesugi, Hiraga et al. (2021b))

market, maybe because financial institutions are reluctant to compete with each other for deposits in a very low interest rate environment.

We next consider the loan HHI for regional financial institutions (regional banks, second-tier regional banks, Shinkin banks, and credit cooperatives). The level of the

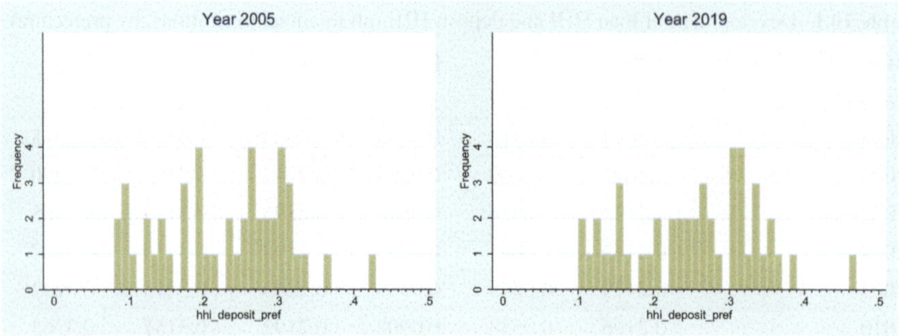

Fig. 10.2 (continued)

loan HHI is clearly higher, reflecting the smaller number of financial institutions present in the market (Table 10.2).

However, the findings that the value of the deposit HHI is higher than the loan HHI and that the average value of the loan HHI has increased over the sample period

Table 10.2 Development of loan HHI and deposit HHI (regional financial institutions, by prefecture)

Year (end of March)	Mean	Min	p5	Median	p95	Max
Loan HHI						
2005	0.2614	0.0369	0.0567	0.2914	0.3772	0.5171
2006	0.2617	0.0286	0.0572	0.2790	0.3688	0.5704
2007	0.2655	0.0265	0.0563	0.2856	0.3769	0.5607
2008	0.2680	0.0266	0.0554	0.2850	0.3727	0.5432
2009	0.2691	0.0238	0.0549	0.2830	0.3723	0.5331
2010	0.2710	0.0264	0.0548	0.2860	0.3774	0.5086
2011	0.2731	0.0226	0.0603	0.2851	0.3804	0.4873
2012	0.2736	0.0225	0.0578	0.2916	0.3860	0.4771
2013	0.2756	0.0223	0.0572	0.2941	0.3848	0.4718
2014	0.2753	0.0235	0.0581	0.2929	0.3891	0.4489
2015	0.2756	0.0226	0.0559	0.2937	0.3933	0.4378
2016	0.2757	0.0242	0.0557	0.2859	0.3941	0.4350
2017	0.2765	0.0271	0.0560	0.2820	0.4131	0.4314
2018	0.2763	0.0241	0.0562	0.2812	0.4112	0.4289
2019	0.2767	0.0246	0.0561	0.2775	0.4185	0.4291
(Reference) Deposit HHI						
2005	0.2845	0.0481	0.0648	0.2993	0.4000	0.5120
2019	0.3090	0.0620	0.0751	0.3190	0.4627	0.5222

Source Uesugi, Hiraga, et al. (2021b)

Table 10.3 Number of MEAs and MCEAs and number of municipalities included

	2005	2010	2015
MEA	109	108	100
Number of municipalities	1278	1122	1106
MCEA	142	121	122
Number of municipalities	480	354	364
MEA+MCEA	251	229	222
Number of municipalities	1758	1476	1328

Source Uesugi, Hiraga et al. (2021b)
Note An ordinance designated city is counted as a city. Tokyo's 23 special wards are counted as one

are the same as what we found with all financial institutions. Further, looking at the quantile values it is the case that the minimum value has become smaller over time although the decline is weaker. On the other hand, the maximum value has decreased over time due to the fact that the HHI declined over the sample period in the Nara prefecture that recorded the highest concentration at the beginning of the period.[14]

10.5.2 Loan HHI by Urban Employment Area—Substantial Heterogeneity Even within the Same Prefecture

The following table contains the results of the HHI calculations when the loan market is defined by urban employment areas (MEAs and MCEAs). Urban employment areas are municipal units and their geographic area is determined by the amount of commuter travel between the central city and the surrounding municipalities, based on the DID population as of 2005, 2010, and 2015, the years in which the census was conducted. Thus, as Table 10.3 shows, the number of MEAs and MCEAs and the total number of municipalities covered change every five years. Over time the number of MEAs and MCEAs has decreased along with the number of municipalities due to mergers among local governments. However, the total number of both is still 222 as of 2015, allowing the HHI to be calculated for these narrower, relative to prefectures, markets.[15]

We first consider, in Table 10.4, the HHI for all financial institutions included in the analysis. We find that the average HHI for the loan market is 0.2629 (2005) and 0.2777 (2019). The level of the HHI is higher than the prefectural HHI due to the smaller geographic area and the fewer financial institutions located there. It is

[14] In Nara Prefecture these large declines are not seen in the loan HHI. It is possible that there has been some changes in lending at Shinkin banks and some other small financial institutions.

[15] On average the geographic scope of MEAs and MCEAs is smaller than that of prefectures. The exception is the MEA with the Special Wards of Tokyo as its central city which, as of 2015, formed a huge urban employment area including 152 cities, wards, towns, and villages.

also the case, just as we found when the HHI was measured by prefecture, that the average HHI, concentration in the loan market, has increased over time. Similarly, the deposit HHI is larger than the loan HHI.

It is not necessarily the case, however, that the individual HHIs for each urban employment area will behave similarly to the prefectural HHI. As an example, take Hokkaido which has more than 20 urban employment areas, including MEAs and MCEAs; it may be that the level and evolution of the HHI differ by employment area even within the same prefecture.

Therefore, in Figure 10.3 we plot the loan HHI for all financial institutions in Hokkaido and in four selected urban employment areas within Hokkaido, Sapporo, Kitami, Rumoi, and Nemuro. Hokkaido overall has the lowest level HHI. Sapporo's HHI is the next lowest, with its movements during the period similar to those of Hokkaido. Since the Sapporo region accounts for a large share of the province's total economic activity financial institutions' lending and its market concentration have a strong influence on what we observe for Hokkaido as a whole. On the other hand,

Table 10.4 Development of Loan HHI and Deposit HHI (all financial institutions, by urban employment area)

Year (end of March)	N	Mean	Min	p5	Median	p95	Max
Loan HHI							
2005	251	0.2629	0.0594	0.1446	0.2588	0.4041	0.5986
2006	243	0.2619	0.0730	0.1463	0.2546	0.3982	0.5401
2007	241	0.2641	0.0693	0.1473	0.2616	0.4031	0.5385
2008	241	0.2664	0.0678	0.1510	0.2589	0.4035	0.5955
2009	240	0.2716	0.0640	0.1574	0.2676	0.4047	0.6415
2010	229	0.2723	0.0626	0.1534	0.2674	0.4206	0.5683
2011	229	0.2728	0.0587	0.1560	0.2646	0.4051	0.5912
2012	228	0.2745	0.0591	0.1551	0.2724	0.4192	0.5931
2013	228	0.2747	0.0591	0.1561	0.2733	0.4054	0.5926
2014	228	0.2744	0.0602	0.1557	0.2714	0.4207	0.5919
2015	222	0.2756	0.0548	0.1599	0.2728	0.4049	0.6109
2016	222	0.2765	0.0539	0.1619	0.2752	0.4089	0.6080
2017	222	0.2789	0.0535	0.1596	0.2754	0.4079	0.6066
2018	222	0.2790	0.0520	0.1586	0.2752	0.4084	0.5858
2019	222	0.2777	0.0541	0.1575	0.2744	0.4018	0.5850
(For reference) Deposit HHI							
2005	251	0.2877	0.0683	0.1469	0.2854	0.4361	0.5539
2019	222	0.3079	0.0951	0.1747	0.3043	0.4498	0.5531

Source Uesugi, Hiraga et al. (2021b)

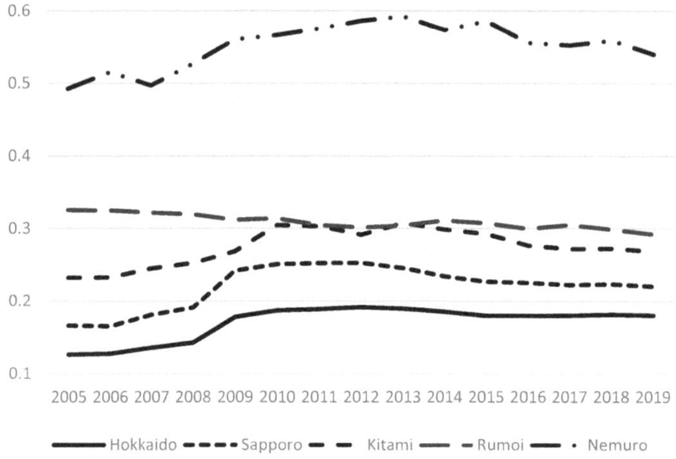

Fig. 10.3 Development of loan HHI in Hokkaido and several urban employment areas (*Source* Processed by the author based on Uesugi, Hiraga, et al. (2021b))

the HHI in other urban employment areas behaved quite differently. In Rumoi, for instance, the HHI declined, while in Nemuro, where the HHI in 2005 was quite high at over 0.5, it rose further until about 2013.

Given the heterogeneity in HHI among urban employment areas within a prefecture, the relationship between the loan market concentration and firms' financing environment may depend on how we define the market geographically. Market concentration in areas within a region that are considered peripheral, in terms of the level of economic activity, may deviate significantly from the region as a whole.

The best way to address this issue is to define the geographic scope of a loan market in a way that more accurately reflects economic reality.[16] In practice, however, most studies analyzing the degree of concentration and competition in loan markets either use administrative divisions within a country or treat the market as an area enclosed by a circle of a certain radius.[17]

---

[16] If a bank in one region does not raise its interest rate because it believes that an increase in the loan interest rate in one region will encourage firms to borrow from banks in the other region then we consider these two regions as belonging to the same loan market. If markets are identified using these criteria, which are referred in the Japan Fair Trade Commission's Guidelines to application of the Antimonopoly Act concerning review of business combination, it is possible to delineate markets that reflect economic reality.

[17] An example of the former is Sapienza (2002) who treats bank mergers in Italy using the province as the unit of measurement, and an example of the latter is Garmaise and Moskowitz (2006) who examine the impact of bank mergers in the US and treat the area of a circle with a radius of 10 miles as belonging to the same loan market.

10.6 Factor Decomposition of Loan HHI

What elements comprise the HHI in the loan market and what factors cause it to vary over time? One approach to answering these questions is to decompose the level of the HHI into the number of financial institutions that have branches in the region and the variation in the share of loans for these institutions. In the following section we use this approach to determine which factor has a stronger impact on changes in the HHI.

10.6.1 Decomposition into Factors Related to Variation in Market Share and the Number of Financial Institutions

The HHI can be decomposed into two parts as shown in Eq. (10.8) below, one relating to the number of financial institutions and the other representing the extent of deviation from the situation where the shares are evenly distributed.[18] Let r be the region, n be the number of financial institutions in the market at time t, and CV be the coefficient of variation (standard deviation divided by the mean) of the share of loans held by these institutions in the region. The following relationship then exists between n, CV, and HHI.[19]

$$HHI_{rt} = {CV_{rt}^2}/{n_{rt}} + {1}/{n_{rt}} \tag{10.8}$$

Equation (10.8) shows that the HHI is higher the smaller the number of financial institutions participating in the market or the greater the variation in the loan share. Thus, by dividing the HHI into two components, the inverse of the number of financial institutions and the variation in the distribution of market share, we can identify which component better explains the level of concentration and its variation over time.

10.6.2 Results of Factor Decomposition

We present the results of a factor decomposition of the loan market HHI by prefecture for all financial institutions. Table 10.5 shows that the coefficient of variation, which

[18] This decomposition is based on the arguments presented in Hannan (1997).

[19] We derive the formula as below:

$$CV^2 = n\sum_{i=1}^{n}\left(\frac{Loan_i}{\sum_i Loan_i} - \frac{1}{n}\right)^2 = \mathrm{n}\sum_{i=1}^{n}\left\{\left(\frac{Loan_i}{\sum_i Loan_i}\right)^2 + \frac{1}{n^2} - \frac{2}{n}\frac{Loan_i}{\sum_i Loan_i}\right\}$$

$$= \mathrm{n}\sum_{i=1}^{n}\left(\frac{Loan_i}{\sum_i Loan_i}\right)^2 - 1 = \mathrm{n}HHI\_Loan - 1$$

reflects variations in market share, explains movements in the HHI better than the inverse of the number of financial institutions located in a prefecture.

Table 10.5 Decomposition of loan HHI (all financial institutions, by prefecture)

Factor of coefficients of variation	Mean	Min	p5	Median	p95	Max
2005	0.1673	0.0628	0.0757	0.1651	0.2450	0.2827
2006	0.1660	0.0663	0.0849	0.1647	0.2397	0.2704
2007	0.1688	0.0587	0.0803	0.1712	0.2474	0.2779
2008	0.1708	0.0546	0.0785	0.1792	0.2516	0.2731
2009	0.1733	0.0407	0.0832	0.1749	0.2565	0.2706
2010	0.1744	0.0401	0.0813	0.1740	0.2548	0.2706
2011	0.1761	0.0368	0.0806	0.1743	0.2547	0.2737
2012	0.1768	0.0370	0.0744	0.1731	0.2492	0.2811
2013	0.1788	0.0364	0.0718	0.1778	0.2515	0.2811
2014	0.1794	0.0381	0.0713	0.1766	0.2516	0.2865
2015	0.1802	0.0371	0.0699	0.1825	0.2513	0.2913
2016	0.1816	0.0362	0.0685	0.1762	0.2564	0.2934
2017	0.1832	0.0358	0.0629	0.1790	0.2839	0.2944
2018	0.1837	0.0343	0.0579	0.1790	0.2825	0.2930
2019	0.1838	0.0362	0.0565	0.1768	0.2874	0.2998
Factor of the number of financial institutions	Mean	Min	p5	Median	p95	Max
2005	0.0426	0.0044	0.0132	0.0400	0.0909	0.1667
2006	0.0433	0.0045	0.0137	0.0417	0.0909	0.1667
2007	0.0437	0.0045	0.0137	0.0417	0.0909	0.1667
2008	0.0441	0.0046	0.0137	0.0417	0.0909	0.1667
2009	0.0445	0.0047	0.0139	0.0435	0.0909	0.1667
2010	0.0452	0.0047	0.0137	0.0435	0.0909	0.1667
2011	0.0454	0.0047	0.0137	0.0435	0.1000	0.1667
2012	0.0453	0.0047	0.0135	0.0435	0.1000	0.1667
2013	0.0457	0.0047	0.0137	0.0435	0.1000	0.1667
2014	0.0458	0.0053	0.0141	0.0455	0.1000	0.1667
2015	0.0458	0.0048	0.0141	0.0455	0.1000	0.1667
2016	0.0456	0.0049	0.0141	0.0455	0.1000	0.1429
2017	0.0455	0.0050	0.0143	0.0455	0.1000	0.1429
2018	0.0460	0.0050	0.0143	0.0476	0.1000	0.1429
2019	0.0463	0.0054	0.0143	0.0476	0.1000	0.1429

Source Uesugi, Hiraga et al. (2021b)

Looking at the average of the factors that affect the development of the prefectural loan HHI, the inverse of the number of financial institutions has increased monotonically over time, from 0.043 (2005) to 0.046 (2019).

The reason for this is that the number of financial institutions with branches in each region has been on a gradual downward trend due to bank consolidation and branch closures. The square of the coefficient of variation divided by the number of financial institutions has also been increasing over time from 0.167 (2005) to 0.184 (2019). Moreover, this factor contributes quantitatively more to the increase in the HHI than the inverse of the number of financial institutions.

However, the picture is different when looking at statistics that represent the left end of the distribution. The minimum and the 5 percentile values of the inverse of the number of financial institutions have increased over the period. This is the same as what was found for the mean, indicating that even in areas where the number of financial institutions was originally large (i.e., where its inverse was small) the number of financial institutions decreased (i.e., its inverse increased) during the sample period. Conversely, the minimum and 5 percentile values of the coefficient of variation are decreasing. When we looked at the overall HHI in Sect. 10.5 we saw that the HHI declined over time in the metropolitan prefectures. The factor decomposition indicates that the decline in the HHI was due to the equalization of loan shares among lender financial institutions, with the share of the top banks declining and the share of the bottom banks rising despite an overall decline in the number of financial institutions in the region.

In summary, the gradual increase in concentration in the loan market in Japan over the last 15 years is more reflective of a greater dispersion in market share than a decline in the number of financial institutions. It could also be the result of financial institutions with relatively large market shares increasing their share by offering lower interest rates. On the other hand, in metropolitan areas, the loan HHI is declining because the degree of variation in loan market share is shrinking while the number of financial institutions is decreasing. The decline in loan HHI in the metropolitan areas, which contrasts with the overall trend of the increase in loan HHI, contributes to the polarization of loan HHI in the country.

10.7 Change in the Loan HHI Due to Financial Institution Mergers

One of the major factors that can cause changes in the HHI over time is mergers between financial institutions. This is because if the merging institutions were active in the same loan market the HHI will invariably increase as loan shares that were divided between two or more institutions are combined into a single institution after the merger. Thus, mergers are expected to increase both of the HHI components discussed in the previous section. The inverse of financial institutions will always increase because the merger will reduce the number of financial institutions in the region by at least one. Similarly, the larger the loan market share of the merging institutions the greater the variation in loan shares after the merger.

In this section we measure how much the HHI has increased at the prefecture and the urban employment area level as a result of bank mergers, which are an important issue for policy making. This allows us to determine how mergers between financial institutions have impacted the evolution of the HHI in the loan market over time. Note that the following analysis focuses on mergers in which one of the legal entities ceases to exist and does not cover mergers in which the participating financial institutions survive under a holding company. In the case of the former, credit standards will be merged across the financial institutions participating in the merger and branches that have been competing in the same market will no longer be competitors after the completion of the merger. In contrast, in the latter case credit standards may differ and competition among branches in the same market may remain.

10.7.1 Analytical Method

Let $\Delta \text{HHI\_Counterfactual}_{\text{rt}-1}$ be the expected increase in the HHI at time t–1 due to a merger of financial institutions at time t in region r. The financial institutions merging at time t are run by different entities prior to that time and are treated as separate financial institutions in the calculation of $\text{HHI}_{\text{rt}-1}$. On the other hand, $\text{HHI\_Counterfactual}_{\text{rt}-1}$ calculates the HHI by assuming that the financial institutions that merge in t are already the same entity at time t–1. The difference between the two, $\text{HHI\_Counterfactual}_{\text{rt}-1} - \text{HHI}_{\text{rt}-1} = \Delta \text{HHI\_Counterfactual}_{\text{rt}-1}$, is positive if both institutions participating in the merger have loans in the same region r. The higher the regional lending share of the merging institutions, or the greater the number of such mergers in the region, the larger the value. Formula (10.9) standardizes this increase:

$$\Delta HHI\_Counterfactual_{rt-1} / HHI_{rt-1} \tag{10.9}$$

10.7.2 Projected Increase in the HHI at the Prefecture Level

We show the results of the calculation in formula (10.9), which is the expected increase in the HHI at the prefecture level following mergers of financial institutions. The expected increase in the HHI is positive for 118 out of 705 prefecture-year observations for the 2005–2019 period. However, many of these positive values are near zero because the merging financial institutions have small lending shares in many prefectures.

Table 10.6 shows the prefecture-year observations that recorded the largest $\Delta HHI\_Counterfactual_{rt-1}/HHI_{rt-1}$. They are also are limited to those whose value is above 1%. When narrowed down in this way the number of prefecture-year observations in which the HHI is expected to substantially increase due to financial institution mergers falls to 28.

We now take a closer look at the mergers which had substantial impacts on prefectural loan markets. The merger of financial institutions in Wakayama Prefecture in FY2006 was expected to increase the loan HHI by over 30% as of the end of March

Table 10.6 Prefecture-year observations where loan HHI is expected to increase due to financial institution mergers (all financial institutions)

Year	Prefecture	ΔHHI_Counterfactual/HHI
2006	Wakayama	0.3032
2005	Tokyo	0.3002
2007	Yamagata	0.2001
2013	Tokyo	0.1735
2008	Hokkaido	0.1689
2012	Gifu	0.1538
2005	Aichi	0.1275
2005	Osaka	0.1196
2019	Osaka	0.0658
2013	Osaka	0.0545
2009	Ibaraki	0.0507
2005	Kanagawa	0.0371
2012	Osaka	0.0361
2009	Aomori	0.0305
2005	Kyoto	0.0284
2015	Fukui	0.0227
2012	Tokyo	0.0214
2013	Aichi	0.0203
2005	Nara	0.0201
2010	Osaka	0.0200
2005	Hyogo	0.0195
2007	Gunma	0.0183
2018	Shizuoka	0.0179
2005	Saitama	0.0164
2018	Mie	0.0155
2012	Aichi	0.0137
2006	Yamaguchi	0.0133
2006	Shimane	0.0131

Source Uesugi, Hiraga et al. (2021b)

2006. This was due to the October 2006 merger between Kiyo Bank, a regional bank, and Wakayama Bank, a second regional bank. Similarly, a merger of financial institutions in Tokyo in FY2005 was also expected to result in an increase of over 30% in the loan HHI. This increase was largely due to the impact of the January 2006 merger of the Bank of Tokyo Mitsubishi and the UFJ Bank.

Looking at Table 10.6 as a whole, the loan HHI was expected to rise substantially in metropolitan prefectures (Tokyo, Osaka, and Aichi prefectures) mainly due to mergers of city banks. On the other hand, there are a certain number of mergers of regional financial institutions that were expected to increase the HHI in non-metropolitan prefectures (e.g., Wakayama prefecture, Yamagata Shiawase Bank and Shokusan Bank in Yamagata prefecture, Hokuyo Bank and Sapporo Bank in Hokkaido, and The Juroku Bank and Gifu Bank in Gifu prefecture).

10.7.3 Projected Increase in the HHI at the Urban Employment Area Level

The results presented here are based on urban employment areas. The number of urban employment area-year observations with a positive expected increase in the HHI associated with financial institution mergers is 133 out of 3,648.

Table 10.7 shows the urban employment area-year observations that recorded a substantial (more than 1%) increase in $\Delta HHI\_Counterfactual_{rt-1}/HHI_{rt-1}$. Since most of the urban employment areas are smaller than prefectures, in terms of market size the loan share of individual financial institutions is larger, which in turn means that an expected increase in HHI after the merger is larger as well. As a result there are 74 urban employment area-year observations in the table.

When examined at the prefecture level a substantial increase in the loan and the deposit HHI was expected only when large financial institutions such as city banks, regional banks, and second-tier regional banks participated into the mergers. The market size of a prefecture was so large that it would have taken a merger between financial institutions of substantial size to have a significant impact on the concentration of the market. In contrast, when we regard each urban employment area as the loan and the deposit market, which is smaller than prefectures, even mergers between Shinkin banks can have a significant impact on the HHI. The examples of such cases include: the Shibetsu region of Hokkaido when Nayoro Shinkin and Shibetsu Shinkin merged in October 2007; the Hamamatsu region of Shizuoka Prefecture when Hamamatsu Shinkin and Iwata Shinkin merged in January 2019; and the Sakata region of Yamagata Prefecture when Sakata Shinkin and Tsuruoka Shinkin merged in March 2008.

Table 10.7 Urban employment area-year observations where loan HHI is expected to increase due to financial institution mergers (all financial institutions)

Year	Urban employment area	ΔHHI_ Counterfactual/HHI	Year	Urban employment area	ΔHHI_ Counterfactual/HHI
2006	Wakayama City	0.37560	2007	Gotemba City	0.04984
2008	Furano City	0.34105	2009	Koga City	0.04666
2005	Tokyo	0.28188	2013	Osaka	0.04474
2007	Nagai City	0.26303	2019	Shimada City	0.04186
2007	Shibetsu City	0.21287	2006	Gojo City	0.04165
2007	Yamagata City	0.20143	2016	Hakodate City	0.03605
2018	Hamamatsu City	0.18890	2008	Kitami City	0.03527
2008	Chitose City	0.17885	2005	Atsugi City	0.03500
2013	Tokyo	0.17691	2006	Ube City	0.03497
2006	Tanabe City	0.17116	2007	Takasaki City	0.03280
2007	Sakata City	0.17089	2012	Osaka	0.03086
2008	Sapporo/ Otaru	0.16294	2008	Nemuro City	0.03083
2008	Takikawa City	0.15929	2005	Aizu Wakamatsu City	0.03044
2012	Gifu City	0.15791	2005	Kyoto City	0.02987
2005	Nagoya/ Komaki	0.15413	2018	Tsu City	0.02822
2008	Hakodate City	0.14785	2012	Seki City	0.02787
2007	Shinjyo City	0.12263	2015	Fukui City	0.02768
2009	Chikusei City	0.11993	2013	Nagoya City	0.02416
2005	Osaka	0.11534	2018	Ise City	0.02306
2008	Kushiro City	0.11185	2010	Osaka	0.02258
2009	Tsukuba/ Tsuchiura	0.11052	2005	Yokkaichi City	0.02243
2007	Yonezawa City	0.10686	2012	Ogaki City	0.02184
2006	Izumo City	0.10568	2012	Takayama City	0.02145
2009	Hitachi City	0.10191	2012	Tokyo	0.02065
2009	Kitami City	0.10178	2012	Nagoya City	0.01943
2006	Shingu City	0.09949	2005	Kobe City	0.01926

(continued)

Table 10.7 (continued)

Year	Urban employment area	ΔHHI_ Counterfactual/HHI	Year	Urban employment area	ΔHHI_ Counterfactual/HHI
2019	Kakegawa City	0.09647	2005	Himeji City	0.01537
2007	Tsuruoka City	0.09605	2005	Yamagata City	0.01315
2008	Tomakomai City	0.09569	2013	Kobe City	0.01223
2009	Kamisu/ Kashima	0.09476	2009	Kyoto City	0.01128
2017	Iwanai Town	0.09220	2009	Mito City	0.01117
2008	Wakkanai City	0.09154	2013	Sendai City	0.01100
2008	Iwamizawa City	0.08943	2017	Sapporo/ Otaru	0.01022
2007	Muroran City	0.07948	2006	Yamaguchi City	0.01017
2019	Shizuoka City	0.06565			
2015	Ogaki City	0.06311			
2008	Asahikawa City	0.06226			
2019	Osaka City	0.05879			
2008	Obihiro City	0.05348			
2008	Muroran City	0.05222			

Source Uesugi, Hiraga et al. (2021b)

10.8 How Long Will the Expected Increase in the HHI Persist?

In the previous section we predicted the extent to which a merger would result in an increase in the loan market HHI based on prior loan balance information for the financial institutions participating in the merger. To understand the impact of the merger on the actual loan HHI it is necessary not only to predict the extent to which the HHI will rise before the merger but also to examine whether the HHI rose as expected after the merger and how long the increase lasted.

10.8.1 Estimates Measuring the Extent to Which the Expected HHI Increase is Realized

Based on the above discussion the extent to which the expected increase in HHI at time t–1 is reflected in the actual change in HHI after time t is examined by estimating Eq. (10.10).

$$\left(\frac{\Delta HHI_{rt+j,t-1}}{HHI_{rt-1}}\right) = \alpha + \beta_j(\Delta HHI\_Counterfactual_{rt-1}/HHI_{rt-1}) + \varepsilon_{rt+j} \quad (10.10)$$

Here j ranges from 0 to 5 and we observe how β_j changes over time. If the share of the merged financial institution in the loan market does not change from the pre-merger level and the share of other financial institutions also does not change then the predicted change in the HHI will actually be realized and the value of estimated coefficient β_j will be 1. On the other hand, if the merged financial institution subsequently reduces its lending share and other financial institutions increase their share, which would result in a smaller amount of variation in loan shares, the anticipated increase in the HHI will not be realized ex-post and the value of the coefficient will be less than 1. Finally, if the merged institution's share increases further ex-post and the degree of variation among financial institutions increases the value of the coefficient will exceed 1.

10.8.2 Post-Merger HHI in the Loan Market

Table 10.8 presents the estimation results of Eq. (10.10). For the loan market the year t–1 is 2005 through 2013 and the table shows the extent to which the expected increase in HHI due to the merger in the ex-ante stage is reflected in the actual change in HHI in each year, from year t of the merger through year t+5, five years later.

Table 10.8 Estimation results on the impact of an expected increase in loan HHI on its actual increase (all financial institutions, by prefecture)

	(1)	(2)	(3)	(4)	(5)	(6)
	Dependent variable: Δloan HHI/ HHI					
	t	t +1	t+2	t+3	t+4	t+5
Δloan HHI_Counterfactual/ loan HHI	0.888***	0.775***	0.654***	0.670***	0.551***	0.509***
Number of observations	423	423	423	423	423	423
R-squared	0.401	0.150	0.066	0.048	0.027	0.019

Source Uesugi, Hiraga et al. (2021b)
Note ***, **, and * represent statistical significance at 1%, 5%, and 10%, respectively

Columns (1) through (6) measure the range of the change in the loan HHI that actually occurred from year t to year t+5, starting with year t–1. These changes are the dependent variables. The coefficient in column (1) indicates the extent to which the expected HHI is actually reflected in the actual HHI in year t is 0.89, which is significantly different from the coefficient of 1 that would be obtained if the expectations made in the year before the merger were fully realized. However, this coefficient declines in the periods following the merger. The coefficient in column (2), which uses the change in the HHI in the year t+1 is 0.78. The coefficients indicating the extent to which the expected HHI is reflected in the actual HHI in later years also tend to decrease. In the loan market where bank mergers occurred, the degree of variation in lending share among financial institutions shrank due to a decrease in the share of the merging banks and an increase in the share of other financial institutions, resulting in a decrease in market concentration.[20]

10.8.3 The Persistence of the HHI Increase is Affected by the Extent of Prior Concentration

The finding that the predicted increase in the HHI is mostly realized immediately after the merger but that the impact diminishes over time has an important policy implication. Even if the degree of competition among financial institutions is moderated by the merger this implies that there are forces at work to restore the HHI to its pre-merger level.

What are the factors that may have caused the HHI to revert to its prior level? We implement an additional analysis considering that the prior concentration in the loan market may have had some effect.

If the loan market is less concentrated and competitive to start then once the HHI rises as a result of a bank merger other financial institutions may aggressively lend to capture the combined bank's market share. In this case the HHI would decline in the years following the merger. Conversely, if the original concentration is high and the degree of competition in the market is moderate then competitive pressure from other financial institutions will be weak after the merger and the HHI, which rose after the merger, would be expected to remain high in subsequent years.

Based on this consideration the loan HHI in Eq. (10.10) is estimated again but this time by splitting the sample into two based on the concentration of the loan market ex-ante in the year of 2005. Columns (1) through (6) of Table 10.9 present estimates only for the prefectures where the 2005 loan HHI was higher than the median value and the degree of competition was considered relatively loose.

Columns (7) through (12) present the results for the prefectures considered to have a relatively high degree of competition with HHI below the median value. We

[20] An examination of the deposit market yields results similar to those obtained here. However, in the deposit market the actual HHI increase in the merger year was larger than in the loan market and the subsequent increases were also more persistent.

Table 10.9 Estimation results on the impact of an expected increase in loan HHI on its actual increase (all financial institutions, by prefecture, by loan HHI in 2005)

	(1)	(2)	(3)	(4)	(5)	(6)
	Dependent variable: Δloan HHI/ HHI					
	For prefecture-year that satisfies HHI_Loan_2005 > median					
	t	t+1	t+2	t+3	t+4	t+5
Δloan HHI_Counterfactual/ loan HHI	0.843***	0.962***	0.826***	0.967***	0.940***	0.848***
Number of observations	207	207	207	207	207	207
R-squared	0.363	0.246	0.126	0.125	0.093	0.064
	(7)	(8)	(9)	(10)	(11)	(12)
	Dependent variable: Δloan HHI/ HHI					
	For prefecture-year that satisfies HHI_Loan_2005 < = median					
	t	t+1	t+2	t+3	t+4	t+5
Δloan HHI_Counterfactual/ loan HHI	0.898***	0.684***	0.553***	0.511**	0.357	0.331
Number of observations	216	216	216	216	216	216
R-squared	0.410	0.114	0.045	0.026	0.011	0.008

Source Uesugi, Hiraga et al. (2021b)
Note ***, **, and * represent statistical significance at 1%, 5%, and 10%, respectively

find contrasting coefficient movements. The coefficient for the high concentration prefectures is between 0.83 and 0.97, a level not significantly different from 1 except at time t, which displays no tendency to diminish in the years following the merger. In contrast, the coefficient for the low concentration prefectures was 0.90, a level not significantly different from 1 at the time of the merger, but it does decline significantly thereafter and after four years the coefficient was not significantly different from 0. These results suggest that the merged bank's market share declined as other financial institutions intensified their lending offensive following the merger.[21]

[21] The same estimation was conducted for the deposit market after dividing the sample and the results showed that in prefectures with low concentration and high competition the increase in the HHI is more persistent than that in the loan market. We also examine the persistence of the HHI increase in the loan market by urban employment area rather than by prefecture. We find that the post-merger increase in the loan market HHI was insignificant at an early stage when we limit the sample to a small number of areas with low prior concentration and a high degree of competition.

10.9 The Impact of the Loan HHI on the Firm Financing Environment

In our previous analysis we assumed that the loan HHI represents the market power of financial institutions and examined its level and changes, as well as the extent to which the HHI increases with financial institution mergers and the persistence of this increase. As shown in Section 10.3, when assuming a Cournot-type oligopoly there is a positive relationship between the HHI and the price-cost margin.[22] We do not know, however, whether the positive relationship is the result of market power or due to a few efficient banks gaining a larger market share.

In the U.S. there have been studies focusing on the relationship between the HHI and deposit and loan interest rates, which examine which of the two possible explanations is true: Hannan (1997), Hannan and Prager (2004), and Berger and Hannan (1989) examined how deposit market concentration impacts deposit and loan interest rates, while Hannan and Berger (1991) focused on the extent to which bank deposit rates change when market interest rates change (the pass-through rate) and found that more concentrated markets have smaller pass-through rates.

In Japan, Hiraga, Manabe, and Yoshino (2017) calculated the loan HHI using the same data employed in this chapter to examine the relationship between concentration and loan interest rates and loan volumes. Uchino (2014), like Hannan and Berger (1991), found that the relationship between pass-through rates and deposit rates is affected by market concentration using Japanese data.

In this section, as in Hiraga, Manabe, and Yoshino (2017), we use the prefecture-level loan HHI and merge it with the borrowing interest rates of local firms and other information aggregated at the prefectural level to investigate whether higher HHI in the loan market leads to higher borrowing interest rates for firms.

10.9.1 Analytical Method

Using prefecture-level panel data we regress aggregate firm borrowing interest rates on the possible determinants in the local loan market, including the loan HHI. The estimation equation is as follows:

$$
\begin{aligned}
Rate_{rt} = \alpha &+ \beta_1 HHI_{rt-i} + \beta_2 ROA_{rt-1} + \beta_3 Cash_{rt-1} + \beta_4 Unemployment_{rt-1} \\
&+ \beta_5 LandPrice_{rt-1} + \beta_6 Growth\_Population_{rt-1} + \theta_r + \mu_t + \varepsilon_{rt} \qquad (10.11)
\end{aligned}
$$

where r is a prefecture, t is a year, and i is one of 1, 2, or 3.

[22] Ojima (2018) estimated price–cost margins for financial institutions in Japan. Using the ratio of current income to total assets and the marginal cost obtained from the estimated translog cost function she obtains P-MC and finds that it has been on a downward trend over the past 30 years.

The dependent variable is the average interest rate paid (Rate) by firms located in each prefecture. We calculate this by dividing the interest that firms pay by the outstanding long- and short-term loan amount. The information on the interest and the loan amount is based on the financial statements collected by one of Japan's largest credit research companies and covers a substantial portion of firms located in a prefecture. From the same data source we obtain firms' return on assets (ROA) and cash holdings (Cash) which are included as explanatory variables.

The key explanatory variable is the prefectural HHI (HHI) of the loan market which has been used in previous analyses. If the HHI is positively correlated with market power then the coefficient on the HHI should be positive assuming no change in the share of marginal cost. However, it may take time for a change in concentration to affect a firm's stock-based borrowing interest rate due to the need to renew loan contracts. With this in mind we not only use the HHI value from the preceding period but also the lagged values of two or three periods before.

The other variables used to represent the level of economic activity in the region are the unemployment rate (Unemployment), log of residential land prices (Land-Price), and population growth rate (Growth_Population). The fixed effects model is employed to control for prefecture-specific factors that do not vary over time.

It is important to note that the HHI is determined by the number of financial institutions that have branches and operate in the region and the variation in the loan volume extended by these institutions. The decision to open a branch in a region and the lending policy and demand for funds by each branch are influenced by variables that also affect the interest rate paid (the explained variable) such as the unobservable credit risk in the region. In these cases the estimated coefficients on HHI are subject to bias.

Unlike decisions by individual financial institutions regarding branch location and lending policies which are affected by regional credit risk, bank mergers are decisions that reflect management performance of the merging banks as a whole, with the impact of regional credit risk on this considered to be relatively small. Therefore, as an additional examination, we also perform an estimation using the predicted increase in the HHI that accompanies bank mergers, rather than the HHI itself, as an explanatory variable.[23] In Section 10.7 we measured the expected increase in the loan HHI associated with financial institution mergers, which is used as the explanatory variable.

[23] This approach follows Garmaise and Moskowitz (2006), however, their unit of analysis is spatially smaller than prefectures (within a 10-mile radius circle) and the extent to which individual local factors influence the merger decisions of financial institutions is likely to be smaller than in this analysis.

10.9.2 Estimation Results

The results of the estimation are presented in Table 10.10. We estimate equation (10.11) first with the HHI itself and then with the expected change in HHI as the explanatory variable. We do this for each of the different lag lengths for a total of six estimations.

Table 10.10 Estimation results on the relationship between loan HHI and borrowing interest rate

Estimation method: Fixed effect model						
Dependent variable: Borrowing interest rate						
	(1)	(2)	(3)	(4)	(5)	(6)
HHI_t–1	0.412*					
HHI_t–2		0.584**				
HHI_t–3			0.678**			
Δloan HHI_ Counterfactual/ loan HHI upon bank mergers_t–2				-0.333		
Δloan HHI_ Counterfactual/ loan HHI upon bank mergers_t–3					0.0945	
Δloan HHI_ Counterfactual/ loan HHI upon bank mergers_t–4						0.216
ROA_t–1	0.992***	0.800***	0.592*	0.819***	0.628**	0.309
Cash holdings_t–1	-1.455***	-1.411***	-1.591***	-1.323***	-1.448***	-1.356***
Unemployment rate_t–1	0.0360***	0.0310***	0.0209**	0.0315***	0.0222**	0.0302***
lnResidential Land price_t–1	0.0325	0.0255	0.0487	0.0112	0.0355	0.0220
Population growth rate_t–1	0.0137	0.0170	0.0127	0.0167	0.0129	0.0128
Year fixed effect	Yes	Yes	Yes	Yes	Yes	Yes
Prefecture fixed effect	Yes	Yes	Yes	Yes	Yes	Yes
Number of observations	658	611	564	611	564	517
R-squared	0.962	0.963	0.962	0.962	0.962	0.956

Source Table 1 in Uesugi, Nguyen, and Hiramine (2021)
Note ***, **, and * represent statistical significance at 1%, 5%, and 10%, respectively

With the HHI as an explanatory variable we find that the coefficient is positive and the longer the lag the larger and more significant it is. If the HHI increases by about 0.07, which is the standard deviation of the loan HHI, the HHI (3-period lag) coefficient in column (3) would indicate an increase in the borrowing interest rate of about 0.05 percentage points (=0.678×0.07) after 3 years. Given the current very low interest rate levels in Japan we may say that the increase of five basis points in the loan interest rate is economically significant.

In contrast, when the estimation is repeated using the expected HHI the coefficient is insignificant at all lags. As the lag length increases the coefficient does change from negative to positive but remains insignificant nonetheless.

What might account for the difference between these results? The first possibility is that the endogenous bias in the HHI is reduced by using the merger-related increase in the HHI. If unobservable economic risk in the region is driving financial institutions to exit, raising the HHI and loan interest rates at the same time, then the estimation using the HHI itself would overestimate β_1. If this is the case then the estimates using the expected HHI would be more accurate and have less bias.

The second possibility is that an increase in the HHI due to mergers and an increase in the HHI due to other factors are the result of different behaviors of financial institutions. Mergers cause the HHI to rise because they reduce the number of financial institutions in the loan market and concentrate lending in the hands of a few institutions. This same increase in the HHI occurs when a financial institution exits the market and the remaining institutions share and assume its business. However, if the merging financial institutions behave differently than before the merger, for example, if post-merger synergies make their operations more efficient and allow them to lend at lower interest rates, the interest rate paid by firms may not rise even if the HHI rises.

To clarify which of the two is occurring, the use of firm-level data, including information on transaction relationships between firms and financial institutions, is required rather than data aggregated at the regional level.

10.10 Summary

In this chapter we attempted to calculate regional financial market concentration using information on the amount of loans at the branch level of financial institutions located in Japan, and to statistically clarify the nature of this concentration. After showing that, under certain theoretical assumptions, market concentration is an indicator related to market power we empirically verify that there is a loan interest rates increase with market concentration.

We not only consider the loan and deposit HHIs at the prefectural level but also look at the urban employment area level defined by the linkages between cities and towns based on the way workers commute over a recent 15-year period. We have the following findings: financial market concentration is on the rise; concentration in the loan market tends to be polarized between metropolitan and non-metropolitan areas;

increased dispersion in market share has contributed more to the rise in concentration than a decline in the number of financial institutions; and mergers of financial institutions increased the loan HHI, although the increase did not persist in regions with a low ex-ante level of loan market concentration.

In Chapter 11 we will turn our focus to mergers between financial institutions. Mergers not only change the degree of market concentration and market power but also change the way the merging financial institutions operate. In addition, because information asymmetries exist between borrower firms and lender financial institutions in the loan market firms and financial institutions often establish relationships in advance to mitigate this problem. For this reason a merger is not expected to have the same effect on all firms in the loan market where the merger occurs but rather to have a stronger impact on firms that transact with the merging bank. We will analyze this issue using the example of a merger between two megabanks which, at the time, was the largest bank merger ever.

Chapter 11
Financial Institution Mergers and Firm Financing

Abstract By comparing firms that used to transact with merged banks with those that did not we measure the impact of financial institution mergers on firm financing in two ways. We first take a close look at a megabank merger. We then conduct a comprehensive examination of how recent financial institution mergers have affected the financing environment of firms. The key results are as follows. First, the 2006 merger between two megabanks, the Bank of Tokyo-Mitsubishi and the UFJ Bank, led to a substantial increase in interest rates among non-listed borrower firms and a decline in their loan ratios. Second, looking at the effects of financial institution mergers since 2004 we find that the financial environment for firms that transacted with merged banks has improved on average, which is the opposite of the findings for the megabank merger. Among all bank mergers since 2004 the finding of higher interest rates is unique to the megabank merger. Mergers in the 2010s resulted in a larger increase in the loan ratio for firms that previously transacted with the merged banks than for firms that did not.

Keywords Financial institution merger · Managerial efficiency · Megabanks · Bargaining power · Borrowing interest rates

11.1 Introduction: Effects of Mergers of Financial Institutions on Firm Borrowing Interest Rates

In Chapter 10, using prefecture-level data, we found that firm borrowing interest rates rise modestly and gradually as concentration in the loan market increases, and that the increase is insignificant when the increase in concentration is attributable to financial institution mergers.

However, since firms and financial institutions transact based on pre-established relationships the impact of a bank merger on a firm's financing is likely to vary depending on the existence of bank-firm relationships. A merger is not expected to have a similar impact on all firms in the loan market but rather to have a stronger impact on firms that transact with the merged bank. Based on this idea the chapter uses

I. Uesugi, *The Economics of SME Finance*, Advances in Japanese Business and Economics 36, https://doi.org/10.1007/978-981-96-3193-3_11

firm-level data, including information on firm relationships with financial institutions, to determine the impact of mergers on the financing of firms, particularly financing of SMEs.

Mergers among financial institutions are not only important for firms' financing environment but also for the future of financial institutions in Japan. In particular, the Japan Fair Trade Commission (JFTC) recently withheld the decision on the proposal of a merger between two regional banks in Nagasaki prefecture which would result in a substantial increase in market concentration in the region. It eventually gave approval to the proposed merger after the merging banks took necessary measures such as the transfer of loans to other financial institutions to resolve the problem of increased market power caused by the merger.

This created an opportunity to discuss the difficult business environment for regional financial institutions which are facing a decline in demand due to the decreasing population and the continued low interest rates brought about by monetary easing. This also led to a discussion about the need to create an environment which facilitates mergers and business consolidations among financial institutions as a means for regional banks to continue providing financial services. As a result of these discussions the Financial Services Agency (FSA) of the government implemented a special law in November 2020 that provides for a temporary exemption from the application of the Antimonopoly Act to regional banks.

The necessary policy response for the time being to the question of whether to allow financial institution mergers, which significantly increase market concentration, has been implemented. However, there is no empirical evidence on whether mergers of financial institutions in Japan have actually improved economic welfare in the loan market as a whole, nor do we know much about how mergers change surpluses for firms which are an integral part of the economic welfare. Empirical research on the effects of financial institution mergers in Japan is limited despite the fact that numerous mergers have taken place. Questions of whether firms' financing will become tighter after bank mergers, and if so to what extent, as well as what types of mergers will substantially deteriorate firms' financing environment, have not been fully addressed.

Given this situation this chapter focuses on recent financial institution mergers in Japan and examines their effect on the firms' financing environment through relationships between firms and financial institutions. We first examine a merger between two Japanese megabanks which at the time was the largest merger in the world in terms of assets. Given that Japanese megabanks have extended loans to firms including many SMEs this merger must have had a massive impact on the financing of SMEs.

Second, we examine all the financial institution mergers since the mid-2000s in Japan. The megabank mergers, including the one we analyze, are just one of many financial institution mergers that have taken place in Japan, albeit they are on a large scale. By comprehensively examining the impact of mergers on the firm financing environment, we clarify the effects of these financial institution mergers to date and provide a basis for discussing the direction and extent to which future mergers will affect financing.

11.2 Overview of Results

We outline our main findings regarding the above two issues, the impact of the megabank merger and that of financial institution mergers overall, below. With megabank mergers the financing environment worsens for firms that had a prior relationships with the merging banks in that post-merger borrowing interest rates rise and the ratio of borrowings to total assets declines. In particular, borrowing interest rates increase by up to 30 basis points (= 0.3%) for firms that had pre-existing relationships with both merging banks relative to firms that did not. The average interest rate paid by firms in the dataset prior to the merger was 2.6% (= 260 basis points), indicating that the margin of the increase in the interest rate was economically significant.

On the other hand, for all financial institution mergers from 2004 to 2018 the decline in borrowing interest rates for firms that used to transact with the merging banks was slightly larger than the decline for other firms, with the increase in the borrowing ratio slightly higher. In this case, mergers have improved the financing environment for firms, albeit only slightly. The findings of a considerable increase in interest rates for the megabank merger is rather unique among all the mergers during the period.

This chapter proceeds as follows. Section 11.3 presents the theoretical framework for analyzing the impact of mergers on economic welfare to show how changes in firms' financial conditions are related to the change in welfare. Section 11.4 discusses the issues that need to be considered when applying the theoretical predictions to the loan market. Section 11.5 outlines the empirical analysis. Section 11.6 presents the results of the analysis of a megabank merger, and Sect. 11.7 presents the results of the analysis of financial institution mergers since the mid-2000s. Section 11.8 summarizes.

11.3 Theoretical Framework

The question of how borrowing firms are affected by changes in the price and supply of loans through mergers of financial institutions is also a question of how consumer surplus changes. The extent of a change in the demand side surplus in the loan market due to bank mergers is affected by the behavior of the supply side and the resulting change in the supply-side surplus. To clarify the relationship between bank mergers and the demand side surplus Williamson's (1968) welfare trade-off framework is helpful. Below is an overview of the arguments presented in Odagiri (2001, Chapters 3 and 11).[1]

Figure 11.1 shows the change in equilibrium in three cases when two of the n financial institutions that provide homogeneous lending services merge under a downward-sloping demand curve. The financial institutions here are expected to follow the assumption in Cournot's oligopoly model: in other words, they act as if

[1] The specifics of the model are explained in the Appendix at the end of this chapter.

the rival bank will not change its loan volume when its own loan volume increases. The pre-merger equilibrium is represented by (q0, r0), the volume of loans and the interest rate, and (q1, r1) is the post-merger equilibrium. The marginal cost is represented by c.

The first effect of a merger is an increase in the market power of financial institutions. At the same time, however, improvements in managerial efficiency at financial institutions may also occur. Mergers can result in a variety of improvements that lead to cost reductions, through economies of scale and scope as well as consolidation of branches, administrative departments, and computer systems. In the figure we consider cost reductions to be reflected in the marginal cost of the financial institution and indicate the extent of the decline as Δc. We consider three cases depending on the size of Δc. In each case we assume that the cost reductions are reflected in the marginal cost of the financial institution. Through the analysis of these cases we can see that the size of efficiency improvement affects the surplus and the financing environment of borrower firms.

The first case, shown as Case 1, is when there is no improvement in the operating efficiency of the financial institution after the merger. Because Δc=0 marginal costs

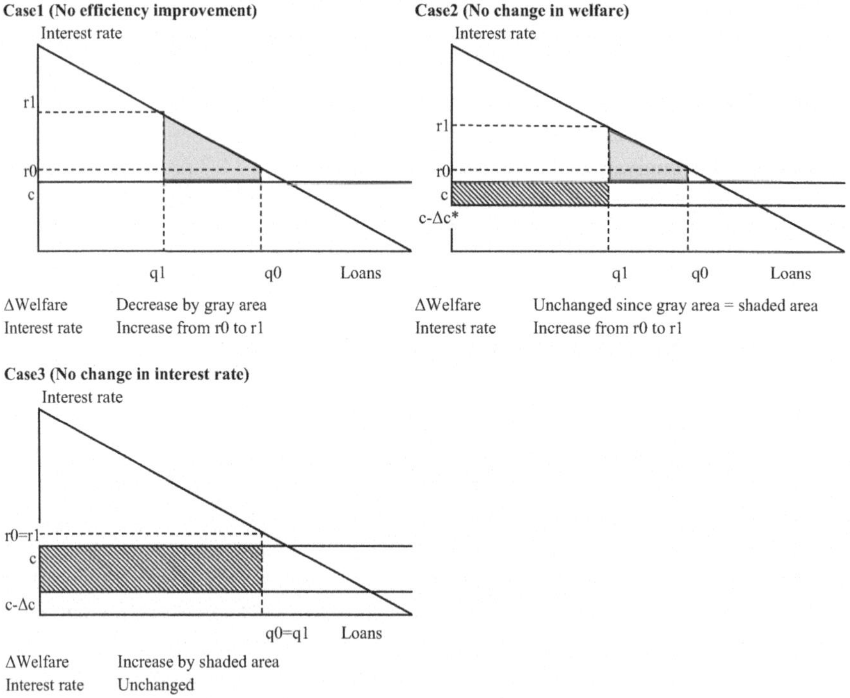

Fig. 11.1 Partial equilibrium analysis regarding the impact of merger on welfare (*Source* Processed by the author based on Fig. 11(1) page 233 of Ogagiri (2001) *Note* We draw the figure based on the same logic in Williamson (1968), while we are different from his in the assumption that a decrease in marginal costs is limited to merged banks)

remain unchanged and only the effect of the merger is an increase in the bank's market power. The interest rate increases from r0 to r1 and the volume of loans decreases from q0 to q1. The social surplus, which is the sum of the borrower firm's surplus and the lender financial institution's surplus, decreases by the amount corresponding to the gray area due to the decrease in the volume of loans.

In Case 3 there is a significant improvement in managerial efficiency after the merger. The decrease in marginal cost is equal to the pre-merger markup and the interest rate remains unchanged. Since the interest rate does not change the volume of loans does not change and the surplus on the borrower firm side remains unchanged. On the lender side the surplus increases by the shaded area, reflecting the efficiency improvement, and overall social welfare also increases by that amount.

Case 2 is the intermediate between Cases 1 and 3. Efficiency improves to some extent, marginal costs decline, and the lending institutions' surplus increases by the shaded area. However, this is not enough to offset the increase in interest rates and in the new equilibrium interest rates rise and the volume of lending declines. Thus, the surplus on the borrowing side decreases by the gray area. Since the overall social surplus is an increasing function of the marginal cost decline Δc, here the shaded and gray areas are the same in size under Δc^* such that there is no change in social surplus before and after the merger.

When Δc is between Cases 2 and 3 the merger increases the interest rate faced by the firms but also increases the social surplus, so it is reasonable to justify the merger from a social welfare perspective. Furthermore, if the decline in marginal costs is larger and exceeds Δc as in Case 3 not only will social welfare increase but the borrowing firms' surplus in the borrowing firm will as well.

Thus, the key question for the firm financing environment after the bank merger is the comparison between the two driving forces: the impact of increased market power and that of improved managerial efficiency.

11.4 How to Empirically Examine Theoretical Predictions

How can the theoretical predictions about the effects of mergers be applied to real mergers of financial institutions? The theoretical framework of Williamson (1968) as outlined above cannot be directly applied to actual mergers, especially bank mergers in the loan market. There are several factors we thus need to consider when we conduct an empirical analysis of the corporate loan market, particularly for SMEs.

11.4.1 Importance of the Transaction Relationship between the Firm and the Financial Institution Prior to the Merger

First, what should be compared in order to measure the effect of a merger as shown in Fig. 11.1? It seems appropriate to compare a loan market in which financial institution mergers such as those shown in the figure have occurred with a market in which there have been no mergers. However, in a loan market for SMEs, where the degree of information asymmetry regarding the attributes and behavior of borrower firms is severe, firms and financial institutions usually do not make spot loan contracts every time the firms would like to obtain loans, but rather they have a persistent lending relationship within which the firms repeatedly obtain loans from the financial institutions. In such cases, since not all financial institutions and firms in the market are equally affected by the increase in market power and the improvement in management efficiency of the merged bank, it is appropriate to measure the effect of the financial institution merger by comparing firms that had a pre-existing relationship with the merged bank with those that did not. Sapienza (2002) and Erel (2011), who conduct their analyses using loan contract-level data in Italy and the US, respectively, also examine how contracts with merging banks differ from those with non-merger banks (rival banks) within the region where the merger is taking place.

However, differences in the degree of a change in market power across loan markets may also affect the results. Previous studies have examined the shares of the merging banks in the loan market prior to a merger and found that the larger the shares in the market the more sizable the difference in the ex-post loan interest rates between merging banks and non-merging banks. Not only the existence of ex-ante transaction relationships between firms and merging banks but also the size of market shares by these merging financial institutions in the market may affect the impact of bank mergers on firms' financing environment.

11.4.2 The Focus of the Analysis is on the Changes in the Firms' Financing Environment

The next issue we address is which of the two changes in surplus shown in Figure 11.1, the change on the demand side and the change on the supply side, should be measured. Based on the figure we may evaluate the overall change in the welfare caused by a financial institution merger by subtracting the gray area from the shaded area and calculating the overall change in the surplus.

However, the main objective of this chapter is to determine the impact of mergers on the financing environment of the demand side of the loan market. In the gray area of the figure we estimate the corresponding change in the demand-side surplus (i.e., the extent to which borrowers' interest rates rise (r1–r0) and their borrowing amount declines (q1–q0)).

Of course, for the evaluation of the merger it is of great importance to not only consider changes in the financing environment on the demand side but also changes in the supply side. Focusing on financial institutions that supply loans, previous studies have found that there exist economies of scale with respect to expense ratios and that merged banks reduce expenses to a greater extent than do non-merged banks.[2]However, in order to conduct a merger assessment, which compares the two surpluses, it is necessary to formulate and estimate the demand and supply structure in the loan market and then produce estimates that show how the surpluses change after financial institution mergers.[3]

11.4.3 Other Changes in the Financing Environment Brought about by the Merger

Figure 11.1 focuses on the factors that affect the firms' financing environment: increased market power through a greater share of loan volume and improved managerial efficiency through increased bank size. However, there are several other changes that may affect the behavior of merged banks which as a result may change firms' financing environment. These include an increase in banks' size and organizational complexity, an increase in the market share, and an expansion of the geographical area of operation of the merged banks which expands the opportunities for diversification.

Corporate mergers, including those of financial institutions, are decided as part of the management policy of the merging firms. Therefore, it is difficult to accurately predict the managerial decisions made at the time of a merger as management has a great deal of discretionary power over its policies. Economics, however, can provide some perspective on what is a rational management policy that maximizes profits based on the changes that accompany a merger. We summarize possible management strategies that financial institutions can undertake in response to the changes that occur as a result of a merger and their impact on the financing environment faced by firms.

---

[2] In Japan, the expense ratio, which is operating expenses (the sum of personnel, property, and taxes) divided by the volume of funds, tends to diminish with the size of the financial institution for regional banks and Shinkin banks (Horie, 2008, p. 145 and p. 234). Ogura (2021), by looking at mergers of regional and second-tier regional banks and Shinkin banks since the 2000s, also shows that the extent of the decline in operating expenses after mergers is greater for regional and second-tier regional banks and Shinkin banks than for non-merger banks. In the U.S. as well, Berger and Mester (1997) find that the average cost of a bank continues to decline until the bank has total assets of about $25 billion, indicating that economies of scale work for financial institutions up to a certain point. A survey by Amel et al. (2004), however, finds that in developed countries the results are not consistent as to whether economies of scale or diseconomies of scale are observed for bank mergers above a certain size.

[3] Regarding the impact of mergers on economic welfare, Chapter 6 in Ohashi (2021) discusses advantages and disadvantages of the reduced form estimations employed in this chapter over the method of structural estimation.

First is a change in lending policies resulting from increased size and organizational complexity. While marginal costs may decrease after a merger through economies of scale and a reduction of overlapping resources, the increased organizational complexity of a merged bank may make it less likely to lend to smaller firms due to a significant degree of asymmetric information.

Because the overwhelming majority of SMEs are privately held their financial information is not publicly available and reports on their business activities often lack details. When these firms borrow from financial institutions they often do so through relationship-based lending in order to mitigate the problems caused by the information asymmetry. On the other hand, financial institutions differ in the extent that they can handle the soft information necessary for relationship lending. Previous studies indicate that smaller financial institutions, which have a flatter organizational hierarchy and are more likely to use soft information for lending decisions, tend to engage in relationship lending. As financial institutions merge and become larger and more complex they may reduce their capacity to handle soft information and may decrease their loans to smaller firms that require soft information to lend to.[4]

Second is the effect on relationship lending of a merger in the same market which increases the market share of the merged bank and reduces the amount of competition. Petersen and Rajan (1995) and Hauswald and Marquez (2006) show that the less competition in the market the more leeway financial institutions have to develop long-term relationships with firms.

Boot and Thakor (2000), however, state the opposite in their theoretical model: the more intense the degree of competition the more likely financial institutions are to engage in relationship-based lending to differentiate themselves from other banks. The existence of conflicting theoretical hypotheses precludes a one-way prediction regarding increases or decreases in lending. However, it is still possible to predict that in the loan markets where mergers of financial institutions significantly increase concentration banks will substantially alter the amount of loans to SMEs, which often rely on firm-bank relationships.[5]

Third, in the case of mergers across different markets merged financial institutions are better able to diversify their loan portfolios across regions. Hughes et al. (1999), Penas and Unal (2004), and Aguirregabiria et al. (2020) examine how the expanded geographic scope of operations associated with a merger can increase profit efficiency through region-specific risk diversification. If merging financial institutions lend more aggressively than before through this loan portfolio diversification channel the

[4] In fact, Ogura and Uchida (2014), using a survey of Japanese SMEs conducted in the mid-2000s, showed in their analysis that the degree of acquisition of soft information decreases for small financial institutions after a merger. In the United States Berger et al. (1998) reported that merged financial institutions tended to reduce their lending to SMEs.

[5] Although not looking directly at the impact of mergers, Carbo-Valverde et al. (2009) use Spanish data to show that the less competitive the loan market the more severe the financial constraints faced by firms.

firms' financing environment may improve.[6] In Section 11.5 we will empirically examine the plausibility of these additional theoretical predictions.

11.5 Empirical Analysis

In the following sections we focus on financial institution mergers in Japan since the mid-2000s and their impact on the firm financing environment. First, we look at the impact of one of the largest mergers during the period in detail. Specifically, we examine the January 2006 merger between Bank of Tokyo-Mitsubishi and UFJ Bank.

To examine the impact of this merger we use information on firm-financial institution relationships and firm-level financial information accumulated by one of the largest Japanese credit research firms to see how firms' borrowing interest rates and loan amounts changed depending on whether or not they had pre-existing relationships with either one or both of the merging banks. Since this was a merger between two megabanks there are a number of firms that fall into each of the following categories in terms of prior relationships with the merging banks: firms that used to transact with both merging banks; those used to transact with the acquiring bank; those used to transact with the target bank; and those used to transact with neither of the merged banks. The analysis will also take into account that firms could be affected differently depending on the categories to which they belong.

While megabank mergers may have a significant impact on firm financing there have been many mergers during this period involving other types of banks such as regional banks, second-tier regional banks, Shinkin banks, and credit cooperatives. As noted in the previous section there is a great deal of discretion in how management changes its lending practices as a result of mergers and a single merger does not provide a complete picture of the impact of a merger on firm financing. Thus, we also examine the impact of Japanese financial institution mergers on firm financing since the mid-2000s using comprehensive information on firm-financial institution relationships and firm characteristics.

Through these two analyses we are able to clarify how mergers of Japanese financial institutions have affected firms' financial environment. Additionally, the analyses provide some insights into the impact of large-scale reorganization among regional financial institutions that is expected in the future.

[6] The operations that can be performed with expanded geographic areas are not limited to lending. It has been pointed out in Japan that a wide-area merger of financial institutions can obtain a wide range of information about borrowers and use that information for matching business succession, corporate mergers, etc. (Nikkei BizGate interview with Professor Hironari Nozaki, Toyo University, September 30, 2020).

11.6 Impact of a Megabank Merger on Corporate Financing

In this section we examine the impact of a financial institution merger on funding conditions in unlisted firms with few alternative sources of funding using firm-level panel data that includes information on the financial institutions with which they do business and their branches. The merger between Bank of Tokyo-Mitsubishi (BTM) and UFJ Bank (UFJ) in 2005–2006 was one of the last of many city bank mergers that occurred in Japan in the late 1990s and early 2000s. The combined loan assets of the two banks amounted to approximately ¥70 trillion, accounting for just under 20% of all outstanding loans to financial institutions in Japan at the time. The Bank of Mitsubishi Tokyo UFJ (BTMU) was the largest in terms of the asset amount not only in Japan but also in the world. Both BTM and UFJ had a substantial number of unlisted borrower firms prior to the merger and it is likely that many changes occurred within these firms as a result of the merger.

11.6.1 Three Hypotheses to Be Tested

Here we divide firms into three groups depending on the firm-financial institution relationship in the pre-merger phase. We present three hypotheses for the firms in each group.

First, we focus on firms that had relationships with both of the merging financial institutions. For these firms the merger would automatically reduce the number of financial institutions with which they do business by one, which would narrow their options regarding funding sources and weaken their bargaining power.

Petersen and Rajan (1994), Harhoff and Körting (1998), and Bonfim et al. (2018) consider the number of financial institutions for each firm as a variable indicating the difficulty of finding alternative lenders. They use the time-series or cross-sectional variation in the number of financial institutions that a firm transacts with to analyze the impact of the number on firms' financing condition. However, previous studies do not account for the possibility that the number of financial institutions and terms of funding are simultaneously determined. In contrast, by focusing on firms in which the number of financial institutions decreases by one exogenously due to a merger we can examine the causal impact of a decrease in the number of financial institutions on funding terms. With these points in mind we set Hypothesis 1 as follows:

> **Hypothesis 1:** Firms that had transaction relationships with both of the merging financial institutions (here BTM and UFJ) will find it more difficult to find alternative lenders as the number of financial institutions with which they transact decreases exogenously

by one due to the merger. As a result they face more stringent financing conditions such as higher interest rates.

Second, we focus on firms that had a relationship with one of the merging financial institutions. Unlike firms that had pre-existing relationships with both of the financial institutions participating in the merger these firms will not experience a decrease in the number of financial institutions with which they transact. However, they may face a change in their financing terms following the merger. For example, as Stein (2002) showed in his theoretical model, if the merged financial institution's organization becomes more complex, making it more difficult to handle soft information, the result will be a decrease in lending to SMEs. This is what Berger et al. (1998) empirically showed for the U.S., that is, the financing environment for firms doing business with the merged financial institution will worsen. Based on these considerations Hypothesis 2 is formulated as follows:

Hypothesis 2: Firms that had a transaction relationship with one of the financial institutions participating in the merger (in this case BTM or UFJ) will obtain more favorable financing conditions than before the merger if the merging institutions' managerial efficiency improvement dominates. On the other hand, if the impact of the increased organizational complexity dominates, firms, especially smaller ones, will face more difficult financing conditions than before the merger.

Third, we focus on firms that had transaction relationships with the target financial institution relative to the acquiring financial institution. As Peek and Rosengren (1998) point out, the lending standard of merged financial institutions after the merger usually follows that of the acquiring financial institution rather than the one that was targeted. As a result firms that used to transact with the target financial institution (UFJ) may face less favorable financing terms than those that transacted with the acquiring financial institution (BTM). Previous studies that have examined this point include Karceski et al. (2005) who focused on Norwegian listed companies that used to transact with the target financial institutions and saw a drop in their share prices after the bank mergers. In our study we focus on unlisted firms that are limited in their funding sources and more likely to be affected by the discriminatory treatment toward the firms that used to transact with the target banks. In addition, we examine changes in funding terms rather than in stock prices which allows us to more directly examine the existence of discriminatory treatment. We therefore set Hypothesis 3 as:

Hypothesis 3: Firms that had a transaction relationship with the target financial institution (here UFJ) will face more stringent financing conditions than firms that had a transaction relationship with the acquiring financial institution (here BTM).

To test these three hypotheses we use a firm-level panel dataset and examine the effects of the financial institution merger. We measure the impact of the merger on firm financing by accounting for the fact that the pre-existing relationship between firms and financial institutions depends on firm attributes among other factors.

For the examination we need to consider the start and the termination of the firm-bank relationship because we assume in the following estimations that the relationship between firms and financial institutions is stable before and after the merger. Degryse et al. (2011) and Bonaccorci di Patti and Gobbi (2007) respectively use loan contract data from Belgium and Italy to examine the determinants of the maintenance or termination of transaction relationships with merged banks after the mergers. It is possible that in Japan firms' prior transaction relationships with the merged banks are terminated after bank mergers.

However, such relationship terminations in Japan are less likely as the average number of transaction years is much longer in Japan than in other countries. Degryse et al. (2009) summarize the results of various studies that examine the duration of transaction relationships between firms and financial institutions in many countries: 15–18 years in Norway; 14 years in Italy; 13 years in Germany; 7–11 years in the U.S.; and 8 years in Belgium. In contrast, the average transaction period in Japan is more than 30 years, suggesting that the transaction relationship is stable here compared to other countries.

In light of the above evidence that changes in transaction relationships after mergers are infrequent in Japan we will proceed with firms that used to transact with the merged banks at the time of the merger as the treatment group. However, by conducting an additional estimation that limits the treatment group to firms that maintained relationships after the merger we will see how firms that dropped out of transaction relationships with the merged banks were treated after the merger.

11.6.2 BTM and UFJ Merger

This section provides an overview of the events leading up to the merger between Bank of Tokyo Mitsubishi (BTM) and UFJ Bank (UFJ) as well as some points to keep in mind as we proceed with the analysis. In order to attribute the pre- and post-merger changes in the funding environment to the bank merger it is necessary to show that there is no reverse causality (i.e., that the banks were forced to merge due to the poor performance of their borrowers) and that the short interval of time between the announcement of the merger and it actually taking place makes it difficult for firms and financial institutions to take actions in advance of the merger. As we will discuss below these conditions were likely met in this merger.

BTM was formed by the merger of Mitsubishi Bank and Bank of Tokyo in 1996 and unlike other megabanks had not participated in any other mergers since that time. UFJ Bank (UFJ), on the other hand, was formed in 2002 through the merger of Sanwa Bank and Tokai Bank and was said to have lagged behind other megabanks in dealing with non-performing loans to some large firms. In fact, in May 2004 UFJ reported a huge deficit associated with the disposal of bad loans to these large firms for the fiscal year ending March 31, 2004. As a result of these losses, among other factors, the capital adequacy ratio fell substantially.

In response, UFJ Holdings, the holding company of UFJ, agreed with BTM in July 2004 to start discussions towards a business integration. Subsequently, in October 2005 MTFG merged with UFJ Holdings to form Mitsubishi UFJ Financial Group and BTM and UFJ became a part of that group. In addition, on January 1, 2006, BTM and UFJ officially merged to form BTMU. At the time BTM and UFJ were the second and fourth largest financial institutions in Japan, respectively, in terms of total assets, making the merged BTMU the largest bank in Japan.

The first thing to note about this merger is that it took place in a relatively short period of time, from the announcement of UFJ's large losses (May 2004) to the start of discussions regarding the integration of the holding companies (July 2004), the merger of the holding companies (October 2005), and the merger between BTM and UFJ (January 1 2006). In particular, the interval between the announcement of the huge deficit due to NPL-related losses and the start of negotiations for the merger between the holding companies of UFJ and BTM was approximately two months.

Admittedly, before May 2004 it had been pointed out that UFJ was lagging behind other megabanks in the disposal of bad loans. But most of the firms and depositors that had transaction relationships with UFJ, as well as most of the employees of UFJ, did not expect UFJ's drastically deteriorating business condition or a major change in its management structure, including a merger with another megabank, even several years before the merger. Therefore, it is difficult to say that lending behavior on the part of merging banks or the behavior of borrower firms were affected by the anticipation of the merger of UFJ and BTM.

A second thing to note about the merger is that UFJ's large losses on NPL write-offs were on a small number of loans to large firms that were considered "too big to fail." While they did realize losses on loans to SMEs and unlisted companies it is difficult to believe that this was the trigger for the merger since the number of loans to SMEs and unlisted companies was relatively small. Table 11.1 also shows that the average performance of the unlisted firms borrowing from UFJ before the merger was not significantly worse than that of unlisted firms that borrowed from BTM. Therefore, it is difficult to say that the performance of the unlisted firms that borrowed from UFJ was directly responsible for the rapid deterioration of UFJ's business condition, or for the merger with BTM.

11.6.3 Data

We obtain data for the analysis from the Teikoku Databank (hereinafter referred to as "TDB") database which covers a considerable number of firms located in Japan and contains basic information such as firm age, number of employees, type of ownership, industry, head office address, as well as names of financial institutions and their branches that a firm transacts with.

Table 11.1 Summary statistics for the megabank merger analysis

		Entire sample	Subsamples (by tranction relationships with the merging banks)				
			No transactions	Transacted with either one of them	Transacted with BTM	Transacted with UFJ	Transacted with both
Firm attributes							
	ln (firm age)	3.1822	3.1215	3.3182	3.3204	3.3164	3.4853
	ln (number of employees)	2.7584	2.5241	3.2701	3.3305	3.2206	3.9754
	Credit score	50.7871	49.7105	53.0562	53.2219	52.9204	56.6779
	Sales growth ratio	0.0383	0.0334	0.0528	0.0522	0.0533	0.0484
	Operating profit ratio	0.0145	0.0088	0.0288	0.0303	0.0276	0.0374
	Cash and deposit ratio	0.2001	0.2043	0.1887	0.1895	0.1880	0.1852
	Fixed tangible asset ratio	0.2677	0.2784	0.2401	0.2327	0.2462	0.2276
	Number of banks firms transact with	3.2372	2.7889	4.1817	4.2816	4.0998	5.6923
Concentration in the loan market							
	HHI	0.1857	0.2057	0.1321	0.1365	0.1285	0.1178
Regional dummies							
	Hokkaido	0.0819	0.1074	0.0117	0.0150	0.0090	0.0035
	Tohoku	0.0774	0.1013	0.0121	0.0145	0.0100	0.0031
	Kanto	0.3228	0.2620	0.4657	0.6752	0.2941	0.6007
	Koshinetsu	0.0595	0.0778	0.0094	0.0178	0.0025	0.0024
	Hokuriku	0.0305	0.0391	0.0068	0.0078	0.0059	0.0046
	Tokai	0.0969	0.0675	0.2025	0.0318	0.3424	0.0958
	Kinki	0.1371	0.1008	0.2306	0.1440	0.3016	0.2717
	Chugoku	0.0880	0.1101	0.0296	0.0437	0.0181	0.0109
	Shikoku	0.0238	0.0295	0.0086	0.0092	0.0081	0.0038

(continued)

Table 11.1 (continued)

		Entire sample	Subsamples (by tranction relationships with the merging banks)				
			No transactions	Transacted with either one of them	Transacted with BTM	Transacted with UFJ	Transacted with both
	Kyushu and Okinawa	0.0820	0.1044	0.0230	0.0409	0.0084	0.0034
Number of observations		122,206	90,212	25,222	11,359	13,863	6,772
	Share in the sample		0.738	0.206	0.093	0.113	0.055

Source Processed by the author based on Table 3 of Uchino and Uesugi (2022)

In addition to this basic information the database contains information on income statement and balance sheet items such as total assets, interest expense, and short-term and long-term loans for a substantial number of firms included in the database. The analysis here is limited to unlisted firms because the impact of financial institution mergers is likely to be more substantial for firms that rely on borrowing from financial institutions and have no means of directly raising funds from corporate bonds or the stock market. In addition, given the fact that UFJ's decision to merge with BTM was triggered by a small number of non-performing loans to listed companies the merger between BTM and UFJ can be considered an exogenous event for unlisted borrower firms.

Note here that in order to examine Hypothesis 1 and the effect of an exogenous decrease in the number of financial institutions that a firm transacts with by one, firms which transact with only one financial institution as of 2005 are excluded from the sample. Furthermore, to accurately measure the effect of the merger between BTM and UFJ, firms involved in other financial institution mergers that took place during the same period are excluded from the sample. As a result of this sample selection we have an unbalanced panel data set for about 120,000 firms.

11.6.4 Empirical Analysis Methodology

To quantitatively examine the effects of financial institution mergers we use the Propensity Score Matching-Difference in Differences (PSM-DID) methodology to estimate the effects. The difference from the previous analyses is that there are three or four types of ex-ante relationships between firms and the merging banks which makes it necessary to pick up two of those groups in order to apply the methodology.

To address this we adopt the method proposed by Lechner (2002). More specifically we implement a multinomial probit model estimation, select one treatment and one control group from the three or four groups of firms, and choose for each treatment firm control firms that are closest in their propensity scores.

To test Hypothesis 1 we choose firms that used to transact with both BTM and UFJ as the treatment group and those that transacted with either BTM or UFJ as the control group. To test Hypothesis 2 we choose firms that used to transact with either BTM or UFJ as the treatment and those that transacted with neither BTM nor UFJ as the control. To test Hypothesis 3 we choose firms that transacted with BTM as the treatment and those with UFJ as the control group.

11.6.5 Descriptive Statistics

Table 11.1 presents descriptive statistics for the sample firms as of 2004, the year prior to the merger, both for the entire sample and for subsamples split by the types of relationships with the merging banks. From this table we see the extent to which firm characteristics differ between groups depending on the types of prior transaction relationships with the merging banks.

While 74% of the firms had no transaction relationships with either BTM or UFJ 21% of the firms had such relationships with either BTM or UFJ. Of these 9% had a relationship with BTM and 11% had a relationship with UFJ. A total of 6% had transaction relationships with both BTM and UFJ.

The attributes of the sample firms vary considerably depending on which group they belonged to: no relationship; relationship with either; and relationship with both. In the following order, variables such as firm age, number of employees, number of financial institutions, and credit scores are larger. Firms that have transaction relationships with megabanks are larger, older, and have a lower credit risk.

Among firms that have transaction relationships with either megabank BTM firms tend to be older, larger, and have higher credit ratings while UFJ firms tend to have higher sales growth rates.[7]

When we look at the region dummies a higher percentage of firms that have transaction relationships with BTM and UFJ are located in the Kanto, Kinki, and Tokai regions compared to those with no transaction relationships. While megabanks have a nationwide network of branches a large number of their branches are located in the Tokyo, Kansai, and Chukyo areas. As a result, firms transacting with the megabanks are more likely to locate in the metropolitan areas than those transacting with neither of them.

Table 11.1 presents the attributes of the sample firms before the merger. Figure 11.2, on the other hand, shows how post-merger financing conditions changed

[7] A credit score is a score given to a firm by a private credit research company, which is a third-party evaluation of the firm's soundness, solvency, and growth potential, ranging from 0 to 100 points. The higher the score the better the firm is considered to be.

after the merger. We see the distribution of interest rates paid by group for 2004, before the merger, and for 2008, three years after the merger. The difference between the two distributions is larger for firms that used to transact with both of the megabanks than those in other groups.

11.6.6 Effects of Mergers on the Financing Environment

Figure 11.2 suggests that the merger of the financial institutions is causing an increase in the interest rate for the merged banks. However, the results are obtained without any firm attributes being controlled for and susceptible to a selection bias. Therefore, it is necessary to use the PSM-DID estimator, described in the empirical analysis methodology, in order to accurately measure changes in the firm financing environment after the bank merger.

Table 11.2 displays the estimation results using PSM-DID. Columns (1), (2), and (4) show the results of the examination of Hypothesis 1, Hypothesis 2, and Hypothesis 3, respectively. Column (3) is added to measure the overall impact of the merger. In each column of the treatment and the control we measure the development of the variable from $t-1$ (one year before the merger) to t through $t+5$. Then we take the difference between the treatment group and the control group for the DID estimates.

In column (1), the increase in borrowing interest rates is 5 to 13 basis points (bp, $1\% = 100$ basis points) larger for treatment group firms that transacted with both banks prior to the merger than for those that deal with either bank. The decrease in the borrowing ratio is 0.7 percentage point to 0.8 percentage point larger for the treatment group firms than for the control group firms. This indicates that the financing environment for firms in the treatment group deteriorated, which was caused by a decline in the firms' bargaining power and is attributed to a decrease in the number of banks with which they transacted by one after the merger. The impact of the more stringent financing environment is also evident in the firms' activity. Estimates for the DID for the tangible fixed asset investment ratio and for the sales amount were negative in the year of the merger although these negative effects last only for that year.

Column (2) shows that the increase in interest rates is 7 to 15 bp larger for the treatment group firms that transacted with one of the merging banks than for those that transacted with neither. The decrease in the borrowing ratio is 0.3 to 1.4 percentage points larger. Hypothesis 2 predicted that interest rates would decline by a larger margin if the merger improved the bank's managerial efficiency and would increase by a larger margin if the merger lessened the availability of funds to SMEs due to, for example, increased organizational complexity of the merged bank. The results imply that it is the latter. In contrast, estimates for the DID for the tangible fixed asset investment ratio and sales are positive when significant. This indicates no clear negative impact on the real side despite the worsening financing environment.

Although the results are not shown here an additional examination by dividing the sample into small and large firms shows that the decline in the borrowing ratio is

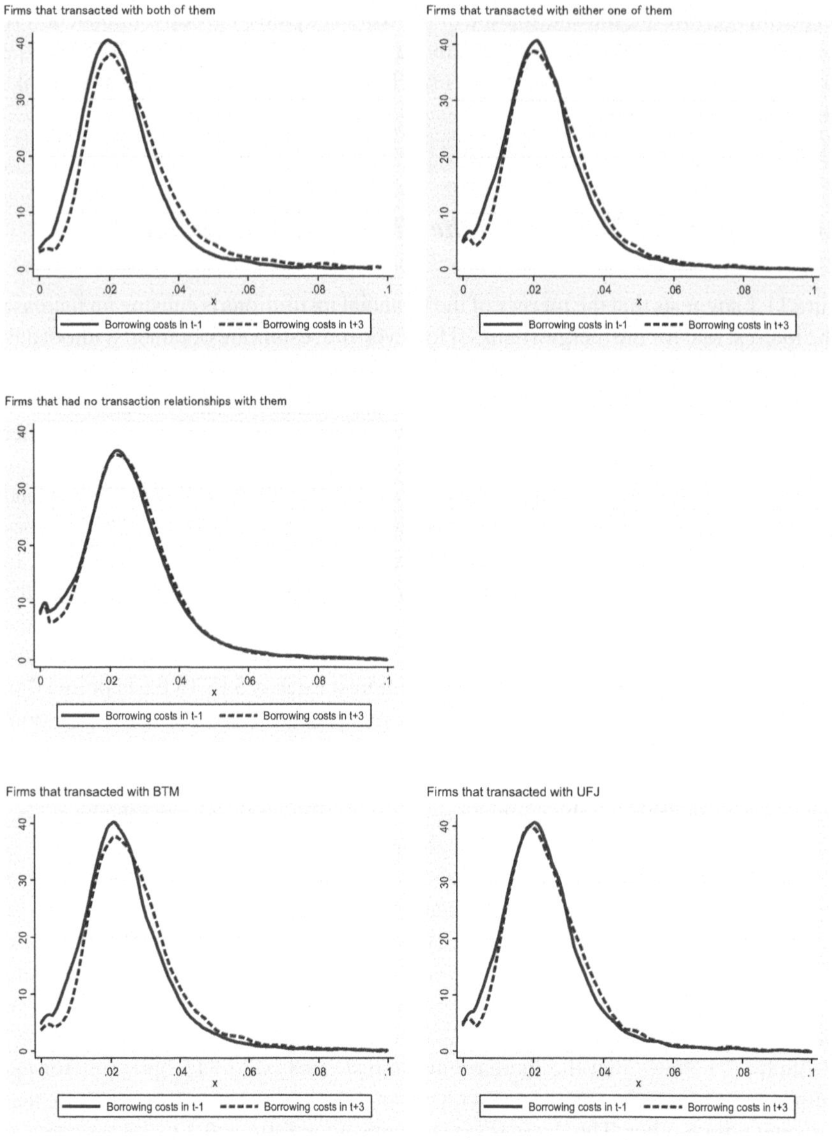

Fig. 11.2 Distributions of interest rates before and after the merger by subsample (*Source* Fig. 11.1 of Uchino and Uesugi (2022) *Note* Observations with interest rates of 10% or more (0.1 on the x-axis) are omitted in the graphs. Horizontal axis represents interest rates and vertial axis represents density)

Table 11.2 Estimation results on the change in firm financing and activities after the merger

		(1)	(2)	(3)	(4)
Treatment =	Firms transacted with	both banks	either one of banks	both banks	BTM
Control =	Firms transacted with	either one of banks	none of banks	none of banks	UFJ
		DID	DID	DID	DID
Interest rate	t	0.0005**	0.0002	0.0008***	−0.0001
	t + 1	0.0004	0.0007***	0.0015***	−0.0002
	t + 2	0.0010***	0.0010***	0.0025***	−0.0005
	t + 3	0.0009**	0.0015***	0.0029***	−0.0004
	t + 4	0.0013***	0.0013***	0.0026***	0.0003
	t + 5	0.0007*	0.0013***	0.0024***	0.0001
Loan ratio	t	−0.0014	−0.0034**	−0.0063**	−0.0025
	t + 1	−0.0075***	−0.0086***	−0.0195***	−0.0031
	t + 2	−0.0070**	−0.0137***	−0.0263***	0.0018
	t + 3	−0.0026	−0.0118***	−0.0159***	0.0008
	t + 4	−0.0049	−0.0106***	−0.0132**	−0.0021
	t + 5	−0.0073*	−0.0108***	−0.0143**	0.0002
Fixed tangible investment ratio	t	−0.0413**	0.0163	−0.0219	−0.0087
	t + 1	−0.0105	0.0084	0.0070	−0.0016
	t + 2	−0.0200	0.0226*	0.0075	−0.0076
	t + 3	−0.0117	−0.0030	0.0176	0.0309
	t + 4	−0.0186	0.0268**	0.0024	−0.0038
	t + 5	−0.0109	0.0105	−0.0009	0.0031
ln (Sales)	t	−0.0070*	0.0031	−0.0089	0.0002

(continued)

Table 11.2 (continued)

		(1)	(2)	(3)	(4)
Treatment =	Firms transacted with	both banks	either one of banks	both banks	BTM
Control =	Firms transacted with	either one of banks	none of banks	none of banks	UFJ
		DID	DID	DID	DID
	t + 1	−0.0066	0.0018	−0.0075	0.0015
	t + 2	−0.0092	0.0066	−0.0021	0.0052
	t + 3	−0.0018	0.0090	0.0026	0.0021
	t + 4	−0.0069	−0.0017	−0.0188	0.0019
	t + 5	0.0060	−0.0080	−0.0138	−0.0020

Source Processed by the author based on Table 6 of Uchino and Uesugi (2022)

Table 11.3 Number of financial institution mergers since 2004

	Number of financial institution mergers	City banks	Trust banks and former long-term credit banks	Regional banks	Second-tier regional banks	Shinkin banks	Credit cooperatives
2004	19			1	2	12	4
2005	13		1			7	5
2006	10	2		2		4	2
2007	7				1	3	3
2008	9		1		1	6	1
2009	7	1				5	1
2010	8		1	2	1	2	2
2011	1					1	
2012	3		1	1		1	
2013	3	1				1	1
2014	1					1	
2015	2		1				1
2016	2					2	
2017	5		1			1	3
2018	6		1	1		2	2

Source Modified by the author based on Table 2 of Uesugi et al. (2021) *Note* In the case of a merger of financial institutions that belong to different categories we classify it in the category for the larger institution

larger for the small size group. The merger may have changed the bank's management in the direction of discouraging lending to small firms.

In column (4), all the results, unlike those in columns (1) through (3) are insignificant. No significant differences exist in interest rates or borrowing ratios between firms that had prior relationships with BTM and firms that had relationships with UFJ. Hypothesis 3 expected that firms that had a relationship with the target bank, UFJ, would be treated unfavorably, resulting in a larger increase in interest rates, but it appears that no such discriminatory treatment occurred.[8]

The estimations whose results are reported in this table include the treatment firms that had relationships with either or both of BTM and UFJ at the time of the merger but terminated the relationships afterward. In an additional test we restricted the treatment group firms to those that continued to transact with the merged bank after the merger and found that the extent of the increase in the borrowing interest rate and the decrease in the borrowing ratio was marginally smaller. This indicates that only

[8] According to those who had the knowledge of the situation at the time, firms that had borrowed from both the BTM and the UFJ were not necessarily subject to the lending standards of the combined bank, BTM, after the merger, but were instead subject to the standards of the bank with the larger loan balance.

a small number of firms terminated relationships with BTMU after the merger and that these firms faced a somewhat more stringent financing environment than those that remained in the relationships.[9]

11.6.7 Summary of Megabank Merger Effects

In summary, the financing environment has deteriorated for firms that used to transact with the merging megabanks in that their borrowing ratios decreased and the interest rates increased after the merger. There are several possible reasons for the more stringent loan conditions such as increased bargaining power due to a decrease in the number of transaction relationships and changes in management policies at the merged banks. In particular, firms that had relationships with both of the banks face more stringent financing conditions because they are affected by both the exogenous decline in the number of banks they transact with and a change in management policy at the merged bank.

Looking at the results in column (3) of Table 11.2, which compares firms that used to transact with both of the merged banks and those that transacted with neither one, the change in the borrowing interest rate is 30 basis points larger at the maximum. Considering the average interest rate paid by the firms in our dataset prior to the merger was 2.6%, the increase of 30 bp is economically significant.

How did such an economically sizable deterioration in loan conditions occur by the megabank merger? When we say that the increase in interest rates was due to increased bargaining power on the part of megabanks it tends to give the impression that the merged banks threatened SMEs with higher loan interest rates and smaller loan amounts and that the borrower SMEs initially resisted such increases but ended up accepting these conditions.

However, media reports during the period indicate that the actual process was more nuanced than we stereotypically expected. Financial institutions as a whole were quite aggressive in extending loans during the period as seen in the following articles: "Blue chip firms enjoy low interest rates: Interviews with SMEs in Sakai, Higashi Osaka, and Amagasaki city" (Nihon Keizai Shimbun, morning edition, January 19, 2007) and "Regional Banks' Lending out of Their Headquarter Prefectures, More Intense Competition for Acquiring New Customer Firms by Establishing New Branches and Offering Low Interest Rates" (Nihon Keizai Shimbun morning edition, March 20, 2007). As far as we could see there were no reports that the merged bank explicitly coerced borrower firms to pay higher interest rates and that the behavior was criticized by the public. Regarding the behavior of the BTMU, the merged megabank, it was reported that regional banks were taking away the BTMU's loan share and that BTMU's outstanding loan amount was declining. It was also reported that the bank's

[9] In a separate analysis conducted by the author who created a dataset similar to the one used here, less than 5% of the firms that had a business relationship with BTMU or UFJ were found to have terminated their relationship with BTMU after the merger and through 2008.

stance was that "it is definitely better to expand its loan base, but we would not compete head-to-head with regional banks for extending loans" ("Bank of Mitsubishi UFJ: 6% decrease in loans to four prefectures in the Chubu region," Nihon Keizai Shimbun morning edition, May 25, 2007). To summarize, what actually occurred during the period is that the merged bank did not increase the interest rate it charged to its SME borrower firms but also did not follow other financial institutions in lowering its interest rates.

It is true that the extent of the increase in borrowing interest rates and the decrease in the borrowing ratio were relatively larger for existing borrowers of the merged bank than for others. As a result there are concerns about the negative impact of the more stringent loan conditions on business activities such as investment and sales.

However, compared to the degree and duration of the more disadvantageous financing environment for firms, the negative effect on firms' real activities is relatively small and of limited duration. As can be seen in Table 11.1 the operating profit margin and credit scores of the merged bank's customers are higher than other firms. These relatively better-performing firms may have used their cash flow to finance capital investments if it was difficult for the firms to raise funds through borrowing.

11.7 Impact of Bank Mergers Including Those of Smaller Financial Institutions

In the previous section we looked at the impact of the largest bank merger in terms of assets in the world on the financing of borrowing firms. However, this merger, despite its size, is one of many that have taken place in Japan. How, if at all, would the results obtained for the megabank merger change if we examine all financial institution mergers? In this section we use a simpler method than that used in Section 11.6 to understand how the firm financing environment has changed by covering all mergers of financial institutions from 2004.

11.7.1 Hypotheses to Be Tested

In this section, as in Section 11.6, we focus on the existence of transaction relationships with the merging banks in the pre-merger stage. However, due to the large number of mergers we deal with we do not divide firms according to the number of transaction relationships they have with the merging banks as we did in the previous section. Rather, we focus only on the existence of a lending relationship and set up a set of empirical hypotheses.

One change that could worsen the financing environment for firms with pre-existing lending relationships with two or more of the merging financial institutions is a decline in their bargaining power due to an exogenous decrease in the number of financial institutions they deal with. In addition, for firms that have transaction relationships with at least one merging financial institution an increase in the size and complexity of the post-merger bank may lead to a decline in lending to SMEs. On the flip side a change that could improve firms' financing environment could be the increased managerial efficiency of banks after mergers which would have a ripple effect on financing conditions of borrower firms. These two possibilities are summarized in the following hypotheses.

Hypothesis 1: Firms with pre-merger relationships with the merging financial institutions will face a more difficult financing environment as the number of financial institutions with which they do business decreases and/or the size and organizational complexity of the merging financial institutions increases.

Hypothesis 1': Alternatively, the financing environment will improve as management efficiency improves at the merging financial institutions.

Based on this set of hypotheses we employ the firm-level panel data set and perform a comprehensive test on the effects of financial institution mergers.

11.7.2 Financial Institution Mergers that Took Place During the Period

Mergers of financial institutions from 2004 to 2018 are included in the analysis and the number of such mergers is shown in Table 11.3. A related forms of business consolidations such as multiple financial institutions joining under a holding company are not included in the treatment group. This is because they are considered a more gradual business combination than mergers and are less likely to result in the behavior of financial institutions we expect in the hypotheses.

11.7.3 Data and Estimation of DID

As in the previous section, in the analysis we use firm-level data obtained from the TDB database. In the previous section we estimated the determinants of transaction status with the merging banks, matched the treatment group firms with control group firms with similar attributes using the propensity score matching (PSM) method, and analyzed the effect of the merger on firms' financing and performance using the difference-in-differences (DID) method.

In this section we do not consider the similarity in attributes when matching control group firms to treatment group firms. In other words, we do not perform PSM but instead calculate DIDs for the variables of interest such as those on firm financing. Specifically, we implement the following procedure.

First, we identify firms that have transaction relationships with merging financial institutions—they are firms in the treatment group. We then calculate the average values of the interest rate paid, the ratio of loans to total assets, and the investment ratio of tangible fixed assets for each group of treatment firms categorized by the financial institution that they transact with, the prefecture that they are located, and the year the firm activities are recorded.[10] We similarly identify firms that had relationships with non-merging financial institutions, which belong to the control group. We again calculate the average values of the relevant variables for these firms at the financial institution they transact with, prefecture, and year level. The treatment and control group firms differ in terms of whether they have experienced a merger or not but the market concentration is the same since they are located in the same prefecture.

Second, we examine financial institution mergers from 2004 until the end of 2018. We consider financial institutions that merged during the period as one financial institution from the beginning to the end of the period and firms that have lending relationships with these institutions are considered to be firms that have transaction relationships with the merging financial institutions. If a financial institution has merged more than once all financial institutions that participated in the merger during the period are considered as one financial institution.

Third, we obtain statistics of treatment group firms and statistics of control group firms. We do this for each group categorized by the financial institution, prefecture, and year.

Fourth, we measure the impact of financial institution mergers by the change in the above difference from the starting point of the financial institution merger year until i years later, that is, by obtaining the DID. For a group of financial institutions that has experienced multiple mergers the starting point is the year of the last merger.[11]

We express the DID obtained through the above procedure by the following Eq. (11.1). By examining the pre- and post-merger changes for each of the treatment and control group firms and comparing the two we can measure the impact of the merger on the firms' financing environment after removing the firm group-specific effects that remain constant over time and the time effects that remain constant across firm groups.

$$DID^{b}_{r\tau+i} \equiv \left(R^{T_b}_{r\tau+i} - R^{C_b}_{r\tau+i}\right) - \left(R^{T_b}_{r\tau} - R^{C_b}_{r\tau}\right) \tag{11.1}$$

[10] This is different from Sect. 11.6 in that here we use aggregate information on firms doing business with a particular financial institution by prefecture rather than by firm. It is important to note that the DID controls for financial institution-prefecture fixed effects but not for firm fixed effects.

[11] The estimations are also performed using the year prior to the merger instead of the year of the merger for the starting point but the results are qualitatively the same.

$R_{r\tau}$ is the interest rate paid by firms as of τ, the year of the financial institution merger in region r. T_b indicates the interest rates paid by the firms that borrowed from financial institution b that merged in year τ (treatment group firms). The database provides up to 10 financial institutions for each firm and if merged financial institution b is included in the database the firm is assumed to be in the treatment group. On the other hand, C_b indicates the interest rates paid by the firms located in the same region but borrowing from institutions other than the merging financial institution b (control group firms). If the merged financial institution b is not included in the database the firm is considered a control group firm. We do not only use the interest rate paid but also employ the borrowing ratio, short-term borrowing ratio, long-term borrowing ratio, leverage ratio, and investment ratio of tangible fixed assets.[12]

The DID measures the effect of the merger on the treatment group firms. If the DID is positive for the interest rate paid it means that the increase in the interest rate paid by firms that borrowed from the merged financial institution exceeded that of firms that borrowed from other financial institutions. We can then say that the financing environment for the borrowing firms worsened due to the merger. What we have not considered so far are firms that had transacted with the financial institutions at the time of their merger but subsequently terminated their relationships for some reason. In this analytical framework, even though these firms were treatment group firms at the time of the merger they are included in the control group from the point when they no longer had a transaction relationship with the merging banks.

However, as discussed in the analysis of the megabank merger in Sect. 11.6, the presence or absence of firms that terminated their transaction relationships with the merging financial institutions makes only a marginal difference in the results. As such, we will not give special consideration to these firms in the following analysis.

11.7.4 Analysis of the Determinants of DID

DID is calculated for several variables including firms' interest rates paid to understand the impact of mergers on the financing environment faced by firms. It is the case, however, that the change in firm behavior measured by DID estimates can vary depending on a variety of factors including the year in which the financial institution merger occurs. To clarify these issues we also provide estimates for the DID by quartile.

The next step is to estimate the determinants of DID. The objective is not only to obtain descriptive statistics of DID by simple summary statistics or cross-tabulation with one variable but also to include various factors in the estimation simultaneously in order to examine their impact on DID. The estimation equation is specified as follows:

[12] Other variables (trade payables ratio, trade receivables ratio, cash and deposits ratio, ROA, operating profit to sales ratio, and tangible fixed assets ratio) were also tabulated but results are not shown.

$$DID_{rt}^{b} = \alpha + \beta_1 MergedBankSize_{rt}^{b} + \beta_2 HHI\_Loan_{rt} + \delta_{t-\tau} + \theta_\tau + \varepsilon_{rt}^{b} \quad (11.2)$$

t ranges from 2005 to 2019, one to five years after the merger year τ. $MergedBankSize_{rt}^{b}$ is the share of the merged bank in terms of the number of borrower firms in the region and HHI_Loan_{rt} is the concentration of the loan market in the region. $\delta_{t-\tau}$ and θ_τ are dummies indicating the number of years since the merger and the merger year, respectively.

11.7.5 Descriptive Statistics

Summary statistics of the DID in Table 11.4 show the degree to which various variables of the merging financial institutions' client firms changed as a result of the merger. Both the average and the median of the interest rate paid was −0.03 percentage points (=−3 basis points), indicating that the margin of interest rate decrease is slightly larger among firms that used to transact with the merged banks than firms that did not.

Borrowing ratios also rose by a larger margin for the client firms of the merged financial institution, with the mean value of DID being + 0.1 percentage points and the median value + 0.6 percentage points. The increase in the loan ratio was driven by a larger increase in the long-term loan ratio rather than by the short-term loan ratio. Based on the results on the interest rate and loan ratio mergers of financial institutions have not necessarily worsened the financing environment for their borrower firms.

While the financing environment slightly improved the investment in tangible fixed assets did not increase after the merger. The decrease in the investment rate is larger for firms that transacted with merged financial institutions (5.7 percentage points for the average and 4.2 percentage points for the median).

11.7.6 Descriptive Statistics by Merger Year

Next we present descriptive statistics for the DID calculated by the year in which the financial institution merger occurs. Of the variables in Table 11.4 we focus on borrowing interest rates and loan ratios. Table 11.5 shows the results for each financial institution merger year. For the interest rate paid, in the sample with 2006 as the merger year the mean is +0.13 percentage points (= +13 basis points), the largest positive value over the period. However, the DID often becomes negative after 2007. The later years in which we observe positive changes have a small impact on the result for the entire sample period due to the small number of mergers or the small size of the merging financial institutions.

For the loan ratio the difference in trend is more evident between the first half and the second half of the sample period in which mergers occur. That is, while the DID is negative in the first half it is positive in the second half.

Table 11.4 Summary statistics for the analysis of all bank mergers

	Number of observations	Mean	Standard deviation	Min.	p25	Median	p75	Max.
Borrowing interest rate (%)	1144	−0.030	0.265	−1.705	−0.157	−0.031	0.112	1.527
Loan ratio	1144	0.001	0.053	−0.260	−0.027	0.006	0.031	0.214
Short-term loan ratio	1144	−0.001	0.024	−0.111	−0.013	−0.001	0.010	0.124
Long-term loan ratio	1144	0.002	0.043	-0.176	−0.020	0.004	0.027	0.175
Leverage ratio	1144	−0.006	0.062	−0.284	−0.036	−0.003	0.029	0.238
Tangible fixed asset investment ratio	1144	−0.057	0.233	−2.050	−0.151	−0.042	0.049	1.395

Source Table 3 in Uesugi et al. (2021)

Table 11.5 Summary statistics by merger year

		Borrowing interest rate (%)			Loan ratio		
	Number of observations	Mean	Standard deviation	Median	Mean	Standard deviation	Median
2004	170	0.0124	0.2247	0.0171	−0.010	0.045	−0.007
2005	35	−0.2282	0.4845	−0.0696	−0.009	0.040	−0.005
2006	260	0.1277	0.2714	0.1210	−0.016	0.063	−0.011
2007	39	−0.0272	0.2900	−0.0193	−0.006	0.045	−0.005
2008	40	−0.1370	0.1793	−0.1120	−0.004	0.051	0.009
2009	155	−0.0869	0.2404	−0.0611	−0.006	0.052	−0.007
2010	65	−0.0469	0.1405	−0.0405	0.007	0.059	0.005
2011	5	0.0093	0.0762	0.0051	0.007	0.019	0.000
2012	81	−0.1923	0.2774	−0.1737	0.027	0.034	0.023
2013	245	−0.0956	0.1811	−0.0905	0.021	0.046	0.023
2014	10	0.0589	0.1671	0.0739	0.032	0.051	0.023
2015	4	0.0538	0.0528	0.0698	0.024	0.006	0.025
2016	9	−0.0036	0.0926	0.0281	0.004	0.050	0.012
2017	17	−0.0223	0.3465	−0.0179	0.058	0.053	0.038
2018	9	−0.0367	0.3608	0.0547	0.011	0.030	0.007

Source Table 4 in Uesugi et al. (2021)

11.7.7 Estimation Results

Table 11.6 presents the estimation results that examine the determinants of several variables that may affect the DID. We employ the DID for the interest rate paid, loan ratio, and tangible fixed asset investment ratio for the dependent variables.

In the interest rate paid estimation result shown in the first column, the merged financial institution's share in the region and the concentration in the regional loan market both yield positive and significant coefficients. The higher the intra-regional share of the merging financial institution and the higher the concentration of the loan market in the region the greater the increase in the interest rate paid by the borrower firms of the merging financial institution. However, the coefficient on the intra-regional share is only economically marginally significant, indicating a 0.11 percentage points (=11 basis points) increase in interest rates when the share of the merging financial institution reaches 100%. The coefficients on merger year dummies are negative in all years when significant except for 2006, the year in which the merger between BTM and UFJ occurred and the coefficient is positive and significant.

The loan ratio estimation result is in the second column. The coefficients on intra-regional share and market concentration are both insignificant. All significant coefficients on the merger year dummies are positive and more likely to be positive

Table 11.6 Estimation results on the determinants of change in firm financing and investment after mergers

	DID_interest rate	DID_loan ratio	DID_fixed tangible investment ratio
Share of merging financial insitutions	0.112*	0.00495	0.00903
Loan HHI in the merger prefecture	0.264***	0.00754	−0.205**
Dummy for two years after the merger (base is one year after)	0.0183	0.00615	−0.0151
three years	−0.0269	0.00257	−0.0177
four years	−0.0236	−0.00364	−0.0391*
five years	−0.0417*	0.00129	−0.0207
Merger year 2005 (base is year 2004)	−0.245***	0.00145	−0.00436
Year 2006	0.114***	−0.00603	−0.113***
Year 2007	−0.0450	0.00415	−0.115***
Year 2008	−0.159***	0.00540	−0.0405
Year 2009	−0.0972***	0.00425	−0.133***
Year 2010	−0.0526	0.0176**	−0.189***
Year 2011	−0.0154	0.0173	−0.141
Year 2012	−0.187***	0.0376***	−0.255***
Year 2013	−0.109***	0.0308***	−0.107***
Year 2014	0.0852	0.0432**	−0.00450
Year 2015	0.0734	0.0353	0.119
Year 2016	−0.0276	0.0124	−0.205***
Year 2017	−0.0245	0.0674***	−0.281***
Year 2018	− 0.0545	0.0226	−0.155**
Constant	−0.0360	−0.0135**	0.109***
Number of observations	1,144	1,144	1,144
R-squared	0.169	0.105	0.094

Source Table 5 in Uesugi et al. (2021)
Note ***, **, and * represent statistical significance at the 1%, 5%, and 10%, respectively

and significant in the second half of the period than in the first, as seen in the summary statistics.

The result for the tangible fixed investment ratio estimation in the third column show that the coefficient on the loan market concentration as measured by the HHI is significantly negative. The financing environment is less conducive to capital investment perhaps due to the effect of higher loan interest rates in areas of high market concentration. The coefficients on the merger year dummies are negative in all years when significant.

11.7.8 Impact on Firm Financing of Financial Institution Mergers Since 2004

An examination of all recent financial institution mergers and the overall result it provides on the effects of mergers on the firm financing environment is rather different from what we saw with the megabank merger of BTM and UFJ.

First, when all mergers are considered the decline in interest rates paid by borrower firms of the merged bank is slightly larger than the decline for other firms by 0.03 percentage points (=3 basis points) which is the opposite of the result for the megabank merger. Similarly, the increase in the loan ratio was 0.1 percentage points larger for firms that transacted with the merged bank. Overall, mergers have led to a slight improvement in the financing environment for firms which implies that the effect of increased management efficiency has been reflected in the financing conditions of the firms.

Of course, the direction and extent of the impact depend on the market share of the merging banks and the year of the merger. First, the higher the market share of the merging banks the greater the increase in market concentration after the merger and the more likely it is to see an increase in interest rates. This result is similar to the empirical analysis for the U.S. (Erel, 2011) and Italy (Sapienza, 2002). It is also important to note that the direction of the impact changes with the year of the merger. In particular, the sign of the effect on the loan ratio changes between the first and second half of the analysis period. That is, while we observe a smaller increase in the loan ratio for firms that used to transact with merging banks than firms that did not in the first half of the period, in the second half we observe the opposite.[13]

11.8 Summary

This chapter measures the impact of financial institution mergers on firm financing by separating firms that have pre-existing transaction relationships with the merging bank from those that do not, even if they are located in the same region, and examining the differences between the two. The study also provides a comprehensive overview of the impact of financial institution mergers over the last 15 years.

The megabank merger that took place between 2005 and 2006 had the effect of increasing the borrowing interest rates of unlisted firms and decreasing their loan ratios. The maximum increase in borrowing interest rates was 30 basis points which

[13] It should be noted that the analysis in this section, which comprehensively examines financial institution mergers since the mid-2000s, is different from the analysis in Sect. 11.6 in the following points. First, it does not use firm attribute information when matching treatment and control groups. Second, it does not separate the sample according to the number of prior transaction relationships with the merged financial institutions. Third, it pools observations with different number of elapsed years after the merger. An analysis within a framework similar to that of Uchino and Uesugi (2022) is an issue for future research.

was substantial compared to the level of interest rates at the time of the merger. However, the real activities of firms such as capital investment ratios and sales were not negatively affected for several years which was in contrast with the negative results for the interest rates and the loan ratio.

Next we look at the effects of all financial institution mergers in Japan from 2004 to 2018, which includes the megabank merger. We find that the firm financing environment has improved on average, indicating that the higher interest rates resulting from the megabank merger were an exception to this general tendency. We compare megabank mergers with those of smaller financial institutions to speculate that there exist two underlying factors. First, megabank mergers may improve management efficiency less than small bank mergers since large banks are already sizable and have limited room to benefit from the economies of scale. Second, megabanks may be able to increase the bargaining power to the borrower firms after the merger more than small merged banks since transactions with megabanks have reputational value to firms, which makes the costs for switching transaction relationships high.

The increase in the loan ratio tends to be larger for mergers of financial institutions in the latter half of the sample period, indicating that the merging financial institutions may be more aggressive in lending to strengthen their own operating base. The results also show that when the market share by the merged bank is high the merger results in a larger increase in interest rates. However, the effect is economically not so significant.

In the first half of the analysis period it appears that many of the merged financial institutions like BTMU took a stance of not embarking on a lending competition by aggressively reducing interest rates. However, from the middle of the period and thereafter it appears that the merged banks shifted their stance to look to aggressively increase their lending. This may reflect the fact that more "forward-looking" mergers are being undertaken to strengthen management bases rather than mergers for the purpose of dealing with nonperforming loans or bailing out distressed financial institutions.

As regional financial institutions continue to merge it is likely that financial institutions will emerge that hold a large share of the market within a prefecture. There is a possibility that due to the significant increase in their bargaining power the merging financial institutions will seek higher interest rates and more favorable transaction terms from them. However, if the aggressive lending stance taken by merging financial institutions that was found in this chapter continues, it seems unlikely that mergers of financial institutions will result in an immediate sharp deterioration of the firm financing environment.

Appendix: The Impact of Financial Institution Mergers on Cournot's Oligopoly Model

Pre-Merger Interest Rates and Loan Volumes in Cournot's Oligopoly Model

We assume that the loan market is an oligopoly consisting of n firms offering homogeneous loan services. The total lending volume is $Q = \sum_{i=1}^{n} q_i$ and the total loan volume by firms other than firm i is written as Q_{-i}.

Solving the problem of maximizing the profit of a financial institution $\pi_i = r(Q)q_i - C_i(q_i)$, the first-order condition is,

$$\frac{\partial \pi_i}{\partial q_i} = \frac{dr}{dQ}(1 + \lambda_i)q_i + r(Q) - \frac{dC_i}{dq_i} = 0 \tag{11.3}$$

where $\lambda_i \equiv \frac{\partial Q_{-i}}{\partial q_i}$, but in the Cournot model this is assumed to be zero for all financial institutions i (i.e., other firms do not respond to changes in their own loan volume). Assuming that the cost function is $C_i = c_i\, q_i + f_i$ and the inverse demand function is $r = a - bQ$, Eq. (11.3) can be written as

$$-2bq_i + a - bQ_{-i} = c_i \tag{11.4}$$

Solving this for q_i yields the reaction function which shows how the firm's optimal loan volume is determined in response to the loan volume of rival financial institutions,

$$q_i = \frac{S_i - Q_{-i}}{2} \tag{11.5}$$

where $S_i = \frac{a-c_i}{b}$. Assuming that the marginal cost c_i is symmetric for all financial institutions we obtain the individual institution's loan volume, overall loan volume, interest rate, and individual institution's profit in equilibrium as follows (we add 0 to the superscript to indicate that this is pre-merger):

$$q^0 = \frac{1}{n+1}S,\ Q^0 = \frac{n}{n+1}S,\ r^0 = c + \frac{1}{n+1}bS,\ \pi^0 = \frac{bS^2}{(n+1)^2} \tag{11.6}$$

where $S = \frac{a-c}{b}$.

Interest Rate Changes Due to Mergers

Consider the case where two of the n firms (i = 1, 2) merge but the marginal cost of the financial institution remains unchanged, which corresponds to Case 1 in Fig. 11.1. After the merger there should be a symmetric equilibrium of n − 1 firms and the new equilibrium is obtained by replacing n in Eq. (11.6) with n − 1. Prices increase and the overall market loan volume decreases.

This would only cause an increase in interest rates due to increased market power but what would happen if the merged financial institution lowers its marginal cost byΔc? Here we assume that marginal costs remain the same for all but the merging financial institution. Using Eq. (11.5) and assuming that marginal costs are equal for the non-merging financial institutions, the response functions for the merging and non-merging financial institutions post-merger are as follows:

$$q_1 = \frac{a - (c - \Delta c) - bQ_{-1}}{2b}, whereQ_{-1} = \sum_{i=3}^{n} q_i$$

$$q_i = \frac{a - c - bQ_{-i}}{2b}, whereQ_{-i} = q_1 + \sum_{\substack{j=3 \\ j \neq i}}^{n} q_j, i = 3, ..., n, \tag{11.7}$$

Non-merging financial institutions provide the same amount of loans in equilibrium. Solving Eq. (11.7) then yields the following equilibrium loan volume and interest rates for the merging institutions, the non-merging institutions, and the aggregate after the merger.

$$\begin{aligned} q_1^1 &= \tfrac{1}{n}\left[S + (n-1)\tfrac{\Delta c}{b}\right] \\ q_i^1 &= \tfrac{1}{n}\left[S - \tfrac{\Delta c}{b}\right], i = 3, ..., n \\ Q^1 &= q_1^1 + (n-2)q_i^1 = \tfrac{1}{n}\left[(n-1)S + \tfrac{\Delta c}{b}\right] \end{aligned}$$

$$r^1 = c - \Delta c + \frac{1}{n}[bS + (n-1)\Delta c] \tag{11.8}$$

For the interest rate to remain constant at the time of merger, r^1 in Eq. (11.8) must equal r^0 in Eq. (11.6), which leads to the following condition:

$$\Delta c = \frac{bS}{n+1} = r^0 - c \tag{11.9}$$

If the improvement in efficiency of the merging institutions is equal to the difference between the interest rate and marginal cost (markup) ex ante the interest rate will remain the same following the merger. This situation corresponds to Case 3 in Fig. 11.1. If the decline in marginal cost is smaller the post-merger interest rate will rise, resulting in the situation in Case 2, and if the decline is greater than the ex-ante markup the interest rate will decline after the merger.

Changes in Social Surplus Due to Mergers

We found that the magnitude of the increase in the interest rate decreases with the extent of the decrease in the marginal cost after the merger and that the interest rate starts to decline when the decrease in the marginal cost exceeds a certain level. How is the change in the social surplus, which is the sum of the surplus of financial institutions on the supply side and the surplus of firms on the demand side, related to the change in the marginal cost?

First, the pre-merger social surplus W^0 is,

$$W^0 = \frac{(n+2)nbS^2}{2(n+1)^2} \tag{11.10}$$

and the post-merger social surplus W^1 is,

$$W^1 = \frac{1}{2bn^2}[(n-1)bS + \Delta c]^2 + \frac{1}{bn^2}[bS + (n-1)\Delta c]^2 + \frac{n-2}{bn^2}[bS - \Delta c]^2 \tag{11.11}$$

When $\Delta c = 0$, which is case 1 in Fig. 11.1, $W^0 > W^1$. The decrease in surplus corresponds to the gray area in the figure; social surplus decreases due to the merger. In Case 3, when $\Delta c = \frac{bS}{n+1}$ we have $W^1 < W^0$. In this case the social surplus increases due to the merger. W^1 is also an increasing function of Δc. From these results we expect that there exists a Case 2 where the interest rate is increasing but the post-merger social surplus is equal to the pre-merger social surplus with Δc^*.

Chapter 12
The Future of SME Finance

Abstract In this chapter, based on the empirical results of previous chapters, we discuss future challenges for SME finance in Japan and some measures to address them.

Keywords Inefficiencies of fund allocation · Role of the goverment · Role of private financial institutions

12.1 Empirical Findings Presented in This Book

Based on the results of Chapters 2 through 11 it is possible to understand the current state of SME finance. Broadly speaking, while the problem of financial constraints on the activities of SMEs is relatively small there is room for improvement in the efficiency of allocation of funds in various aspects of the loan market.

12.1.1 Financial Constraint for SMEs in Recent years in Japan is Relatively Less Stringent Than Before

In the firm sector, including SMEs, the inclination toward excess savings has been entrenched since the mid-1990s and the number of zero leverage firms has increased over time, especially in the 2000s. Although the COVID-19 pandemic was a significant, temporary negative shock to cash flows the number of bankruptcies was relatively low due to government support measures (Chapter 2). Looking at the reallocation of funds among firms, the extent of a decline in borrowing for SMEs was smaller during recessions than in normal times (Chapter 3) which is consistent with the finding that the credit crunch was limited to a short period even during the Japanese financial crisis in the late 1990s. Trends in the regional allocation of funds within each financial institution show not only an increase in holdings of assets other

I. Uesugi, *The Economics of SME Finance*, Advances in Japanese Business and Economics 36, https://doi.org/10.1007/978-981-96-3193-3_12

than loans in response to an increase in deposits but also a large amount of cross-border lending outside of one's own prefecture (Chapter 4). In terms of government involvement in the loan market the large credit guarantee programs implemented during past crises have improved the credit availability for SMEs (Chapter 6), and direct lending by government-affiliated financial institutions has increased firms' loan ratios and capital investment in both crisis and normal times (Chapter 7). In Japan the concentration of the loan market has increased through mergers of financial institutions from the mid-2000s to the present (Chapter 10) but interest rates have not risen and borrowing ratios have not declined, except in the case of mergers between megabanks (Chapter 11).[1]

12.1.2 Inefficiencies Exist in the Allocation of Funds for SMEs in Many Ways

Despite numerous adverse shocks to SME financing, such as crises and financial institution mergers, the supply of funds to SMEs by financial institutions, including those involving the government, can be described as ample in general. However, that does not necessarily mean that the allocation of funds has been perfectly efficient.

First, the percentage of SMEs that are in negative net worth in terms of book value has remained high relative to large and medium-sized enterprises. While the ratio of zombie firms, firms which have difficulty continuing operations without support from financial institutions and other sources, declined after Japan's financial crisis and the Global Financial Crisis, it began to rise again in the wake of the COVID-19 pandemic (Chapter 2). Further, an efficient flow of funds, whereby the supply of funds to low-productivity firms decreases while the supply to high-productivity firms increases, is less clearly observed for SMEs than for large firms (Chapter 3). Cross-border lending is inefficient in that the flow increases from regions with increasing productivity to those with declining productivity. In addition, credit-guaranteed loans are more likely to be delinquent when they are extended across prefectural borders (Tsuruta, 2021) (Chapter 4). Finally, both credit-guaranteed loans and direct loans by government financial institutions decrease the profit ratio of the user firms and increase their probability of falling into financial distress (Chapters 6 and 7).

Addressing these inefficiencies in the allocation of funds is an important medium-to long-term issue for SME finance in the post-pandemic era. In addition, although not necessarily inefficient, there are many firms that are unwilling to invest and thus become zero leveraged (Chapter 2). Stimulating the demand for funds among these firms is a major challenge. By addressing these issues finance can contribute

[1] It does not mean that there are no financially constrained SMEs, even when the financial constraint problem is relatively minor for SMEs. As indicated in Chapter 2, it is not clear whether microenterprises have always tended to be in excess saving. Thus, they are more likely to be unable to borrow even if they want to than are firms of larger sizes. In addition, based on the SME Agency's 2018 Basic Surveys of SMEs, about 5% of SMEs with funding needs have their borrowing applications rejected or loan amount reduced by their main banks.

to improving the productivity of SMEs. Below we discuss possible measures from four different perspectives: business revitalization; interregional allocation of funds; the role of the government; and the role of financial institutions.

12.2 Business Revitalization

In order to address the problem of a large number of zombie firms and that the allocation of funds to SMEs is not necessarily in line with their productivity it is necessary for SMEs in poor business conditions to take early steps to revitalize their businesses, choosing to survive or exit on their own and to consider methods of revitalization.

At the end of the SME Financing Facilitation Act (March 31, 2013) the number of firms that had their loan terms modified and the number that were in need of restructuring were 300,000 to 400,000 and 50,000 to 60,000, respectively, according to the document from the Financial Services Agency. However, it is not yet clear, due to a lack of empirical evidence, to what extent the zombie firms, which are identified by several criteria under the definition of "difficult to survive without support from financial institutions," overlap with the firms in need of a turnaround, and what kind of externalities SME zombie firms have on other firms. However, given the increase in the number of firms whose debt ratios rose as a result of the government financial support measures in response to the COVID-19 pandemic, and the fact that many firms are hesitant to make major changes due to increased uncertainty, there is an increasing need to promote restructuring among zombie firms and firms with poor financial performance.

There are two types of business revitalization: judicial bankruptcies and private out-of-court debt workouts, with the latter being more common than the former in Japan in recent years. Among the out-of-court debt workouts there are several methods in which financial institutions take the lead in business revitalization. Some financial institutions are actively working in cooperation with the SME Revitalization Support Councils (SMERSC) which are located in each prefecture. However, even though the support by the SMERSC is most widely used when firms undertake out-of-court workouts the number of cases supported by the SMERSC is still small compared to the total number of firms in need of revitalization.

In the case of these out-of-court debt workouts, whether or not the current management decides to move ahead with the business revitalization is important, along with coordination among creditors and the search for business sponsors, as well as the involvement of government. For example, the stipulation of the Guidelines on Management Personal Guarantees allows managers who provide personal guarantees to retain a certain amount of assets upon debt restructuring, encouraging managers to take early steps toward business revitalization.

A further boost to the business revitalization would be to find substitutes for personal guarantees, which managers of SMEs usually pledge when their firms borrow. The results obtained in Chapter 9 suggest that loan covenants could be used to discipline firms even in the absence of personal guarantees.[2] We expect that managers of firms with loan contracts that do not require personal guarantees will be more likely to take steps to revitalize their businesses as soon as possible.

Another important factor in encouraging early turnaround is to dispel the negative impression that the term "revitalization" has. Currently, the term "revitalization" is associated with negative connotations such as "bankruptcy," "failure," and "no hope of recovery." SME owners, many of whom have established their reputations in the community and are concerned about the possible loss of such, are reluctant to take steps into the business revitalization. However, compared to postponing the response to a deteriorating business condition, which often leads to bankruptcies and liquidations of the entire business, a firm's early decision to undertake revitalization measures may be more beneficial to the local economy and to the local financial institutions.[3] Sharing the common understanding that business revitalization is essential to the local economy and society will change the mindset of business managers. If through these efforts the notion that "companies and managers are separate" and "business turnarounds are very positive for the local economy" becomes widespread then the psychological barrier to business revitalization by managers will be greatly reduced.

The policy of minimizing corporate bankruptcies through government financial support measures in response to the COVID-19 pandemic cannot continue forever. At some point firms will be forced to choose between survival and closing the business as a result of debt repayment. By then it is desirable to create an environment in which firms with good business prospects can survive and those with poor prospects can either close the business or restructure to remain viable.

12.3 Allocation of Funds Across Regions

Chapter 4 discussed the negative relationship between productivity and the flow of funds, with deposits to be provided as loans moving from productivity-increasing regions to productivity-decreasing regions. Also, credit guaranteed loans are more likely to be delinquent when regional financial institutions extend these loans beyond the prefectural borders of their headquarters (Tsuruta, 2021).[4] This inefficient cross-border lending may be attributed to the following two factors: (1) financial institutions

[2] Tsushima (2017) presents a unique perspective that personal guarantees have forced managers to make up their mind to make their best effort, which strengthen their bargaining power over their employees and business partners. However, few small business owners are likely to be able to make this level of management effort.

[3] For an example of a regional financial institution taking such a stance, see Yasuaki Saito, "How to support firms with deteriorating performance," Speech Material prepared by the Shizuoka Bank at the Tokai Local Finance Bureau, June 24, 2021.

[4] At this point, however, there has not yet been an analysis of whether non-credit guaranteed cross-border lending is being conducted efficiently using the information on borrower firms. This is an issue for future research.

which seek to lend outside of the prefecture due to a lack of local demand for funds but want to avoid high screening costs prefer to use credit guarantees; and (2) high credit risk borrower firms seek funds from outside their prefecture because they are unable to obtain loans from local financial institutions because of their high risk.

However, the inefficiencies of cross-border lending could be overcome through cooperation of local financial institutions. Instead of each financial institution incurring the costs for its own cross-border lending monitoring costs can be saved if financial institutions headquartered in other prefectures extend loans to borrowers endorsed by local financial institutions based on their own screening and monitoring. Since the screening and monitoring capabilities of local financial institutions are utilized there would be no need to rely on credit guarantees.

Furthermore, if financial institutions located in different regions not only cooperate but also merge they will be able to identify highly productive firms across a large area that they operate and then extend loans to these firms using deposits collected in areas with low productivity. Of course, there is a concern that the increased market power that results from mergers of financial institutions will reduce the welfare of borrowers. However, if funds are allocated and information is produced more efficiently through the use of a cross-regional branch network the benefits may outweigh the costs of the increased market power.[5]

It should be noted that the interregional flow of funds, as represented by cross-border lending, is affected by the aging of the population and the savings rate in each region. Although the location of firms that demand funds also plays a role the current pattern of deposits flowing out of rural areas to metropolitan areas in the form of loans may be reversed in the future as the savings rate declines in regional areas where the proportion of elderly citizens is increasing. Financial institutions will need to consider this as they build their own branch networks and other business infrastructures.

12.4 The Role of the Government

Based on the evaluation of government involvement in SME financing as discussed in Chapters 5 through 9 we can identify several ways in which the role of government can be improved.

[5] Studies analyzing mergers across different loan markets (out-of-market mergers) have reported that effects of improved managerial efficiency and those of increased bargaining power on borrowers loan conditions are tenuous (e.g., Sapienza, 2002). Under these circumstances, improvements in the efficiency of interregional fund allocation due to bank mergers may outweigh other effects caused by the mergers.

12.4.1 *The Impact of Government Policies on SME Financing and Firm Performance*

Government support measures, whether credit-guaranteed loans or direct loans from government financial institutions, often have a negative effect on firm performance while still improving the credit availability for SMEs. Considering the diminishing rate of return of firms' investments it may be natural for the ROA to decline for firms that make investments with new loans supported by the government. However, if the deterioration in performance leads to a higher probability of financial distress such as negative net worth and default it is necessary for the government to take necessary measures to prevent the firm's performance from getting worse. There are several possible ways to do so.

First, we focus on the measure to improve the performance of firms that receive credit guaranteed loans. The way in which private financial institutions extend loans determines the performance of firms that receive funds. Therefore, if the government gives appropriate incentives for private financial institutions to properly screen and monitor borrowers when the financial institutions extend credit-guaranteed loans the firms' performance may improve. The incentive may include preferential treatment of financial institutions in the credit guarantee application process based on the ex-post performance of the credit guaranteed loans they extended. For example, the government may allow private financial institutions that record a low subrogation payment ratio to apply for credit guarantees with simpler application procedures. With such an incentive in place financial institutions may be more willing to monitor SMEs and thus improve ex-post firm performance.

Second, we point out the possibility that both credit guarantees and direct lending by government-affiliated financial institutions can improve the performance of relatively high-risk firms through intensive efforts for business revitalization. A major obstacle in the past had been the inability of credit guarantee corporations and government-affiliated financial institutions, which are publicly funded, to agree to debt forgiveness in out-of-court workouts. In recent years, however, the reluctance of these institutions to accept debt forgiveness has reportedly diminished.[6] During the recent COVID-19 pandemic firms that were suffering from its immediate effects as well as firms that were financially distressed prior to the pandemic took advantage of the support measures including credit-guaranteed loans and government bank loans (Chapter 2). There is an increasing need for the government to be actively involved in the business revitalization given that zombie firms or firms in distress use interest-free, unsecured loans supported by the government more frequently than other firms.

Until now, risk-taking through the provision of funds in times of crisis has been regarded as the government's responsibility. Going forward, the raison d'etre of

[6] Fujiwara (2020) emphasizes, in particular, that credit guarantee corporations have shifted to a more proactive stance towards business revitalization.

government-affiliated financial institutions will probably be to focus on management improvement and business restructuring for underperforming firms after provision of funds. Rather than worrying about public–private competition at the time of extending loans there may be more room for cooperation with private-sector financial institutions in terms of how to improve the management of firms after lending.

12.4.2 Long-Term Impact of Government Involvement

We examined the existence of substitution between private financial institutions and government-affiliated financial institutions in Chapter 8, that is, whether loans by the private sector would decline once government-affiliated institutions increased their loans. Even though we found no supporting evidence for substitution between government loans and private sector loans, active government involvement in SME financing may, in the long run, discourage private financial institutions from undertaking innovative activities. As examples, we discuss how commitment lines, business continuity plans (BCPs), and new lending technologies based on fintech have been used.

Uesugi, Ono et al. (2021) conducted a survey on firm behavior during the COVID-19 pandemicand found that only 20% of firms that had commitment line agreements with financial institutions actually used those lines to borrow. Government intervention resulted in private financial institutions and government-affiliated institutions providing loans with good terms, including interest-free and unsecured loans. This suggests that many SMEs took advantage of this government-provided liquidity and did not tap into their own previously established lines of credit.

In the same survey a comparison of firms that had prepared a business continuity plan (BCP) and those that had not as of May 2020, after the outbreak of the COVID-19 pandemic, shows no difference in sales levels. Although there are many ways to interpret this one possibility is that, in response to the shock, the government provided ample cash flow support to firms regardless of whether or not they had prepared a BCP in advance, meaning there was no observable difference in performance.[7]

The impact of the government's generous measures is also casting a shadow over the operations of fintech companies that provide working capital quickly to SMEs. An example is the electronic factoring business in which a fintech factor company processes and purchases accounts receivable electronically and supplies funds to firms. According to the company that provides this service, the increase in short-term demand for factoring by firms during the pandemic was very limited due to the large scale provision of public support measures such as interest-free unsecured loans.

The examples of commitment lines, BCPs, and new fintech lending techniques indicate that the presence of government emergency support measures reduces the need for firms and financial institutions in the private sector to prepare their

---

[7] Another interpretation is that the BCP had no effect on changing firm performance.

own financing measures for shocks. If the government provides generous support measures repeatedly for many years to come we do not expect an increasing demand for new and innovative financing measures provided by the private sector. Emergency measures adopted by the government have side effects once they have served the purpose of providing liquidity to firms. To avoid such side effects it may be necessary to limit the length of the period in which special government support measures are provided. It is also worth shortening the maturity of credit-guaranteed loans and government bank loans as much as possible.[8]

12.5 The Role of Private Financial Institutions

Finally, we discuss efforts of financial institutions to efficiently provide funds in the SME loan market. As Sect. 12.1 of this chapter indicates, we know the circumstances in which SME finance becomes inefficient. At this point, however, it is difficult for us to make decisive recommendations to financial institutions to fix the inefficiencies.

The FSA has been paying particular attention to regional financial institutions that lend to a large number of SMEs and has recommended these institutions promote "relationship banking," "community-based finance," and "lending based on business prospect assessments." What these terms imply is that financial institutions should not be overly dependent on collateral and personal guarantees but should accurately assess the nature of the borrower firms' businesses and their growth potential based on information obtained from long-term relationships with these firms. As a result these financial institutions can provide financial services that not only help their borrower SMEs but also increase the profitability of these financial institutions. Many regional financial institutions are striving to realize the objective and Hashimoto (2016) provides several examples of financial institutions that extend loans based on accurate business prospect assessments.

The question, however, is whether the average Japanese regional financial institution has enough resources to collect the information which would allow them to make loans based on business prospect assessments, and whether they would earn a return commensurate with the resources invested. Regarding human resource constraints Ono (2007) compared the number of borrower firms per financial institution staff member and found that the number was much higher in Japan than in the United States. This has not changed significantly to date.[9]

Furthermore, nearly two decades after the FSA presented its Action Program on Strengthening Relationship Banking Functions the average Japanese regional financial institution has yet to improve its own profitability. Ojima (2018) notes that

[8] As discussed in Chapter 6, a temporary crisis-related guarantee program has been introduced since the reform in the credit guarantee scheme in 2018.

[9] Chapter 2 in Part 2 of SME Agency (2016) shows the number of borrower firms per financial institution officer, and states that the bank officers also conduct business other than lending, such as selling mutual funds and insurance products.

markups at regional financial institutions have been declining almost continuously since the mid-2000s. Although mergers among financial institutions appear to be a promising solution to this problem the results in Chapter 11 indicate that this does not necessarily translate into increased market power and higher loan interest rates.

The Bank of Japan (2019) simulated what would happen to regional banks, second-tier regional banks, and Shinkin banks in the event of a major negative shock after several years of declining profitability, and cited the possibility that some financial institutions would experience a large drop in their capital ratios and substantially reduce their lending in an attempt to raise their capital ratio. What these findings mean is that regional financial institutions which are responsible for a large portion of Japan's SME financing may not have the human resources or management strength to continue providing loans based on business prospect assessments, as recommended by government authorities. In order to address this issue it would seem to make sense for these institutions to concentrate management resources to enable lending and consulting based on business prospect assessments, and to provide products and services that would generate demand for new loans on the part of firms.[10]

As indicated by the SME Agency (2005) it is common for Japanese SMEs to transact with multiple banks. In other words, firms obtain loans from no less than two financial institutions simultaneously, which is important for SMEs to increase their bargaining power and obtain more favorable borrowing terms. However, as a result, the number of borrower firms per financial institution officer increases when transactions with multiple financial institutions prevail as compared to transactions with a single financial institution. All of this means the average regional financial institution has limited resources to adequately screen and monitor its clients, even though such screening and monitoring is necessary for business prospect assessments. To improve this situation financial institutions may concentrate their resources on the relationships with firms that are willing to pay more interest and fees for the products and services provided based on close business relationships.[11]

It is important for financial institutions to offer new products and services that will generate demand for new loans because creating loan demand allows financial institutions to earn higher interest rates and fees. For this purpose a financial institution and a borrower may sign a detailed loan contract which requires close mutual communication and a large amount of information exchange.

[10] Although we do not go into details, Sato (2017) compares the lending practices of commercial banks in the United States and Japan and provide perspectives for Japanese financial institutions to learn from the United States. Specifically, he compares Union Bank of California and Bank of Tokyo-Mitsubishi UFJ in Japan and points out several substantial differences: extent of the link between credit ratings and lending decision criteria, areas of risk-taking, and the procedures and the speed of risk-taking decisions.

[11] As an example of a bank that has implemented such an approach, we can cite a bank that has improved its performance by changing its personnel evaluation from one that targets only loan volume to one that includes interest rates, and by reshuffling their borrower firm portfolio to a considerable degree (Nikkei Business, March 16, 2020, "How to Survive Japan's Smallest Bank: How to Avoid "War of Attrition" Sales Competition, Saga Kyoei Bank").

Kinoshita (2005) compared the relationship between firms and financial institutions in Japan and the U.S. He found that loan contracts by financial institutions in the U.S. were much more detailed than those in Japan, mainly in terms of covenants, and that the contents of these contracts were based on close communication between firms and financial institutions, including business status reports submitted by firms. In Japan, covenant-based loans, described in Chapter 9, are provided by government-affiliated financial institutions and some regional financial institutions. The process of communication between the financial institution and the firm regarding the initial introduction of covenants and the ex-post monitoring of their status facilitates a mutual understanding. In this way financial institutions may be able to provide firms with unique services based on the in-depth information they obtain about the firms when they sign detailed loan contracts and monitor the covenants contained in these contracts.

Recently, commitment lines have been used more frequently in Japan whereby financial institutions extend loans to firms given certain conditions are met and the firms request the loans. Since commitment lines impose an obligation on banks to provide loans up to the pre-committed amount it is often the case that covenants are often imposed on user firms and that banks check compliance with the covenants when they are requested by the firms to provide funds. It is expected that the use of commitment lines will expand among Japanese SMEs if the current regulation is relaxed. If that is the case there will a simultaneous increase in the number of commitment lines and loan contracts that include covenants.[12]

However, intensive communication through bank-firm relationships is not possible for all SMEs because firms and banks need to incur fixed costs for such communication and many relatively small SMEs may not pay for such costs. For banks that transact with these SMEs it may be better to consider providing transaction type lending rather than lending that requires close firm-bank relationships. It has been noted in the literature that fintech companies are better at substituting loans made by large banks than those extended by small banks (Balyuk et al., 2020). This means that these fintech companies are able to extend transaction loans to relative small SMEs.

Finance has the power to change the allocation of resources in the economy. We hope that financial institutions and the government will play their respective roles and that as a result SME finance will help boost the growth of the Japanese economy.

[12] See Honda (2020) for a discussion of the current status and institutional issues related to commitment lines in Japan.

References

Agarwal, Sumit and Robert Hauswald (2010) "Distance and private information in lending," Review of Financial Studies, Vol. 23, No. 7, pp. 2757–2788.
Aguirregabiria, Victor, Robert Clark and Hui Wang (2020) "The geographic flow of bank funding and access to credit: Branch networks, local synergies, and competition," Working paper.
Amel, Dean, Colleen Barnes, Fabio Panetta and Carmelo Salleo (2004) "Consolidation and efficiency in the financial sector: A review of the international evidence," Journal of Banking and Finance, Vol. 28, No. 10, pp. 2493–2519.
Angelini, Paolo, Roberto Di Salvo and Giovanni Ferri (1998) "Availability and cost of credit for small businesses: Customer relationships and credit cooperatives," Journal of Banking and Finance, Vol. 22, No. 6–8, pp. 925–954.
Arping, Stefan, Gyöngyi Lóránth and Alan D. Morrison (2010) "Public initiatives to support entrepreneurs: Credit guarantees versus co-funding," Journal of Financial Stability, Vol. 6, No. 1, pp. 26–35.
Atkinson, David (2019) Kokuun no Bunkiten Chusho Kigyo Kaikaku de Futatabi Kagayaku ka Chugoku no Zokkoku ni Naruka (A Turning Point in the Nation's Fortunes: Shine Again with Small Business Reforms or Become a Dependency of China). Kodansha plus alpha Shinsho.
Balyuk, Tetyana, Allen N. Berger and John Hackney (2020) "What is fueling FinTech lending? The role of banking market structure," Working Paper.
Banerjee, Abhijit V. (1997) "A theory of misgovernance," Quarterly Journal of Economics, Vol. 112, No. 4, pp. 1289–1332.
Banerjee, Ryan N. and Boris Hofmann (2020) "Corporate zombies: Anatomy and life cycle," BIS Working Papers, No. 882.
Barlevy, Gadi (2003) "Credit market frictions and the allocation of resources over the business cycle," Journal of Monetary Economics, Vol. 50, No. 8, pp. 1795–1818.
Becsi, Zsolt, Victor E. Li and Ping Wang (2005) "Heterogeneous borrowers, liquidity, and the search for credit," Journal of Economic Dynamics and Control, Vol. 29, No. 8, pp. 1331–1360.
Behr, Patrick, Lars Norden and Felix Noth (2013) "Financial constraints of private firms and bank lending behavior," Journal of Banking and Finance, Vol. 37, No. 9, pp. 3472–3485.
Bennedsen, Morten, Francisco Pérez-González and Daniel Wolfenzon (2020) "Do CEOs matter? Evidence from hospitalization events," Journal of Finance, Vol. 75, No. 4, pp. 1877–1911.
Berger, Allen N. and Timothy H. Hannan (1989) "The price-concentration relationship in banking," Review of Economics and Statistics, Vol. 71, No. 2, pp. 291–299.
Berger, Allen N. and Loretta J. Mester (1997) "Inside the black box: What explains differences in the efficiencies of financial institutions?" Journal of Banking and Finance, Vol. 21, No. 7, pp. 895–947.

I. Uesugi, *The Economics of SME Finance*, Advances in Japanese Business and Economics 36, https://doi.org/10.1007/978-981-96-3193-3

Berger, Allen N., Anthony Saunders, Joseph M. Scalise and Gregory F. Udell (1998) "The effects of bank mergers and acquisitions on small business lending," Journal of Financial Economics, Vol. 50, No. 2, pp. 187–229.

Berglöf, Erik and Gérard Roland (1997) "Soft budget constraints and credit crunches in financial transition," European Economic Review, Vol. 41, No. 3–5, pp. 807–817.

Besanko, David and Anjan V. Thakor (1987) "Collateral and rationing: Sorting equilibria in monopolistic and competitive credit markets," International Economic Review, pp. 671–689.

Bessler, Wolfgang, Wolfgang Drobetz, Rebekka Haller and Iwan Meier (2013) "The international zero-leverage phenomenon," Journal of Corporate Finance, Vol. 23, pp. 196–221.

Bester, Helmut (1985) "Screening vs. rationing in credit markets with imperfect information," American Economic Review, Vol. 75, No. 4, pp. 850–855.

Board of Audit (1999) "Tokutei Kensa Taishou ni Kansuru Kensa Jokyo: Daihachi Chusho Kigyo Kinyu Anteika Tokubetsu Hoshou Seido no Jisshi Jokyo ni tsuite (Status of inspections regarding specified inspection targets: 8th implementation of the Special Guarantee Program for Financial Stabilization of SMEs)." Report on the 1998 Financial Inspection, Chap. 4.

Bonaccorsi di Patti, Emilia and Giorgio Gobbi (2007) "Winners or losers? The effects of banking consolidation on corporate borrowers," Journal of Finance, Vol. 62, No. 2, pp. 669–695.

Bonfim, Diana, Qinglei Dai and Francesco Franco (2018) "The number of bank relationships and borrowing costs: The role of information asymmetries," Journal of Empirical Finance, Vol. 46, pp. 191–209.

Boot, Arnoud W. A. and Anjan V. Thakor (1994) "Moral hazard and secured lending in an infinitely repeated credit market game," International Economic Review, Vol. 35, No. 4, pp. 899–920.

Boot, Arnoud W. A. and Anjan V. Thakor (2000) "Can relationship banking survive competition?," Journal of Finance, Vol. 55, No. 2, pp. 679–713.

Boot, Arnoud W. A., Anjan V. Thakor and Gregory F. Udell (1991) "Secured lending and default risk: Equilibrium analysis, policy implications and empirical results," Economic Journal, Vol. 101, No. 406, pp. 458–472.

Bruche, Max and Gerard Llobet (2014) "Preventing zombie lending," Review of Financial Studies, Vol. 27, No. 3, pp. 923–956.

Caballero, Ricardo J. and Mohamad L. Hammour (1994) "The cleansing effect of recessions," American Economic Review, Vol. 84, No. 5, pp. 1350–1368.

Caballero, Ricardo J. and Mohamad L. Hammour (2005) "The cost of recessions revisited: A reverse-liquidationist view," Review of Economic Studies, Vol. 72, No. 2, pp. 313–341.

Caballero, Ricardo J., Takeo Hoshi and Anil K. Kashyap (2008) "Zombie lending and depressed restructuring in Japan," American Economic Review, Vol. 98, No. 5, pp. 1943–1977.

Calomiris, Charles W., Mauricio Larrain, Jose Liberti and Jason Sturgess (2017) "How collateral laws shape lending and sectoral activity," Journal of Financial Economics, Vol. 123, No. 1, pp. 163–188.

Carbo-Valverde, Santiago, Francisco Rodriguez-Fernandez and Gregory F. Udell (2009) "Bank market power and SME financing constraints," Review of Finance, Vol. 13, No. 2, pp. 309–340.

Cetorelli, Nicola (1999) "Competitive analysis in banking: Appraisal of the methodologies," Federal Reserve Bank of Chicago Economic Perspectives, Vol. 23, No. 1, pp. 2–15.

Chamley, Christophe and Celine Rochon (2011) "From search to match: When loan contracts are too long," Journal of Money, Credit and Banking, Vol. 43, No. s2, pp. 385–411.

Chaney, Paul K. and Anjan V. Thakor (1985) "Incentive effects of benevolent intervention: The case of government loan guarantees," Journal of Public Economics, Vol. 26, No. 2, pp. 169–189.

Cole, Rebel A. (1998) "The importance of relationships to the availability of credit," Journal of Banking and Finance, Vol. 22, No. 6–8, pp. 959–977.

Davis, Steven J. and John C. Haltiwanger (1992) "Gross job creation, gross job destruction, and employment reallocation," Quarterly Journal of Economics, Vol. 107, No. 3, pp. 819–863.

Davis, Steven J., John C. Haltiwanger and Scott Schuh (1996) Job Creation and Destruction. MIT Press.

De Aghion, Beatriz Armendariz (1999) "Development banking," Journal of Development Economics, Vol. 58, No. 1, pp.83–100.

De Meza, David and David C. Webb (1987) "Too much investment: A problem of asymmetric information," Quarterly Journal of Economics, Vol. 102, No. 2, pp. 281–292.

DeAngelo, Harry, Linda DeAngelo and Toni M. Whited (2011) "Capital structure dynamics and transitory debt," Journal of Financial Economics, Vol. 99, No. 2, pp. 235–261.

Degryse, Hans, Moshe Kim and Steven Ongena (2009) Microeconometrics of Banking: Methods, Applications, and Results. Oxford University Press.

Degryse, Hans, Nancy Masschelein and Janet Mitchell (2011) "Staying, dropping, or switching: The impacts of bank mergers on small firms," Review of Financial Studies, Vol. 24, No. 4, pp. 1102–1140.

Degryse, Hans and Steven Ongena (2005) "Distance, lending relationships, and competition," Journal of Finance, Vol. 60, No. 1, pp. 231–266.

DenHaan, Wouter J., Garey Ramey and Joel Watson (2003) "Liquidity flows and fragility of business enterprises," Journal of Monetary Economics, Vol. 50, No. 6, pp. 1215–1241.

Devos, Erik, Upinder Dhillon, Murali Jagannathan and Srinivasan Krishnamurthy (2012) "Why are firms unlevered?," Journal of Corporate Finance, Vol. 18, No. 3, pp. 664–682.

Dewatripont, Mathias and Eric Maskin (1995) "Credit and efficiency in centralized and decentralized economies," Review of Economic Studies, Vol. 62, No. 4, pp. 541–555.

Diamond, Douglas W. (1984) "Financial intermediation and delegated monitoring," Review of Economic Studies, Vol. 51, No. 3, pp. 393–414.

Diamond, Douglas W. (1991) "Monitoring and reputation: The choice between bank loans and directly placed debt," Journal of Political Economy, Vol. 99, No. 4, pp. 689–721.

Diamond, Douglas W. (2001) "Should Japanese banks be recapitalized?," Monetary and Economic Studies, Vol. 19, No. 2, pp. 1–19.

Doi, Takero. (2005). "Yushi, Hosho, Hojokin wo Meguru Seisaku Kinyu ni Kansuru Hikaku Bunseki (Comparative analysis of government financial support regarding loans, guarantees, and subsidies)." In the Report of Research Group 2 of the Financial Research Council: On the reform of government financial support, Chap. 3.

Dore, Timothy E., Tetsuji Okazaki, Ken Ohnishi and Naoki Wakamori (2021) "Firm growth, financial constraints, and policy-based finance," CIRJE Discussion Papers, CIRJE-F-1170.

Eisfeldt, Andrea L. and Adriano A. Rampini (2006) "Capital reallocation and liquidity," Journal of Monetary Economics, Vol. 53, No. 3, pp. 369–399.

El Ghoul, Sadok, Zhengwe Fu and Omrane Guedhami (2021) "Zombie firms: Prevalence, determinants, and corporate policies," Finance Research Letters, Vol. 41, 101876.

El Ghoul, Omrane Guedhami, Chuck Kwok and Xiaolan Zheng (2018) "Zero-leverage puzzle: An international comparison," Review of Finance, Vol. 22, No. 3, pp. 1063–1120.

Erel, Isil (2011) "The effect of bank mergers on loan prices: Evidence from the United States," Review of Financial Studies, Vol. 24, No. 4, pp. 1068–1101.

Foster, Lucia, John C. Haltiwanger and C. J. Krizan (2001) "Aggregate productivity growth: Lessons from microeconomic evidence," New Developments in Productivity Analysis, ed. Charles R. Hulten, Edward R. Dean and Michael J. Harper, pp. 303–372. University of Chicago Press.

Fukao, Kyoji (2012) Ushinawareta 20 Nen to Nihon Keizai: Kozoteki Genin to Saisei e no Gendoryoku no Kaimei (The "Lost Two Decades" and the Japanese Economy: Unraveling the Structural Causes and Driving Forces for Revival). Nihon Keizai Shimbun.

Fukao, Kyoji and Hyeog Ug Kwon (2006) "Why did Japan's TFP growth slow down in the lost decade? An empirical analysis based on firm-level data of manufacturing firms," Japanese Economic Review, Vol. 57, No. 2, pp. 195–228.

Fukasawa, Eiji (2007) "Chiho Jichitai no Chusho Kigyo Muke Seido Yushi ga Chokumen shite iru Kadai (Challenges facing local government institutional loans to SMEs)." National Diet Library Research and Legislative Review Bureau Reference, 77–95.

Fukuda, Shin-ichi (2015) Ushinawareta 20 Nen wo Koete (Beyond the "Lost Two Decades"). NTT Publishing.

Fukuda, Shin-ichi, Hiroshi Teruyama, Akihiro Kamiya and So Kei (1995) "Seizogyo ni Okeru Seisaku Kinyu no Yudou Kouka (Effects of government financial support to the manufacturing industry)." Economic Analysis, Vol. 140, 1–55, Economic Research Institute, Economic Planning Agency.

Fukuda, Shin-ichi and Jun-ichi Nakamura (2011) "Why did 'zombie' firms recover in Japan?," The World Economy, Vol. 34, No. 7, pp. 1124–1137.

Fukuda, Shin-ichi and Satoshi Koibuchi (2006) "Furyo Saiken to Saiken Hoki Mein Banku no Choka Futan (Non-performing loans and loan forgiveness: Excess burden on main banks)," The Economic Review, Vol. 57, No. 2, pp. 110–120.

Fukuda, Shin-ichi and Koki Okumura (2021) "The aging society, savings rates, and regional flow of funds in Japan," Journal of the Japanese and International Economies, Vol. 62, 101165.

Fujiwara, Keizo (2020) "Jissen-teki Chusho Kigyo Saisei Ron Dai 3 Han (Lectures on Practical SME Revitalization, 3rd ed.)." Kinyu-zaisei Jijo Kenkyukai.

Gale, William G. (1990) "Federal lending and the market for credit," Journal of Public Economics, Vol. 42, No. 2, pp. 177–193.

Gale, William G. (1991) "Economic effects of federal credit programs," American Economic Review, Vol. 81, No. 1, pp. 133–152.

Gande, Amar, Manju Puri, Anthony Saunders and Ingo Walter (1997) "Bank underwriting of debt securities: Modern evidence," Review of Financial Studies, Vol. 10, No. 4, pp. 1175–1202.

Garmaise, Mark J. and Tobias J. Moskowitz (2006) "Bank mergers and crime: The real and social effects of credit market competition," Journal of Finance, Vol. 61, No. 2, pp. 495–538.

Genda, Yuji (2004) Jobu Kurieishon (Job Creation). Nihon Keizai Shimbun.

Giannetti, Mariassunta and Andrei Simonov (2013) "On the real effects of bank bailouts: Micro evidence from Japan," American Economic Journal: Macroeconomics, Vol. 5, No. 1, pp. 135–167.

Gilje, Erik P., Elena Loutskina and Philip E. Strahan (2016) "Exporting liquidity: Branch banking and financial integration," Journal of Finance, Vol. 71, No. 3, pp. 1159–1184.

Goto, Yasuo and Scott Wilbur (2019) "Unfinished business: Zombie firms among SME in Japan's lost decades," Japan and the World Economy, Vol. 49, pp. 105–112.

Guner, Nezih, Gustavo Ventura and Yi Xu (2008) "Macroeconomic implications of size-dependent policies," Review of Economic Dynamics, Vol. 11, No. 4, pp. 721–744.

Hadlock, Charles J. and Joshua R. Pierce (2010) "New evidence on measuring financial constraints: Moving beyond the KZ index," Review of Financial Studies, Vol. 23, No. 5, pp. 1909–1940.

Hamao, Yasushi and Takeo Hoshi (2000) "Bank underwriting of corporate bonds: Evidence from Japan after the financial system reform of 1993," Columbia University CJEB Working Papers, 179.

Hanazaki, Masaharu and Kazuyo Hachisuka (1997) "Kaigin Yushi to Kigyo no Setsubi Toshi (Loans by the Japan Development Bank and corporate capital investment)." In Asako and Ohtaki (Eds.), Gendai Makuro Keizai Dougaku (Modern Macroeconomic Dynamics), Chap. 11, 377–413. The University of Tokyo Press.

Hannan, Timothy (1997) "Market share inequality, the number of competitors, and the HHI: An examination of bank pricing," Review of Industrial Organization, Vol. 12, No. 1, pp. 23–35.

Hannan, Timothy and Allen Berger (1991) "The rigidity of prices: Evidence from the banking industry," American Economic Review, Vol. 81, No. 4, pp. 938–945.

Hannan, Timothy and Robin A. Prager (2004) "The competitive implications of multimarket bank branching," Journal of Banking and Finance, Vol. 28, No. 8, pp. 1889–1914.

Harhoff, Dietmar and Timm Körting (1998) "Lending relationships in Germany-Empirical evidence from survey data," Journal of Banking and Finance, Vol. 22, No. 10–11, pp. 1317–1353.

Hashimoto, Takunori. (2016). Suterareru Ginko (Abandoned Banks). Kodansha Gendai Shinsho.

Harimaya, Kozo and Yasufumi Ozaki (2017) "Chiiki Kinyu Kikan no Kyoso Kankyo ga Jigyosho no Kaihai Gyo ni Ataeru Eikyo (Impact of the competitive environment of regional financial institutions on business openings and closings)." RIETI Discussion Paper Series, 17-J-047.

Hauswald, Robert and Robert Marquez (2006) "Competition and strategic information acquisition in credit markets," Review of Financial Studies, Vol. 19, No. 3, pp. 967–1000.

Herrera, Ana, Maria, Marek Kolar and Raoul Minetti (2011) "Credit reallocation," Journal of Monetary Economics, Vol. 58, No. 6–8, pp. 551–563.

Higano, Mikinari (1986) Kinyu Kikan no Shinsa Noryoku (Ability of Financial Institutions to Screen). The University of Tokyo Press.

Hiraga, Kazuki, Masashi Manabe and Naoyuki Yoshino. (2017). "Chiikikinyu Shijo deha, Kasendo ga Takamaru to Kashidashi Kinri ha Agarunoka (In regional financial markets, do lending rates increase as the degree of oligopoly increases)". Financial Services Agency Financial Research Center DP 2016–5.

Holmstrom, Bengt and Jean Tirole (1997) "Financial intermediation, loanable funds, and the real sector," Quarterly Journal of Economics, Vol. 112, No. 3, pp. 663–691.

Honda, Tomohito (2020) Nihon Kigyou wo Taisho to Shita Komittomento Rain ni Kansuru Jisshou Bunseki (An empirical analysis of commitment lines for Japanese firms). Doctoral dissertation (Economics), Hitotsubashi University.

Honda, Tomohito, Kaoru Hosono, Daisuke Miyakawa, Arito Ono, and Iichiro Uesugi (2023) "Determinants and effects of the use of COVID-19 business support programs in Japan," Journal of the Japanese and International Economies, Vol. 67, 101239.

Honjo, Yuji, Arito Ono and Daisuke Tsuruta (2019) "The effect of physical collateral and personal guarantees on business start-ups," RIETI Discussion Paper Series, 19-E-087.

Horie, Yasuhiro (2008) Chiiki Kinyu Kikan no Keiei Kodo: Keizai Kozo Henka eno Taiou (Management behavior of regional financial institutions: Responding to changes in economic structure). Keiso Shobo.

Horie, Yasuhiro. (2015). Nihon no Chiiki Kinyu Kikan Keiei (Management of Regional Financial Institutions in Japan). Keiso Shobo.

Horie, Yasuhiro and Ritsuko Arioka. (2021). Chiiki Kinyu Kikan no Shueki-ryoku: Keiei Saihen to Shorai Zou (Profitability of Regional Financial Institutions: Management Restructuring and Future Vision). Keiso Shobo.

Horiuchi, Akiyoshi and Qing-Yuan Sui (1993) "Influence of Japan Development Bank loans on corporate investment behavior," Journal of the Japanese and International Economies, Vol. 7, No. 4, pp. 441–465.

Horiuchi, Akiyoshi and Qing-Yuan Sui (1994) "Joho Seisan-sha to shite no Kaihatsu Ginko: Sono Kinou to Genkai (Japan Development Bank as an information producer: Its functions and limitations)." In Kaizuka and Ueda (Eds.), Henkakuki no Kinyu Shisutemu (Financial System in Transition), 143–172. The University of Tokyo Press.

Hoshi, Takeo and Anil Kashyap (1999) "The Japanese banking crisis: Where did it come from and how will it end?," NBER Macroeconomics Annual, Vol. 14, pp. 129–201.

Hoshi, Takeo, Daiji Kawaguchi and Kenichi Ueda (2022) "Zombies, again ? The COVID-19 business support programs in Japan," Journal of Banking and Finance, 106421.

Hosono, Kaoru, Miho Takizawa and Kotaro Tsuru (2017) "Size-dependent policy and firm growth," RIETI Discussion Paper Series, 17-E-070.

Hughes, Joseph P., William W. Lang, Loretta J. Mester and Choon-Geol Moon (1999) "The dollars and sense of bank consolidation," Journal of Banking and Finance, Vol. 23, No. 2–4, pp. 291–324.

Hyun, Junghwan and Raoul Minetti (2019) "Credit reallocation, deleveraging, and financial crises," Journal of Money, Credit and Banking, Vol. 51, No. 7, pp. 1889–1921.

Ikeo, Kazuto (1998) "Seifukei Kinyu Katsudo no Yakuwari: Rironteki Seiri (Role of government financial activities: theoretical considerations)". In Iwata and Fukao (eds.), Zaisei Toyushi no Keizai Bunseki (On Economic Analysis of Fiscal Investment and Loan Program) (Chap. 2). Nihon Keizai Shimbun.

Imai, Kentaro (2016) "A panel study of zombie SMEs in Japan: Identification, borrowing and investment behavior," Journal of the Japanese and International Economies, Vol. 39, pp. 91–107.

Imai, Masami (2009) "Political influence and declarations of bank insolvency in Japan," Journal of Money, Credit and Banking, Vol. 41, No. 1, pp. 131–158.

Imai, Masami (2018) "Government financial institutions and capital allocation efficiency in Japan," Wesleyan Economic Working Papers, No. 2018–002.

Innes, Robert (1991) "Investment and government intervention in credit markets when there is asymmetric information," Journal of Public Economics, Vol. 46, No. 3, pp. 347–381.

Iwamoto, Yasushi (2001) "Nihon no Zaisei Toyushi (Fiscal investment and loan program in Japan)," The Economic Review, Vol. 52, No. 1, pp. 2–15.

Jiangli, Wenying, Haluk Unal and Chiwon Yom (2008) "Relationship lending, accounting disclosure, and credit availability during the Asian financial crisis," Journal of Money, Credit and Banking, Vol. 40, No. 1, pp. 25–55.

Kaizuka, Keimei. (1981). "Kinyuu ni okeru Kangyo to Mingyo (Public and private sectors in finance)," Contemporary Economics Quarterly, Vol. 45, pp. 42–50.

Kalemli-Ozcan, Sebnem, Ariell Reshef, Bent E. Sorensen, and Oved Yosha (2010) "Why does capital flow to rich states?" Review of Economics and Statistics, Vol. 92, No. 4, pp. 769–783.

Kanemoto, Yoshitsugu and Kazuyuki Tokuoka (2002) "Nihon no Toshiken Settei Kijun (Criteria for the Metropolitan Areas in Japan)," Journal of Applied Regional Science, Vol. 7, pp. 1–15.

Kang, Jun-Koo and Wei-Lin Liu (2007) "Is universal banking justified? Evidence from bank underwriting of corporate bonds in Japan," Journal of Financial Economics, Vol. 84, No. 1, pp. 142–186.

Kano, Masaji and Yoshiro Tsutsui (2003) "Geographical segmentation in Japanese bank loan markets," Regional Science and Urban Economics, Vol. 33, No. 2, pp. 157–174.

Karceski, Jason, Steven Ongena and David C. Smith (2005) "The impact of bank consolidation on commercial borrower welfare," Journal of Finance, Vol. 60, No. 4, pp. 2043–2082.

Kinoshita, Nobuyuki (2005) Ginko no Kino to Houseido no Kenkyu: Nichibei no Kinyu Seido no Keisei to Shorai (A Study of Banking Functions and Legal Systems: The Formation and Future of Financial Systems in Japan and the U.S.). Toyo Keizai.

Khoo, Joye and Robert B. Durand (2017) "Japanese corporate leverage during the Lost Decades," Pacific-Basin Finance Journal, Vol. 46, Part A, pp. 94–108.

Kondo, Takanori. (2014). "Enkatsuka-Ho ga Chusho Kigyo Kinyu ni Ataeru Eikyo ni Tsuite no Jissho Kenkyu (An empirical study on the impact of the Financing Facilitation Act on SME financing)," Review of Monetary and Financial Studies, Vol. 36, pp. 24–42.

Kondo, Takanori (2018) Seifu no Ginkou Kashidashi eno Kanyo ha Nihon no Chushou Kigyo wo Tsuyoku Shita ka: Enkatsuka Ho, Shinyou Hosho Seido, Shihon Chunyu Seisaku no Kouka ni Tsuite no Jisshou Kenkyuu (Has Japanese Government Involvement in Bank Lending Strengthened Japanese SMEs: An Empirical Study of the Effects of the Facilitation Act, the Credit Guarantee System, and the Capital Injection Policy). Koyo Shobo.

Konno, Sayako (2014) "Kinyuu Kiki Go no Kokusaiteki Yousei wo Uketa Shikin Junkan Toukei no Seibi to Kakuju (Development and improvement of Flow of Funds statistics in response to international demands after the Financial Crisis)," The Bank of Japan Review, 2014-J-6.

Kroszner, Randall S. and Raghuram G. Rajan (1994) "Is the Glass-Steagall Act justified? A study of the US experience with universal banking before 1933," American Economic Review, Vol. 84, No. 4, pp. 810–832.

Kroszner, Randall S. and Raghuram G. Rajan (1997) "Organization structure and credibility: Evidence from commercial bank securities activities before the Glass-Steagall Act," Journal of Monetary Economics, Vol. 39, No. 3, pp. 475–516.

Kurose, Naohiro (2021) "Atkinson-shi no Chushou Kigyo Saihensei Ron wo Hihan Suru (Criticism against Mr. Atkinson's argument for the SME reorganization)," Kigyo Shindan, Vol. 68, No. 7, pp. 14–17.

Kwon, Hyeog Ug, Futoshi Narita and Machiko Narita (2015) "Resource reallocation and zombie lending in Japan in the 1990s," Review of Economic Dynamics, Vol. 18, No. 4, pp. 709–732.

La Porta, Raphael, Florencio Lopez-de-Silanes and Andrei Shleifer (2002) "Government ownership of banks," Journal of Finance, Vol. 57, No. 1, pp. 265–301.

Lanteri, Andrea (2018) "The market for used capital: Endogenous irreversibility and reallocation over the business cycle," American Economic Review, Vol. 108, No. 9, pp. 2383–2419.

Lechner, Michael (2002) "Program heterogeneity and propensity score matching: An application to the evaluation of active labor market policies," Review of Economics and Statistics, Vol. 84, No. 2, pp. 205–220.

Li, Wenli (1998) "Government loan, guarantee, and grant programs: An evaluation," Federal Reserve Bank of Richmond Economic Quarterly, Vol. 84, No. 4, pp. 25–51.

Lin, Yupeng, Anand Srinivasan and Takeshi Yamada (2017) "The effect of government bank lending: Evidence from the financial crisis in Japan," Available at SSRN 2544446.

Longhofer, Stanley D. and João A. C. Santos (2000) "The importance of bank seniority for relationship lending," Journal of Financial Intermediation, Vol. 9, No. 1, pp. 57–89.

Mankiw, Gregory N. (1986) "The allocation of credit and financial collapse," Quarterly Journal of Economics, Vol. 101, No. 3, pp. 455–470.

Manove, Michael, Jorge A. Padilla and Marco Pagano (2001) "Collateral versus project screening: A model of lazy banks," RAND Journal of Economics, Vol. 32, No. 4, pp. 726–744.

Maruyama, Tomoya (2021) "How competitiveness evolved in the Japanese bank loan market between 1977–2020," Japan and the World Economy, Vol. 69, 101232.

Micco, Alejandro and Ugo Panizza (2006) "Bank ownership and lending behavior," Economics Letters, Vol. 93, No. 2, pp. 248–254.

Micco, Alejandro, Ugo Panizza and Monica Yanez (2007) "Bank ownership and performance. Does politics matter?," Journal of Banking and Finance, Vol. 31, No. 1, pp. 219–241.

Minato, Tetsuo (2021) "Chusho Kigyo wa Keizai Seichou no Ashikase ka?: Atkinson "Setsu" no Kosatsu (Are SMEs a stumbling block to economic growth? A comment of Atkinson's argument)," Commercial Finance, Vol. 71, No. 1, pp. 7–17.

Ministry of Internal Affairs and Communications. (2003). Seifu Kinyu Kikan To ni yoru Koteki Shikin no Kyokyu ni Kansuru Seisaku Hyoka Sho (Policy assessment report on the provision of public funds by government financial and other institutions).

Mitsui, Itsutomo (2020) "Chusho Kigyo ni totte no Shin no "Seisansei Kojo" to ha (What is true "productivity improvement" for SMEs)." Small and Medium Business Industrial Research Institute Report January 2019 Subgroup Report, 72–75. https://www.asahi-net.or.jp/~MQ7I-MTI/productivity2020G.pdf

Miwa, Yoshiro (2011) "Are Japanese firms becoming more independent from their banks?: Evidence from the firm-level data of the "Corporate Enterprise Quarterly Statistics," 1994–2009," CIRJE Discussion Paper, No. F-808.

Montgomery, Heather and Satoshi Shimizutani (2009) "The effectiveness of bank recapitalization policies in Japan," Japan and the World Economy, Vol. 21, No. 1, pp. 1–25.

Muramoto, Tsutomu (2015) Chusho Kigyo Shien Seisaku Shisutemu: Kinyuu wo Chushin to shita Taikeika (SME Support and Policy System: Systematization Focusing on Finance). Sotensha.

Nagata, Kunikazu. (2017). "Shihon Chunyu ga Chiiki Ginko no Kashidashi Kodo ni Ataeru Eikyo (Impact of capital injection on lending behavior of regional banks)." RIETI Discussion Paper Series, 17-J-046.

Nakamura, Jun-ichi. (2017). "Nihon Kigyo no Shikin Yojo to Kyasshu Furo Shito: Hojin Kigyo Tokei Chosa Hyou Deta ni Motozuku Kibo Betsu Bunseki (Cash surplus and use of cash flow by Japanese firms: An analysis by size based on data from the Corporate Statistics Survey of Corporations)," Financial Review, Vol. 132, pp. 27–55.

Nakashima, Kiyotaka (2016) "An econometric evaluation of bank recapitalization programs with bank-and loan-level data," Journal of Banking and Finance, Vol. 63, pp. 1–24.

Nakata, Masao and Shigehiro Adachi (2006a) "Seifu Kei Kinyu Kikan Yushi wa "Karinikui Chiiki" e Tekisetsu ni Haibun sarete iru ka?: Fukanzen Kyoso ni Kiin suru "Shijo no Shippai" no Hokan Kino ni Kansuru Jisshou Bunseki (Are government loans appropriately allocated to "hard-to-borrow" areas? An empirical analysis of the complementary function to deal with "market failure" caused by imperfect competition)." PRI Discussion Paper Series, No.06A-27, Policy Research Institute Ministry of Finance.

Nakata, Masao and Shigehiro Adachi (2006b) "Kashidashi Kinri no Chiiki Kan Kakusa wa Naze Kaishou Sarenai no ka?: Daini Chihou Ginko, Shinyou Kinko no Paneru Deeta ni yoru Jisshou

Bunseki (Why the regional disparity in lending rates has not been eliminated?: An empirical analysis based on panel data from second-tier regional banks and shinkin banks)," Financial Review, Vol. 86, pp. 161–193.

Nakata, Tetsuo (2013) Tsusho Sangyo Seisaku Shi 12: Chusho Kigyo Seisaku (History of Trade and Industrial Policy 12: Small and Medium Enterprise Policy). Research Institute of Economy, Trade and Industry.

Nemoto, Tadanobu (2015) "Ri-man Shokku Iko no Obei Shokoku ni Okeru Chusho Kigyo Muke Seisaku Kinyu (Policy Financing for SMEs in Western Countries after the Global Financial Crisis)," Japan Finance Corporation Review, Vol. 27, pp. 63–97.

Nemoto, Tadanobu, Hikaru Fukanuma and Wako Watanabe (2006) "Sogyo Ki ni Okeru Seifu Kei Kinyu Kikan no Yakuwari (Role of government-affiliated financial institutions in the start-up phase)." RIETI Discussion Paper Series, 06-J-004.

Nguyen, Hoai-Luu Q. (2019) "Are credit markets still local? Evidence from bank branch closings," American Economic Journal: Applied Economics, Vol. 11, No1, pp. 1–32.

Nishimura, Kiyohiko G., Takanobu Nakajima and Kozo Kiyota (2005) "Does the natural selection mechanism still work in severe recessions?: Examination of the Japanese economy in the 1990s," Journal of Economic Behavior and Organization, Vol. 58, No. 1, pp. 53–78.

Nishimura, Yoshimasa (2011) Kinyu Shisutemu Kaikaku 50 Nen no Kiseki (50 Years of Financial System Reform). Kinyu Zaisei Jijo.

NTT Data Institute of Management Research (2019) "Kinyu Sabisu no Riyo Doko Chosa (Survey of Usage of Financial Services)."

Odagiri, Hiroyuki (2001) Atarashii Sangyo Soshiki Ron: Riron, jissho, seisaku (Lecture on New Industrial Organization: Theory, Evidence, and Policy). Yuhikaku

OECD (2009) "The impact of the global crisis on SME and entrepreneurship financing and policy responses," A report prepared by a team of the SME and Entrepreneurship Division of the OECD Center for Entrepreneurship, SMEs and Local Development, together with Lorraine Ruffing.

Ogura, Yoshiaki (2012) "Lending competition and credit availability for new firms: Empirical study with the price cost margin in regional loan markets," Journal of Banking and Finance, Vol. 36, No. 6, pp. 1822–1838.

Ogura, Yoshiaki (2018) "The objective function of government-controlled banks in a financial crisis," Journal of Banking and Finance, Vol. 89, pp. 78–93.

Ogura, Yoshiaki (2020) "Intensified lending competition and search-for-yield under prolonged monetary easing," Journal of the Japanese and International Economies, Vol. 56, 101076.

Ogura, Yoshiaki (2021) Chiiki Kinyu no Keizaigaku: Jinkou Gensho Ka no Chihou Kasseika to Ginkogyo no Yakuwari (The Economics of Regional Financing: The Role of the Banking Industry in the Revitalization of Local Areas Under a Declining Population). Keio University Press.

Ogura, Yoshiaki and Hirofumi Uchida (2014) "Bank consolidation and soft information acquisition in small business lending," Journal of Financial Services Research, Vol. 45, No. 2, pp. 173–200.

Ohashi, Hiroshi (2021) Kyousou Seisaku no Keizaigaku Jinkou Gensho, Dejitaruka, Sangyo Seisaku (Economics of Competition Policy Population Decline, Digitalization, and Industrial Policy). Nihon Keizai Shimbun.

Ojima, Mayumi (2018) "Chiiki Kinyu Kikan ni okeru Kyousou Gekika to Kinyu no Anteisei (Increased competition among regional financial institutions and financial stability)," Review of Monetary and Financial Studies, Vol. 41, pp. 1–18.

Okazaki, Tetsuji and Takeo Hoshi (2002) "1980 Nendai no Ginko Keiei: Senryaku, Soshiki. Gabanansu (Bank management in the 1980s: strategy, organization, and governance)." In Muramatsu and Okuno (Eds.), Heisei Baburu no Kenkyu (A Study of the Heisei Bubble) (Part 1). Toyo Keizai Inc.

Ono, Arito (2007) Shin Jidai no Chusho Kigyo Kinyu (SME Finance in the New Era). Toyo Keizai Shimposha.

Ono, Arito (2019) "Hosho Jisseki De-ta wo Yomitoku (Interpreting data on the use of credit guarantees)," Gekkan Kinyu Journal, May 2019, 74–79.

Ono, Arito, Yukiko Saito, Koji Sakai, and Iichiro Uesugi (2023) "Does Geographical Proximity Matter in Small Business Lending? Evidence from Changes in Main Bank Relationships," Asia-Pacific Journal of Financial Studies, Vol. 52, pp. 819–855.

Ono, Arito, Koji Sakai and Iichiro Uesugi (2012) "The effects of collateral on firm performance," Journal of the Japanese and International Economies, Vol. 26, No. 1, pp. 84–109.

Ono, Arito, Hirofumi Uchida, Gregory F. Udell and Iichiro Uesugi (2021) "Lending pro-cyclicality and macroprudential policy: Evidence from Japanese LTV ratios," Journal of Financial Stability, Vol. 53, 100819.

Ono, Arito and Iichiro Uesugi (2009) "Role of collateral and personal guarantees in relationship lending: Evidence from Japan's SME loan market," Journal of Money, Credit and Banking, Vol. 41, No. 5, pp. 935–960.

Ono, Arito, Iichiro Uesugi and Yukihiro Yasuda (2013) "Are lending relationships beneficial or harmful for public credit guarantees? Evidence from Japan's emergency credit guarantee program," Journal of Financial Stability, Vol. 9, No. 2, pp. 151–167.

Ono, Arito and Yukihiro Yasuda (2017) "Forgiveness versus financing: The determinants and impact of SME debt forbearance in Japan," RIETI Discussion Paper Series, 17-E-086.

Osada, Takeshi (2010) "Shihon Chunyu Seisaku no Kyapitaru Kurannchi Sokushin Kouka (Capital injection policy's effect on promoting capital crunches)." Review of Monetary and Financial Studies, Vol. 31, pp. 49–68.

Osotimehin, Sophie and Francesco Pappadà (2017) "Credit frictions and the cleansing effect of recessions," Economic Journal, Vol. 127, No. 602, pp. 1153–1187.

Ozaki, Michitaka, Takuto Konno, Haruhiko Hiroyama and Saiki Tsuchiya (2019) "Chiiki Ginkou no Ekkyou Kashidashi no Doukou (Trends in cross-border lending by regional banks)." The Bank of Japan Review, 2019-J-4.

Peek, Joe and Eric S. Rosengren (1998) "Bank consolidation and small business lending: It's not just bank size that matters," Journal of Banking and Finance, Vol. 22, No. 6–8, pp. 799–819.

Peek, Joe and Eric S. Rosengren (2005) "Unnatural selection: Perverse incentives and the misallocation of credit in Japan," American Economic Review, Vol. 95, No. 4, pp. 1144–1166.

Penas, María Fabiana and Haluk Unal (2004) "Gains in bank mergers: Evidence from the bond markets," Journal of Financial Economics, Vol. 74, No. 1, pp. 149–179.

Petersen, Mitchell A. and Raghuram G. Rajan (1994) "The benefits of lending relationships: Evidence from small business data," Journal of Finance, Vol. 49, No. 1, pp. 3–37.

Petersen, Mitchell A. and Raghuram G. Rajan (1995) "The effect of credit market competition on lending relationships," Quarterly Journal of Economics, Vol. 110, No. 2, pp. 407–443.

Petersen, Mitchell A. and Raghuram G. Rajan (2002) "Does distance still matter? The information revolution in small business lending," Journal of Finance, Vol. 57, No. 6, pp. 2533–2570.

Puri, Manju (1996) "Commercial banks in investment banking conflict of interest or certification role?," Journal of Financial Economics, Vol. 40, No. 3, pp. 373–401.

Rajan, Raghuram G. and Andrew Winton (1995) "Covenants and collateral as incentives to monitor," Journal of Finance, Vol. 50, No. 4, pp. 1113–1146.

Rajan, Raghuram G. and Luigi Zingales (1995) "What do we know about capital structure? Some evidence from international data," Journal of Finance, Vol. 50, No. 5, pp. 1421–1460.

Ramey, Valerie A. and Matthew D. Shapiro (1998) "Costly capital reallocation and the effects of government spending," Carnegie-Rochester Conference Series on Public Policy, Vol. 48, pp. 145–194.

Regional Banks Association of Japan (2017) "Shoko Chukin no Arikata ni Tsuite (The presence of Shoko Chukin Bank)." Materials distributed at the second meeting of the Study Group on the Presence of Shoko Chukin Bank organized by the Small and Medium Enterprise Agency.

Saito, Kuniyoshi and Daisuke Tsuruta (2018) "Information asymmetry in small and medium enterprise credit guarantee schemes: Evidence from Japan," Applied Economics, Vol. 50, No. 22, pp. 2469–2485.

Sakai, Koji and Iichiro Uesugi (2021) "The extent and efficiency of credit reallocation during economic downturns," RIETI Discussion Paper Series, 19-E-004.

Sakai, Koji and Iichiro Uesugi (2024) "The extent and efficiency of credit reallocation during economic downturns," Journal of Risk and Financial Management, Vol. 17, No. 12, pp. 574.

Sakai, Koji, Iichiro Uesugi and Tsutomu Watanabe (2010) "Firm age and the evolution of borrowing costs: Evidence from Japanese small firms," Journal of Banking and Finance, Vol.34, No.8, pp.1970-1981.

Sakuragawa, Masaya and Takeo Hoshi (2009) "Mondai Ooi Chusho Kigyo Kinyu Enkatsuka Hoan (Problematic SME Financing Facilitation Act)." Nihon Keizai Shimbun, Keizai Kyoshitsu, 13 Nov 2009.

Sapienza, Paola (2002) "The effects of banking mergers on loan contracts," Journal of Finance, Vol. 57, No. 1, pp. 329–367.

Sapienza, Paola (2004) "The effect of government ownership on bank lending," Journal of Financial Economics, Vol. 72, No. 2, pp. 357–384.

Sato, Mitsuru (2017) Yushi Gyomu Saisei no Shohosen: Beigin to Hogin no Yushi Kanri wa Doko ga Chigau ka (Prescription for Revitalizing Loan Operations: What are the Differences Between Loan Management at U.S. and Japanese Banks). Kinyu zaisei jijo kenkyukai.

Sekine, Toshitaka, Keiichiro Kobayashi and Yumi Saita (2003) "Forbearance lending: The case of Japanese firms," Monetary and Economic Studies, Vol. 21, No. 2, pp. 69–92.

Sekino, Masahiro and Wako Watanabe (2014) "Does the policy lending of the government financial institution substitute for the private lending during the period of the credit crunch? Evidence from loan level data in Japan," RIETI Discussion Paper Series, 14-E-063.

Sekino, Masahiro and Wako Watanabe (2016) "Does the policy lending of a government financial institution to mitigate the credit crunch improve firm performance? Evidence from loan level data in Japan," RIETI Discussion Paper Series, 16-E-056.

Sharpe, Steven A. (1990) "Asymmetric information, bank lending, and implicit contracts: A stylized model of customer relationships," Journal of Finance, Vol. 45, No. 4, pp. 1069–1087.

Shleifer, Andrei (1998) "State versus private ownership," Journal of Economic Perspectives, Vol. 12, No. 4, pp. 133–150.

Shleifer, Andrei and Robert W. Vishny (1994) "The politics of market socialism," Journal of Economic Perspectives, Vol. 8, No. 2, pp. 165–176.

Small and Medium Enterprise Agency (2005) 2005 Nenban Chusho Kigyo Hakusho (2005 White Paper on Small and Medium Enterprises). Gyosei.

Small and Medium Enterprise Agency (2016) 2016 Nenban Chusho Kigyo Hakusho (2016 White Paper on Small and Medium Enterprises). Nikkei Printing.

Small and Medium Enterprise Agency (2018) 2018 Nenban Chusho Kigyo Hakusho (2018 White Paper on Small and Medium Enterprises). Nikkei Printing.

Small and Medium Enterprise Agency (2020) 2020 Nenban Chusho Kigyo Hakusho (2020 White Paper on Small and Medium Enterprises). Nikkei Printing.

Small and Medium Enterprise Agency (2021) 2021 Nendo Ban Chusho Kigyo Shisaku Riyo Gaido Bukku (FY2021 Small and Medium Business Policy Guidebook). Small and Medium Enterprise Agency.

Smith, Bruce D. and Michael J. Stutzer (1989) "Credit rationing and government loan programs: A welfare analysis," Real Estate Economics, Vol. 17, No. 2, pp. 177–193.

Stein, Jeremy C. (2002) "Information production and capital allocation: Decentralized versus hierarchical firms," Journal of Finance, Vol. 57, No. 5, pp. 1891–1921.

Stiglitz, Joseph E. and Andrew Weiss (1981) "Credit rationing in markets with imperfect information," American Economic Review, Vol. 71, No. 3, pp. 393–410.

Strebulaev, Ilya A. and Baozhong Yang (2013) "The mystery of zero-leverage firms," Journal of Financial Economics, Vol. 109, No. 1, pp. 1–23.

Stulz, René M. and Herb Johnson (1985) "An analysis of secured debt," Journal of Financial Economics, Vol. 14, No. 4, pp. 501–521.

Sugiyama, Toshihiro (2020) "Heisei no 30 Nenkan ni Okeru Ginko Gyo no Kokunai Tenpo su no Hensen (Changes in the number of branches of the banking industry in Japan over the past 30 years of the Heisei Era)," Bulletin of Edogawa University, Vol. 30, pp. 115–134.

Takata, Hajime (2018) "Kigyo Shueki Shijo Saiko wo Koshin Jisshitsu Mushakkin Hiritsu Yaku Roku Wari Kigyo ha Toshika ni (Corporate earnings hit an all-time high, 60% of firms have become effectively zero-leverage and investors)." Mizuho Research Institute Research TODAY, 20 Sep 2018.

Takami, Shigeo. (2013). "Zero Rebarejji Kigyo no Jittai: Nihon no Jojo Seizogyo 822 Sha wo Taisho to shite (The reality of zero-leverage companies: a survey of 822 listed manufacturing companies in Japan)," Rissho Management Review, Vol. 46, No. 1, pp. 57–92.

Tanaka, Kazuho (2018) "Nihon Kouko ga Mezasu Chiiki Kinyu Kikan tono Renkei no Katachi (Cooperation with regional financial institutions that JFC is aiming for)." Shukan Kinyu Zaisei Jijo, 30 Apr 2018–7 May 2018, 34–38.

The Bank of Japan (2016) "Chiiki Kinyu Kikan no Kashiyagyo Muke Kashidashi to Yoshin Kanri no Kadai: Anke-to Chosa Kekka kara (Regional financial institutions' lending to the rental housing industry and credit management issues: results of a questionnaire survey)." Financial System Report Supplement.

The Bank of Japan (2019) Kinyu Shisutemu Repo-to 2019 Nen 4 Gatsu Gou (Financial System Report April 2019).

Tsuruta, Daisuke (2016) "No lending relationships and liquidity management of small businesses during a financial shock," Journal of the Japanese and International Economies, Vol. 42, pp. 31–46.

Tsuruta, Daisuke (2020) "SME policies as a barrier to growth of SMEs," Small Business Economics, Vol. 54, pp. 1067–1106.

Tsuruta, Daisuke (2021) "Distant lending for regional small businesses using public credit guarantee schemes: Evidence from Japan," RIETI Discussion Paper Series, 21-E-083.

Tsuruta, Daisuke and Hirofumi Uchida (2019) "The real driver of trade credit," Pacific-Basin Finance Journal, Vol. 57, 101183.

Tsushima, Koichi (2017) Okane wo Kakenai Jigyo Shokei: Kawaii Kokeisha niwa "Kojin Hoshou" wo Tsugasero (Money-saving business succession: If you love your successor, let him/her take over your "personal guarantees"). Doyukan.

Uchida, Hirofumi (2016) "A comparison of the lending technologies between private and public banks," RIETI Discussion Paper Series, 16-E-023.

Uchida, Hirofumi and Yoshiro Tsutsui (2005) "Has competition in the Japanese banking sector improved?," Journal of Banking and Finance, Vol. 29, No. 2, pp. 419–439.

Uchida, Hirofumi, Iichiro Uesugi and Hiromichi Iwaki (2017) "Adverse selection versus moral hazard in financial contracting: Evidence from collateralized and non-collateralized loans," RIETI Discussion Paper Series, 17-E-058.

Uchida, Hirofumi, Iichiro Uesugi and Masaki Hotei (2010) "Repayment enforcement and informational advantages: Empirical determinants of trade credit use," RIETI Discussion Paper Series, 10-E-041.

Uchino, Taisuke (2014) "Bank deposit interest rate pass-through and geographical segmentation in Japanese banking markets," Japan and the World Economy, Vol. 30, pp. 37–51.

Uchino, Taisuke and Iichiro Uesugi (2022) "The effects of a megabank merger on firm-bank relationships and loan availability," Journal of the Japanese and International Economies, Vol. 63, 101189.

Uesugi, Iichiro (2008) "Seifu ni yoru Tokubetsu Shinyo Hosho niha Kouka ga atta no ka (Was the credit guarantees by the government effective?)". In Watanabe and Uesugi (Eds.), On Verification an Empirical Analysis of the "Unsubstantiated Common Beliefs" of SME Finance (Chap. 6). Nihon Keizai Shimbun, Inc.

Uesugi, Iichiro, Arito Ono, Tomohito Honda, Shota Araki, Hirofumi Uchida, Yuki Onozuka, Daiji Kawaguchi, Daisuke Tsuruta, Hikaru Fukanuma, Kaoru Hosono, Daisuke Miyakawa, Yukihiro Yasuda, and Nobuyoshi Yamori (2021) "Shingata Korona Uirusu Kansensho Ka niokeru Kigyo Jittai Chosa no Gaiyo (Summary of the survey of companies under the COVID-19 pandemic)." RIETI Discussion Paper Series, 21-J-029.

Uesugi, Iichiro, Arito Ono, Tomohito Honda, Shota Araki, Hirofumi Uchida, Yuki Onozuka, Daiji Kawaguchi, Daisuke Tsuruta, Hikaru Fukanuma, Kaoru Hosono, Daisuke Miyakawa, Yukihiro Yasuda and Nobuyoshi Yamori (2022) "Korona Shokku he no Kigyou no Taiou to Seisaku Shien Sochi (Corporate responses to the COVID-19 Shock and policy support measures: An analysis based on survey research)," The Economic Review, Vol. 73, No. 2, pp. 133–157.

Uesugi, Iichiro, Hikaru Fukanuma, Arito Ono, Peng Xu, Daisuke Tsuruta, Tadanobu Nemoto, Daisuke Miyakawa, Yukihiro Yasuda, Nobuyoshi Yamori, Wako Watanabe, and Hiromichi Iwaki (2015) "Kinyuu Enkatsuka Hou Shuryougo ni okeru Kinyu Jittai Chousa Kekka no Gaiyou (Financing after the end of the Financing Facilitation Act: summary of the results of the survey on the actual financial situation)." RIETI Discussion Paper Series, 15-J-028.

Uesugi, Iichiro, Kazuki Hiraga, Masashi Manabe and Naoyuki Yoshino (2021a) "Interregional Flow of Funds in Japan via Loans and Deposits of Financial Institutions, and its Determinants," Financial Services Agency Financial Research Center DP2020–10.

Uesugi, Iichiro, Kazuki Hiraga, Masashi Manabe, and Naoyuki Yoshino (2022) "Measuring Concentration in the Japanese Loan and Deposit Markets," Japan and the World Economy, Vol. 63, 101148.

Uesugi, Iichiro, Hirofumi Uchida, Yoshiaki Ogura, Arito Ono, Peng Xu, Daisuke Tsuruta, Tadanobu Nemoto, Hideaki Hirata, Yukihiro Yasuda, Nobuyoshi Yamori, Wako Watanabe, and Masaki Hotei (2009) "Kinyukiki Ka niokeru Chusho Kigyokinyu no Genjo 'Kigyo Kinyukikan tono Torihiki Jittai Chosa (2008nen 2gatsu Jisshi), 'Kinyukiki Ka niokeru Kigyo Kinyukikan tono Torihiki Jittai Chousa (2009nen 2gatsu Jisshi)' no Kekka gaiyou (The current state of SME financing under the Financial Crisis: summary of the survey of transactions between firms and financial institutions (conducted in February 2008), and the survey on transactions between firms and financial institutions under the Financial Crisis (conducted in February 2009))." RIETI Discussion Paper Series, 09-J-020.

Uesugi, Iichiro, Hirofumi Uchida and Hiromichi Iwaki (2015a) "Mutanpo Kashidashi to Kigyo no Shikin Chotatsu Pafomansu (Unsecured loan and corporate financing and performance)," Journal of Economics & Business Administration, Vol. 212, No. 6, pp. 21–37.

Uesugi, Iichiro, Hirofumi Uchida and Hiromichi Iwaki (2015b) "Mutanpo Kashidashi no Dounyuu ga Kigyou no Shikin Choutatsu to Pafo-mansu ni Ataeru Koukano Kensho (The effects of unsecured lending on corporate financing and performance)." HIT-REFINED Working Paper Series, No.18.

Uesugi, Iichiro, Hirofumi Uchida and Hiromichi Iwaki (2016) "Tanpo Yoryoku wo Kouryoshita Mutapo Kashidashi ni Kansuru Bunseki (The analysis of unsecured loan with consideration of collateral capacity)." Part II of the report submitted to the SME-Unit of the Japan Finance Corporation Study Group.

Uesugi, Iichiro, Hirofumi Uchida and Hiromichi Iwaki (2018) "Muhoshonin Kashidashi no Dounyu to Kigyo no Shikin Chotatsu Pafo-mansu (The introduction of nonguaranteed loans and firm financing and performance)," Review of Monetary and Financial Studies, Vol. 40, pp. 27–53, Japan Society of Monetary Economics.

Uesugi, Iichiro, Hirofumi Uchida and Hiromichi Iwaki (2020) "Seifukei Kinyuu Kikan ni yoru Kinri Settei ga Takinyuu Kikan no Kariire Kinri Kashidashi Gaku ni Oyobosu Eikyou (Impact of interest rate setting by government-affiliated financial institutions on other financial institutions' borrowing and lending)," The Economic Review, Vol. 71, No. 4, pp. 333–357.

Uesugi, Iichiro, Hirofumi Uchida and Yuta Mizusugi (2016) "Nihon Seisaku Kinyuu Kouko to no Torihiki Kankei ga Kigyou Pafo-mansu ni Ataeru Kouka no Kenshou (Examining the effects of business transactions with JFC on corporate performance)," The Economic Review, Vol. 67, No.1, pp. 238–260.

Uesugi, Iichiro, Kaoru Hosono, Daisuke Miyakawa, Arito Ono and Hirofumi Uchida (2018) "Reallocation of tangible assets and productivity," RIETI Discussion Paper Series, 18-E-048.

Uesugi, Iichiro and Koji Sakai (2017) "Nihon Kigyo no Shikin Saihaibun (Credit reallocation of Japanese firms)," RIETI Discussion Paper Series, 15-J-035.

Uesugi, Iichiro, Koji Sakai and Guy M. Yamashiro (2006) "Effectiveness of credit guarantees in the Japanese loan market," RIETI Discussion Paper Series, 06-E-004.

Uesugi, Iichiro, Koji Sakai and Guy M. Yamashiro (2010) "The effectiveness of public credit guarantees in the Japanese loan market," Journal of the Japanese and International Economies, Vol. 24, No. 4, pp. 457–480.

Uesugi, Iichiro, Nguyễn Thùy Linh and Yoshiki Hiramine (2021) "Chiiki Kinyu Shijo ni okeru Shuchudo ya Kinyukikan Gappei ga Kigyou no Shikin Chotatsu ni Oyobosu Eikyo (The impact of concentration in regional financial markets and financial institution mergers on corporate financing)." CAREE Discussion Paper Series, J-2021–03.

Uchida, Hirofumi (2011) "Kigyou Kan Shinyou no Kinou (Function of trade credit)," Gendai Finance, Vol. 29, pp. 3–48.

Uchida, Hirofumi (2018) Kinyu: Tei Seicho Ka no Nihon no Kinyu Shisutemu – Baburu•Kiki•Teitai Ka no Antei (Financing: Japan's financial system under low growth: Bubble, crisis, and stability under stagnation). In Fukao, Nakamura and Nakabayashi (Eds.), Iwanami Koza Nihon Keizai no Rekishi (Iwanami Lectures: History of the Japanese Economy), Vol. 6 Chap. 2.

Vogel, Robert C. and Dale W. Adams (1997) "The benefits and costs of loan guarantee programs," The Financier, Vol. 4, No. 1&2, pp. 22–29.

Wang, Gang, R. Michael Holmes Jr., In-Sue Oh and Weichun Zhu (2016) "Do CEOs matter to firm strategic actions and firm performance? A meta-analytic investigation based on upper echelons theory," Personnel Psychology, Vol. 69, No. 4, pp. 775–862.

Wang, Teng (2021) "Local banks and the effects of oil price shocks," Journal of Banking and Finance, Vol. 125, 106069.

Watanabe, Tsutomu and Iichiro Uesugi (2008) Kensho Chusho Kigyo Kinyu "Konkyo Naki Tsusetsu" no Jissho Bunseki (Examining SME Finance: An Empirical Analysis of the "Unfounded Common Beliefs"). Nihon Keizai Shimbun.

Wilcox, James A. and Yukihiro Yasuda (2019) "Government guarantees of loans to small businesses: Effects on banks' risk-taking and non-guaranteed lending," Journal of Financial Intermediation, Vol. 37, pp. 45–57.

Williamson, Oliver E. (1968) "Economies as an antitrust defense: The welfare tradeoffs," American Economic Review, Vol. 58, No. 1, pp. 18–36.

Yabushita, Shiro and Tomoo Bushimata (2006) Chusho Kigyo Kinyu Nyumon (Introduction to SME Finance). Toyo Keizai Inc.

Yamada, Kotone, Yukio Minoura, Jouchi Nakajima and Tomoyuki Yagi (2022) "Kigyo Kinyu Shien to Shigen Haibun: Kenkyu no Chouryu to Shingata Korona Uirusu Kansen Sho Kakudai gono Doko (Corporate financial support and resource allocation: trends in research and after the spread of COVID-19)," Bank of Japan Working Paper series No.22-J-4.

Yamori, Nobuyoshi (2007) "Nihon Kigyou no Kinyuu Ishiki Kodo no Kettei Yoin: Kansai Kigyo Anketo ni Motozuku Bunseki (Determinants of financial awareness and behavior of Japanese firms: An analysis based on a questionnaire survey of firms in the Kansai region)," RIETI Discussion Paper Series, 07-J-016.

Yamori, Nobuyoshi (2012) "Chusho Kigyo Kinyu Enkatsuka Hou no Koka to Kadai: 2010 Nen Chusho Kigyo Kinyu no Jittai Chosa Kekka ni Motozuite (Effects and challenges of the SME financing facilitation law: Based on the results of the 2010 SME financing fact-finding survey)," Financial Structure Research, Vol. 34, pp. 99–114.

Yamori, Nobuyoshi (2016) "Minkan Kinyu Kikan oyobi Seifu Kei Kinyu Kikan no Katsudo ni Taisuru Chusho Kigyo no Hyoka: Kigyou Nenrei ni yoru Sai ha Aru ka? (SMEs' assessment of the activities of private and government financial institutions: are there differences by firm age?)," RIETI Discussion Paper Series, 16-J-021.

Yamori, Nobuyoshi (2021) "Sekinin Kyoyu Seido no Moto de no Kinyu Kikan no Shinyou Hosho Riyou Taido (Attitudes towards credit guarantee usage by financial institutions under the loss-sharing system)." In Yamori, Support for Business Succession by Regional Financial Institutions and Credit Guarantee Associations (Chap. 1), Institute of Economics and Business Administration, Kobe University.

Yamori, Nobuyoshi, Hirofumi Uchida, Iichiro Uesugi, Yoshiaki Ogura, Kenya Takaku, Kei Tomimura, Tadanobu Nemoto and Wako Watanabe (2007). "Chusho Kigyo Kinyu no Kankyou Henka no Moto de no Seisaku Kinyu no Yakuwari to Kadai: "Kinyu Kikan ni Taisuru Chusho Kigyo no Ishiki Chosa" no Kekka wo Moto ni (The roles and challenges of policy finance under the change in the SME finance environment: Based on "the survey of SMEs' attitudes toward financial institutions")," Research & Documentation, Vol. 119, pp. 1–95.

Yasuda, Takehiko (2004) "Sogyoji no Ryudosei Seiyaku to Sogyo Douki Seisaku Kinyu no Kouka (Liquidity constraint, motivation to start businesses, and the impact of government financial assistance for startup firms)," RIETI Discussion Paper Series, 04-J-032.

Index

I. Uesugi, *The Economics of SME Finance*, Advances in Japanese Business and Economics 36, https://doi.org/10.1007/978-981-96-3193-3

The manufacturer's authorised representative in the EU is Springer Nature Customer Service Centre GmbH, Europaplatz 3, 69115 Heidelberg, Germany. If you have any concerns regarding our products, please contact ProductSafety@springernature.com

Printed and bound by CPI Group (UK) Ltd, Croydon, CR0 4YY
01/10/2026
02225931-0004